D0220093

These Englands

These Englands

A conversation on national identity

Edited by
Arthur Aughey and Christine Berberich

MANCHESTER UNIVERSITY PRESS
Manchester and New York

distributed in the United States exclusively
by Palgrave Macmillan

Copyright © Manchester University Press 2011

While copyright in the volume as a whole is vested in Manchester University Press, copyright in individual chapters belongs to their respective authors, and no chapter may be reproduced wholly or in part without the express permission in writing of both author and publisher.

Published by Manchester University Press
Oxford Road, Manchester M13 9NR, UK
and Room 400, 175 Fifth Avenue, New York, NY 10010, USA
www.manchesteruniversitypress.co.uk

Distributed in the United States exclusively by
Palgrave Macmillan, 175 Fifth Avenue, New York,
NY 10010, USA

Distributed in Canada exclusively by
UBC Press, University of British Columbia, 2029 West Mall,
Vancouver, BC, Canada V6T 1Z2

British Library Cataloguing-in-Publication Data
A catalogue record for this book is available from the British Library

Library of Congress Cataloging-in-Publication Data applied for

ISBN   978 07190 7960 3 hardback
ISBN   978 07190 7961 0 paperback

First published 2011

The publisher has no responsibility for the persistence or accuracy of URLs for any external or third-party internet websites referred to in this book, and does not guarantee that any content on such websites is, or will remain, accurate or appropriate.

Typeset in Minion and Optima
by Action Publishing Technology Ltd, Gloucester
Printed in Great Britain
by TJ International Ltd, Padstow

To the next generation:

Sky Aughey and Lucas Finnegan Stefanuti

Contents

Tables

Notes on Contributors

Arthur Aughey is Professor of Politics at the University of Ulster and a Fellow of the Royal Society of Arts. He is a Senior Fellow at the Centre for British Politics at the University of Hull and Fellow of the Institute for British Irish Studies at University College Dublin. His recent publications include *Nationalism Devolution and the Challenge to the United Kingdom State* (2001), *Northern Ireland Politics: After the Belfast Agreement* (2005) and *The Politics of Englishness* (Manchester University Press, 2007). He is currently Leverhulme Major Research Fellow and gratefully acknowledges its financial assistance in the writing of this book.

Matt Beech is Lecturer in Politics and Director of the Centre for British Politics in the Department of Politics and International Studies at the University of Hull. He has published widely on British Social democracy and Conservatism. His latest book is a collection of essays co-edited with Simon Lee, entitled *The Conservatives under David Cameron: Built to Last?* (2009).

Christine Berberich is Senior Lecturer in English Literature at the University of Portsmouth. Her main research interest focuses on national identity construction, and here in particular 'Englishness'. She has published widely on authors such as Evelyn Waugh, Kazuo Ishiguro, Anthony Powell, George Orwell, Julian Barnes and W.G. Sebald. Her monograph *The Image of the English Gentleman in Twentieth-Century Literature: Englishness & Nostalgia* was published in 2007. She is currently co-editing a book on *Land & Identity*.

Christopher G.A. Bryant is Emeritus Professor of Sociology at the University of Salford and an Academician of the Social Sciences. His interests are in social theory (especially positivism and structuration theory) and political sociology (with particular reference to pluralism, civil society and national questions in the Netherlands, Poland before and after 1989, Britain, and, latterly, England). His most recent books are *The Contemporary Giddens* (2001; co-editor David Jary) and *The*

Nations of Britain (2006). He gave the 2010 O'Donnell Lecture at the University of Wales on 'Reconfiguring Britain'.

Susan Condor is Professor of Social Psychology at Lancaster University. She is currently director of the Social Conflict and Solidarity Research Unit, and a member of the Governing Council of the International Society of Political Psychology. Her research focuses on everyday understandings of historical and political processes. Since the early 1990s, she has been investigating the ways in which ordinary social actors understand England and Englishness, and the factors that influence the ways in which people are inclined to claim and to display their own sense of national identity.

Colin Copus is Professor of Local Politics and Director of the Local Governance Research Unit in the Department of Public Policy, De Montfort University. His main research interests are local party politics, local political leadership, the changing role of the councillor and small party and independent politics. He also researches and writes on English national identity and English governance. He has recently concluded two major research projects: the first a Leverhulme funded project exploring the role and impact of small political parties, independent politics and political associations in local government; the second, a Nuffield funded comparative project examining the roles, responsibilities and activities of councillors across Europe. Colin is the author of two major books: *Leading the Localities: Executive Mayors in English Local Governance* (Manchester University Press, 2006) and *Party Politics and Local Government* (Manchester University Press, 2004). He has also served as a councillor on a London Borough council, a county and a district council and three parish councils.

John Curtice is Professor of Politics at Strathclyde University and a Research Consultant to the National Centre for Social Research (NatCen). During the course of the last decade, he has undertaken extensive research in all four territories of the UK on how public opinion has reacted to the advent of devolution. Recent publications include *Has Devolution Worked* (co-editor) and *The Scottish Elections 2007: Revolution or Evolution* (co-author).

Gary Day is a Principal Lecturer in English at De Monfort University and a Fellow of the Royal Society of Arts. He oversees the Theatre Archive Project, which is based at De Montfort and the British Library. He is also co-editor, with Jack Lynch, of *The Wiley Encyclopaedia of British Literature 1660–1789*. His publications include *Class* (2001), *Literary Criticism: A New History* (2008) and, most recently, *Modernist Literature 1890–1950* (2010).

Stephen Ingle is Emeritus Professor of Politics at the University of Stirling. He took the Chair at Stirling in 1991 to re-establish Politics and remained Head of Department until 2002. His research interests are principally in the relationship between politics and literature and in adversarial (especially British) politics. His recent publications include *Narratives of British Socialism* (2002), *The Social and Political Thought of George Orwell* (2006) and *The British Party System* (4th edn, 2008).

Simon Lee is Senior Lecturer in Politics and Director of the Centre for Democratic Governance, at the University of Hull. He is the author of *Boom and Bust: The Politics and Legacy of Gordon Brown* and co-editor (with Matt Beech) of *Built to Last? The Conservatives under David Cameron* and *Ten Years of New Labour*. His next book, *The Nation We're In: The State of England*, will be published in autumn 2011.

Philip Norton is Professor of Government, and Director of the Centre for Legislative Studies, at the University of Hull. He sits in the House of Lords as Lord Norton of Louth and was the first Chairman of the House of Lords Select Committee on the Constitution. He is the author or editor of twenty-eight books, covering comparative legislatures and British politics, especially parliament, the constitution and the Conservative Party.

Patrick Parrinder's books include *Science Fiction: Its Criticism and Teaching* (1980), *James Joyce* (1984), *Shadows of the Future* (1995) and *Nation and Novel: The English Novel from its Origins to the Present Day* (2006). He is General Editor of the forthcoming multi-volume *Oxford History of the Novel in English* and co-editor, with Andrzej Gasiorek, of volume 4 in the series, *The Reinvention of the British and Irish Novel 1880–1940* (2010). He is also a Vice-President of the H.G. Wells Society and has edited ten of Wells's scienc fiction titles for Penguin Classics, including *The Country of the Blind and Other Selected Stories* (2007). He is Emeritus Professor of English at the University of Reading.

Julia Stapleton is Reader in Politics at Durham University. Her research is focused on British intellectual history in the twentieth century, with particular reference to political thought and national identity. Her publications include *Englishness and the Study of Politics: The Social and Political Thought of Ernest Barker* (1994), *Sir Arthur Bryant and National History in Twentieth-Century Britain* (2005) and *Christianity, Patriotism and Nationhood: The England of G.K. Chesterton* (2009).

Paul Thomas is a Senior Lecturer in Youth and Community Work at the School of Education and Professional Development, University of Huddersfield, UK. Previously, Paul was Youth Campaigns and Policy

Officer at the Commission for Racial Equality in the north of England, has campaigned against racism and xenophobia amongst football fans and worked for a national voluntary-sector youth work organisation. Paul's research focus is on multiculturalism, young people and Community Cohesion, with a forthcoming monograph titled *Youth, Multiculturalism and Community Cohesion.*

Preface

Krishan Kumar

What a mystery the English are, to themselves and others. Unlike their continental neighbours, the French, Germans and Italians, or even their nearer neighbours, the Welsh, Scottish and Irish, they have never established a strong sense of national identity. What is more, they have not shown much interest in inquiring, in any systematic way, into the character of themselves as a nation. Nor is there much evidence of 'English nationalism' – the very term sounds un-English. What we are left with is a series of confusions – 'English' for 'British', 'this island race' to represent the English as all of Britain, an 'English monarchy' which denies not just its British character but an even more distant provenance.

For some people, the absence of English concern with nationhood, national identity and nationalism is a source of strength, not weakness. There is a very English way of thinking of nationalism as a sort of tribalism, suitable perhaps for mobilizing people to throw off alien rule but something that civilized people should have gone beyond. An indifference to nationalism, it is said, betokens a kind of openness to the world, a certain cosmopolitanism that sits well with a country that at one time presided over the fate of a quarter of the world's population and administered a quarter of its territory. The British empire is no more, but perhaps it has left a legacy of thinking in global, not local or parochial, ways. In this view, a concern with nation and national identity must mean a regressive narrowing of outlook, a throwback to a more primitive age.

There is still a lot that seems attractive in this view, and perhaps, in the end, it will be justified. But in the meantime there is the 'English Question' – the effect on the English of recent constitutional changes that have given a considerable degree of autonomy to the Scots, Welsh and Northern Irish but seem to have ignored the English. Where do the English stand in this? What, if any, is their cause? What way of life might they want to assert, and to defend? What case can they make for being treated as a separate nation, on a par at least with the Scots, Welsh and Irish? Here the lack of a tradition of reflection on the national character comes back to haunt the English. The badge of superiority in one respect, in another it marks a poverty of resources that can be drawn upon to mount a case in the urgency of the moment.

Still, that is perhaps to put it too strongly. As the editors of this volume argue, and the various contributors show, there is an English tradition, if not an English nationalism. Drawing enterprisingly and engagingly on the social and political philosophy of Michael Oakeshott, they skilfully draw out the various 'intimations' of that tradition, showing the various voices that make up the English 'conversation'. This is an attractive and persuasive way of furthering a discussion that often seems in danger of becoming repetitive and sterile. It avoids the problematic concept of 'national character', and it denies the need to identify any kind of 'core' to the national culture or identity. Instead it points to the diversity that is inherent in any living tradition, one that can change, sometimes radically, without losing the character and continuity that gives it identity and recognition. The contributors to this volume show that while it may be useful to stress 'these Englands' rather than 'this England', it is in the inter-action and mutual relationship of these various Englands that we can best understand what, if anything, there is of English national character and an English national tradition.

This is therefore a volume to be welcomed, as making not just a valuable addition to the burgeoning literature on Englishness, but doing so from an unusual and refreshing vantage point. It covers politics, history and literature. The editors contribute a searching introduction of their own that incisively maps out the approach of the volume as a whole, and that serves as a substantial appetiser to the varied dishes that follow. They have certainly given us a rich feast to digest.

Acknowledgements

The idea for this book was conceived some considerable time ago. Tony Mason, from Manchester University Press, reacted enthusiastically to our initial idea and was encouraging throughout the whole process of writing and editing. We want to thank him for his unfaltering support and understanding. Special thanks go to our copy-editor, Graeme Leonard, who worked efficiently and reliably, and who kept calm at a critical moment.

We also want to thank all the contributors to this book – for their enthusiasm for the project and for the quality of their chapters. This made the process of editing itself a lively intellectual conversation.

Arthur Aughey gratefully acknowledges the support of a Leverhulme Trust Major Research Fellowship which he held during the writing of this book. He would also like to thank Dr Julia Stapleton for her intellectual support, and Sky Aughey and Sharon Glenn for sharing conversations about and journeys in England. The encouragement of the Social Science Research Institute at the University of Ulster, in particular its Director Dr Cathy Gormley-Heenan, is also greatly appreciated.

Christine Berberich would like to thank former colleagues at the University of Derby and present colleagues at the University of Portsmouth for intellectual support and good cheer. Gerdi Berberich provided invaluable practical help throughout the project and Lucas Finnegan Stefanuti offered timely reminders that there are things other than work.

Introduction: these Englands – a conversation on national identity

Arthur Aughey and Christine Berberich

A very intelligent book on the British political tradition (Rhodes, Wanna & Weller, 2009: 75–6) claimed that: 'The Scots, the Welsh, and the Northern Irish can and do debate national identity at length and with arms. The English can mount the occasional sortie but, like sex and religion, it is not deemed a suitable dinner table topic.' That may well be true but, alternatively, it could be argued that the English always *have* discussed their national identity at length, if not 'with arms' (in both senses of that word), and rarely at the dinner table. We argue that they have done so in such a distinctive manner that it is frequently and unselfconsciously repeated in attempts to define what England means. This chapter introduces the diversity of reflection on Englishness in a number of stages. Firstly, we consider that distinctive manner of discussing national identity that often comes in the form and shape of what we will call 'listing'. It has been asked (Ribeiro, 2002: 15) if 'perhaps the making of such lists is a peculiarly English idiosyncrasy?', and the answer to this question appears to be a resounding 'yes'. The narrative device of 'the list', here in particular its use to define and explain national identity, deserves some elaboration. When all else fails, a simple listing of things, events, places and people can be offered in place of a proper definition. Dominic Head (2006: 19), for example, has pointed out the 'empirical habit of cultural commentators who resort to lists of things that might define that national character by drawing together its disparate elements'. Here, we aim to explore how that is done.

Secondly, we attempt to show how that diversity also involves a common reference to England. 'Versions' of England are particularly apparent when reading contemporary travel writing on and about England. While Sebald, Raban, Theroux, Bryson and others write about England, they describe what they *see* and *experience* as individuals – and that is different from book to book; so different, in fact, that they seem to be writing about *different* Englands altogether. If we identify these differences of perspective we also try to specify what makes England, as George Santayana noted (1922: 4), 'a distinctive society'. For Santayana, people 'are at once entangled in a mesh of instrumentalities, irrelevance, misunderstanding, vanity and propaganda' (1922: 27). But when, 'being naturally akin' and each alone in their own heaven, it is also possible for people to '*soliloquize in harmony*', if only because 'their hearts are similar'. This is the basis for society's 'friendship in the spirit', one which achieves some unison across 'the void of separation', the condition for English freedom and independence. Santayana believed that in England the many voices did soliloquise in harmony and that even frantic, perhaps fanatic, poses tended to 'neutralize one another and do no harm on the whole' (1922: 5). This assumes, to use E.P. Thompson's term (1978), that talking about England is conducted in a distinctive *idiom* and one that assumes mutual understanding. To capture this idiomatic notion, we use Pierre Bayard's thesis in *How To Talk About Books You Haven't Read* where culture – and by extension, national identity – is a matter of orientation amongst the artefacts of Englishness.

Thirdly, we try to complete the picture by adapting two ideas from the work of the English philosopher Michael Oakeshott. The first of these is the metaphor of the 'dry wall' which was originally used to explain the character of historical change. We use it here to suggest how the varieties of Englishness stand in relation to one another and to the whole. The second is the idea of politics as conversation. Here we propose that Englishness can be understood as a conversation, an imaginative rather than a purely functional engagement, with the country's history, culture and society, where what is conversed about, explicitly or implicitly, is the meaning of England itself. The conversation changes, of course, but there is discursive continuity as well which can illustrate a 'tradition' of talking about the nation. The conversation involves a plural notion of *these* Englands (an assumption of diverse, if related, 'lists' which stand in national relation) rather than the singular notion of *this* England (as the patriotic magazine of that name would have it). We refer to Oakeshott because his Englishness is transparent, his own list expressing a 'fondness for homely metaphors drawn from cookery, cricket, horse racing and such like, has meant that he was always something of an acquired taste, especially for those who find this Englishness alien or parochial' (Horton, 2005: 24). Conversation, according to Oakeshott, involved exploring the 'intimations' of a tradition of behaviour and Englishness, as the essays in this book reveal, can also be understood as just such a tradition of behaviour, and one with many intimations. Oakeshott observed (1991: 61) that a tradition of behaviour is tricky to get to know. It 'is neither fixed nor finished; it has no changeless centre to which understanding can anchor itself; there is no sovereign purpose to be perceived or invariable direction to be detected; there is no model to be copied, idea to be realised, or rule to be followed. Some parts of it may change more slowly than others, but none is immune from change. Everything is temporary'. However 'flimsy and elusive' tradition is not without identity – and the identity, we suggest, lies in how the various elements stand in relation and in how they conduct the conversation. Everything is temporary, yes, but Oakeshott adds the crucial qualification that 'nothing is arbitrary'. It is, rather, 'a flow of sympathy', and we attempt to explain here what that might mean in England's case.

Listing

David Willetts (2009: 54) observed how national ties have not been diminished in an era of globalisation but mean as much as ever. In England, though, 'we have celebrated these ties with nothing as vulgar as a clear theory'. Instead, Willets argued, the English tend to offer 'lists of associations'. The first list which he cited was taken from Vita Sackville-West's novel *The Edwardians* (1930), where she imagines what thoughts are going on in the heads of the congregation at the coronation of King George V: 'England, Shakespeare, Elizabeth, London; Westminster, the docks, India, the Cutty Sark, England; England, Gloucester, John of Gaunt; Magna Carta, Cromwell, England'. The second was the familiar reference from T.S. Eliot's *Notes towards the Definition of a Culture* (1930): 'Derby Day, Henley Regatta, Cowes, the Twelfth of August, a cup final, the dog races, the pin table, the dart board, Wensleydale cheese, boiled cabbage cut into sections, beetroot in vinegar, 19th Century Gothic churches and the music of Elgar'. Sackville-West poignantly asked what her list could mean to a foreigner and it is possible to suggest one contemporary meaning: such lists have *a* meaning for foreigners insofar as they are promoted by the heritage industry and therefore required for those tourists wanting an 'authentic experience' of the country. Eliot, suggested that people can make their own lists as indeed they have. For example, George Orwell's list (1941: 11) is familiar too: 'solid breakfasts and gloomy Sundays, smoky towns and winding roads, green fields and red pillar-boxes, the pub, the football match, the back garden and the "nice cup of tea"'. These lists are not of mere historical interest. It is possible to cite more recent examples, for they are frequently invoked.

Take just a few random examples. Over seven pages of listing those things without which 'England wouldn't be England', Alan Titchmarsh (2007: 130–6) refers to (amongst many other things): cucumber sandwiches (no crusts), the National Trust, inglenooks, knotted handkerchiefs, Melton Mowbray Pork Pies, the Shipping Forecast, *Gardeners' Question Time*, the Dowager Duchess of Devonshire, Betty's Café and Guy Fawkes Night. Ian Dury & The Blockheads in their song 'England's Glory' (1977) list such glorious lines as 'Frankie Howerd, Noël Coward and garden gnomes/Frankie Vaughan, Kenneth Horne, Sherlock Holmes' and 'Winkles, Woodbines, Walnut Whips/Vera Lynn and Stafford Cripps'. As the final chorus claims: 'And every one could tell a different story/And show old England's glory something new'. Politicians and political commentators also have a fondness for lists when it comes to what England means to them. For John Redwood (http://whatengland-meanstome.co.uk/?p=38), England means 'a summer's day by a river in a wooded valley, an afternoon on the cricket field, strawberries at Wimbledon, and well kept gardens in leafy suburbs. It is seeing Shakespeare enacted at the Globe, hearing William Byrd and Handel'. While for Iain Dale (http://whatenglandmeanstome.co.uk/?p=119) it is 'the green landscape, the village shop, the pub, the Daily Telegraph'. Similarly, acknowledged 'foreigners' might compile their own lists of Englishness in an attempt to situate themselves in their adopted country (the naturalised Eliot is here a case in point), or simply to summarise what it is the term 'England' conjures up for them. The German researcher Anna Rettberg, for example, whose research focuses on rebranding and rewriting national identity in contemporary literature, explains that she borrows 'a typically English form' to present her ideas, and then offers a list of her own personal markers of Englishness that includes 'red telephone and letter boxes, double decker buses, queues and many apologies ... (littered) canals with narrowboats, red-bricked terraced houses, rows of chimneys with seagulls, single-glazed windows, fenced gardens ... mist and fog, rain showers, a nice drizzle and sunny spells ... obscure cricket rules and village greens ... oaks and sheep on green fields, rolling hills, hedges and stone walls, a day out, Ordnance Survey maps, public footpaths, gates and stiles' (http://whatenglandmeanstome.co.uk/?p=355). Are these lists nothing more than quaint eccentricities, eccentricity being itself a traditional self-definition eliciting not only national approval but also evoking the national 'genius', with an equal tendency towards being insufferably twee? Or are these lists alternatively evidence only of the old adage that 'twice makes custom', encouraging imitators to stand self-consciously (and so almost like a historical list) in line with Eliot and Orwell? These things may be true but there is something else at work which is worth reflecting on. As Willets insightfully observed (2009: 54), the meaning of lists is that they 'tell us we are members of a club with few explicit rules, or rather rules so subtle that they can only be caught by knowing references'. There are four points which can be made about the distinctiveness of listing as a source of English identity.

Firstly, they nearly always contain concrete, rather than abstract, references. In his *England: An Elegy*, Roger Scruton also noted this tradition of constructing 'eccentric lists of ephemera'. For him, recourse to listing suggests that England is 'not a nation or a creed or a language or a state but a *home*'. He goes on in language that would have been familiar to Stanley Baldwin: 'Things at home don't need an explanation. They are there because they are there. It was one of the most remarkable features of the English that they required so little explanation of their customs and institutions' (2000: 16). This expresses a truth rarely theorised but frequently encountered. Thus, when John Betjeman tried to describe what England meant to him he resorted to the evocation of place names like Huish Champflower and Kingston Bagpuise, a tradition followed by Flanders and Swann in their post-Beeching lament, *The Slow Train*, for the railway stations at Midsummer Norton and Mumby Row. Like Flanders and Swann – who also mention Selby and Goole – Betjeman admitted that for others England 'may stand for something else, equally eccentric to me as I may appear to you, something to do with Wolverhampton or dear old Swindon or wherever you happen to live' (1943: 296). His literary, even romantic, view of things would appear to be confirmed by modern empirical research. English people can associate with abstractions like common values but they do identify more readily with 'common orientations towards, or rootedness in, place – be it the homeland as a whole, the rural idyll of the British countryside, or another of the multiplicity of geographical referents of the nation' (Wallwork & Dixon, 2004: 35). That is why evocative lists of England as a place and a home are likely to continue to find a popular response in the future while, for example, former Prime Minister Gordon Brown's praise of 'British values' was always unlikely to achieve the same effect.

Secondly, the relationship between references is implicit rather than explicit. They only make sense in an association *distinctively* English, even though what may be *representative* of that association changes. Patrick Parrinder, for example, remarks in his *Nation and the Novel* (2006: 16) how, in English literature, 'associations of Englishness are built up' – such that, for example, 'Falstaff's green fields are English by habitual association' not because anyone else's fields (like those of Ireland, for instance) are any *less* green. And as an example of Parrinder's claim, Julian Barnes, in his novel *England England*, uses traditional icons of Englishness but deconstructs them for his own means. By building his novel around different lists of Englishness, he not only ridicules this idea in the first place but also shows up those lists precisely for what they are: artificial constructs conveying a few stereotypes of the nation. Their shortcomings, he intimates, are clear to see: most of the markers of Englishness compiled in the book's '50 Quintessences' are traditional, backward-looking, and nostalgic (1998: 83–5). They do not provide a version of a contemporary England in miniature, but one of an England of times gone by, a mythical version of England. With this, Barnes lampoons the contemporary heritage and tourism industry that, rather than really furthering a healthy patriotism, 'Disneyfies' the past and turns it into a fiction (Berberich, 2009). However, what is 'real' – insofar as England is an 'imagined community' – is far from clear. Barnes certainly exaggerates only one part of English self-understanding and recruits it to stand in for the whole. Similarly, James Hawes, in his dystopian novel *Speak for England* (2005), resorts to lists in order to give a sense of self – or rather to firmly link the idea of 'self' to the idea of 'place'. His female character George, who has grown up far away from England amidst a group of 1950s English plane-crash survivors who have fathered a new colony of little Englanders, chants English place names while having sex with the *English* hero, Brian. Her increasingly frantic litany of 'Trafalgar Square ... Horse Guards, Whitehall, the Houses of Parliament ... Windsor, Oxford, Stratford-upon-Avon ... The White Cliffs, the White Horse, Stonehenge. Oh, Hadrian's Wall and Offa's Dyke, Ullswater, Long Mynd, Simmon's Yat' that, predictably, culminates in a jubilant 'England, oh England' (2005: 149–51) suggests that she seeks to find security in – for her – quasi-mythical places of a 'motherland' she has never seen for herself, and it is in this that the irony of Hawes' text lies: for the stranded 'colonists' in Papua New Guinea, England has turned into a fabled land, far removed from the rather disillusioning reality of the early twenty-first century. 'Listing', for George, is the only way of trying to get 'close' to England.

Another example shows how one study of the Cotswolds revealed how that area's idea of itself has been influenced by changing ideas of Englishness and vice versa because 'regional identities construct and are constructed by national identity' (Brace, 1999: 503). The dream of England captured in the rural landscape of places like the Cotswolds, and the reality of England displayed in its predominantly urban life – the distinction between idealisation and the real which Barnes was drawing absolutely – can represent two worlds that either exclude or complement. The most influential cultural readings of Englishness, including Barnes's, have argued the former case and used this as a metaphor for England's social, political and economic backwardness (see Nairn, 1977; Wiener, 1981a; Wright, 1985). We would argue that this is a misreading of a much more complex relationship between notions of England because in the popular imagination the particular can substitute for the whole or the whole can be found in the particular but together they can form a stable, if complex and changing, sense of nationhood.

Thirdly, if the changing concrete references in the lists do suggest something ephemeral – the fragments of experience – continuity of association is also evoked. Take, for instance, Ernest Barker's conclusion to *The Character of England*. He thought that it was possible to be too seduced by change and to miss the larger picture. 'But this long slow movement of the character of England', he asked, 'has it not something enduring?' (1947: 575). The answer, of course, was in the question. And if that answer seems familiar it is because Orwell had made a similar point, describing England as 'an everlasting animal stretching into the future and past, and, like all living things, having the power to change out of recognition and yet remain the same' (1941; 2001: 277). And there are affinities also with Anthony Powell's reflection on English sensibilities in *A Dance to the Music of Time*: 'Everything alters, yet does remain the same' (1997: 358). As T.S. Eliot sensed in the chapel of Little Gidding, connecting the ephemeral to the permanent meant that history is now and England. This tradition of reflection may be a consequence of the English craving for the picturesque and suspicion of the sublime – that whereas the German looked to metaphysical union in the state, the Englishman 'loves his country, is proud of his nation, but distrusts the state' (Gelfert, 1992: 41). Again, unlike Gordon Brown's 'values' – which were more appropriate to the metaphysical union of the British state – Englishness requires something more concrete and less sublime. That may overstate things, but the distinctively a-political character of

Englishness is one which has intrigued scholars. A recent example is Krishan Kumar's *The Making of English National Identity* (2003). For Kumar 'there are virtually no expressions of English nationalism' and 'no native tradition of reflection on English national identity', at least until the late nineteenth century. Even then, expression of national consciousness is typically cultural and distinct from the nationalisms of its European neighbours. 'The enigma of English nationalism', according to Kumar (2003: 34), 'lies in the fact that though the English must have *a* sort of nationalism, they puzzle everyone by thinking that they do not'. Roy Hattersley possibly captures this disposition succinctly in his own collection of essays, *In Search of England* where he proudly proclaims himself to be English but sees no point in making a fuss about it: 'Indeed, not making a fuss about being English seems to me an essential ingredient of Englishness' (2009: 2). Theoretically elusive English nationhood may be but that is to look for it in the wrong places.

Fourthly, what remains the same is a feeling of personal connection – for good or ill – with England. What constitutes Englishness may be understood as a conscious – or even unconscious – relationship with others both past and present. Oakeshott (1938: 359) put this well. 'Just as there are English poets (Blake perhaps) who appear to stand on the edge of the English poetic tradition, so there are philosophers (Hobbes, for example) who appear anxious to detach themselves from the philosophic tradition; but Blake is as impossible without Shakespeare and Milton and much that he himself had never read, as Hobbes without Aristotle, Epicurus and Aquinas.' Englishness, in short, is another way of talking about that 'standing-in-relation', irrespective of whether particular cultural 'products' are individually recollected or not (Boucher, 1991: 721). A recent exposition of a similar notion can be found in Pierre Bayard's (very French) thesis with the provocative title *How To Talk About Books You Haven't Read* (2007).

For Bayard, culture is all a matter of orientation. It is about 'being able to find your bearings within books as a system, which requires you to know that they form a system and to be able to locate each element in relation to the others'. This mastery is 'a command of relations' but not of every book in isolation (which even for the most studious is impossible anyway). Thus it is possible to feel oneself part of the national conversation even if one is ignorant of 'a large part of the whole' (2007: 10–12) or, one could add, critical of it. Just as we may be ignorant of much of 'our' history or of 'our' politics – and most of us are – without in any way feeling that we have no sense of nationality, so we may be ignorant of 'our' culture without in any sense feeling that it is alien to us or that we cannot speak of it intelligently. Similarly, the literature which may have played important roles in our imaginative lives – one naturally thinks here of Shakespeare – we may never have read. 'But the way other people talk to us or to each other about these books, in their texts and conversations' allow us to make sense of their connection (Bayard, 2007: 33). For Bayard, this is what constitutes our 'virtual library' and the trick is to define a book's place in that library 'which gives meaning to it in the same way a word takes on meaning in relation to other words' (2007: 117). He proposes that 'talking about a book is less about the book itself than about the moment of conversation devoted to it' (2007: 163), concluding with the reflection that the diversity of culture is both revealed and enhanced whenever a book 'participates in a conversation or a written exchange, where it is animated by the subjectivity of every reader and his dialogue with others, and to genuinely listen to it implies developing a particular sensitivity to all the possibilities that the book takes on in such circumstances' (2007: 181).

Scholars of literature or art may devote themselves with great effort and with great erudition to the work of an author or artist and, like scholars in history, philosophy and politics, come to know a great deal of which the non-scholar remains entirely ignorant. For most people, however, such knowledge and such detail are irrelevant to a sense of nationhood, even when (as Oakeshott argues of Blake) they feel disconnected from it. Therefore, when Oasis sings of 'Don't Look Back in Anger' its members are, of course, making a very conscious literary reference and also evoking a tradition of angry young men. Those who listen to it may not get that reference and may never have heard of John Osborne but they are, nevertheless, participating in a practice with a distinctive (English) voice and it is interesting to note the rattle bag of cultural and historical references which people do carry around in their heads (see Condor, 2000). And those who have participated in a pub-quiz will understand how difficult it is to give answers in one particularly interrogative context to those questions about which, in a general context, one already 'knows'. This is one example of St Augustine's rule of thumb: that when one doesn't have to speak of something, one knows it; but when one does, one realises that one doesn't know it. In the case of cultural knowledge, at least, these are two rather different types of knowing – in Bayard's terminology, knowledge of the actual book and a command of the relations of books. The second is the cultural knowledge which most people seem to have and is what generally passes for a national identity. What constitutes that knowledge is always changing. One's cultural formation is not exclusively national of course, but there is an inescapably national inflection to what one knows and experiences, even as things change. As the novelist Andrea Levy once put it: 'If Englishness does not define me, then redefine Englishness' (cited in Nünning, 2004: 150). That is true up to a point, the point being that those claiming that England should redefine itself also undergo redefinition in terms of the England in which they find themselves. There is only one grand illusion, as Oakeshott famously observed, and that is to think that there is a harbour for shelter or a floor for anchorage, a starting-place or an appointed destination – in other words, the illusion that there will be a final definition, that there is an origin or essence specifying authenticity, or that there is some objective towards which everyone is headed. Or, to change metaphors, national culture 'is not a groove within which we are destined to grind out our helpless and unsatisfying lives' (1991: 63). There are many grooves and lives are in constant adjustment. 'Culture', as Eliot remarked (1972: 94), 'can never be wholly conscious – there is always more to it than we are conscious of; and it cannot be planned because it is also the unconscious background of all our planning'.

Listing, we suggest, is a way of talking about England without having to theorise it, for the enumeration of the references already requires a personal command of relations, conscious and unconscious. If there is a larger moral here it is possibly the one which Robert Colls (following Santayana) makes in the conclusion to *The Identity of England*: 'the nation's propensity for seeing itself as diverse should not be allowed to outstrip its propensity for seeing itself as unified' (2002: 380). In this regard, listing again seems a very English way to acknowledge diversity but also to imply its own unity not as a transient 'common enthusiasm or a common purpose' (Eliot, 1972: 51) but as a complex association. As the blogger Paul Watterson (http://whatenglandmeanstome.co.uk/?p=51) argued: 'England is a jigsaw puzzle of many diverse and disparate parts, but like any jigsaw puzzle, the picture is only truly complete when all those parts are present and fitting together.' The image of the jigsaw is, incidentally, one that Barnes also applies in *England England* (1998): the protagonist Martha's earliest memory is, allegedly, that of sitting at the kitchen table, assembling her 'Counties of England' jigsaw. While Martha is still learning about her sense of self and the role of 'place' for it, her father suddenly leaves the family, accidentally taking the piece for Nottinghamshire with him. Like her jigsaw, Martha's understanding of what England means to her remains incomplete.

How, then, can continuity in change – or sameness in difference – of Englishness be intelligibly expressed? Here is our first analogy taken from Michael Oakeshott, the metaphor of the 'dry wall'.

Dry wall

Oakeshott (1983) uses the image of a feature of the rugged country-side, the 'dry wall', to conjure up how historical events are related to each other. It is history of no premeditated design, but one in which events are related one to another by their particular interlocking shapes. The value of that particular image is that it evokes historical change in terms of historical continuity. But this continuity is not the continuity of permanent traits or fated behaviour but of contiguity, a contiguity that has space for events which appear to challenge much of what went before. Moreover, a nation remains stable (or not) by virtue of the touching shapes of practices rather than by the mortar of national purpose, deeply held values or collective destiny (which is not to deny that some people *do* see nationality in that way). The parts of a nation 'stand-in-relation' to one another and for Oakeshott the term designates an intelligible connection between related circumstances and not *mere* accident. As Ernest Barker, a close friend of Oakeshott, described the nation, it is one 'united by the primary fact of contiguity', its members being led by such contiguity to develop forms of 'mental sympathy'. These forms of mental sympathy constitute a common capital of thoughts and a common will to live together. Barker makes it clear that 'common' does not mean 'one-idea' and, following Aristotle, he proposes that 'social thought proceeds by the way of a plurality of ideas, by the way of debate and discussion between the different ideas, "when they meet together" and come into contact with one another, and by the way of a composition of ideas attained through such debate and discussion'. In short, a nation is 'some composition of the different threads of thought' but a composition that is neither finished nor completed (Barker, 1961: 76). In an England ever more plural than Barker could have imagined, this seems a remarkably apt reflection. Moreover, it is one which also recommended itself to J.B. Priestley, who thought – and here we can witness the English legend of 'common sense' – that the 'essence of Englishness, the great clue, the guiding thread in the maze' of its history is the preference for 'the open-ended' as opposed to the 'closed-in creations of pure rationality' (1973: 12). Of course, it is easy to get carried away by self-referential hubris and self-regard though Priestley was concerned to point out that this characteristic does not make the English any better or worse than anyone else, only, 'as so many foreign observers have testified, it does make them *different*' (1973: 12).

Oakeshott further identified two conceptions of historical identity. The first is an argument according to foundations or origins. It is, he argues, 'the theory of identity without difference, the theory by which difference of any sort destroys identity'. But where is to be found, he asked, 'this absolute original which, unchanged, is the real thing?' (1993b: 65) The second is an argument according to 'unchanging substance' which holds that identity requires an authentic core, a centre which persists through change. Oakeshott believed both of these arguments, while they have their articulate advocates, are unsatisfactory. For him, identity must indeed be discovered in history but not as original founding or unchanging substance. Change is continuity and continuity, change. 'Identity, so far from excluding differences, is meaningless in their absence, just as difference or change depend upon something whose identity is not destroyed by that change' (Oakeshott, 1993b: 65–7). And this would rule out two options for understanding Englishness – either the elaboration of a changeless centre to which the present generation can anchor itself, or the hankering after some authentic original to which it can return – which, again, is not to claim that some people do not see these as possible lines of political action.

Those intelligibly related circumstances compose in different periods what Oakeshott calls a 'character', formed by human choices but recognisable according to certain recurrences. 'It is not to be expected that this activity will not at some future time reach out towards something new, that it will not add to its stock' but 'what is already there' at any one time may become regarded as its current 'character' (Oakeshott, 1993b: 31). It may even be that so powerful is the character in any one period that its particular 'what is there' is often confused with the whole of a national tradition, when the historical character of which becomes rigid caricature and conveyed by generalisations such as: 'The English are, or do, this or that'. This sort of generalisation often acts as a marker of identity in popular culture, especially in Hollywood films. While these are caricatures, they may indeed capture something which is distinctive if not necessarily representative of national life and this provides a more sympathetic perspective on heritage listing than Barnes's. They may do so because, while some things do change, some things also stay the same, giving people a sense of how they do, or should, behave (Fox, 2005), since according to Santayana, nationality is too intertwined with our moral sense to be changed and too accidental to be worth changing (1922: 4). A good example of this insight can be found in a short essay by G.K. Chesterton, 'French and English', one which illustrates the subtleties which constitute the complex elements which compose an identity. Chesterton proposed that if an outsider (in this case the French) were to adopt the aristocratic manner of the English elite what they would imitate would be only the vice of snobbishness without its virtue. They 'would not understand those elements in the English which balance snobbishness and make it human'. To understand what Santayana believed to be England's 'national discipline', required 'all the leisure and the life of England through many centuries, to produce at last the generous and genial fruit of English snobbishness' (Chesterton, 1925: 289). Ian Buruma (1999) makes similar observations about those European Anglophiles for whom snobbishness, and the ordered deference it assumed, was an essential part of their enchantment. And if this seems a time-bound reflection inappropriate to modern England consider the story told by John Denham MP at an IPPR/Our Kingdom seminar on Englishness in November 2010. He recalled a train journey from Durham to London with a National Union of Mineworkers delegation during a national strike. Its members were going to London to lobby in support of their radical leader, Arthur Scargill. When he asked what they were doing afterwards, they said they were going to Buckingham Palace. They always did just in case they would catch a glimpse of the Queen.

The dry wall analogy, itself a long 'list' of different social, political and cultural dispositions, may seem too thin for a national identity. To assume that the glory of England – at least, according to Ian Dury – is a collection of different stories and not some grand narrative can sometimes provoke disquiet. Surely there must be more to England than the mere accumulation of stones in the wall? Such disquiet may bring about a search for the essential England, a quest to define the mortar of purpose holding the wall together, to find those permanent foundations which keep it all up. And these journeys to find the heart of England could well indicate a failure of national nerve in the stability of the construct. For example, Paul Kingsnorth's *Real England: The Battle against the Bland* is a cry for his beloved country, an England becoming ever more inauthentic as the 'globalised, placeless world spreads', where 'the spreading plastic of the consumer machine' grinds the people of England into 'citizens of nowhere' (2008: 16). His book tracks the struggles of those 'fighting the cause of the real England' – from the struggle to keep up the traditions of 'real ale' in the 'traditional English pub' (2008: 237) – and not in the *traditional* English pub, which, like *traditional* fish and chips, can often mean the very opposite, a fact already bemoaned by George Orwell in his article 'The Moon Under Water' (1968). And it is interesting to note that Kingsnorth's radicalism also echoes Roger Scruton's (2000) conservative attack on the modern 'forbidding of England'. In both cases, we can detect the desire to elaborate either a changeless centre to which the present generation can anchor itself or the hankering after some authentic original to which it can return

But consider Julian Baggini's journey into the English mind, the distillation of which he calls the English philosophy, a product of his having lived in England's *Everytown* (which turns out to be Rotherham). Baggini (2007: 72–3) addressed the question that the arrangement of this untidy national dry wall could not function if people were living differently. Did England not require deeper emotional attachments? This is a question made even more relevant by the impact of radical Islam. Baggini thought that worries about insufficient national glue holding society together were misplaced and 'the shared values we all need to sign up to are actually pretty minimal and civic'. If the English differed in their strength of feeling about Englishness this was to be expected and not to be deplored because it reflected strength, not weakness. For Baggini, toleration (one could say respect for where and how people stand in relation to one another) was the best one could do and that in England it still worked, not perfectly but adequately. The country had been – and continued to be – reasonably good at providing people with often 'incompatible ideals about how society should be run', the space to rub along together. In short, Baggini's experience led him to conclude that those who 'wring their hands over the question of national identity' were missing the point. They mistook the need for people to feel they belonged to England with the need for everyone to feel the *same kind* of belonging to England. Baggini was confirmed as a *dry wall* patriot, where Englishness was a tolerant but tolerable 'live and let live' and toleration, he believed, 'is England's dominant philosophical concept for maintaining a harmonious society' (2007: 74).

There was no need for deep brotherly love in this society of strangers and the dry wall only looked precarious if this intense commonality was indeed necessary for national solidarity. Nevertheless, how does the diversity acknowledge some form of unity? This condition is conveyed by the second of the analogies we have adapted from Oakeshott: Englishness as 'conversation'.

Englishness as conversation

Conversation has been termed Oakeshott's 'great image' where the human condition is nothing other than people 'acting and speaking in response to one another' (Minogue, 2004: 244). It is an attempt to show how Santayana's mesh of instrumentalities, irrelevance, misunderstanding, vanity and propaganda can also 'soliloquize in harmony'. Conversation, of course, has become a cant political and bureaucratic term, its overuse rendering it almost meaningless. Indeed, there is popular suspicion that, by conversation, politicians, bureaucrats and perhaps even academics really mean something very different from colloquial usage. As former Deputy Prime Minister John Prescott once put it: 'Conversation means you have a two-way exchange. You ask the question and I answer it. It's called conversation' (cited in Coleman, 2004: 116). Public cynicism rests on the assumption that the answer is an authoritatively pre-determined one and that conversation is entirely utilitarian, a means to achieve a desired political end. Guaranteeing everyone a say, of course, is not the same as guaranteeing everyone a hearing. Some may not be listened to, not because what they say is unimportant but because what they say is uncongenial to those who decide what *is* important. In other words, the popular suspicion is that you can speak all you like but you will only be listened to when you say what the powerful wish to hear. As Oscar Wilde said, 'I delight in talking politics. I talk them all day. But I can't bear listening to them' (cited in Gambetta, 1998: 19). Oakeshott's use of the term, as one would expect, is more subtle and complex. We argue that to say anything meaningful about Englishness as conversation, as it is implied in the frequent use of that term, it is worth attending to Oakeshott's considered thoughts. His starting point is the colloquial meaning but he goes beyond it to capture the relationship between various modes of discourse which, in the arts, sciences and practice, compose a national tradition like Englishness.

The art of conversation for Oakeshott has 'a dialectic of its own; circular, without beginning or end' (Oakeshott, 2004: 187). This image of conversation assumes political discourse without sovereign purpose or appointment with destiny, a view which complements the dry wall analogy of history and identity. According to Minogue, when Oakeshott talks of conversation 'he is thinking of the local pub, not Oscar Wilde at the Café de Paris' (2003: 10), and both Wilde and the Irish in general do receive admonishment for their prefabricated wittiness and epigrammatic flourish, 'conversation as a kind of intellectual bottle-party at which the welcome guests are those who come

with some exotic contribution' (Oakeshott, 2004: 188). However, this
is not a reprise of Matthew Arnold's distinction between the romantic
Celt and the rational Anglo-Saxon. It is not some clichéd English
solidity or sobriety which is favoured but the open-endedness of the
engagement. The enemies of conversation are 'the noisy, the quarrelsome, the disputatious, the thrusters, the monopolists and the
informers who carry books in their pockets and half-remembered
quotations in their heads' (Oakeshott, 2004: 189). And if this is
thought to be a one-sided conservative deformation of English traditions, it is reminiscent of Orwell's (very English) depiction of the
communist agitator in *The Road to Wigan Pier* as a character half
gangster, half gramophone. For Oakeshott, like Orwell, 'absolute
dogmatism' and 'absolute omniscience' destroy the conversational
basis of politics which has defined English self-understanding
(Baggini's toleration). He identifies it as the most civilised of the arts
but not the greatest, 'a mean between extremes and therefore appropriate to the civilised man, who is neither a genius nor fool' (2004:
191). As such, it is not for the powerful, who find conversation a
distraction, for instance Gordon Gekko's comment in Oliver Stone's
Wall Street: 'It's all about bucks, kid. The rest is conversation' (20th
Century Fox, 1987). Nor is it for the dullard (for reasons nothing to
do with self-protection as in Seamus Heaney's [1975] rendering of the
Ulsterman's 'Whatever you say, say nothing') because from the
dullard's point of view – unlike the wary Ulsterman's deflective loqua-
tiousness – there *is* little that is worth saying. 'Conversation, in short,
is a disposition of the human soul; it may often reveal itself in talk, but
it is capable of civilising any of the activities in which human beings
engage' (Oakeshott, 2004: 193). What is required is forbearance from
dogmatism and some give and take, 'internal discipline combined with
the absence of a route to be taken or a conclusion to be reached'
(Oakeshott, 2004: 197). The political implication which is drawn from
this conversational imagery hardly varies, and what he was later to call
'ambulatory conversation' is always to be preferred to the certainties
of rationalism in politics (Oakeshott, 1975: 324). This is a familiar
ideal of political Englishness and is not specifically conservative.

If there is one activity, argued Oakeshott, which has benefited from 'the
civilising touch of conversation, it is politics' (2004: 194). Significantly,
he believed this to have been the mark of English achievement and a
considerable contribution to modern civilisation for 'remarkably
enough it was Englishmen (who are otherwise not greatly disposed
towards conversation) who first explored the recognition that politics is

supremely eligible to be a conversational art' (2004: 195). The civilities informing the English habit of parliamentary debate were only slowly cultivated when 'dogmatic intelligence was met by conversational intelligence, and what we now call "politics" is the byproduct of this encounter' (2004: 195). Here is the philosopher's version of Balfour's introduction to Bagehot's *The English Constitution* (Balfour, 1927: xxiv) where he observed that the raucous bickering of English political life required the sharing of common sentiments and a disposition towards compromise. Conversation *as Englishness* – a plurality of voices within a common tradition of behaviour – is therefore very different from the sense in which Conor Cruise O'Brien (1994) wrote of the 'ancestral voices' of religion and nationalism in Ireland: dangerously dogmatic and uncompromising in effect. It is also very different from the Jacobin (and Puritan) quest where truth is in contest with error and where speech is nothing but argument, only permitted until truth is achieved. The conversational style, which Oakeshott believes to inform the English parliamentary tradition, puts truth not against error but against lies. Reputable political behaviour 'is not dependent on sound philosophy'. Rather 'constitutional tradition is a good substitute', and in this respect English politics has been remarkably rich. And it is notable that here is another 'concrete' reference. Parliamentary democracy is not an abstract idea but 'a way of living and a manner of politics which first began to emerge in the Middle Ages'. Out of that era was fashioned a way of life and manner of politics, 'an outline which has since been enlarged by experience and invention and defended against attack from without and treason from within' (Oakeshott, 1948: 476). This view is not universally shared, of course, but it is part of the legend of Englishness, even on the left.

For example, Colls (2007b: 525) has argued that: 'National identity, or "personality", is clearly connected to constitutional practice.' If that practice was not always democratic it was generally popular. This can be illustrated by a modern reference to Billy Bragg's *The Progressive Patriot* where he writes self-consciously in this idiom of English conversational politics. Abandoning absolute oppositions, Bragg can acknowledge virtue in the work of those with whom he would disagree politically, like Roger Scruton, and to accept that modifying the institutional inheritance of the past is preferable to smashing it. The Englishness of Bragg's politics is actually confirmed by what he denies and what he denies is 'The Whig Interpretation of History', an interpretation he can only associate with the deluded or disingenuous 'traditionally correct brigade'. Macauley's idea of English history as one of physical, moral and intellectual improvement is dismissed only to re-emerge in 'The Bragg Interpretation of History' which charts the road to popular liberty from Magna Carta to the Welfare State. Furthermore, his story of improvement does not rely on 'foreign philosophies or imported ideas' but is 'part of the core fabric of our nation', something of which Bragg is 'immensely proud'. He has found a reason to belong because he can identify with 'values of fairness, tolerance and decency', those very values which, Herbert Butterfield argued in *The Englishman and his History* (1944), made for dubious history but for good politics (like Baggini's tolerant English). Bragg's history may not be sound but his politics, even in dissenting mode, form part of a national conversation of decency. And it is interesting to note here that Peter Ackroyd tracks the emergence of English political stability and cultural liveliness to seventeenth- and eighteenth-century trends for conversation to 'become the single most important medium for understanding' and where 'with its unique form and its formidable strength the essay itself takes its place as a true feature of the English imagination' (2002: 318).

This conversational understanding of political discourse evokes open-endedness and flexibility. It does not mean that there are no arguments in politics, even violent ones, but it does mean that even ideological politics are implicitly traditional in that they cannot be abstracted from the larger 'goings on' within a national community. What may appear to be a revolutionary and radical change comes often to look, in retrospect, like the modification of particular circumstances, the continuities just as obvious to the historian as the changes. And to use a very English analogy, those radical voices in Anthony Powell's *A Dance to the Music of Time* – Quiggins, Bagshaw, Widmerpool and others – speak a recognisable language and form part of a familiar world in that lifetime of literary conversation without in any way diminishing their radicalism. The theoretical framework of conversation, in short, does not exclude the fiercest debate or dispute, it only excludes the expectation of an argument to end arguments. This is not a peculiarly conservative or even exclusively English perspective. For example the radical American constitutional theorist Bruce Ackerman has argued that, for all its historical contingency and imperfection, 'constitutional language has set the terms within which previous generations have disagreed with one another, and sometimes has allowed them to move beyond disagreement to a transformed understanding of their political commitments'. He thought this was particularly appropriate for national identity, which is neither atemporal nor momentary but involves the 'situated understanding one might reach after a good conversation' (1989: 477–8).

This open-endedness goes quite some way towards dealing with the related criticism that conservatism is a necessary consequence of understanding Englishness as conversation. There is much in Oakeshott that we can find in the work of other theorists who are certainly neither philosophically nor politically conservative and one can trace the notion in the work of, for example, Bikhu Parekh (2008) and Chantal Mouffe (2005; see also Isaacs, 2006: 169–73). However, an appropriate reference (in a double sense) can be made here to David Miller. In *On Nationality*, Miller argues that the process of national change 'should consist in a collective conversation in which many voices can join'. In this conversation, he restates a venerable radical proposition that no voice should have a privileged status: 'those who seek to defend traditional interpretations enter the conversation on an equal footing with those who want to propose changes'. And this proposition of equality distinguishes the radical from the conservative who believes that the authority of established practice *should* have a privileged voice. For Miller, 'liberal freedoms play a vital role in providing the conditions under which conversation can continue' though he is historically less assured than Oakeshott in accounting for those liberal freedoms (1995: 127–8). Indeed, Miller's use of the term conversation has been described by one commentator as a very *English* way of thinking about nationality. 'How many other countries in Europe, not to mention elsewhere, have enjoyed more than a few decades of the kind of peaceful evolution and tolerance that Miller wants to defend?' (Benner, 1997: 199). Certainly this is not a universal condition and conversations about nationality, as Miller understands them, require institutionalised agreement on norms that all citizens respect, the very thing which Oakeshott's Englishness patriotically assumes. Others, particularly Canadians, appear to appreciate the explanatory value of a conversational understanding of nationality. Charles Blattberg, for example, has identified patriotic conversation as the basis of sound democratic politics, one based on intimations from practice rather than abstract theory. The assumption is 'that there is already some sharing, some integration, between the conflicting parties to begin with' (2003: 163), but it is only because of the differences that there is a conversation at all.

If nations are, as Benedict Anderson has asserted, imagined communities (Anderson, 1991), then conversation is all the more important for a *shared* imagination of the nation; and this is where novels contribute to our understanding. Parrinder writes that 'fictional narrative gives us an inside view of a society or a nation' and that 'the novel's representation of Englishness . . . reflect[s] what seems

to be the national characteristic of unity-in-division' (2006: 1). Since
the novel's eighteenth-century beginnings and its quick rise to fame, a
preoccupation with nation, nationhood and national identity has been
evident – from the likely writers such as Defoe and Disraeli, to those
who had a more hidden political agenda, such as Jane Austen or
Charlotte Brontë. The conversation between novel and reader might
not be obvious at first glance, but if theorists such as Roland Barthes
are to be believed, then it is only the reader who instils a novel with a
meaning, a point that Virginia Woolf similarly expounds in one of her
last essays, aptly entitled 'The Reader', in which she explains that the
reader 'can read directly what is on the page, or, drawing aside, can
read what is not written' (Woolf, 1979: 429). In this sense, a novelist
might inscribe a novel with national ideas and ideals, but it is, effectively, the reader who not only decodes this message but adopts – or,
as the case may be – *adapts* it for his or her own means. This active
engagement with the text – or, we could say, this 'conversation'
between novelist and reader – has changed considerably over the past
century. Kumar links the creation of a national canon of literature
directly to the idea of nationhood: 'English culture, at its deepest level,
is seen as created by a series of "national" poets, dramatists, and
novelists. Their writing embodies values, whole ways of life, which
express the aspirations of the national culture at its best and highest'
(2001: 49). Literature, especially in the nineteenth century, had a
didactic function in that it aimed to educate (perhaps 'indoctrinate'?)
its readers in nationally acceptable norms and values – one only has to
think of the continuous Francophobia that can be found in early nineteenth-century novels (all of the otherwise enlightened Charlotte
Brontë's novels are a case in point here), or the casual anti-Semitism
displayed by acknowledged 'Greats' such as Dickens. The second half
of the twentieth century saw a new trend, aided, on the one hand, by
decolonialisation, and, on the other, by the emergence of literary post-
modernism. Writers from the former colonies provide a new
dimension to the writing on and about English national identity by
presenting the dichotomy of the mythical England they learnt about,
predominantly, from books and the 'real' and, in most cases, entirely
different England – Andrea Levy's *Small Island* (2004) being a particularly pertinent recent example. Other contemporary novelists
actively toy with their readers' expectations: authors such as Julian
Barnes, Kazuo Ishiguro, James Hawes or Rupert Thomson have
created literary works that *appear* to uphold traditional notions of
Englishness on the surface, only to subvert and challenge them. The
resulting dystopias of contemporary England involve the reader in a

continuing debate about national mores and identity construction. 'Novels are the source of some of our most influential ideas and expressions of national identity', according to Parrinder (2006: 6). The very diverse nature of fictional writing on and about England is proof of the on-going conversation about England that sees its continuity in politics, the media, the arts and film.

Organisation of the book

On the one hand, the sense of English national continuity often evokes a settled identity or national character. And that character is, of course, a suggestive abstraction from the diverse and complex 'goings on' in any stable political community. It can encourage the thought that the 'English' think or behave in a certain way, that 'England' acts in a certain manner or that 'Englishness' is composed of timeless and permanent features. For example, when talking about 'those books they haven't read', the English are advised not to be enthusiastic since among them 'insincere enthusiasm is easily spotted' (Hitchings, 2008: 21). This can also be expressed perhaps as 'heritage', as something authentic or original, a singular sort of narrative. On the other hand, the contingency of events and identifications encourages scepticism about such national characters, reminding us of the diversity of English attitudes, of the difficulty of attributing activity to England, the meaning of which is constantly changing. We have argued that the relationship between the claims of continuity and the claims of change, as Oakeshott and Orwell in their different ways understand them, can be captured by understanding Englishness as conversation. We have also suggested that nationality is the placing of oneself (or finding oneself) in relation to a particular history, politics and culture. Some may feel that national belonging requires a common purpose and commitment, that nationality is 'ethnic' rather than 'civic'. On the other hand, others may understand themselves to be cosmopolitan rather than national. Indeed, they may feel alienated from much of what 'tradition' or 'heritage' represents. The chapters which follow elaborate how these matters have contributed to the making of modern Englishness in its diversity and in its commonality, a conversation between past and present; between continuity and change; between party and nation; between identity and imagination; between people and belief; between majorities and minorities. This book brings together insights from English history, politics, constitutional affairs, literature, psephology and social psychology to provide a digest of current reflection and is divided into three complementary parts.

In the first part, *Englishness in Discourse and Opinion*, the nuances and subtleties of Englishness are explored in Susan Condor's chapter on the conversational etiquette of national identification amongst the ethnic majority population in which those characteristics frequently referred to in discussions of the English – lack of national consciousness, confusion of British and English and absence of reflection on national identity – are revealed as a distinctive mode of conversing about these matters. This is not the same thing as a lack of national self-consciousness, for what is assumed in such conversation is as important as what is actually said. John Curtice's chapter assesses the extent to which devolution to the nations of the United Kingdom – with the exception of England – has affected English political identity. The survey evidence he cites confirms Condor's insights into the subtleties of how Englishness is publicly expressed, showing that the link between national identity and nationalism is far from obvious. Colls has argued that neither ethnic nationalism nor centreless pluralism make much sense in contemporary England and he thought that the challenge to political imagination intent on inclusiveness was not to deny patriotic sentiment but to increase 'the number of the points of origin, and loosening the terms of tenure' (2002: 371). Christopher Bryant's chapter explores the conceptual structure and sociological texture of what such a cosmopolitan England – neither ethnically particular nor abstractly universal – would look like. This open and convivial England is already intimated in the experience of London, though the positive, 'light side' of cosmopolitan London is not the whole of English experience. For there is a 'dark side' of intolerance and ignorance, and it is one which is not exclusive to the white ethnic majority. However, contemporary England is sufficiently open, progressive and accommodating for a cosmopolitan English 'community of sentiment' to be more than a 'mere idea'. Paul Thomas's study of the religious, cultural and racial tensions between Muslim and white youths in the North-West of England reveals both the dark and the light sides. Positive experiences of multiculturalism are uneven and prejudices are deeply rooted but the situation is not hopeless. Thomas argues that it is impossible to imagine a modern Englishness which does not embrace diversity and he shows that the convivial England which Bryant theorises is not a 'mere theory' either. Despite the divisions he uncovers, the conversational etiquette of Englishness which Condor identifies and Baggini discovered, remains as a major constraint on incivility.

The second part considers *Englishness in Politics and Institutions*. There are two aspects of received wisdom about the politics of Englishness which require attention. It has been argued, firstly, that politics in England is a 'state of mind, not a consciously organised political institution' (Rose, 1982: 29). Agreeing with Rose, Bogdanor believes it still to be the case that 'England does not at present feel the need to have her identity legitimised by institutions'. Disavowing political nationalism and 'delightfully reluctant' to make an issue of their character as a nation 'the English simply refuse to acknowledge that there is a question, remaining content to repeat Disraeli's aphorism that England is governed not by logic but by Parliament' (Bogdanor, 2009: 108). Secondly, Jim Bulpitt once claimed that traditional British statecraft intentionally mis-recognised England and 'attempted to relate to (or distance itself from) all parts of the periphery in similar fashion. For the Centre then, if not for the English, England was part of the periphery' (1983: 237–8). If the English did not feel any need for their identity to be legitimised, it may have been because they already assumed there existed a correspondence between the governing institutions and Englishness. After 1997, the Labour government believed that devolution to Scotland, Wales and Northern Ireland dealt with England in the appropriately English way: pragmatic adjustment without provocation. It assumed that devolution's asymmetry would disturb neither the constitution's ability to adapt nor the English citizen's capacity to accommodate change. This is the context for Simon Lee's chapter. Its argument is that the old confusion of British with English works now to deny England such that it has been doubly disadvantaged. It has been disadvantaged *nationally* because Labour's British Way denied the distinctiveness of England and it has been disadvantaged *civically* because democratic participation and accountability have been sacrificed to centralised convenience. Here is a challenge to the conventional wisdom about England as a state of mind (alone) and to that venerable Disraelian wisdom. This really is *News from Nowhere*. And those familiar with Morris's work will recognise the ironic passage: 'I must now shock you by telling you that we have no longer anything which you, a native of another planet, would call a government.' The English 'are very well off as to politics, – because we have none'. But this is no longer an English utopia. It is an English dystopia. The call to action is to politicise England and to give it a government. Lee can make a strong moral claim, captures a certain English mood but, as Condor and Curtice have shown, this has certainly not become a nationalist movement. However, the points he raises are unlikely to go away and Colin Copus addresses the effect on local government of the centralisation Lee criticises. His institutional analysis touches directly on that grand anxiety about which

Scruton and Kingsnorth have written, that England is no longer 'home' because of the atrophy of local identification. As Copus shows, the civic disengagement which politicians frequently bemoan may have much to do with the way in which both 'local' and 'government' have been deprived of substantial meaning by a long process of centralisation. The central institution of English political identity has been parliament at Westminster, the heart of what was once called the *English* constitution. Philip Norton traces the history of Westminster's significance in England's political imagination but also the difficulties this English understanding has encountered adjusting to claims to self-government in Scotland, Wales and Northern Ireland. Today there exists a distinctive English Question – what sort of recognition should be given to England within the contemporary reformed *British* constitution. It is interesting to note that Norton concludes with a very English answer: there is no rational solution, the question may remain unresolved, but Westminster will be pragmatic, adapt to new political realities and, despite all the recent challenges to parliamentary authority, this shows institutional self-confidence.

What of the legend of English conservatism which is the subject of Stephen Ingle's chapter? On the one hand, as one critic put it, English political culture '*is* a Tory culture' and 'there are some ways in which it exists more as this embodiment than it does as a political party' (Johnson, 1985: 234–5). On the other hand, T.E. Utley once asked: 'Is it not the great merit of English Conservatism that it comes to terms with reality and the great merit of the Tory party that it confines itself to the role of a midwife to history' (Moore & Heffer, 1989: 73–4)? Ingle's essay captures these ambiguities in the conservative reconciliation of Northern and Southern 'metaphors', a geographical reference with longstanding English political and cultural meanings. Few Conservatives, however, have felt comfortable with modern Britain, and for one of them it was luck, rather than any (illusory) dominant conservative culture, that made the Conservative Party the 'Great Survivor' (Bulpitt, 1991: 7). Nonetheless, the conciliatory legend of English politics (as it appeared) meant that power was ceded but also retained. In 1950, A.J.P. Taylor thought it rather amusing to suggest that: 'We are all Tories nowadays' (1977: 21). Almost fifty years later Lord Blake observed that one is unlikely to say of English politics that 'we are all conservatives nowadays'. But, he thought, 'it would be true, all the same' (1998: 416). However, what Conservatism now means and what its Englishness entails is far from clear, as Ingle demonstrates. And as Matt Beech argues in his discussion of the intellectual influences of R.H. Tawney, J.M. Keynes and Anthony Crosland, the interpenetration of class, religion and ideas formed a distinctive mix of English radical thought collectively known as social democracy. As he tracks its transformation – and diminishment – in the materialism and secularisation of English society, it is obvious that it too has lost much of its ethical fervour and justification.

The third part, *Englishness in History and Imagination*, reprises themes discussed in the first two parts, this time with a historical and literary emphasis. In *The Picture of Dorian Gray*, Oscar Wilde conjured the character of Lord Fermoy, a Tory except when the Tories were in office, 'during which period he roundly abused them for being a pack of Radicals' and blamed them for England going to the dogs. 'Only England', Wilde wrote, 'could have produced him.' He also identified the profession of Sir Thomas Burdon who, 'in accordance with a wise and well-known rule', thought with the Liberals and dined with the Tories. These may be taken as effusions of Wilde's brilliantly paradoxical style certainly but, as the preceding parts suggest, it captures truths about English dispositions that recur in its history and its literature (and possibly in its politics after the 2010 general election). There is another more serious, and possibly alienating, aspect here and it is the perceived dis-association of liberty and order, of legitimacy and power, of democracy and government, an aspect very much at odds with that very English ideology which, to use Watson's expression, proclaims the reconciliation of ordered liberty, of legitimate power and of constitutional stability – 'the idea of liberty expressed through parliamentary institutions' (Watson, 1973: 1). Wilde's England is the England of its elites – whose ideology this is – but there is another England that is written of, the England of virtuous people distinct from their elites, people who may very well think that the country *really is* going to the dogs and have no time for the Fermoys and Burdons of this world. Who are the people and who speaks for them? That of course is a question with many answers and Julia Stapleton outlines those given by two prolific and influential writers, Arthur Mee and G.K. Chesterton, the latter of whom especially targeted Wilde's aesthetic decadence in the name of English popular vitality. She recalls something which is all too often forgotten now that England has become distinctive in its public secularism (a point of controversy during Pope Benedict XVI's visit to the United Kingdom in September 2010) and that is a former self-understanding which providentially bound together Christian faith and English progress. This perspective complements that partial loss of larger purpose which religious traditions once contributed to English political discourse.

In the literary imagination as well one can find a tradition of reflection that England is going to the dogs, and this is explored in Day's and Parrinder's respective chapters. They chart and assess the representation of England in literature from the late nineteenth to the early twenty-first century. Kumar (2003) has asserted that Englishness, especially in the turbulent nineteenth century, was a predominantly cultural construction, and that literature was the primary tool to disseminate the idea of 'this England'. However, in an earlier publication he also makes it clear that these Victorian certainties regarding the nation crumbled in the twentieth century, and here in particular in its second half: 'The empire was gone, as was Britain's position as an industrial world power'. Now largely bereft of a major world role, Britishness 'capitulated' in the face of assertions of renewed 'Scottish, Welsh, and Irish nationalism. England, the core nation, stood exposed, no longer protected by a surrounding carapace of Britishness'. As a consequence, England has been forced 'to reassess itself and its future identity' (Kumar, 2001: 52). Day's contribution in Chapter 11 picks up on particular post-colonial anxieties and uncertainties regarding modern Englishness. He shows how the post-colonial 'Other' are affected when they arrive in England only to realise that the Motherland they have always taken for granted does not live up to their expectations. It is no longer 'real' in that imagined sense but 'hyper-real', having turned itself into a marketable commodity of the sort lamented by Kingsnorth and Scruton. Parrinder's contribution shows succinctly how literary presentations of England feed and build on each other, from the Victorian novelist on the cusp of Modernity, Thomas Hardy, via Edward Thomas, nature lover and Great War veteran, to that maudlin but accurate chronicler of an England in flux and decline, Philip Larkin whose influence still looms large, as can be seen in Parrinder's discussion of the contemporary poet Grace Nichols. His conclusion returns us to our beginning: of England in conversation with itself about politics, history, change, expectation and memory.

Part I

Englishness in discourse and opinion

Sense and sensibility: the conversational etiquette of English national self-identification

Susan Condor

English national identity: the incitement to discourse

By reason of some strange, obscure elements in him the Englishman remains, as he has always been, a somewhat incomprehensible being. (Dixon, 1931: 33)

In his historical analysis of the idea of English national character, Peter Mandler tracked the path of this 'slippery and flexible' (2006: 2) construct over the course of the past two centuries. In this chapter I will focus on a contemporary variant of this discourse: the idea of English national identity. The terms 'national character' and 'national identity' are often treated as synonymous. However, for the purposes of this chapter, I shall take 'national character' to refer to the psychological traits or cultural habits of a national people, and 'national identity' to refer to the ways in which members of a national group reflexively understand themselves.

Explicit conversation concerning the distinctive psychological qualities of particular national peoples has, to some extent, fallen out of fashion. In his account of the frontiers of British identity, Robin Cohen asserted that, 'Nowadays, it would be quite impossible in scholarly circles to get away with grand generalisations about national character' (1994: 2). Similarly, Mandler (2006) noted how debates concerning English national character declined over the course of the twentieth century. It might be reasonable to suppose that, as a subject of public debate, the topic of English national identity would circumvent a good deal of the normative opprobrium currently associated with explicit talk about English national character.

In public conversation, as in everyday talk, it is necessary to establish the reportability of any offering, if only to ward off the possible response of 'Why are you telling me that?' (Sacks, 1992: 12). Mandler (2006) documents a long tradition of casting English national character as extraordinary or enigmatic. Similarly, in more contemporary debates, English national identity may be cast as remarkable, problematic or perverse in a variety of ways. Historical narratives may be used to construct stories of lost identity, or to present English national self-conception as lagging hopelessly behind the post-Imperial, post-Devolution times:

> With the loss of the British Empire, large-scale immigration, the call of Europe, and renewed nationalist movements that threaten the 'break-up' of Britain, it is the English who find themselves most acutely faced with questions of national identity. (Kumar, 2006: 428)

International comparisons may be invoked to cast English orientations to national identity as extra-ordinary ('*unlike the rest of us*'):

> I recall spending an evening ... talking to a prominent English novelist about identity. I mentioned that I could not understand the reticence of English people, unlike the rest of us on the island, to talk about what it meant to be English. The novelist replied testily that it was like asking people about their religion and sex lives, something they were very reluctant to do. (McCrone, 2006: 276)

Talk about English national identity may be wrapped in moral-panic rhetoric, with the speaker suggesting that some facet of English national self-consciousness (or the absence of national self-consciousness) represents a threat to democratic governance:

> Former Home Secretary David Blunkett has called on the English to reclaim their sense of national identity ... Mr Blunkett said: 'There is a real danger that if we simply neglect or talk down national identity – people's sense of common belonging and shared values – we risk creating a festering, resentful national identity, an identity based not on confidence but on grievance'. (politics.co.uk, Tuesday 15 March 2005)

> What one most needs is to re-establish what we mean by being English, and when we have done that, we can see what the overlap of that identity is with a British identity. The consequences to politics of a country losing its identity is equivalent to an individual losing their own mind, and we all know what the outcome in those circumstances is. (Frank Field MP, 2009)[1]

Significantly, commentators often seek to establish the newsworthy status of their observations by suggesting that their own discussion of English national identity is filling a discursive vacuum. Krishan

Kumar noted in the preface of his scholarly treatise, *The Making of English National Identity*, that '[t]here is no native tradition of reflection on English national identity' (2003: x). In a rather more circumspect manner, David McCrone (2006) added a question mark to the title of his review of recent texts on Englishness: 'A nation that dares not speak its name?' In political debates, it is common for a speaker to couple his or her own remarks on English national identity with a quotation from G.K. Chesterton's *The Secret People*: 'you do not know us. For we have not spoken yet' (1915: 243).

Extending this line of argument, it is often suggested that the problem of English national identity (whatever it may be) may be addressed through further incitement to discourse.[2] The past few years have witnessed the development of a range of strategies for extorting more, or better, talk about national identity from the English people. These include technologies used to monitor the national subjectivities of the population of England (illustrated, for example, by the inclusion of questions on national self-definition as a regular feature of the annual British Social Attitudes surveys). Less formally, English people may be encouraged to publicly broadcast their national sentiments, fantasies and desires through some medium of mass communication (exemplified by the *What England Means to Me* website).[3]

The research interview as incitement to discourse

In this chapter I will focus on one particular device currently used to elicit talk about English national identity: the research interview. It has been claimed that we now live in an 'interview society' (Atkinson & Silverman, 1997) and, according to most estimates, interviews are currently used in about 90 per cent of social scientific research. It is, then, hardly surprising that a number of researchers (myself included) have used interviews and focus groups to study the national identity of the white ethnic majority population of England.[4] Some of this research has employed heterogeneous samples of adults (Abell, et al., 2006; 2007; Condor, 1996; 1997; 2000; 2006; 2010; Condor & Abell, 2006a; 2006b; Mann, 2006; Mann & Fenton, 2009; Skey, 2009; 2010) or young people (Carrington & Short, 1998; Faas, 2008; Fenton, 2007). Other studies have concentrated on particular sub-groups such as elite women (Edmunds & Turner, 2001); mothers in London (Byrne, 2007); soldiers (Gibson & Abell, 2004; Gibson & Condor, 2009); and English people in North Wales (Day et al., 2006), Scotland (Bechhofer et al, 1999; Kiely et al., 2005a; 2005b) and Berwick-upon-Tweed (Kiely et al., 2000).

Broadly speaking, researchers can view the talk that takes place in interviews and focus groups in two ways (see Abell & Myers, 2008). I shall term these the Confessional Model and the Conversational Model.

Researchers who adopt the Confessional Model treat the interview as a period of time-out from mundane social life, a context in which the respondent is given the opportunity to reflect upon, and provide testimony concerning, their everyday experiences. The interview encounter is designed in such a manner as to minimise so-called 'interviewer effects', treating the interviewer as a neutral presence charged simply with the task of encouraging informants to disclose personal information. Social scientists who approach interview talk in this way tend to focus on the semantic content of the respondents' accounts, which are generally interpreted as relatively straightforward reports of what the individual 'thinks about being English and British', their 'lived and felt aspect of national identity', and so forth.

In contrast, the Conversational Model treats research interviews as instances of situated social interaction. Researchers who adopt this kind of approach do not typically presume that interview talk provides definitive and unmediated ('depth') insight into what people actually think or feel at a particular point in historical or biographical time.[5] Rather, they are interested in what interview conversations may reveal about the ideological and rhetorical resources that participants use to manage their self-presentation, to construct narratives of identity, and to describe, explain and cast judgement upon the social world. Analysts who approach interview accounts as instances of talk-in-action do not necessarily take the semantic content of talk (what linguists would term the *sense* of the utterances) at face value. Rather, they are also attentive to pragmatic aspects of meaning (what linguists would term the *force* of the utterances), often conveyed through conventions of non-literal signification, such as implicature, ellipsis and irony.

In this chapter, I will consider some of the ways in which white English people talk about national identity in interview encounters, basing my observations on a corpus of transcripts of conversational interviews conducted in England between 1995 and 2009.[6] For the purposes of this chapter I will not be especially concerned with what the respondents say their national identity is (for example, whether they say that they regard themselves as English or British). Rather, I shall consider how the respondents go about articulating claims to, or denials of, national identity, with a view to explicating what people are *doing* when they set about answering questions about national identity.

Four traffic rules of English national self-identification[7]

Researchers regularly report that interview respondents in England often display difficulties answering questions concerning national identity. For example, respondents may produce 'silly' answers; they may offer contradictory replies within a couple of minutes of conversational time; they may deny any sense of national identity or disclaim any interest in the subject; they may express a measure of confusion over whether they should say that they are British or English. The conventional way of interpreting these kinds of accounts is to treat them as a source of information concerning the speaker's interior mental life. However, a focus on the manner and situations in which these accounts are actually voiced affords a different sort of interpretation. It seems that these kinds of answers often reveal less about how English people subjectively understand themselves than about the respondents' understanding of the social etiquette of talk about national identity.

Deborah Cameron has noted the reflexive character of talk in contemporary British societies:

> [w]e live in what might be called a 'communication culture' ... a culture that is particularly self-conscious and reflexive about communication, and that generates large quantities of metadiscourse about it. For the members of such a culture it is axiomatically 'good to talk' – but at the same time it is natural to make judgements about what kinds of talk are good and which are less good. (Cameron, 2000: viii)

When I reconsidered my corpus of interview transcripts for the purpose of this chapter, I was struck by the fact that the respondents were rarely treating their accounts of national identity as introspective self-reports. More often than not, respondents were talking about the act of talking.[8] Sometimes this involved metadiscursive commentary on the ongoing interview dialogue (for example, references to the interviewer's act of posing a question, or their own act of formulating an answer). Sometimes this involved references to conversations on national identity taking place at other times or in other places.

In addition, it was clear that the interview participants were routinely orienting to, and were often explicitly invoking, normative judgements concerning the right and wrong ways to talk about national identity.[9] In the following pages I will outline four general rules of conversational etiquette to which speakers typically oriented in the course of talk about national identity.[10]

Rule 1: don't state the obvious

Social scientists who attempt to solicit testimony concerning national identity from white people in England often report difficulty sustaining their respondents' engagement with the topic for any length of time.[11] The interviewer's task can be rendered especially difficult when a respondent appears unwilling or unable to talk about their national identity at all. An example of this sort of situation is presented in extract 1.[12]

> **Extract 1: 'I know how to speak.'**
> I   Would you describe yourself as English?
> LW   I've always been, I am what I am, not, I, I know how to speak, and I know how to speak properly. When I moved from Romford to Brighton, all the girls at school, I went to a girls' school, they all took the mickey out the way I spoke.

In this case, the semantic meaning of the interviewer's question would, on the face of it at least, appear relatively transparent. However, LW's reply would be difficult to classify using conventional social scientific schema for coding answers to questions concerning national identity. The standardised items on national identity used in the British Social Attitudes surveys, for example, do not include: 'I know how to speak properly', amongst the permitted response options.

So what should we make of LW's reply? Is she suffering from some sensory deficit? (Did she mishear the interviewer?) Is she suffering from some cognitive or discursive deficit? (Does she not understand the semantic meaning of the phrase, 'describe yourself as English'?) Does she have such a low level of awareness of, or concern with, matters of national identity that she is not cognitively primed to understand the interviewer's question in these terms?

Of course, any or all of these explanations could be correct. However, it should be noted that LW did not generally display difficulties of hearing or comprehension, and later in her interview LW talked about England and Britain at some length. Consequently, a more likely explanation for her response in extract 1 is that, at this point in the conversation, LW was treating her national identity as a conversational 'given'. Sacks has noted how, in cooperative conversation, 'it is your business not to tell others what you can suppose they know' (1992: 14).[13] By the same token, of course, it is incumbent upon us not to ask questions to which we already know the answers.[14] In the case of extract 1, LW may have been assuming that the interviewer, having already heard her talk about her life and background, would be aware of the fact that she is (and knows herself to be) English. Under these circumstances, LW might well have inferred that the interviewer intended her question to be interpreted figuratively.

Although the exchange in extract 1 is rather idiosyncratic, it illustrates a more general phenomenon, whereby white ethnic majority interview respondents in England are inclined to treat national identity as a taken-for-granted fact of life, rather than as a suitable topic for conversation (see also Mann, 2006). Social scientists who adopt a confessional approach to interview talk are inclined to cast situations in which national identity is treated as both figuratively and literally unremarkable as presenting the social scientists with an insuperable barrier to research. Further, they are inclined to presume that settings in which people treat national identity as unremarkable are also contexts in which people lack a clear sense of national self-awareness (see Bechhofer & McCrone, 2009: 5). From the perspective of the Conversational Model of interview talk, both of these assumptions are questionable. As Billig's (1995) analysis of 'banal' national consciousness demonstrated, when people's accounts are treated as samples of discourse it is possible to treat the taken-for-granted as an analytic topic in its own right. Moreover, the tendency to treat national identity as common knowledge need not be interpreted as evidence that the speakers necessarily lack clear, reflexive, understanding of the subject.[15]

More generally, social scientists have noted that – far from indicating some social pathology, discursive deficit, or conceptual absence – the capacity to establish tacit understandings (or 'common ground') represents an essential precondition for mutual comprehension (Clark, 1996). Further, the very process of relying upon shared tacit knowledge enables conversationalists to display intersubjectivity, and thereby serves as an essential mechanism for cementing social bonds. Goffman, for example, noted two ways in which rhetorical ellipsis may contribute to the delicate choreography of social interaction. First, the act of taking particular social facts for granted minimises a speaker's imposition upon his or her audience: 'if we could not rely on our listeners grasping the point without extended elaboration, we could hardly afford the time to say anything; similarly, if they could not depend on our taking into consideration what they already know, they could hardly afford the time to listen' (1983: 2).

Second, through the very practice of presuming a measure of shared understanding, dialogic partners are able to display empathy and attention to each other's needs. Hence, not only is it often unnecessary to state the obvious, but doing so can also constitute a breach of civility in so far as this may be taken to imply the absence of consideration for, or understanding of, one's audience. As Goffman noted, 'one's cognitive presuppositions about the … capacities of others present can become closely mingled with politeness understandings' (1983: 29).

In his own fieldwork, Goffman focused on the ways in which people claim and attribute identities in everyday social encounters. Significantly, he noted that people rarely report their identities directly. Rather, information about identity is typically *given off* nonverbally during the course of mundane social action. Similarly, Billig (1995) argued that people do not always need to report their nationality explicitly, since they are typically able to give off cues to this identity through accent and linguistic deixis.

A consideration of ways in which the respondents in my corpus of interview transcripts conveyed information concerning their national identity through pronoun use (*we, us*), revealed complex laminations of meaning that could easily be overlooked if a researcher were to accept the propositional content of their accounts at face value. For example, in extract 2 EG claims not to think of himself as English, whilst also displaying awareness of his status *as* English through the use of a speaker-inclusive notional '*we*':

Extract 2:
EG   I don't think of myself as English because **we** do some twatty things.

Similarly, in extract 3, SM denies '*feeling anything*' about being English or British, but then justifies this stance using a speaker-inclusive national '*we*' and '*us*':

Extract 3a: 'Absolutely wholeheartedly not British or English in the slightest.'
I   Tryna see really if you're British or English.
SM   I feel absolutely wholeheartedly not British or English in the slightest.
I   Not British? Why not?
SM   No, not not British, and I don't feel anything like there's anything brilliant or proud to be about being British or English. I'm sorry, I
I   That's fine, that's interesting.
SM   I, I cannot bear, I can't express this strongly enough.
I   We've hit a nerve here.
SM   No. No. No. No.
((*laughter*))

It's, just, I just felt that the Conservative Party hit a new depth when they started going on about this [...] Because, things like, I mean, it's just, things like, **we** in this country have the best British, er best steel industry in the world, except it is not competitive because **we're** not in the Euro, and I just think that small minded mentality is just, you, it's just, I absolutely abhor it, and I just think, what is great to be about English? [...] I just think that the images that people from abroad have of **us** aren't images that are particularly helpful or anything I absolutely want to be associated with.

Cases like this alert us to the problems that can arise when a researcher interprets fragments of people's verbal accounts apart from the precise context in which they were voiced. Specifically, it seems that when white people who have been born and are resident in England tell an English interviewer that they do not think of themselves, feel, or see themselves as English or British, they do not always intend their words to be interpreted literally.

In the case of extract 3a we can see how the non-literal status of a national identity denial can also be signalled by the use of hyperbole, or what conversation analysts call 'extreme case formulations' (see Edwards, 2000). In his immediate response to the interviewer's question, SM asserts baldly: '*I feel absolutely wholeheartedly not British or English in the slightest.*' In isolation, this might be taken as evidence that SM did, indeed, not feel British or English in the slightest. However, this interpretation is undermined both by SM's subsequent use of a speaker-inclusive national '*we*', and also by his explanation, in which he uses the phrase '*feel* [British or English]' as a figurative reference to Conservative, xenophobic nationalism. In this case, then, the use of an extreme case formulation ('*absolutely wholeheartedly not ... in the slightest*') is designed to display his investment in his rejection of national chauvinism, not to flag the literal truth of his denial of national identity.

The non-literal nature of SM's categorical national identity denial also becomes apparent when, a little while later in the conversation, the interviewer raises the '*British or English*' question again. At this point, SM displays a revised understanding of the question ('*Yeah. I see, I see*'), and offers a revised response in which he first acknowledges the common-sense status of his English identity ('*obviously ...* '), and then goes on to assert, '*I see myself very much as being English*':

Extract 3b: 'Obviously I see myself as English.'

I   So, I guess, in national terms, you don't see, you don't see yourself
        as English? Or as British?

SM   Yeah. Yeah. I see, I see, I suppose, that, yeah, obviously, I see myself
        as English. As, as, no, I suppose, I make the distinction, I see
        myself very much as being English.

Rule 2: do not make an issue of your national identity

Sperber and Wilson distinguished two ways in which an idea, object or
event may be referred to in the course of conversation, which they
term *use* and *mention*: 'USE of an expression involves reference to what
the expression refers to; MENTION of an expression involves
reference to the expression itself' (1981: 303). Situations in which
speakers tacitly allude to their national identity (through pronoun use
or implication) involve the discursive *use* of the construct. Conversely,
situations in which speakers *talk about* their sense of national identity,
the construct of national identities, or the language used for denoting
national identities, involve *mention* formulations.

From the interview transcripts, it was clear that respondents were
generally more willing to allude to their national identity in the course
of discussing some other issue than they were to treat their sense of
national identity as a topic of conversation in its own right. As we have
seen, in so far as a speaker could assume that their audience was
already aware of their national identity, the very act of mentioning it
could breach the *don't state the obvious* rule. In addition, respondents
were inclined to treat the act of mentioning one's national identity as
subject to additional normative prescriptions concerning decorum
and demeanour. Faced with the task of answering a direct question
concerning national identity, respondents often attempted to
inoculate themselves against a possible charge of inappropriate discursive conduct. They commonly stressed that their act of mentioning
their national identity had been specifically occasioned by the interviewer's question ('*since you ask* . . . '), and should not be interpreted
as a spontaneous utterance. They also commonly suggested that, in
the general course of everyday life, uninvited public assertions of
English or British national identity constitute a potential affront to
others:

Extract 4: 'If ... someone from abroad says "Where are you from?" ... '

BR I mean, I'm English. But only in so much as if someone turns round to me and says, 'Where are you from?' Say, someone from abroad says, 'Where are you from?' I'm from England, all right. But that's it. [...] You get people who take it too far, you get people who are, like, 'I am English,' and 'I want you to know I'm English', so to do that I've got to be like so against you, it's untrue.

In addition, respondents were inclined to stress the need to regulate verbal proclamations of national identity in the interests of public civility:

Extract 5: 'No need to make a song and dance about it ...'

GH Well, if somebody actually asked me then yes, I'd say I'm British. But I wouldn't be one of those people who goes around sounding it from the rooftops.

I Why not?

GH Well, I suppose I know I'm British, and that's what matters. No need to make a song and dance about it.

Extract 6: 'I don't stand up and shout.'

I So do you see yourselves, you talk about being, talking about England, whatever, do you see yourselves then as, I'm tryna think with you having travelled abroad, do you see yourselves still as British?

TB Well, yeah, but I don't, some people, I don't, I don't particularly

MB I don't stand up and shout

TB No I don't

MB 'I am British', and

TB I don't stand up and shout 'I'm British', and

MB 'don't do this', and 'we'll fly the Union Jack from here, there and everywhere', you know.

In extracts 4, 5 and 6, the respondents all emphasise their personal adherence to norms of discursive civility through contrast with '*people who take it too far*'; '*people who go sounding it from the rooftops*'; '*some people*' who '*stand up and shout*'. This can be seen as an example of a general tendency whereby people in England construct national self-imagery through the use of intranational comparisons (Condor, 1996; 2006; Condor & Abell, 2006a; 2006b). That is, rather than define themselves in contrast to a foreign Other, people from England are more inclined to judge their own orientation to national identity through contrast to an imaginary class of compatriots located in the past, in different places (North vs. South, urban vs. rural locations), in different social classes, generations or amongst people of different political persuasions.

Of course, interview respondents do not always display, or report, restraint in national self-identification. Take, for example, the stretch of talk reported in extract 7, below. The respondent, HW, was a member of the far right British National Party, and the position that he adopted exemplified the kind of stance that BR (extract 4) attributed to his nationalist Other. In order to emphasise his investment in being – and being recognised as – English rather than British, HW presents the interviewer with an emblematic example involving an incident that occurred when he was serving in the (British) army during the Troubles in Northern Ireland:

Extract 7: 'I'm not fucking British, I'm fucking English.'

HW I've been petrol bombed, bottles of piss thrown at me, bags of shit, you name it, I've had it thrown at me. And I was like walking down the street on a night patrol one night, and I heard this 'You fucking Brit bastard'. I'm not fucking British, I'm fucking English. So I told them and they don't like that then, see? [. . .] I'm English, and they called me a Brit bastard. I said, 'No I'm not. I'm English', and they don't like that.

Three things are worth noting about this stretch of talk. First, this sort of account was statistically exceptional: it was rare for the respondents to report energetically asserting their national identity in social encounters, and the people who did so tended to belong to distinctive subgroups.[16] Second, HW is orienting to the fact that his reported actions breach conventional norms of discursive decorum: he casts his vigorous assertion of his English identity as an act of verbal aggression, produced in response to exceptional provocation. Third, extract 7 is also unusual in so far as HW treats his public assertion of national identity as an act of 'telling': that is, of literal self-disclosure. As we shall see in the next section, white ethnic majority respondents in England were generally less inclined to view national identity avowals as a means by which to assert their authentic self-concepts, than to view them as a means by which to display consideration and respect for their audience.

Rule 3: national identity avowals should be recipient-designed

In ordinary social life, conversational offerings tend to be designed with a view to the assumed knowledge, and purposes, of the addressee (Garfinkel, 1967). As we have seen, English interview respondents are often inclined to treat their national identity as common knowledge: that is, as information that was already shared with their English interviewer. However, respondents often invoked two exceptional situations in which it may be appropriate to explicitly mention one's national identity: during travel abroad, and on ceremonial occasions in which one is required to answer a question about nationality for bureaucratic purposes. Both of these situations were associated with normative prescriptions concerning the 'right' way to answer a question. And in both cases, respondents generally understood a 'right' answer to be one which was designed to be intelligible to, and to fit the purposes of, the addressee.[17]

Rule 3a: semantic accommodation (use language that your addressee will understand)

In extract 8, respondent LH explains why she reported 'saying' that she is English with reference to the likely perspective of a foreign audience:

Extract 8: 'I'm responding to the way I feel that they're thinking.'

LH   Do you know what? Do you know one of the reasons why I say 'English'?

I   Mm.

LH   I'm, I'm, I only really answer that question obviously when I'm abroad, and I think it's because foreigners use the term English rather than British. Maybe because of the language.

I   Yeah, yeah.

LH   Yeah, so I don't actually think it means anything other than perhaps I'm responding to the way I feel that they're thinking. Like the French call Britain Angleterre don't they?

It was not unusual for an interview respondent to answer a direct question concerning national identity with the phrase, '*it would depend*', or the metadiscursive comment, '*it's a difficult one*'. Interestingly, in most cases, when a respondent uttered these phrases, they were not commenting on their subjective experience of national identity. Rather they were reflecting on the difficulty of producing a definitive answer to a question about how they 'describe' their national identity, or what they 'call' themselves, in view of the need to accommodate to the various perspectives that might be adopted by a foreign conversational partner:

Extract 9: 'It would depend on who I was talking to and where I was and what I was responding to.'

MC: I think a lot would depend on who was asking me really. It's a difficult one, because when we were travelling. I think when people used to come up and, you know, they knew where you were from obviously but, you know, but if I were being asked, like in America, I would have been more inclined to say British. In Australia or New Zealand I'd have been more inclined to say English because of the history. Do you know what I mean?

I   Yeah.

MC: I think for Americans, you know, Britain is like about this big anyway ((gestures a small area with hands)), so I mean, you know what I mean? I would use both of those names but I feel it would depend on who I was talking to and where I was and what I was responding to.

Rule 3b: pragmatic accommodation (tailor your answer to the questioner's purposes)

In England, questions about national 'identity' are capable of being interpreted in two different ways. On the one hand, they can be understood as requests for information about the addressee's ontological (for example citizenship) status ('*what are* you?'). On the other hand, they can be understood as enquiries about the addressee's self-concept ('*how do you feel* about being ... ?'). In their interview accounts, respondents often suggested that their understanding of the force of a request for information concerning national identity could vary as a function of conversational content. We have already noted how, in real or imagined face-to-face interactions with another English person, speakers were liable to treat their ontological status as English as a conversational given. Consequently, in this kind of setting, speakers were disposed to interpret questions about their sense of national identity as questions about their subjective self-image. In other imagined contexts – such as conversations taking place abroad or written communication – speakers were inclined to interpret questions concerning their national identity as requests for information about their citizenship status.

There was also some evidence that interview respondents' preferred interpretations of questions about national identity varied according to their social class and level of education. Generally, people from working-class backgrounds or with relatively low levels of formal education were liable to interpret questions about national identity as invitations to self-disclose. In contrast, people from middle-class backgrounds or with relatively high levels of education were more inclined to regard questions concerning national identity as requests for information about citizenship status.

Extract 10 reports a stretch of interview dialogue between an interviewer and two elderly sisters. Both agree that the only time the question of national identity '*ever crops up*' is for the purpose of foreign travel. However, their understanding of the force of the question (and hence what would constitute a felicitous reply) differs. KG, an ex-teacher, treats the procedure of filling out a passport application form as a ceremonial context requiring a standard response. In contrast AG, an ex-factory worker with no post-compulsory education, justifies her choice of answer with reference to '*how I think of myself*'.

Extract 10: 'I think British is what people expect.'

KG The only time it ever crops up is when you have to fill in a passport. You know when you are travelling (inaudible) you never discuss–

I It doesn't crop up?

KG No.

AG No.

KG If there was a question that asked your nationality, then we would definitely put–, but unless (.)

I So, so you'd put English rather than British, would you?

AG Oh yes.

KG I've <u>started</u> to put British but I used to <u>always</u> write English.

AG Oh no, I still write English.

I Why?

AG I suppose that's how I think of myself.

I Why have you started to put British?

KG Well, because I've decided – I think it's the more acceptable (.) nowadays

AG Well, maybe, but I think I'm–

[…]

KG I don't know. But I think British is what people expect.

When people interpreted questions relating to national identity as bureaucratic requests for information about citizenship, they could cast replies designed to assert the speaker's authentic self-concept as uncooperative and self-indulgent:

> **Extract 11: National self-assertion versus pragmatic cooperation**
> PJ I remember the customs guard up on the bus in France, and looked round and he said 'Anglais?' And these two, two Scottish lecturers came up and said, 'Ecosse!' and, and, and the customs guard just kind of raised his eyebrows as if to say 'yeah of course, of course, of course'. But I wonder if the French, for example, I mean (.) what's the French for British, I don't know if there is a French–?
> I I don't, I don't know.
> PJ Whether they think of England and Scotland as the same, that's what I'm saying, 'no, they're Anglais' [...] Anyway I imagine that customs guards are not really that bothered about what people [...] personally prefer to be called. I'd hazard a guess that if you are a customs guard you'll really be a bit more interested in knowing how many cigarettes someone is allowed to be carrying.

Awareness of the dialogic quality of public conversations in liberal democracies should, of course, caution us against assuming that accommodation between everyday and bureaucratic discourses of national identity involves a one-way process. At the time of writing, moves are afoot to reword the English Census item on nationality in response to a perceived preference on the part of the public to interpret this as an invitation to report their subjective sense of identity. As explained by the National Statistician.[18]

> With the new devolved administrations, there has been an increasing interest in 'national' consciousness with many people wanting their 'national' identity to be acknowledged. Many people in the White British ethnic group feel that their national identity is English. The Office for National Statistics encourages organizations to collect data on national identity and recommends the following question:
>
> 'What do you consider your national identity to be?'
>
> The question allows respondents to choose more than one identity (if they think of themselves as having more than one). This is because national identity is self-defined, i.e. it is something that is subjectively meaningful to the person concerned. (*Hansard*, 4 July 2005, column 128 W).

It is, of course, unlikely that this bureaucratic response will accomplish permanent conversational closure. On the contrary, this revised form of wording has already prompted objections on the grounds that it precludes the possibility that Englishness might be construed as an objective civic status.[19]

Rule 4: design your national identity avowals with a view to the sensitivities of the actual or potential audience

In previous work, my colleagues and I have considered how national identity claims are often made with a view to impression-management or, to use Goffman's terminology, establishing and maintaining the 'face' of the speaker. We have suggested, for example, that whereas people in Scotland often attempt to project a positive face *through* a strong claim to national identity, speakers in England are more inclined to treat national self-identification as a potentially face-threatening act, and consequently are often inclined to project an image of themselves as rational and moral individuals *despite* their acknowledgement of their national identity (Condor & Abell, 2006a; 2006b).

In everyday social encounters, rules of facework are typically treated as reciprocal. In the course of social interaction, people do not simply act to maintain their own face, but also act in such a way as to protect, or enhance, the face of the other participants. One interesting aspect of the interview discussions of national identity related to the ways in which speakers were inclined to import national Others into the interview conversation, typically positioning foreigners either as co-conversationalists or as ratified overhearers. We have seen how respondents could invoke an imaginary foreign audience when describing situations in which explicit national identity avowals might reasonably be expected. In addition, respondents often replied to questions about national identity with a reference to the imagined sensitivities of a generalised foreign Other. The default assumption was that any strong, or uninvited, national identity claim could be viewed as a potential threat to the face of national Others (see for example extract 4 above). Even those respondents who claimed a strong sense of national identity commonly prefaced their assertion with a disclaimer to the effect that this was not intended as an insult to others:

Extract 12: 'It's not meant to be an affrontery.'
ST: I say I'm English, you know, it's not to be an affrontery to them, because the Scots, the Irish, the Welsh, but, they do it the other way round, don't they? Very quick to let you know that their origin is Welsh or Scottish, and, yeah, I think I'd be the same.

Interview respondents could orient to the potential sensitivities of various classes of Other: the other UK nations; other nations in the British Isles; British citizens or denizens of different national heritages; People outside the British Isles. In addition, respondents could endorse different views concerning the likely preferences of these Others. For example, speakers could justify '*saying British*' on the grounds that this displayed sensitivity to their black and ethnic minority compatriots:

Extract 13: 'because ... ethnic minorities say they are British.'
I   In terms of nationality, what would you say you were? (.)
CK   Oh, er, British.
I   Not English?
CK   Well obviously I am English. I could hardly deny it ((*laugh*)) but I'd probably be more likely to <u>say</u> British.
I   Because?
CK: Because it's more inclusive. Black people and ethnic minorities say they are British. British is everyone.

On the other hand, people could justify describing themselves as English on the grounds that this displayed appropriate tactful deference to the sensitivities of both ethnic and national UK minorities:

Extract 14: 'I don't want to presume a commonality.'
I   What would you describe yourself then as nationally?
PV   English.
I   English.
PV   Yeah.
I   Why are you English? What makes you say that?
PV   Erm. Well, I suppose cos I'm kind of aware that, you know, there's people who describe themselves as Scottish and Welsh, and to try and describe yourself as British, is trying to identify, you know, I, I just think it's more accurate, really, and I mean, all this stuff about language, and stuff. It's all, you know, it's, it's, yeah, I think it's more accurate, and so I tend to say it.
I   Is that because
PV   So I was almost to say, 'I'm from England, Pakistan, Scotland or Wales.'
I   Mm. (.) So is that because you don't feel any kind of erm commonality I suppose for people in Scotland and Wales? Is it because you want to be seen as distinct?
PV   No. Well, I don't know if I, I wouldn't presu– well I suppose, I dunno, I dunno
((*laughter*))

maybe I'm not pres– no, no, no, no, but maybe I'm not presuming
it, I don't want to presume a commonality with these people really.

I   Mm. (.) Mm.

PV   That's very generous of me, isn't it?

I   I think it's a lovely thing.

((*laughter*))

PV   It's like stepping on their

((*laughter*))

     I dunno.

Sometimes people suggested that the best way to display affinity with
Scotland was to '*say British*':

Extract 15: 'Because I ... feel an affinity for Scotland.'

JJ   I used to say I was English just because I hadn't really thought
about it. When I actually thought about it, I thought, well, I am
British, actually. So, I got myself into the habit of saying 'I'm
British' when somebody else asks what nationality I am, which
doesn't happen very often, so it wasn't very easy to go round saying
that ((*laughs*)) but, yeah, that was something I deliberately did
because of those things, because I sort of do feel an affinity for
Scotland.

In other situations people suggested that the right way to display sensitivity to the population of Scotland was to '*say English*':

Extract 16: 'That's what they would prefer.'

I   What would you say your nationality was?

SE   Oh English, very much. I – I'd say I was English.

I   Why English? English more than British?

SE   I think I would have always said British but because the Scottish
don't want to be any part of that, then probably I'd say English
now. Not because I feel any different from someone who lives in
Scotland or Ireland or anything else, but that's what they would
prefer so that's what my – my response would be probably.

Sometimes people spontaneously mentioned the problem of attempting to display tactful sensitivity to the imagined sensibilities of all
Other people all of the time:

Extract 17: 'Other people would take offence.'

I   What do you see as your country?

PG   As my country?

I   Yes.

PG   Yes, that's a hard one. I don't know because I'd like to say – I'd like to say it's the U – well, I can't say the UK because I think other people would take offence at that I can't call myself – I don't like to think of myself as like, you know, English as in I am not the same or not part of the same people as the Scottish, the Welsh, cos really we are, it's just that, but then, you know, I mean someone from Northern Ireland might take offence at me saying I was like, you know– I like to think of my country as like the United Kingdom rather than – which is fair enough because, you know, I dunno.

On other occasions, a respondent's recognition of the ambiguous connotations of particular forms of national self-labelling could be prompted by the interviewer. For example, shortly after SE had explained that she would '*say English*' with reference to the preferences of '*someone who lives in Scotland or Ireland or anything else*' (extract 16 above) the interviewer asked, '*what about ethnic minorities?*':

Extract 18: 'There isn't a correct answer, is there?'
I   So what about ethnic minorities?
SE   Erm. Oh yeah. I think that perhaps they would prefer British. Yeah they would. Erm. Oh God
((laughter))
       Fuck. So what's the right answer then? Oh fuck. There isn't a correct answer, is there?
((laughter))

Lost in translation: (mis)understanding interview conversations on English national identity

The social dynamics of communication in research interviews
In this chapter I have been adopting a rather literal take on the notion of a 'conversation' on English national identity. Specifically, I have been focusing on the kind of talk that takes place when an interviewer asks a white person from an ethnic majority background, born and currently resident in England, to describe and to account for their personal sense of national identity.

Social scientists who elicit conversations on English national identity through 'qualitative', 'depth' or 'conversational' interviewing typically remark on a tendency on the part of respondents to disclaim a strong sense of national identity and to express confusion over whether they should call themselves English or British. Those researchers who adopt what I termed a confessional approach to interview discourse are apt to conclude that people who respond in this way are dispositionally uniterested in matters relating to nationality, or that they possess a non-salient, weak, ill-defined or confused sense of national identity.

In this chapter I have been questioning the value of this kind of approach. I suggested that in so far as research interviews constitute a form of conversation, we would not necessarily expect to be able to understand respondents' accounts by attending simply to the literal sense of the words that they utter. As in all conversational contexts, the meaning of an interview response will depend on the precise context and intonation in which the statement is made. More generally, successful communication in interview encounters, as in other forms of conversation, is likely to rely upon the ability of the participants to establish common ground, and to accommodate to each other's perspectives.

Clark and Brennan (1991) outlined three grounding mechanisms that people use to coordinate their understanding in everyday conversational contexts: the heuristic of co-presence (used in particular to establish the meaning of indexical referents like 'here', 'now' and 'we'); the heuristic of linguistic copresence (by virtue of which participants treat information that has already been introduced into a conversation as shared common ground); and the heuristic of community membership (according to which participants employ cultural stereotypes to gauge the likely level and content of their conversational partner's prior knowledge and beliefs). In this chapter I have shown how interview respondents can also be seen to employ these heuristics when they answer questions about national identity. For example, when speaking with an English interviewer, English people are inclined to treat their ontological status *as* English and *as* British as something that goes without saying. In so doing, they are using the heuristic of copresence (assuming that the interviewer will be able to interpret the identity markers that they are giving off through accent and pronoun use); the heuristic of linguistic copresence (assuming that an interviewer will remember what they have already said earlier in the interview about their place of birth etc.); and the heuristic of community membership (respondents make this clear when they mention how their accounts are likely to depend, quite literally, upon where their audience is coming from).

Grounding mechanisms are not only used to establish the sense-in-context of any particular contribution to an ongoing conversation. They are also used to determine the kind of speech act (Austin, 1962) that a speaker is performing: what is it that they are *doing* when they direct a particular statement to a particular person in a particular context. Researchers adopting the confessional approach to interview talk tend to presume that their respondents will (conveniently) be solely engaged in the act of literal self-disclosure. However, as we have seen, attention to the precise ways in which white respondents in England formulate their avowals or denials of national self-identity in interview exchanges suggests that they are in fact often engaging in displays of social sensibility. What is at stake is not so much the accuracy or authenticity of their national self-descriptions, as their ability to display socially appropriate forms of intersubjectivity, empathy, tact and decorum.

Miscommunication in the research process

The fact that conversationalists routinely employ grounding mechanisms to coordinate their understandings does not, of course, guarantee that they will always succeed. Instances of miscommunication can be especially common in exchanges between people who do not share what Clark and Schober term 'cultural common ground' (1992). Consequently, it is not surprising to find that misunderstandings regularly arise in research contexts in which the interviewer and respondent differ in age, ethnic, national or social class backgrounds (see Abell et al., 2006, for an example of a misunderstanding between a Scottish interviewer and an English respondent).[20] Troubles in interview conversations between people from similar backgrounds can also occur when interviewer and respondent have a different understanding of the point of the conversation, or when they are using vague words (like 'English', 'national' or 'identity') in different ways. We have seen one example of this kind of breakdown in communication in extract 1, in which the respondent misunderstands the interviewer's question, 'Would you describe yourself as English?' as an invitation to discuss the class-marking of her accented speech.

Research conversations are not, of course, restricted to the local exchange that takes place between interviewer and interviewee for the purposes of collecting data. Academic discourse involves an extended process of communication within and between various networks of participants, conducted through a variety of different media, and extending across long stretches of time and large expanses of geographical space. During the process of dissemination and translation, transformations in meaning can occur at any stage. Breakdowns in communication regularly occur in the course of academic communication (for example, when one author 'misrepresents' the work of another), and information is often lost or distorted in translation between academic, media, political and popular realms of discourse. In the interests of brevity, I shall limit my concern to the ways in which misrepresentations of respondents' meanings can arise in the course of analysing interview discourse at a distance from the immediate conversational context for which the talk was originally designed.

One obvious danger is that researchers who analyse records of research interviews may not attend sufficiently closely to *what*, precisely, a respondent was actually saying at a particular moment in conversational time. Analysts are often keen to identify segments of the interview data that correspond with their own (theoretically-derived) analytic categories. When this is the case, the analyst may treat the precise wording of a respondent's account as an irrelevance. When they come to present 'quotations' to their readers, the author may not be especially concerned about reproducing the micro-details of a speaker's original utterance[21]. Similarly, in the course of presentation, authors often summarise their respondents' accounts using gist-formulations, translating the speaker's original words into their own preferred terminology.

The potential dangers of lexical re-glossing become apparent once we recognise how, in its original conversational context, the meaning of a statement often hinges on what Billig (1995: 93) described as 'small', 'prosaic' and 'routine' words. Billig's interest was in the way national representations may be conveyed through pronouns ('here', 'us', 'them') or nonspecific nouns like 'people'. In this chapter I noted how a failure to attend to a speaker's apparently incidental use of pro-terms like 'we' and 'us' might lead to misleading interpretations of 'denials' of national identity.

Similarly, speakers can convey important information through their precise choice of, and artful slips between, verbs used to designate the psychological condition of self-identity. In some contexts, whether a respondent says that they 'say', 'feel' or 'are' English may be crucial to the sense of their utterance (see Condor et al., 2006). In this chapter I noted how, when answering questions about national self-labelling ('*English or British?*'), interview respondents often interpret the phrases 'say you are', 'describe yourself as' or 'call yourself' as a reference to the act of public self-pronouncement *as opposed to* private self-conception. Consequently, their replies often take the form of metadiscursive reflections concerning the traffic rules of talk about national identity, rather than reports of their subjective sense of self.[22]

The risk of misrepresenting respondents' accounts of national identity at the point of analysis is not restricted to the danger of over-looking the finer details of the transcript record. Paradoxically, the techniques that are commonly used to transform interview conversations into useable data, and to ensure the validity and reliability of social scientific analyses, involve stripping away a good deal of the information that the original conversationalists would have been using to establish mutual comprehension.

On the one hand, the procedure of recording interviews, and then translating the auditory record into written form, facilitates compari- son and classification in so far as it renders the conversations mobile, and enables the researcher to assemble a corpus of conversations together in a single 'centre of calculation' (Latour, 1987). On the other hand, the very fact that the analytic process is distanced both temporally and spatially from the immediate situation in which the talk originally took place compromises the analysts' ability to employ the heuristic of co-presence. The process of audiorecording interviews involves a loss of information concerning the body posture, gaze and facial expression of the interlocuters. The conventions used for tran- scribing these recordings often strip the original utterances of their prosodic features, including speed and volume of delivery, inflection and emphasis. Most established methods used for analysing interview accounts involve the segmentation of transcripts, thereby compromis- ing the analyst's ability to employ the heuristic of linguistic copres- ence.

Faced with the task of interpreting shards of conversation as stand- alone utterances, and deprived of most of the information concerning context, tone and manner of delivery which would have been available to the original conversationalists, it is hardly surprising that researchers should sometimes resort to the heuristic of community membership. After all, even if they canot see or hear the speakers, and are not aware of the conversation preceding the utterance in question, the researcher does at least know that the respondent (their own identity claims notwithstanding) *is* white and English. The tendency to interpret denials and mitigations of national self-conception as evidence of the abnormalities – and possibly deficiencies – of English national identity may, then, often owe less to the researcher's grounded appreciation of what the speaker actually meant, than to their preconceptions concerning the polymorphous perversities of English national character.

Notes

1 www.frankfield.co.uk/campaigns/devolution. All websites in Chapter 1 were accessed on 12 December 2010.
2 Concerns over the repression of talk regarding English national identity have historically coincided with a veritable discursive explosion on the

subject. This situation parallels the kind of process that Foucault (1979) observed in discourses of sexuality in the nineteenth and twentieth centuries.

3 http://whatenglandmeanstome.co.uk/?page_id=2.

4 Research on the national self-perceptions of minority racial or ethnic individuals in England has typically been discussed as a matter of 'British identity' (see Condor et al., 2006). The recent flurry of political and media interest in questions of national identity as they relate specifically to England has tended to focus on the white ethnic majority population. For the purposes of this chapter I shall be focusing exclusively on the interview discourse of this specific sub-group.

5 Social psychologists who adopt the Conversational Model typically assume an agnostic stance concerning the validity of respondents' accounts. Psychological research has shown that people's autobiographical memories, their description of their mental states, and the explanations that they provide for them, are often highly unreliable. With specific regard to the topic of national identity, recent experimental work has, for example, demonstrated that people who sincerely endorse civic understandings of nation may nevertheless display an unconscious tendency to construe national identity in ethno-racial terms (Devos & Ma, 2008).

6 The corpus currently comprises transcripts of 1862 lightly structured ('conversational') interviews conducted between 1995 and 2009. This includes interviews collected for the project *Nationals and Migrants*, within the Constitutional Change and Identity programme funded by the Leverhulme Trust (Grant Number 3511), and for the project *Orientations of Young Men and Women to Citizenship and European Identity* (EC, contract no. HPSE-CT-2001–00077). For further details on the procedures used to conduct and analyse the interviews, see Condor (2006; 2010).

7 I am borrowing the phrase 'traffic rules' from Goffman (1955).

8 Jackie Abell and I (Condor & Abell, 2006a) have noted how the perspectives adopted by social scientists typically mirror the dominant vernacular assumptions about national identity held by members of their national communities. Significantly, the stance that I am adopting in this chapter – treating interview discourse as a situated conversation rather than a device for exposing speakers' private psychological states – parallels the kind of orientation that interview respondents in England commonly adopted towards their own talk about national identity.

9 Clearly, if we treat interview talk as situated dialogue, it follows that we should treat the interviewer as an active participant in the unfolding conversation. Unfortunately, space constraints preclude my fully explicating how the interviewers orient to the same normative concerns as the respondents.

10 These four principles tended to be accepted by people from a wide variety of backgrounds. In addition, people tended to adhere to these principles irrespective of whether they expressed a strong or weak sense of national

identity, or whether they chose to describe themselves as English, British, both or neither.

11 It can also prove very difficult to initiate a research conversation about national identity in England. The interviews in my corpus were all conducted as (relatively) respondent-directed conversations. The interviewer tried not to prime the topic of national identity, but rather attempted in the first instance to elicit 'spontaneous' talk on the topic by steering the conversation round to matters such as home and mobility, political change, the monarchy, holidays and foreign travel, 'the war', football, and so forth. In practice, however, respondents in England very rarely talked explicitly about their own sense of national identity in response to such prompts. Consequently, the interviewer typically had to resort to eliciting, or to maintaining, nation-identity talk through direct questioning.

12 For the purposes of this chapter I am using a simplified form of transcription notation, based on Jefferson's (2004) system:

underline	Stress on syllable or word.
CAPITALS	Material spoken louder than surrounding talk.
dash–	Abrupt cut off.
'inverted commas'	Intonation of quotation.
question mark?	Rising inflection.
(2)	Pause measured to the nearest second.
(.)	Hearable pause of less than one second.
((brackets))	Transcriber's note of something hard to represent phonetically.
Bold	Word or phrase of especial analytic significance.
[...]	Omitted material.

13 This idea is also central to Grice's (1975) conversational maxims of quantity ('Do not make your contribution to the conversation more informative than is required') and manner ('Be brief [avoid unnecessary prolixity]').

14 Interviewers also oriented to this presumption when – as was often the case – they prefaced their requests for information concerning national identity with the softener, 'This may sound like a silly question, but' (see also Mann, 2006).

15 In his account of banal national consciousness Billig (1995) adopts the term 'mindless'. With hindsight, this is possibly regrettable, since the term carries connotations of irrationality. More recently, social psychologists have been inclined to describe the kind of well-established (often early-learned) knowledge that can be used without being brought to the forefront of the mind or mentioned in conversation by the less loaded term, 'implicit'.

16 Specifically, they tended either to be people who held far-right political views, or to be people with experience of living in Scotland, where we might surmise they had habituated to different normative traffic rules of national self-identification (see Condor & Abell, 2006a).

17 A good deal of recent research in England has been prompted by concerns relating to whether, and how, national identities may be changing in response to UK constitutional change. The data set that I am using here includes transcripts of interviews conducted before, during, and after the establishment of the Scottish Parliament. In many respects, the ways in which people in England orient to questions relating to national identity has remained remarkably consistent over time. People interviewed relatively recently may, like AG in extract 10, refer to having changed the ways in which they answer a question about their national identity. However, on inspection, it appears that the changes that the respondents are describing usually pertain to norms relating to 'the right thing to say', rather than to transformations in their subjective sense of self (for further examples, see extracts 15 and 16).

18 Note that this concern to (re)design a census item on 'identity' to accommodate (perceived) public concerns over subjective experience is currently confined to the bureaucratic category of nationality. There are apparently no analogous plans to include 'What do you consider your gender/age to be?' as census items.

19 Britology Watch: Deconstructing 'British Values'. 25 October 2009. http://britologywatch.wordpress.com/2009/10/24/the-2011-census-and -the-suppression-of-english-identity/. The author of this piece also takes issue with the way in which the 'national' identity question has been formulated for Census purposes as a question about (white) 'ethnic' identity.

20 This observation might lead us to question the common conceit that cultural distance grants epistemic privilege, as illustrated for example by Kumar's (2003) well-known contention that English national identity 'cannot be understood from the inside out but more from the outside in'.

21 It is also common practice for transcribers and/or researchers to clean up interview transcripts and even to 'correct' a respondents' wording.

22 It is a social scientific cliché that all national identities are constructed *vis-à-vis* an Other. As Bechhofer and McCrone (2009: 65) recently put it, 'Having a sense of who you are in national identity terms involves knowing who you are not.' Traditionally, social scientists have adopted what we might term a Saidian perspective, according to which national Others are understood to represent the ontological counter to, or antithesis of, the national Self. However, attention to the ways in which the English respondents discussed matters relating to national identity in the conversational interview context points to the possibility that national Others may also be represented in a Meadian or Bakhtinian sense, that is, as imagined dialogic partners. In this case, recognition of Difference may not be cast as grounds for ontological self-celebration, but rather as a precondition for mutual perspective-taking.

2

Is the English lion ready to roar?

John Curtice

For many of its unionist critics, England was potentially the Achilles' heel in Labour's plans, eventually implemented in 1999, to extend devolution to Scotland and Wales. They feared the move would generate an 'English backlash'; the normally quiescent people of England would begin increasingly to roar their disapproval (Hitchens, 1999; Marr, 2000; Redwood, 1999). Now that devolution has been in place for a decade we can begin to assess whether those fears have been realised.

One of the fears raised by devolution's critics concerned identity. They argued that having separately elected political institutions in Edinburgh and Cardiff would foster and promote the distinctive Scottish and Welsh identities that were already relatively common-place in those parts of the United Kingdom (UK) (Thatcher, 1998) and thus might encourage people in England to become more aware of their own distinct nationality too (Paxman, 1998). As a result, those people's sense of being British, an identity that encouraged them to regard those living in Scotland and Wales as 'us' rather than 'Other' (Tajfel, 1978), would be supplanted by increasing adherence to a separate English identity that might come to regard Scotland and Wales as 'Other' rather than 'us'.

A second fear was that devolution would generate resentment. Scotland and Wales would after all be granted a degree of self-govern-ment that was to be denied to England itself (Wright, 2000). Beyond that obvious disparity there were two particular apparent anomalies that it was argued would prove a touch paper for resentment. First, MPs from Scotland would continue to have a vote on and a say in laws concerning England's domestic affairs, such as health and education, whereas MPs from England would no longer have any influence over equivalent laws passed for Scotland because these would now be the responsibility of the Scottish Parliament (Dalyell, 1999 [1977]). Second, not only would pubic spending per head be higher in Scotland (and Wales) than it was in England (McLean, 2005; McLean et al., 2008) – a state of affairs that had long predated devolution – but now Scotland (and Wales) would be free to decide how to spend much of that apparently generous allocation for itself. If the devolved institutions opted to provide more generous public services than existed in England, then people in England might come to question whether public expenditure was being distributed fairly (see, for example, Heathcoat Amory, 2007; Heffer, 2007).

Moreover, these two reactions might well be linked. If people in England were to develop a distinctive sense of English national identity then they might feel that this identity should be reflected in the creation of distinctively English political institutions. After all, expression of national identity appeared to be one of the impulses behind the demand for devolution in Scotland and Wales (Curtice, 1999). Those with a distinctive English identity might be expected to be particularly ready to question the right of Scottish MPs to vote on 'English' laws and to wonder why Scotland and Wales enjoy higher levels of public spending. And even if English national identity were not to become more commonplace following the introduction of devolution, identity might still play an important role in fostering resentment. For it might well be those who already felt 'English' rather than 'British' amongst whom concerns about the equity of the devolution settlement were most likely to grow.

In any event, any such changes in the pattern of identity or the incidence of resentment might be expected to affect attitudes towards how England should be governed. One possibility is that people in England come to feel that their country should now be granted a significant degree of self-government too. That might not pose an immediate threat to the continuance of the Union, but the difficulties of maintaining the Union if the domestic affairs of what is by far its largest component were to be determined by an England-only body are often thought to be considerable (Bogdanor, 2009; Hazell, 2006). But another more dramatic possibility could be that people in England come to tire of the Union and decide that their country should be left to determine its own affairs entirely, thereby leaving the remaining parts of the United Kingdom to fend for themselves (Heffer, 1999; Nairn, 1981; 2000). Such a development would certainly seem to sound the death knell for the Union.

In this chapter we assess whether and how far these fears expressed by unionist critics of devolution have come to be realised. First we look at trends in national identity in England. We then turn to the two particular potential sources of resentment identified by those critics – the continued ability of Scottish MPs to vote on English laws, and the distribution of public spending across the UK. Thereafter, we assess whether the attitudes of people in England towards the way in which they are governed have changed. Finally we pay particular attention to the role that adherence to an English national identity plays in the patterns that we have uncovered. Are those who adhere to an English identity more likely to be critical of the current devolution settlement? And is there any evidence that the link between identity and such critical views has strengthened since the advent of devolution? In short, is there any sign that a new conversation is emerging within England in which Englishness is acquiring a political dimension that might yet pose a challenge to the continuance of Britain and 'Britishness'?

Identity

Much of the evidence upon which this chapter is based comes from the British Social Attitudes (BSA) survey, a high quality survey that is conducted each year by the National Centre for Social Research (Park et al., 2010) and which has paid particular attention to identities and attitudes in England following the advent of devolution in Scotland and Wales in 1999 (Curtice, 2009). Although the survey is conducted throughout Great Britain, all of the figures quoted here are based on the replies of just those respondents living in England. One question asked regularly by BSA invites people to state which, if any, of the set of national identities they feel describes how they think of themselves. In so doing they are asked to choose from a list that includes all of the national identities associated with one or more parts of the United Kingdom, together with 'European'. In recognition of the fact that in a multi-national state such as the United Kingdom people may have multiple identities – and thus feel both 'British' and 'English' – they are invited initially to choose more than one identity if they wish.

In practice, most people in England chose one or both of two identities, 'English' and 'British', and so Table 2.1 focuses on the incidence of those particular responses. Three key patterns are immediately apparent. First, a substantial minority of people in England voluntarily acknowledge both identities – typically in recent years constituting between a third and two-fifths of the adult population. Secondly, of the two identities it is 'British' that is the more commonly acknowledged, albeit not dramatically so. Thirdly, however, it appears that the pattern of identity has been somewhat different since the advent of devolution than it was beforehand. In three readings taken before the creation of devolved institutions in Scotland and Wales, the proportion saying they were English was never higher than 55%. Since then it has

Table 2.1 Trends in free choice national identity, 1996–2009 (%)

	1996	1997	1998	1999	2000	2001	2002	2003	2004	2005	2006	2007	2008	2009
English	52	50	55	65	59	63	57	59	55	60	67	57	60	59
British	71	68	70	71	67	67	73	70	69	70	68	68	67	67
Both	29	26	34	44	35	39	37	38	33	38	45	34	38	37
Base	1,019	1,153	2,695	2,718	2,887	2,761	2,897	3,709	2,684	3,643	3,666	3,517	3,880	2,917

Sources: 1997: British Election Studies; 1996, 1998–2009: British Social Attitudes (respondents living in England only)

never been less than that, and typically has been around 60% or so. It would appear that the advent of devolution did serve to stimulate somewhat greater willingness to acknowledge an English identity, although this seems to have been a one-off change rather than a continuing process.

Still we might wonder what is the relative importance of the two identities, and especially so amongst those who are willing to acknowledge both. Perhaps their British identity is – or has become – the weaker of the two, perhaps representing little more than an acknowledgement of citizenship rather than an expression of identity. We can establish whether there is any evidence to that effect by looking at the pattern of responses that pertains once those who acknowledge more than one identity are asked to state which is the one identity they feel would best describe how they think of themselves if they had to choose only one. If their sense of being English is the more important for those who acknowledge a dual identity, we might find that 'English' now appears to be the more popular identity of the two.

The first row of Table 2.2 thus shows the proportion who either only acknowledge an English identity or, when asked to choose just one out of the several identities that they acknowledge, opt for 'English'. The second row shows the same information for 'British'. In practice this exercise does little to alter the impression painted by Table 2.1. In particular it remains the case that slightly more people in England apparently regard themselves as 'British' than consider themselves to be 'English'. At the same time, however, it also remains

Table 2.2 Trends in forced choice national identity, 1992–2009 (%)

	1992	1996	1997	1998	1999	2000	2001	2002	2003	2004	2005	2006	2007	2008	2009
English	31	34	33	37	44	41	43	37	38	38	40	47	39	41	41
British	63	58	55	51	44	47	44	51	48	51	48	39	47	45	46
Base	2,125	1,019	3,150	2,695	2,718	2,887	2,761	2,897	3,709	2,684	3,643	3,666	3,517	3,880	2,917

Sources: 1992 and 1997: British Election Studies; 1996, 1998–2009: British Social Attitudes (respondents living in England only)

the case that since 1999 consistently more people have opted to call themselves English than did so beforehand. Whereas before that date only around one in three said that they were English, more recently the figure has hovered around 40% or so. Once again, however, this growth in English identity appears to have been a one-off development rather than a continuing trend.

Meanwhile, we should consider the possibility that perhaps the figures in Table 2.1 understate the incidence of dual identities in England. After all, the form of questioning behind those figures requires people to go to the trouble of deliberating and picking out both English and British if they wish to acknowledge a dual identity. Just picking one may seem the simpler and more straightforward option. To assess this possibility BSA has on occasion also asked a more detailed question about national identity that reads as follows:

Some people think of themselves first as British. Others may think of themselves first as English.

Which, if any, of the following best describes how you see yourself?

English not British
More English than British
Equally English and British
More British than English
British not English

As Table 2.3 indicates this line of questioning, first used in Spain and often known as the 'Moreno question' (Moreno, 1988), suggests that the proportion who are willing to acknowledge some combination of being 'English' and 'British' is closer to two-thirds than one-third. At the same time it would appear to cast doubt on the evidence presented so far that has suggested that rather more people acknowledge a British than claim an English identity. In our most recent reading, for example, taken in 2007, one-third (33%) say either than they are 'English not British' or else that they are 'more English than British', while only just over a quarter (26%) state that they are 'British not English' or 'More British than English'. Moreover, the balance of popularity between these two sets of answers has been much the same every time that the question has been asked. The explanation for the discrepancy, however, is straightforward. Nearly everyone who says they are wholly or mostly English is classified as English in Table 2.3. Equally most of those who say they are wholly or mostly British appear amongst the ranks of British identifiers in that same table.

However, around twice as many of those who say they are 'equally British and English' claim, when forced to choose, that they are British than say that they are English. Dual identity is indeed commonplace, but it seems that ultimately it is a British identity that has the slightly stronger hold amongst most people in England.

Table 2.3 Trends in Moreno national identity, 1997–2007 (%)

	1997	1999	2000	2001	2003	2007
English not British	7	17	18	17	17	19
More English than British	17	14	14	13	19	14
Equally English and British	45	37	34	42	31	31
More British than English	14	11	14	9	13	14
British not English	9	14	12	11	10	12
Base	3,150	2,718	1,928	2,761	1,917	859

Sources: 1997: British Election Study; 1999–2007 British Social Attitudes (respondents living in England only)

In any event, there is one respect in which the evidence in Table 2.3 is consistent with the picture we have painted so far. In 1997 a little less than a quarter (24%) said that they were wholly or mostly English. But since 1999 that proportion has consistently been closer to a third. So here is further evidence that there was a once-off increase in adherence to an English identity at around the time that the devolved institutions came into being in Scotland and Wales, but that subsequently there has not been any sign of a continuing trend in that direction.

So we have uncovered some change in the pattern of national identity in England, albeit perhaps not one that we anticipated at the beginning of this chapter. English national identity has become more commonplace following the advent of devolution. But it appears that this was a once and for all shift rather than a gradual change. Moreover, it seems that we should be wary of presuming that this change has supplanted or undermined the sense of British identity in England. Many, if not most people in England acknowledge being both English and British. Meanwhile it seems that British may still be somewhat the more popular or stronger of the two. Still, there are clearly sufficient people in England who do feel English that we cannot presume that some of the apparent anomalies created by the advent of devolution in Scotland and Wales have not seemed increasingly irksome. So we now turn our attention to possible sources of resentment.

Resentment

In our earlier discussion we identified two aspects of the devolution settlement that might be expected to give rise to resentment in England. The first was the fact that MPs representing Scottish constituencies could still vote on laws that only affect England even though MPs in England no longer had any say in equivalent legislation for Scotland. Table 2.4 indicates that most people in England do not feel that this situation is equitable. On each of four occasions on which the issue has been addressed by BSA, around three in five have indicated that they feel that Scottish MPs should not be allowed any longer to vote on laws that only apply to England.[1] However, it would appear that resentment about the issue has not grown over time even though since the late 1990s there have been a number of well publicised instances (such as the introduction of foundation hospitals and university 'top-up' fees) whereby votes cast by Scottish MPs have been crucial in the passage of legislation that did not apply north of the border (Russell & Lodge, 2006). Meanwhile, we might wonder too whether at least some of those who feel that Scottish MPs should not be able to vote in English laws would have been of the same view even before devolution was in place.

The second potential source of resentment that we identified was the financial settlement under which Scotland and Wales are free to spend as they wish a block grant that helps provide for a higher level

Table 2.4 Attitudes towards the 'West Lothian' question, 2000–07 (%)

	2000	2001	2003	2007
Now that Scotland has its own parliament, Scottish MPs should no longer be allowed to vote in the UK House of Commons on laws that only affect England:				
Strongly agree	18	19	22	25
Agree	45	38	38	36
Neither agree nor disagree	19	18	18	17
Disagree	8	12	10	9
Strongly disagree	1	2	1	1
Base	1,695	2,341	1,530	739

Source: British Social Attitudes (respondents living in England only)

of spending per head than pertains in England. On this subject it would seem that there is plenty of evidence from a wide variety of polls to confirm the fears of devolution's unionist critics. For example, when in December 2006 ICM asked people in England, 'Government spending per head of population is higher in Scotland than in England. Do you think this is justified or unjustified', no less than 60% said it was unjustified. Similarly, 62% said the position was unjustified when in January 2007 ICM asked the same question once more, but then added the rider 'with English taxes subsidising public spending in Scotland'. More recently, a YouGov poll conducted in April 2010 asked its respondents, 'Scotland currently receives 20% more public spending per head of population than England. Do you think Scotland gets more than its fair share of government spending, pretty much its fair share given Scotland's large land area and the costs that arose from this, or less than its fair share', in response to which as many as 59% said more than its fair share.

We should, however, note one important feature of these questions. In each case they actually tell respondents that public spending per head in Scotland is higher than it is in England. The questions would thus seem to beget the answer they receive. Perhaps, though, people in England are largely unaware of the differences in the level of spending in the two countries. If so, those differences may not be as potent a source of resentment as those poll questions would apparently have us believe.

An alternative approach that is more likely to identify whether there really is widespread resentment about Scotland's share of public spending is simply to ask people whether they think Scotland secures more or less than its fair share of public spending without providing any further information or prompt. This is the approach that has been adopted consistently by BSA, the results of which are shown in Table 2.5 overleaf.

Two important points emerge. First when asked in this way the proportion of people in England who feel that Scotland gets more than its fair share is well under half, and thus far lower than suggested by the opinion poll questions cited above. However, the table also reveals that resentment about the issue does seem to have grown in recent years. Between 2000 and 2003 only between a fifth and a quarter said that Scotland received more than its fair share of public spending. But by 2007 that figure had reached nearly one-third (32%), and subsequently it has increased further to around two-fifths. Although apparently still a minority concern, it appears that the

Table 2.5 Attitudes towards Scotland's share of public spending, 2000–09 (%)

	2000	2001	2002	2003	2007	2008	2009
Compared with other parts of the UK, Scotland's share of government spending is …							
… much more than its fair share	8	9	9	9	16	21	18
… little more than its fair share	13	15	15	13	16	20	22
… pretty much its fair share	42	44	44	45	38	33	30
… little less than its fair share	10	8	8	8	6	3	4
… much less than its fair share	1	1	1	1	1	*	*
Don't know	25	23	22	25	22	23	25
Base	1,928	2,761	2,897	1,917	859	982	980

Source: British Social Attitudes (respondents living in England only)

perception that Scotland gets more than a fair deal out of the current financial arrangements has grown in recent years. Here at least would seem to be a potential source of growing tension between the two principal partners to the Union.

Preferences

One possible way of addressing the perception that Scotland secures more than its fair share of public spending would be to introduce a closer link between the level of such spending in Scotland and the amount of money raised in taxes north of the border. Table 2.6 suggests that such a move would be popular in England.[2] Around three-quarters agree with the idea that Scotland should pay for its services out of taxes collected in that part of the UK. Moreover, although there is little sign that the already relatively high proportion of people in favour of that view has increased, the figure for those who say that they 'strongly agree' has increased somewhat, from 20% in 2001 to 28% at the time of the most recent reading in 2007. So not only has resentment about Scotland's share of public spending grown, but the demand that spending should be tied to taxes paid in Scotland has also become somewhat more insistent.

Still, all that this demonstrates is that England would apparently like to see a change in the way in which the devolved institutions in Scotland (and perhaps Wales) are financed. It does not constitute evidence that people in England have changed their minds about how their own part of the UK should be governed. We suggested earlier that in that respect there were two possible developments of interest.

Table 2.6 Attitudes in England towards the financial relationship between England and Scotland, 2001–07 (%)

	2001	2003	2007
Now Scotland has its own parliament, it should pay for its services out of taxes collected in Scotland:			
Strongly agree	20	22	28
Agree	53	52	47
Neither agree nor disagree	12	12	14
Disagree	11	10	5
Strongly disagree	1	*	1
Base	2761	1917	859

* Less than 0.5%

Source: British Social Attitudes (respondents living in England only)

The first was that England might have increasingly come to want some form of devolution for itself. The other is that England might wish to be separated from the rest of the UK and become an independent country on its own. We consider each of these possibilities in turn.

The debate about devolution in England has been more fractured than that in either Scotland or Wales. In those two countries the only form of devolution that has ever been seriously considered is some form of parliament or assembly for the whole of the nation. In contrast, in England advocates of devolution have been divided into camps (Hazell, 2006). Some have argued that England should have its own parliament similar to that now enjoyed by Scotland and Wales. Others, however, including at one time the 1997–2010 Labour government, argued that rather than having one body with responsibility for England as a whole, each region of England (that is, each of the nine 'government office regions' into which the country has been divided) should have its own devolved regional assembly. Ideally, therefore, any survey question designed to tap attitudes towards devolution for England should refer to both of these possibilities.

This, however, has not always been the practice. In particular, a number of surveys have simply asked people whether or not they think England should have its own parliament – and in so doing have reminded people that Scotland and Wales already enjoy a measure of devolution, thereby potentially leading respondents towards one particular answer. So, for example, in November 2006 an ICM survey asked people whether they would be in favour of 'the establishment of an English Parliament within the UK, with similar powers to those currently enjoyed by the Scottish Parliament'. No less than 68% said they were in favour. Similarly the following April, the same company reminded its respondents that, 'You may have seen or heard that a separate Scottish Parliament, a Welsh Assembly and a Northern Ireland Assembly have been established', and then proceeded to ask, 'Do you think that England should or should not have its own parliament or assembly?' Again, 67% said they were in favour. Equally in a survey conducted (in England) just before the 2007 devolved elections, Populus found that 65% agreed that, 'now that Scottish devolution is well established – and may be extended – England should now have its own parliament too'.[3] Given the responses to these three surveys, it is perhaps surprising that, in January 2007, an ICM poll found that only 51% believed that there should be 'a parliament for England only' given that 'there is now a Scottish Parliament, and devolved assemblies in Wales and Northern Ireland', and as many as 41% were opposed. Perhaps the idea of a parliament for England 'only' seems less attractive than one for England 'too'.

That such figures run the risk of painting a distorted picture is evident from one exercise conducted by ICM in December 2007, which asked people to choose between a number of possible options, of which a devolved English parliament was only one. In this instance, just 21% chose an English parliament within the framework of the UK. In contrast as many as 32% favoured the status quo, while another 26% reckoned that laws for England should continue be made by the House of Commons although only English MPs should be allowed to vote on them. This is much the same picture as that obtained by a question that BSA has asked on a regular basis, a question that, as Table 2.7 shows, has invited people to choose between the status quo, an English parliament and a set of regional assemblies. Typically over half have opted for the status quo, while those who support devolution have been divided more or less equally between those who support an English parliament and those who instead want regional devolution. The impact of such demand as there is for devolution in England has evidently been significantly dissipated because the protagonists cannot agree on what form that devolution should take.

However, opinion on devolution for England has not been static. First, it seems that since the public voted against the idea of an elected regional assembly for the North-East in a referendum held in November 2004 (Sandford, 2009), support for the idea of elected regional assemblies has waned while that for an English parliament has grown. Now almost twice as many people (29%) back an English parliament as favour elected regional assemblies (15%); indeed support for having a parliament has now apparently reached a record high. Second, the proportion favouring the status quo has fallen below half for the first time ever. Apparently the idea that England should have its own devolved national political institutions too is finally beginning to resonate a little.

Table 2.7 Attitudes towards how England should be governed, 1999–2009 (%)

	1999	2000	2001	2002	2003	2004	2005	2006	2007	2008	2009
With all the changes going on in the way different parts of Great Britain are run, which of the following do you think would be best for England?											
England governed as it is now, with laws made by the UK parliament	62	54	57	56	50	53	54	54	57	51	49
Each region of England to have its own assembly that runs services like health*	15	18	23	20	26	21	20	18	14	15	15
England as whole to have its own new parliament with law-making powers	18	19	16	17	18	21	18	21	17	26	29
Base	2,718	1,928	2,761	2,897	3,709	2,684	1,794	928	859	982	980

Source: British Social Attitudes (respondents living in England only)
Note: In 2004–06 the second option read 'that makes decisions about the region's economy, planning and housing'. The 2003 survey carried both versions of this option and demonstrated that the difference of wording did not make a material difference to the pattern of response. The figures quoted for 2003 are those for the two versions combined

But what of the Union itself? Are there any signs that England is losing patience with that too? The answer to this question once again depends on the wording of the survey question that is asked. In one poll, conducted by ICM in November 2006, as many as 48% said that they favoured 'England becoming an independent country from [sic] Scotland, Wales and Northern Ireland', while only 43% said they were opposed. However, what was meant by 'independence' was not spelt out. As soon as it is made clear that independence implies England separating from the rest of the UK, a rather different picture emerges. Thus, when in December 2007 ICM asked, 'Would you like the Union between England and Scotland to come to continue as it is or would you like it to come to an end so that both England and Scotland become independent of each other?', as many as 69% said that they wanted the Union to continue and only 24% preferred it to break up. Equally, independence for England emerges as a relatively unpopular option when pitted against other possible options such as an English parliament within the Union, or not allowing Scottish MPs to vote on English laws; when ICM conducted such an exercise in December 2007, only 16% favoured independence.

This finding is also reflected in the 2007 BSA, which is the only occasion to date on which that survey has asked explicitly about independence for England. Asked which of two options would be 'better for England', just 16% said 'for England to become an independent country, separate from the rest of the United Kingdom', while no less than 77% preferred 'for England to remain part of the United Kingdom, along with Scotland, Wales and Northern Ireland'. Whatever their discontents about the devolution settlement, it seems that people in England still regard the Union as of benefit to themselves, irrespective of whatever advantages it might bring to the other parts of the UK.

The level of support for the maintenance of the Union amongst people in England can also be gauged by ascertaining their attitude towards Scotland becoming independent. The BSA survey in particular has asked such a question on a number of occasions, thereby giving us an indication as to whether support for the maintenance of the Union may have declined over time. It seems as though it has not. As Table 2.8 shows, the proportion saying that Scotland should become an independent country has consistently been around no more than one-fifth or so.[4] Meanwhile, the same table shows that most people in England accept that Scotland should have some form of devolution, although that support seems to have waned somewhat in the reading taken in 2007. Granting devolution to Scotland (and Wales) but not to England may not have upset England as much as might have been anticipated simply because many people in England accept that the move was a good idea for the rest of the UK even if they do not necessarily want it for themselves.

Still, we should perhaps not overestimate the strength of the commitment of people in England towards the maintenance of the Union. In 2003 and again in 2007 BSA asked people the following question designed to tap the strength of their emotional attachment to the Union. It read: '*If in the future England, Scotland and Wales were all to* **become separate independent countries**, *rather than all being part of the United Kingdom together, would you be pleased, sorry, or, neither pleased nor sorry?*' Only a few people say they would be pleased by such an outcome. In 2003 only 9% proffered that response, and in 2007

Table 2.8 Attitudes towards how Scotland should be governed, 1997–2007 (%)

	1997	1999	2000	2001	2002	2003	2007
Scotland should ...							
... become *independent*, separate from UK and EU, or separate from the UK but part of the EU	14	21	19	19	19	17	19
... remain part of the UK, with its own elected parliament which has *some* taxation powers	38	44	44	53	41	50	36
... remain part of the UK, with its own elected parliament, which has *no* taxation powers	17	13	8	7	11	8	12
... remain part of the UK, *without* an elected parliament	23	14	17	11	15	13	18
Don't know	8	8	11	10	14	11	15
Base	2,536	902	1,928	2,761	1,924	1,917	859

Sources: 1997: British Election Study; 1999–2007: British Social Attitudes (respondents in England only)

only 8%. At the same time, however, less than half said that they would actually be 'sorry'. Just 49% said that that would be their reaction in 2003, while in 2007 the figure fell to 44%. Instead a large proportion – 42% in 2003 and 46% in 2007 – said that they would be 'neither pleased nor sorry'. It would seem that while most people in England cannot see any good reason why the Union should be ended, they may not necessarily be strongly committed to its maintenance in the event that significant tension did break out between England and one or more of the other parts of the UK.

It would appear, then, that the worst fears of devolution's critics have not been realised. There is little sign that support in England for the maintenance of the Union has eroded in the wake of devolution, even if people do not necessarily have a strong emotional attachment to it. Moreover, most people would apparently still prefer England to be governed from Westminster, albeit perhaps with less interference from Scottish MPs, even though they recognise and accept the wish of other parts of the UK to enjoy some form of devolution. However, there are signs that perhaps support for the status quo has begun to erode and that support for some form of devolution is beginning to coalesce around the idea of an English parliament. Perhaps England is about to stir after all.

Identity, resentment and preferences

So far we have established that, since 1999 at least, there seems to have been little sign of a change in the pattern of national identity in England. At the same time, however, we have ascertained that in recent years there appears to have been growing concern about Scotland's share of public spending and increased support for the idea of an English parliament. Self-evidently, then, these two latter trends cannot have been caused by an increase in adherence to an English national identity. However, perhaps it is amongst those who already felt English rather than British that these two trends have been particularly apparent. Even if the pattern of identity in England has not changed, perhaps identity has become more important because it is amongst those with an English identity in particular that the current asymmetric devolution settlement has become increasingly acceptable.

Table 2.9 considers this possibility so far as it relates to concern about Scotland's share of public spending. It does so by showing separately the attitudes of those who, when forced to choose, said they were 'British' and those who said they were 'English'. When attitudes towards spending were first addressed by BSA in 2000 there was in fact virtually no difference between the views of the two groups at all. In both cases the proportion of people who felt that Scotland secures more than its fair share of spending was just over one-fifth. Thereafter there did appear to be some sign that concern about Scotland's share of public spending had grown most rapidly amongst those who said they were 'English'. In 2008 as many as 50% of this group said that Scotland secured more than its fair share, compared with only 37% of those who stated they were British. But in 2009 the proportion that said that Scotland obtained more than its fair share was again virtually identical in the two groups. Whatever may have been responsible for the growth in the perception that Scotland secures more than its fair share of spending, evidently it is not a resentment that emerges out of a sense of English identity that has increasingly come to regard Scotland as 'Other'.

Table 2.9 Perceptions of Scotland's share of spending by forced choice national identity, 2000–09 (%)

	2000		2003		2007		2008		2009	
	British	English	British	English	British	English	British	English	British	English
Compared with other parts of UK, Scotland's share of govt spending is ...										
... more than fair	22	23	19	26	29	37	37	50	42	43
... pretty much fair	43	42	46	45	43	35	38	30	30	30
... less than fair	10	11	8	8	6	8	3	2	3	4
Base	877	822	898	760	408	346	435	428	427	436

Source: British Social Attitudes (respondents living in England only)

In contrast to attitudes towards Scotland's share of public spending, it has always been the case that those who say that they are English have been more likely to back the idea of an English parliament (and less likely to support the status quo) than those who regard themselves primarily as British. Thus, as Table 2.10 overleaf shows, in 2000 21% of those who said they were English supported an English parliament, compared with 14% of those who considered themselves British. Although this was hardly a sharp division of opinion, it suggests that some people at least support the idea of an English parliament because they feel that England's distinctive nationality should be reflected in distinctive political institutions. And perhaps that feeling has now become more popular.

Of this, however, there is also no consistent sign. True, by 2007 support for an English parliament amongst those who said they were English had increased to 27%, while it had fallen back somewhat to 11% amongst those who regarded themselves as British. However, in the subsequent two years support for an English parliament actually increased most amongst those who stated they were British. It seems that even when it comes to the issue of how England itself should be governed, attitudes have relatively little to do with identity. Maybe England is becoming attracted to the idea of an English parliament because the English do not want to be left out of the devolution settlement rather than because creating distinctively English political institutions is regarded as an essential embodiment of English identity.[5]

Table 2.10 Constitutional preferences for England by forced choice national identity, 1999–2009 (%)

	2000		2003		2007		2008		2009	
	British	English	British	English	British	English	British	English	British	English
Which would be best for England?										
England governed as it is now, with laws made by the UK parliament	67	60	52	49	69	50	56	45	58	45
Each region of England to have its own assembly that runs services like health	14	15	27	24	12	16	14	16	12	17
England as whole to have its own new parliament with law-making powers	14	21	16	23	11	27	22	34	23	34
Base	1,186	1,208	1,785	1,447	408	346	435	428	427	436

Source: British Social Attitudes (respondents living in England only)

Conclusion

Although many of the fears raised by devolution's unionist critics appear to have been unfounded, it seems that the advent of devolution in Scotland and Wales has made a mark on the attitudes of people in England. To a long-standing reluctance to having Scottish MPs voting on English laws there has more recently been added a growing concern that Scotland obtains more than its fair share of public spending. Meanwhile, although there still seems to be little sign of much wish to break-up the Union, some people in England are, it seems, beginning to ask themselves whether they should not have devolution too. And although at present such an outlook still appears clearly to be a minority view, it is a demand that might in practice prove difficult to meet without threatening the future of the United Kingdom.

Yet what remains unclear is how much any of this has to do with feelings of 'Englishness'. True, in 1999 there was a one-off increase in willingness to identify as English rather than British, an increase that has never been reversed. But equally there is no sign of that change continuing further, while many people in England still recognise and accept both identities. Meanwhile adherence to an English identity seems to make no more difference now to how people feel about the Union or how England should be governed than it did a decade ago. England may be beginning to have a conversation with itself about devolution, but it seems to be more of a debate about the future of England as a territory rather than Englishness as a national identity.

Notes

1 In contrast to the position described in respect of other topics below, the findings obtained by BSA on this topic are broadly in line with those of other polls, even though the wording on other polls was somewhat different. For example, three polls conducted by ICM in November 2006, January 2007 and December 2007 found that 62%, 53% and 61% respectively felt that English MPs should not be able to vote on Scottish laws.

2 A significant move in that direction was indeed recommended by an all-party commission established under the chairmanship of Sir Kenneth Calman (Commission on Scottish Devolution, 2009), whose proposals are now being implemented by the UK government (Cabinet Office, 2010).

3 During this period (which coincided with the 300th anniversary of the Anglo-Scottish Union) a poll conducted by Opinion Research Business in January 2007 also found much the same result as these. Its question began by stating, 'In 1998 [*sic*] the creation of a Scottish Parliament and a Welsh Assembly gave these countries certain powers that were previously held by the UK parliament in Westminster.' It then asked, 'Do you think an English Parliament should now be established?' As many as 61% said it should.

4 Again question wording can be crucial. In November 2006, 59% told ICM that they approved of 'Scotland becoming an independent country'. Similarly in a second ICM poll conducted in January 2007, 48% said that they backed Scottish independence.. But in a Populus poll conducted in May 2007, no less than 55% of respondents in England and Wales rejected the proposition that 'Scotland should have full independence and no longer be part of Great Britain'. Equally, a YouGov poll, conducted in January 2007 found that just 28% backed Scottish independence when told this meant that it would not just have 'a devolved parliament' but would be 'separate from the rest of the United Kingdom'. Once again when the meaning of independence and its implication for the future of the Union begins to be defined, support for independence falls away.

5 This conclusion is also supported by further analysis of the BSA data that suggests that support for an English parliament has in recent years become more closely linked to perceptions that Scotland secures more than its fair share of public spending. See Ormston and Curtice (2010). We might also note that although strong support for disbarring Scottish MPs from voting on English laws is somewhat higher amongst those who

say they are English rather than those who indicate they are British, as is support for Scottish independence, there is no evidence that the views of those who say they are English have grown further apart from those who indicate they are British.

3

All white? Englishness, 'race' and ethnic identities

Paul Thomas

Introduction

As the previous chapters of this book chart, debates and arguments over the meaning/s and relevance of 'Englishness' have grown steadily since the late 1990s, running in tandem with the emerging 'facts on the ground' of New Labour's devolution policies and the significant movement in public attitudes that have accompanied them. The new political realities in Scotland, Wales and Northern Ireland have inevitably shifted attention towards Englishness, to what it means and how much people living in England identify with it, in comparison to the over-arching 'British' identity now perceived to be under serious threat. Debates about national identity have the dangerous potential to become racialised and exclusionary, especially at a time when a far-right party, the British National Party, has made significant political advances, The current 'conversations' about Englishness have also been triggered by mainstream political and media discourses questioning the national identity and loyalty of non-white British (and English) citizens at a very basic level. This chapter aims to discuss the meaning/s of Englishness for non-white ethnic minorities in the context of wider political debates and developments around multiculturalism, citizenship and Community Cohesion and offers thoughts about the potential for genuinely inclusive and non-racial understandings of Englishness taking greater hold than at present.

Firstly, the chapter provides a brief context of non-white ethnic minority communities in relation to debates about national identity and belonging, followed by discussion of the key political developments under New Labour that have raised questions about the national affiliation of such minority communities. Here, there is a specific focus on Muslim communities in the wake of the 2001 disturbances in Oldham, Burnley and Bradford in northern England which led directly to the new policy priority of Community Cohesion, and the 7/7 London bombings of 2005 and subsequent terror plots that have suggested a profound antipathy to national identity amongst some young Muslims. To develop this focus, the chapter draws on the understandings of Britishness and Englishness held by young Muslims in the context of wider debates over cohesion, segregation and racial tension (Thomas and Sanderson, 2009). This suggests that, potentially, conversations on Englishness can truly be focused on belonging to place and (multi-ethnic) space, rather than 'race'.

A multi-racial nation?

One of the most profound influences on changes to the ways national identity/ies have been understood within the UK since the mid-twentieth century has been non-white immigration and settlement, leading to what some commentators have termed 'the irresistible rise of multi-racial Britain' (Phillips and Phillips, 1998). The belief that, prior to the labour shortages of the late 1940s that drove this immigration, Britain was an unchanging, homogenous country with a clear sense of its own identity is a myth, with the reality of immigration and initial hostility to new arrivals being a continual thread throughout the history of these islands (Winder, 2004). Nevertheless, the presence of non-white communities in the UK has posed significant questions about the meaning and inclusivity of national identity/ies (Gilroy, 2004; Solomos, 2003). These debates have impacted overwhelmingly on England, with the vast bulk of Asian and African-Caribbean settlement being in London, the Midlands and across the north of England. The results of this period of immigration from the late 1940s to the early 1970s (now, more than half of non-white citizens are UK-born [Finney and Simpson, 2009]) are that many of England's larger cities are ethnically diverse, with some projected to become 'plural cities' over the next couple of decades, whereby no one ethnic group forms an absolute majority of the local population, although white English will remain the largest ethnic group (Finney and Simpson, 2009). This significant ethnic diversity means that '[to] a much greater extent than arguments over Scottish, Welsh or Northern Irish identity, debates about Englishness are dominated by the question of race' (Perryman, 2008b: 29).

It is not possible to discuss the meaning and possibility of 'Englishness' for that nation's non-white communities without discussing their experience of and relationship with the over-arching identity of Britishness dominant for so long. Post-war immigrants from different parts of the British Empire were invited to come and fill labour shortages, but politicians were still shocked when they actually exercised their right as subjects of the Empire to take up British citizenship. The political reaction was to progressively tighten immigration from the early 1960s, accompanied by policies of assimilation – the assumption being that new immigrants would leave their own cultures, languages and traditions at the point of embarkation. The daily reality for many of these immigrants was racial discrimination and prejudice, with outbursts of violence such as the 1958 Notting Hill and Nottingham riots (Solomos, 2003). In the face of rising racial tension, the 1964–70 Labour government accepted that assimilation had not worked and ushered in the policy of 'multiculturalism' whereby ethnic diversity was tolerated and a partial anti-discrimination legal framework provided. Whilst representing progress, much of the popular discourse continued to see ethnic minorities as 'alien' 'others', with media and police racism making it difficult to be black *and* British (Gilroy, 2002).

The depth of this ethnic rift was shown in the urban disturbances across English cities in the early 1980s that exposed the alienation of Black young people, and the ineffectiveness of multiculturalism. The result was a gear shift in 'race relations' policies (Solomos, 2003), with more hard-edged policies of anti-racism and equal opportunities first pioneered by local authorities and then gradually accepted by central government. Such policies continue to develop today, for example the Equality Impact Assessments required by the Race Relations Act 2000, and these have had real impacts on the opportunities and experiences of non-white citizens, to the extent that a number of Britain's ethnic minority communities are out-performing white young people in terms of educational attainment (Modood et al, 1997). Such differentiated experiences do question the extent to which 'race' still determines life experiences, despite the continuing reality of racial prejudice. Further evidence of successes in ethnic integration is highlighted by considerable numbers of inter-marriage and mixed partnerships, with a major study finding that 'half of Caribbean men, a third of Caribbean women and a fifth of Indian and African Asian men had a White partner' (Modood et al, 1997: 355). The result of this is that 'dual heritage' or 'mixed' is the fastest growing ethnic category in Britain and the third largest ethnic group overall. This reality, and the vibrant, multi-influenced nature of the country's music, art and literature all leads to the suggestion that 'England is not only one of the most diverse countries in the world, it is also one of the most hybrid' (Weight, 2008: 99).

This seems to indicate that England (and Britain) is moving progressively towards an inclusive national identity based around a 'convivial culture' (Gilroy, 2004: 153). However, that has not been the perception, or the tone of political discourse, of the past few years. Indeed, there have been suggestions that government are 'looking both ways' on ethnic diversity and identity (Back et al, 2002), or are even lurching back towards assimilationism (Kundnani, 2002). Such fears are prompted by the emergence of specific policy agendas around Community Cohesion and Integration (Cantle, 2001), and Preventing Violent Extremism (PVE) (DCLG, 2007a) and the accompanying attacks on 'multiculturalism' that have all painted pessimistic pictures of the state of ethnic relations and (the lack of) shared identities. These policy discourses have focused explicitly on Muslim communities and on their relationships with wider society, leading to suggestions that government has been fanning the flames of differentiated 'racisms' (Back, 1996) through a racialised policy analysis (Alexander, 2004) that has actually made the development of shared identities significantly harder. For this reason, this chapter focuses explicitly on the national identity of Muslim communities, using empirical evidence to suggest more general realities about the possibility of shared and inclusive national identity/ies.

Over the past few years, the 'identity', loyalty and affiliations of British Muslims, particularly the younger generations, has come under repeated scrutiny. The serious urban disturbances in Oldham, Burnley and Bradford in the summer of 2001 all involved Pakistani and Bangladeshi young men clashing with the police, and at times with white English people. The resulting inquiry (Cantle, 2001) suggested that such disturbances, and the ethnic segregation and tension they revealed, were symptomatic of wider national realities. The analysis here was that profound physical and cultural ethnic segregation had led to 'parallel lives' (Ritchie, 2001) and a lack of shared identities or values. Within this Community Cohesion analysis and policy prescription (LGA, 2002; Home Office, 2005) was an explicit suggestion that the communities under scrutiny lacked a commitment to or engagement with national institutions or identities (Cantle, 2001). One clear result was a renewed debate about 'Britishness' (Brown, 2007b) and the need to promote it, something given added urgency by the international and domestic terrorist atrocities of 9/11 and 7/7. The latter events, suicide bombings carried out by young British Muslims, seemed to confirm the fears held in some political quarters about the profound alienation from 'Britishness' amongst young Muslims.

A number of subsequent terror plots and convictions, all similarly involving young British Muslims, suggests support for this perspective, and led the government to launch the Preventing Violent Extremism initiative (DCLG, 2007a; Thomas, 2009), a 'hearts and minds' approach aimed explicitly at young Muslims within the wider 'CONTEST' counter-terrorism strategy. These developments suggest that there is a profound problem with 'British' identity amongst young Muslims: that they are not British enough, and that, furthermore, a significant proportion of young Muslims are actively hostile to British identity, values and policies. Such a position claims that misguided policies of 'multiculturalism' have allowed separate and oppositional ethnic / religious identities to strengthen at the expense of overarching and collective national identities, consequently weakening the country (Prins and Salisbury, 2008). This chapter explores such claims, drawing on empirical evidence from field research to discuss whether there are really any grounds for suggesting that young Muslims do not feel British, and what this suggests for the possibility of an inclusive, meaningful 'English' identity to develop.

Not British enough?

Recently, Community Cohesion has emerged as the clear priority for policy (Home Office, 2005). A number of themes can be detected within Community Cohesion, the most important of them being the damaging effects of physical and cultural ethnic segregation (Cantle, 2001). The implicit suggestion that 'segregation' is in itself damaging and that it is getting worse are highly contested (Finney and Simpson, 2009), but it is beyond dispute that there is significant ethnic segregation in many of Britain's towns and cities, and that young people experience this as a real and negative constriction on their lives (Back, 1996; Thomas, 2003). The result is a lack of shared understandings, values and experiences, with communities having little meaningful contact with each other, and hence separate 'identities' and priorities. Consistent with New Labour social policy (Levitas, 2005), a communitarian analysis is applied here by government, to these deepening 'parallel lives'. The active involvement and will of individuals and communities is required in order to overcome this segregation. Community Cohesion analysis suggests past 'race relations' priorities, especially those post-1981 developments popularly understood as 'anti-racism' or equal opportunities, have had the unintended consequence of making this situation worse by emphasising and prioritising 'difference' rather than commonality. Here, the post-1981 acceptance of the reality of structural racism and racial inequality led policy makers at the national and local level to focus on 'appropriate' facilities and provision for each separate ethnic group, rather than on common needs and issues.

For advocates of Community Cohesion, this policy direction cast aside the parallel priority of early race relations approaches, that of 'promoting good relations' between different groups: 'equality' for each group was prioritised over unity and commonality (Cantle, 2005). Whilst some would see this as an unintended consequence of policy, others saw it as a deliberate divide and rule tactic to encourage ethnic separatism, with echoes of colonial rule (Kundnani, 2007). The result was that the focus on each separate ethnic community, its needs and facilities, undermined cross-ethnic alliances against racial inequality, and inspired a growth in separate ethno-religious identities, rather than over-arching national, or even solidarity-based identities of 'black' or 'Asian' (Kundnani, 2007). This narrative provides an explanation for the apparent growth in 'Muslim' identity amongst Pakistani and Bangladeshi communities which is in conflict, from some perspectives (Prins and Salisbury, 2008), with a 'British' or 'English identity.

Arguably, the Community Cohesion reports (Cantle, 2001; Denham, 2001) and the accompanying political discourse (Travis, 2001) echoed such a perspective, for example in Cantle's call 'for the minority, largely non-white community, to develop a greater acceptance of, and engagement with, the principal national institutions' (2001: 19), and in its focus on the universal use of English, on equal rights and opportunities for women (2001: 5.1.11 and 5.1.13 respectively), and on 'cultural practices' (Denham, 2001: 20), a term that only ever seems to be applied to ethnic minority groups (Alexander, 2004). Accompanied by suggestions of 'self segregation' (Ouseley, 2001), some critics saw this Community Cohesion discourse to imply that ethnic minorities, especially Muslim communities had chosen isolation and separate identities, with the answer being a return to assimilationism (Alexander, 2004; Kalra, 2002). The fact that Britain's leading 'official' Equality advocate declared Britain to be 'sleep-walking to segregation' and that 'multiculturalism' was to blame (Phillips, 2005) gave further strength to this claim and seemed to make official this perspective of dangerous, separate identities and the need to overcome them. Accompanying the development of this Community Cohesion perspective and its operationalisation (Home Office, 2005; 2007) has been government concern with 'Britishness' and the need to promote it, suggesting that some British citizens are currently not 'British enough'(Kundnani, 2007).

This political concern with the 'separate identity' of Muslim communities was given a much sharper focus by the terrorist bombings and failed attempts of July 2005 and by subsequent plots and convictions. The political response has included the PVE initiative aimed at Muslim communities generally, and at young Muslims in particular. Whilst only small numbers of Muslim youths have been involved in these plots, the PVE policy agenda focuses squarely on Muslim communities as a whole, with government insisting on PVE activity in all local authority areas with a Muslim population of 4,000 people or above (Thomas, 2009). Within these communities, the programme is supposedly aimed at those most at risk of recruitment or 'grooming' by extremists, or at those 'justifying or glorifying violent extremist ideologies and terrorism' (DCLG, 2007a: 7). Whilst many of the PVE documents go out of their way to talk about a 'minority of extremists' and to highlight the government's work with the Muslim 'mainstream', the language and approaches elsewhere appear to contradict this: 'The key measure of success will be demonstrable changes in attitudes among Muslims, and wider communities they are part of, locally and nationally' (DCLG, 2007b: 7). The fact that the government's initial, 'light touch' evaluation of the first year of PVE activity (DCLG, 2008a) talks proudly of working with almost 44,000 people suggests a much broader concern with and focus on the 'identity' of young British Muslims.

Empirical data

The policy developments and discourse outlined above suggest an urgent need to know more about how Muslim young people view 'Britishness' and 'Englishness', and how this relates both to other forms of identity relevant to them, and to how other young people feel about national identity. The evidence base is limited here, with previous research amongst young adults, admittedly in an area with a limited Muslim population, suggesting that young people of all ethnic and social backgrounds are indifferent, or even hostile, to national identity (Fenton, 2007). Other surveys amongst adults have suggested stronger support for 'Britishness' rather than 'Englishness' amongst non-White ethnic minorities, but were too small-scale to make firm judgements (CRE, 2005). As a response to this need, the University of Huddersfield initiated the Youth Identity Research Project (Thomas and Sanderson, 2009), with the aim of investigating young peoples' experiences and understandings of 'identity', cohesion and ethnic segregation.

The case study area for this Project was Oldham and Rochdale, Greater Manchester. Both Oldham and Rochdale have significant Muslim populations from a Pakistani and Bangladeshi background, originating in a 1960s and 1970s immigration wave due to workforce shortages in the local textile industries. The decline of this industry (with jobs, ironically, often moving to South Asia) meant social exclusion and poverty for all ethnic communities in the area, and both towns face significant ethnic segregation using the 'index of dissimilarity', and racial tension. The project employed an action research approach, working in partnership with youth work agencies to train youth workers in research approaches and to devise a range of qualitative research approaches appropriate for the wide range of abilities of young people aged 13–19. In total, over 800 young people took part in one form or other of research activity, generating significant amount of data of various types, much of which is still being analysed. For the purpose of this discussion, the data focused on is from the 'Identity ranking' exercise, and the section of the questionnaire dealing with the issue 'proud to be British?' Additionally, participants in the questionnaire were asked to do word association and sentence completion exercises focusing on expressions such as 'British' and 'English people are . . .?' (Thomas and Sanderson, 2009).

Utilising the existing relationship between youth workers and young people, the Youth Identity Project hoped to maximise the openness and honesty of young people, though aware of the dangers of conformity and compliance in any group-based research process (Albrecht et al, 1993). Youth Work's historic concern with disadvantaged youth has been sharpened by the 'social exclusion' focus of the New Labour government (Mizen, 2004), meaning that any Youth Work-based research process will over-represent socially excluded young people. This might appear to 'skew' any data, but arguably issues of alienation from national identity, or attraction to aggressive and oppositional counter identities, whether Islamic or White racial supremacist, are precisely related to young people and communities who have 'lost' from the economic re-structuring of post-industrial globalisation (May, 1999). Clear differences emerged in the type of identity seen as important by young people. Virtually all of the young people of Pakistani / Bangladeshi origin involved in the research saw their religion as the form of identity most important to them but, for most of them, this Islamic identity is *not* incompatible with British national identity – the overwhelming majority of young Muslims were happy to identify themselves as 'British Muslim' or 'British Asian'. The fact that a smaller number of Asian young people were prepared to say that they are 'Proud to be British' can be related to their concern with, and criticisms of, domestic racism and British foreign policy positions. The emphasis of young Asian people on 'British' rather than 'English' contrasted to the views of young white English people, who clearly favoured 'English' identity. These views are discussed below, with the affiliations 'AYP' (Asian Young Person) and 'WYP' (White Young Person) used to indicate Asian and white young people respectively; some quotes are from focus group interviews and are acknowledged as such. All quotes and supporting material are drawn from The Oldham and Rochdale Youth Identity Project Final Report (Thomas and Sanderson, 2009).

The importance of 'Muslim' identity

Islam / faith was seen as the most important form of identity for *all* Asian young people taking part, consistent with other research nationally, and in strong contrast to all other ethnic / faith backgrounds. This clearly gave a lot of Muslim young people a strong and positive sense of identity: 'Pakistani Muslim ... I'm a very strong believer in all religious rules' (AYP, Rochdale); 'British Muslim – I'm very religious' (AYP, Rochdale).

Respondents were asked to rank eight possible labels for the sources of their identity: British, English, their local town, their ethnicity, their status as a Northerner, their religion, their local area within the town, or their status as a European. One of the clearest distinctions between the different identified ethnic groups was the significance of religion as a source of identity. Self-ascribed ethnic categories were grouped together to facilitate meaningful comparison, and responses ranking identity factors 1 or 2 were also aggregated to allow for those with a shared religious / national identity to emerge. The findings are given below in Table 3.1. Table 3.1 represents a qualification to the positive responses given to the findings that the Muslim sample were proud to be British, in that for this group, unlike their counterparts, religious identity trumps national identity

'Britishness' and 'Englishness'

For the majority of Muslim young people, this primary faith-based identity was compatible with being 'British' (contrary to alarmist suggestions of anti-Britishness amongst Muslim young people): 'British: Me' (AYP: Rochdale). Some 63% of those self-identifying as 'Muslim' definitely agreed with the statement 'I am proud to say that

Table 3.1 Significance of religious and national identity for different groups (%)

Self-ascribed ethnicity	Rank Religion 1 or 2	Rank English 1 or 2	Rank British 1 or 2
White British, English, white, white English, White Christian, British (N = 57)	7	75	56
Asian Pakistani, British Muslim, Pakistani, Kashmiri, Pakistani, British Asian, Bangladeshi/Bengali, British Bengali, British Asian (N = 54)	93	3	20
Black African, black British, mixed race, other (N=16)	44	56	44

Source: Thomas and Sanderson, 2009: 22

I am British'(less than the 80% of the 'non-Muslim' group), and only 10% definitely disagreed, indicating that misgivings about foreign policy frequently expressed in group discussions did *not* have an alienating effect on the majority of Muslim young people:

> British mean[s to] live with different people
> British means loving your country
> British means being loyal to England and not being a terrorist and
> blowing it up
> British means you can be multi-cultured yet keep your identity
> (Asian young people, Rochdale)

For Asian young people Britishness is more positive than Englishness: 'I suppose because British is more inclusive, that's how people can relate to that more than just the St George flag' (AYP, Rochdale). This could be a function of Britishness being associated with ideas about inclusive citizenship, as expressed in this word association: 'British means you live in Britain, abiding laws, treating each other respectfully, a citizen of Britain, having rights in Britain'

By contrast, Englishness appeared to be more associated with socio-cultural traits. The last respondent identified English people as 'sometimes racist, to blame for the war on Iraq, good at football, good cricketers, to blame for street crime' (AYP, Rochdale). In the following example, 'Englishness' is seen more negatively, as it is viewed as being about 'being White'.

English people are the opposite of us
English people are White people
(AYP, Rochdale)

This is clearly problematic, as most young White English people see 'English' as a more important identity than 'British', as indicated in Table 3.1. This focus on 'Englishness' amongst young white English people may well reflect the challenges to past notions of 'Britishness' posed by devolution, European Integration and inward migration, all of which has made it harder to hold on to unexamined, 'taken for granted' notions of Englishness (Perryman, 2008b).

Impact of foreign affairs

Despite their acceptance of 'British' national identity, British involvement in military operations in Iraq and Afghanistan, and domestic media and political discussion of them, has had a clear impact on how some Asian young people view national identity:

British means attacking other countries
Muslim people are targeted, victimised
English people are to blame for the war in Iraq
(Asian Young People, Rochdale)

The impact of Islamaphobia and anti-Muslim sentiments related to these international political events amongst some sections of British politics and the media have also impacted on some Muslim young people, with a number of very thoughtful, or even plaintive, comments:

Muslim people are not terrorists
Muslim people are misled by extremists as well as world leaders
(Asian young people, Rochdale)

Problematic 'Muslim' identity

It is clear from the data above that the strong 'Muslim' identity amongst Pakistani and Bangladeshi-origin young people surveyed in Oldham and Rochdale is not viewed as in conflict with British identity, and that British identity remains strong, and relatively unproblematic for these young people, despite the real and ongoing geo-political events taking place. However, this also gave a minority of young British Muslims a basis to judge negatively the morals and lifestyles of non-Muslims. The extreme negativity and prejudices towards white people from some

Asian young people was often expressed in moral or religious terms, suggesting that the importance of religious identity for all young Muslim people was being used by a minority to judge and label others in highly disrespectful ways, with terms such as 'drunkenness' and 'godless' being utilised, as this excerpt from the exercise completed by one youth group in Rochdale shows: 'White people: Shameless, not believing in God, no respect for other people' (AYP, Rochdale).

Such prejudices were particularly exposed by the 'Word Association / Sentence Completion' exercises, with responses suggesting that racist language and stereotypes are part of 'everyday' life for some young people of all ethnic backgrounds. Here, the evidence would support the view of the Community Cohesion reports (Cantle, 2001; Ritchie, 2001) that within segregated communities overt prejudices and negative language can become part of the open and 'taken for granted' way of acting and thinking.

A strong 'Muslim' sense of identity meant that the perceived position of Muslims nationally and internationally, and emotive political issues, such as the Iraq and Afghanistan military involvements, played a signifi-cant role in the way Asian young people viewed 'British' and 'English' identity, as well as the way they understood themselves. This suggests that more overt work and discussions at appropriate stages with young Muslims about their identity and its links to political issues like 7/7and the Iraq war could be positive as those issues are already at the front of young people's minds. Nationally, most educational work within the PVE / Prevent agenda has avoided overt engagement with such contentious topics (Thomas, 2009), what then-DCLG Minister Hazel Blears characterised in December 2008 as the 'hard-edged debate' of the PVE agenda (DCLG, 2008b). This evidence suggests that some Muslim young people want and need to engage in citizenship / political education-based dialogue around these issues, as they are already discussing them. It also suggests that inter-faith work amongst young people may be a positive vehicle for Cohesion. The strength of 'Muslim' identity amongst Asian-origin young people surveyed, and the level of their concern about international political events also needs to be understood in terms of how non-Muslim communities have understood such events through 'White' political and media discourse and 'projected' feelings and prejudices about them: the word association exercise carried out with white young people on 'Muslim' produced responses which identified religious markers (headscarves, beards, funny clothes, Qu'ran), disapproval of religious observance (too strong in their faith), and references to terrorism and the language of popular tabloid newspapers (bombs, ragheads). These were in addition to more timeworn references to cultural traits and the size of the population. The strength and regularity of such prejudiced comments from some young white English people highlighted the 'taken for granted' status of such opinions within white communities, and the influence of racist campaigning organisations in these areas (Copsey, 2008).

Discussion

At first sight, the case study evidence discussed above might seem to support the right-of-centre thesis that there is indeed a problem with the way some young Muslims view their national identity. The overwhelming importance put on 'religion' by the Asian young people surveyed leaves no doubt about the fact that 'Muslim' is first and foremost how they see themselves. The strength and consistency of this religious identity explains this concern with Britain's role in Iraq and Afghanistan, and with the West's failure to rein in Israel's actions in Gaza and on the West Bank – these are understood as attacks on fellow Muslims and upon Muslim countries. This is, of course, very interesting in itself, because this association and concern with Palestine and other Muslim countries was not evident amongst Britain's Asian communities in the 1970s and 1980s, with the *Satanic Verses* controversy of 1989 arguably proving to be a turning point (Malik, 2009). That is not the focus of this chapter, but the suggestion that Britain's Pakistani and Bangladeshi communities feel strong and deep attachments to co-religionists in other countries, and that they side with those co-religionists against the policies and values of their own nation is the conclusion drawn by some commentators (Prins and Salisbury, 2008). However, that view is refuted by this evidence, with young Muslims in exactly the sort of tense, ethnically segregated and socially excluded northern towns seen as capable of producing violent Islamist extremists being entirely comfortable with describing themselves as 'British'. The overwhelming focus on religious identity does beg the question of how important 'British' national identity is to these young Muslims in relation to their 'religious' identity, and there clearly needs to be more detailed research activity on their relative strengths. Also, the judgemental nature of some comments about non-Muslims and the language sometimes used to express it, suggests that this 'Muslim' identity is as much a 'cultural' identity as an authentically 'religious' one. Nevertheless, the very significant support amongst these young Muslims, despite very real concerns about international political events, for the statement 'I'm proud to be British' suggests that the political and media discourse questioning the loyalties of young British Muslims is misplaced. These localised findings from Oldham and Rochdale are supported by large-scale survey evidence from the Open Society Institute, a think-tank funded by billionaire financier George Soros. This found that UK Muslims are more patriotic than co-religionists in any other country: 'on average 78% of Muslims in the UK consider themselves to be British, compared with 49% in France and 23% in Germany' (Rahman, 2009), with the suggestion that an authentic, positive British Islamic identity is gradually developing thanks to Britain's long-term multi-culturalist approach (Rahman, 2009).

This also seems to counter other evidence around the 'indifference' of young adults to national identity (Fenton, 2007), with both Asian and white young people giving positive support for, albeit different, forms of national identity. Arguably, the overt recent focus on ethnic tension and segregation in the north of England (Cantle, 2001) has led young people to be more aware of such debates.

This data does suggest a number of things about the reality and possibilities of 'English' identity for non-white ethnic minorities. Firstly, the data supports evidence from a previous small-scale survey about the clear preference of non-white English people for British over English (CRE, 2005), and confirmed by a more recent Ipsos Mori survey of young people, which found that ethnic minority youth '[do] not identify themselves as being English and consider Englishness to be exclusively [for] people who are White or come from White parentage and lineage' (Ipsos Mori, 2007: 41).

Both of these surveys found different experiences in Scotland and Wales, with non-white ethnic minorities significantly happier to identify themselves as Scottish or Welsh. This could suggest that the devolved nations have been much more successful in developing an inclusive national identity focused on place, not 'race', although their non-white populations are much smaller than England's. Whilst it must be acknowledged that debates about who and what is 'English' are far behind nationality debates in Scotland or Wales, there are also practical blocks on English identity developing for non-white citizens, such as the lack of English political institutions and processes. Not only has public policy arguably encouraged ethnic/religious affiliation rather than national identity (Cantle, 2005), but the ethnic monitoring data on which policy is presaged does not allow 'Asian English' or 'Black English':

> It appears that young people living in England have no choice but to adopt a 'British' identity. However, Scottishness is not seen in the same

way. For instance, young people of Pakistani origin feel comfortable saying they are 'Scottish Asian'. It is this sense of authenticity, of having the right to be called Scottish or Muslim that has emotional signifi-cance. (Ipsos Mori, 2007: 101)

That survey found some evidence of non-white as well as white young English people using English and British interchangeably, as did our own research in Oldham and Rochdale. This confirms that debates about the meaning and relevance of Englishness have yet to engage with most people (Perryman, 2008a). The evidence around ethnic minorities and the key symbols of Englishness, such as the flag of St George, is mixed. Previous research (Bagguley & Hussain, 2005) amongst young Muslims in Bradford has suggested considerable support for and display of the flag, but field research was carried out during the 2002 World Cup and the associated 'spike' in flag display. That much of this display was by Muslims involved in the 'night-time economy' of taxi firms and restaurants may well be seen as a defensive tactic against the possibility of racial harassment: 'for some, flying the flag of St George can be an act of survival as much as one of national celebration' (Burdsey, 2008: 216).

There is also some anecdotal evidence from our research that the permanent display of English flags in some white housing areas is part of the racialised 'neighbourhood nationalism' (Back, 1996) in situa-tions of racial tension and housing segregation (Cantle, 2001). The fact that so many English people appear uncomfortable with displays of their own national flag arguably makes it a subliminal racialised sign (Perryman, 2008a), with some anti-racists arguing passionately for a mainstream 'embrace' of the Flag of St George as a way of squeezing the political 'space' available to far right groups trying to exploit that symbol (Bragg, 2006). One of the few 'spaces' for overt displays of Englishness comes during major sporting events and tournaments, especially those involving the England football team. Here, the evidence can be seen as encouraging, with a very significant number of Asian and black fans travelling to Germany to support England in the 2006 World Cup (Perryman, 2006). These findings stand in direct contrast to those suggested by Burdsey above (2008) and imply that those displays of the flag are of a voluntary rather than a defensive nature.

Of course, the attachment of non-White ethnic minorities to Englishness is not just determined by their own 'choices', but also by the attitudes, understandings and behaviour of the white majority, and by government. Some encouraging evidence about the possibility of non-white citizens being viewed as English (or Scottish) is supplied by a survey carried out with white and non-white people in Bristol and Glasgow (Kyriakedes et al., 2009). This highlights the growing interplay between racialised and hybridised codes of national belonging in Britain and suggests that Muslims are only stigmatised and excluded by white people if identified as 'foreign'. Here, 'local' accents, use of English and hybridised dress and lifestyles are determinants of the degree of acceptance as 'one of us' by the other white, and non-white, communities: 'Muslims who display perceived hybridised cultural norms of Englishness and Scottishness are included; Muslims who display perceived foreign cultural characteristics are excluded by both "White" and "non-Whites" alike' (Kyriakedes et al., 2009: 299). Whilst clearly highlighting continued prejudices and stereotypes within communities, this research does suggest that increasingly hybridity is interrupting racialised and exclusive understandings of Englishness, meaning that 'Asian Muslims can be English, albeit in a narrowly defined space' (Kyriakedes et al., 2009: 300). Such evidence also suggests that Englishness as an identity is something that can be 'chosen', and not dependent on immutable racial characteristics or blood lineage, as highlighted by a White woman interviewed in Bradford for a recent article on 'Englishness': 'If you're born here, you're English. What I don't understand is why the Asians who have been born here want to fly the Pakistan flag? They're English' (Manzoor, 2009: 5).

This focus on 'choice' and hybridity obviously questions the very stress put on Islamic identity by Muslim respondents, and implies that such a religious identity is an overt block to the development and acceptance of an inclusive 'Englishness' for both Muslims and non-Muslims alike. Certainly, some critics of the new policy priority of Community Cohesion see it as an overtly assimilationist attempt to force Muslims to downplay their own identity and to embrace a national identity not up for negotiation or interpretation (Alexander, 2004; Kundnani, 2007). However, empirical evidence suggests that it is not presaged on assimilationism. Instead, it accepts the reality and positive strength of different identities and works with them to create the conditions for meaningful direct contact and dialogue to encourage positive and common over-arching identities (Thomas, 2007). This understanding of the government's Community Cohesion agenda places it in the context of New Labour's efforts to create decentred and inter-sectional forms of identity in a 'human rights' framework (McGhee, 2006). Here, 'hot' forms of exclusive ethnic, class and religious identities that are inevitably going to be in tension with each other in an increasingly fluid and multicultural society need to be replaced by 'cooler', weaker forms of identity. From this perspective, respect and equality between religious and ethnic identities cannot be viewed as progress if those identities are intolerant of gay and lesbian lifestyles or of gender equality. This policy approach can be seen as a departure from previous debates on 'multiculturalism' which stressed the perspective of a 'community of communities' (CFMEB, 2000: 2). By contrast, this new focus necessitates weakening such essentialised ethnic identities and the development of multiple identities, the precondition for 'hybridity' (Hall, 2000). The fact that the young Muslims surveyed here are comfortable with a 'British' identity alongside their 'religious' affiliation might be seen as a tentative but positive development in this direction, perhaps with the development of an inclusive, multi-cultural Englishness a necessary further step.

Developing an inclusive Englishness

This book and the other recent literature it draws on illustrates that debate about the meaning/s and importance of 'Englishness' is growing. This is clearly not a discussion that is going away, with the latest British Social Attitudes survey suggesting that '4 in 10 people in England now regard themselves as solely or primarily English' (Ward and Carvel, 2007), especially as devolution and the re-making of Britain gathers pace. As the empirical data from Oldham and Rochdale discussed here (Thomas and Sanderson, 2009) and other surveys (CRE, 2005; Ipsos Mori, 2007) suggest, this growing affiliation is not yet shared by non-white ethnic minorities for a number of reasons. This is partially because, despite positive evidence (Kyriakides et al., 2009) to the contrary, some white people do not accept ethnic minorities as 'English'. This may seem surprising, given the extent of ethnic diversity in England and the claim that most English people support an inclusive understanding of national identity, 'with this popular majority constructed out of an everyday, mainly, urban experience of multiculturalism' (Perryman, 2009: 16). The problem here is that experiences of multiculturalism in England are very uneven, with cities highly diverse, but many suburban and rural areas remaining largely monocultural. In significant parts of urban areas, the experience is a duo cultural one, rather than multi-cultural, with segregated and suspicious working-class Asian and white communities not feeling that they have shared identities (Cantle, 2001). In both situations, the opportunistic far-right British National party have taken advantage of existing prejudices to add further fuel to them, rather than tackle the real cause of social problems. This all suggest that the government's Community Cohesion and social exclusion policies are a vital component of a greater shared sense of 'Englishness'.

Gary Younge, one of the most thoughtful commentators on the links between 'race' and national identity has commented that 'It is now no longer possible, or desirable, to forestall the inevitable – it is time to find an accommodation between blackness and Englishness' (2000: 112). Whilst community-based cohesion and integration activity can help here, the onus cannot solely be on ethnic minority communities to embrace 'Englishness'. At the moment, there is no real celebration or acknowledgement of Englishness outside major football tournaments, with an apparent reluctance of many English people to even acknowledge or embrace Englishness (Bragg, 2006; Perryman, 2008b). Coupled with government approaches to ethnic monitoring and identification that do not allow non-white ethnic minorities (or anyone else) to choose 'English' as an identity, it is hardly surprising that there is currently limited enthusiasm for Englishness amongst non-white ethnic minorities. The experience of Welsh and Scottish devolution is that an inclusive national identity can successfully be developed (CRE, 2005), and the question now is whether a similarly inclusive and multi-ethnic notion of national identity can be encouraged in the more challenging environment of England. The way forward here is surely not a prescriptive, top-down list of national values to be adhered to (Brown, 2007b). Instead, the multiple and inherently fluent understandings of identity underlying the government's approach to policy (McGhee, 2006) are surely the way forward, where more young people can happily see themselves as, for example, a Brummie English Muslim (Ipsos Mori, 2007). These approaches not only reflect the developing multicultural present of England, but its past as 'It is precisely this "new" hybridity of Englishness that has always been its defining characteristic' (Carrington, 2008: 127).

Such a view suggests that the way forward towards an inclusive Englishness that allows people of all ethnic backgrounds to 'belong' is one that focuses on place, not 'race' and which positively celebrates England's historic engagement with the world and the world with England, the engagement that has given us the 'mongrel glory' (Colin MacIness, in Weight, 2008: 103) responsible for the hybridised music, art, and literature that has had so much impact, as well as for the dynamic, multicultural reality of so many English towns and cities. In short, it is impossible to imagine a modern English identity emerging that doesn't embrace ethnic diversity as a central tenet. The alternative will not be the lack of an English identity, but a racist, monochrome and melancholic Englishness that denies the reality of its own land (Gilroy, 2004).

4

Towards a cosmopolitan England?

Christopher G.A. Bryant

Introduction

In January 2008 David Marquand argued in a posting on the Open Democracy website that the campaigns for an English parliament and the lesser alternative of English votes on English laws were unworthy of support because 'no one has put forward a positive case for devolution to England, based on a moral vision of what England and the English stand for or might come to stand for' (2008b: np). The Scots had their inspirational myth of popular sovereignty and the Welsh their myth of Celtic socialism, but the English had long forgotten their republican tradition of Milton and Blake and had nothing else. In a second posting that month he went further. Until campaigners for an English parliament recovered and regenerated 'the tradition of the Levellers, of Milton, of Tom Paine, of the Chartists, of John Bright, of the pre-1914 syndicalists, of George Orwell and R.H. Tawney', he would 'continue to regard them as barbarous reactionaries' (2008c: np). It is not my intention here to readdress the inequity of England's exclusion from devolution and what should be done about it (see Bryant, 2008). I also do not subscribe to Marquand's new constitutional doctrine that national self-determination is justifiable only if it is also an instrument for something worthier. Even so I shall outline an argument that Marquand's disdain for the English is unwarranted insofar as they are generating a cosmopolitan England of growing prominence and rich potential. England is notably and increasingly cosmopolitan, more so than other parts of the United Kingdom, and cosmopolitanism affords a moral vision as admirable as any Scottish popular sovereignty or Welsh socialism – albeit one in need of more realistic and citizen-friendly articulation. There is already some evidence of English pride in England's 'multiculturalism' and its cosmopolitanism could become a cause for celebration. Such a future is not guaranteed but cosmopolitan England already has enough substance to allow rejection of Marquand's supercilious charge that England has not even the potential to stand for anything worthwhile.

This chapter belongs to the genre Anthony Giddens (1990: 154) calls utopian realism. It is utopian insofar as it treats cosmopolitan England as a good thing, an England whose desirable characteristics and possibilities outweigh its undesirable ones. And it is realist in that it recognises that the formation of a cosmopolitan England has already started and might credibly be expected to continue.

So what does a cosmopolitan England consist of? Answers depend in part on what is meant by 'cosmopolitan'. In earlier writings I have just taken a cosmopolitan England to be one that is perceptibly constituted in significant measure by people, practices and ideas from around the world (2003; 2006; 2008). This is consistent with the first definition of 'cosmopolitan' given by the *Concise Oxford Dictionary* (8th edn, 1990) – 'of or from or knowing many parts of the world' – and I have assumed that it is also consistent with an ordinary language understanding of the word. It is a usage that is atheoretical. The *COD* has, however, a second definition of 'cosmopolitan' – 'free from national limitations or prejudices' – which is nearer to cosmopolitan theory as articulated in philosophy and the social sciences since the 1990s (1990). The idea of cosmopolitanism dates from the ancient Greeks and was developed further during the Enlightenment (Delanty, 2006). Today's cosmopolitan theory attempts to specify what the cosmopolitan consists of and why it is good. It has philosophical and social scientific components, and it also has connections with arguments about globalisation. The debate about cosmopolitanism has proved dauntingly convoluted and highly contentious and it still continues (Beck & Sznaider, 2006; Fine & Boon, 2007; Ossewaarde, 2007).

Some formulations of cosmopolitan theory point to an ultra-cosmopolitanism and as such are unsociological, even anti-sociological; they do not apply to real worlds inhabitable by real people. Others offer a real cosmopolitanism of more practical value to social scientific analysis and empirical research. The last part of this chapter asks whether there is a contemporary cosmopolitan England understood in terms of not only (atheoretical) ordinary-language cosmopolitanism but also (theorised) real cosmopolitanism. Particular attention will be paid to: multi- and inter-culturalism; attitudes to diversity; ethnic diversity in London; and bi- and multi-lingualism.

Cosmopolitan theory: ultra-cosmopolitanism and real cosmopolitanism

Most arguments for and against cosmopolitanism make claims with respect to three continua: first, the human and the social; second the universal and the particular; and third, the cosmopolitan and the local. The first continuum has at one pole people who have overcome all attachments to particular societies and culture and who are thus defined exclusively by their humanity, and at the other people who are only attached to particular societies and cultures and who are thus defined exclusively by their sociality. The second continuum has at its poles the universal, that which is common to all persons, and / or all societies and cultures, and the particular, that which is peculiar to an individual person, society or culture. The third continuum has at one pole the cosmos understood as the globe or the world as a whole, and at the other the most local of locals understood as the smallest community identifiable (presumably the dyad). All really existing people, societies and cultures are located somewhere between the poles of the three continua. Advocates of ultra-cosmopolitanism seek to progress by maximising the human and the universal and attending only to the global and by minimising the social and the particular and disregarding the local. They want us to become exclusively citizens of the world devoid of local loyalties, and they regard all sub-global loyalties from the supranational (such as the European Union) through loyalties to the state and / or nation, to loyalties to the region, city, town, village or street as just more or less local. Alternatively they want us to become exclusively citizens of the world unconcerned to privilege any particular social or cultural characteristics or local attachments we retain over and above the particular social and cultural characteristics or local attachment others retain. This second alternative is sociologically more credible than the first insofar as it concedes retention of the social, the particular and the local, but it is still sociologically incredible insofar as it treats all differences in the social, the particular and the local as matters of fact but not matters of value worth protecting or promoting in competition, or even by comparison, with matters of value to others.

World citizenship is all inclusive. 'World citizens do not belong to a particular group, do not accept the institutions that result from group experiences, but identify themselves with "humanity" alone' (Ossewaarde, 2007: 375). The political philosophers' ideal of an ultra-cosmopolitan utopia is a social scientist's nonsensical dystopia, but it is still worth asking whether there are aspects of life in contemporary societies which can usefully be characterised as 'cosmopolitan' in a sense which is relatable to both the *COD*'s second definition of 'free from national limitations or prejudices' and the political philosophy of cosmopolitanism. Jürgen Habermas's discourse ethics indicates how one might proceed. Habermas distinguishes between moral principles *(Moralität)* which are universal and ethical life *(Sittlichkeit)* which is context specific, and he acknowledges that the application of general principles to real situations requires interpretive skill and sensitivity to context. The morality of, in this case, cosmopolitan principle, which is universal, has necessarily to be mediated by experience of actual social relations and associations which are particular. What Alan Wolfe calls the 'republic of the head' (1989: 124) has always to engage with what Robert Bellah et al. (1985), following Alexis de Tocqueville (1835–40), calls the 'habits of the heart', if real cosmopolitanism is to ensue.

William Smith argues that 'cosmopolitanism as a political project requires a corresponding account of cosmopolitan virtue' (2007: 49) if it is to progress. 'Such an account should indicate the dispositions and qualities that will make us aware of our cosmopolitan obligations and make us more likely to discharge them' (Smith, 2007: 49). This is what Bryan Turner intends when setting out the following five components of 'cosmopolitan virtue':

> *irony*, both as a cultural method and as a contemporary mentality in order to achieve some emotional distance from our own local culture [after Richard Rorty 1989]; *reflexivity* with respect to other cultural values; *scepticism* towards the grand narratives of modern ideologies; *care for other cultures*, especially aboriginal cultures, arising from an awareness of their precarious condition and hence acceptance of cultural hybridization; and *an ecumenical commitment to dialogue* with other cultures, especially religious cultures. (Turner, 2001: 150; emphasis mine)

Turner's cosmopolitans as ironists only ever hold provisional views about social and cultural matters because knowledge has no sure foundations or final form and the need to revise, reformulate or reject is a constant possibility. The ironist's social and cultural loyalties are necessarily cool and, given that 'modern societies are organized around the marketplace of anonymous strangers, where these strangers are mobile and disconnected', his or her patterns of solidarity are invariably thin (Turner, 2001: 148). It is a society of strangers that beckons.

Instead of irony, Smith, following Hannah Arendt (1959; 1977; 1990) speaks of worldliness. Worldliness has three aspects. The first involves adoption of a self-reflexive mode of being in the world. Cosmopolitans form attachments and make commitments, but they are also able to step back and distance themselves from them. The second involves cultivation of 'a heightened feeling or care for the world' (Smith, 2007: 46). It is about 'world-building ... devising durable institutions that will actualise cosmopolitan aspirations to entrench human rights, promote global distributive justice, protect cultural diversity and reignite democracy' (Smith, 2007: 46). The cosmopolitan, subscribing to an ethic of care, supports and campaigns for cosmopolitan causes. The third 'pertains to the skills we exhibit during our interactions with the world' (Smith, 2007: 47). The cosmopolitan performs skilfully by combining cosmopolitan virtue with sensitivity to context. There is no formula for doing this well, but doing it well is indispensable to effective civil society activism. Worldly men and women, so defined, are for Smith the virtuous and astute cosmopolitan citizens that cosmopolitan progress depends upon. Citizens of the world are not, however, citizens of a polity with a formal constitution. Smith's cosmopolitan citizenship may be commendable but in the circumstances of the present it is often a rhetorical conceit.

Undeviating cosmopolitans always engage respectfully with difference, but never accept any fundamentalism, religious or otherwise, on its own terms. They regard everything as open to criticism, and nothing as beyond criticism. (In Durkheimian terms nothing is sacred, everything is profane.) Their irony, reflexivity, scepticism, respect for the other, and commitment to dialogue are absolute. Such paragons of virtue are, of course, the rarest of beings and the prospect of a common citizenry exclusively cosmopolitan in its mentality and action, whether in England or anywhere else, is a fantastical one. Nevertheless there are citizens who do on occasions exemplify elements of cosmopolitan virtue. It is thus possible to treat the cosmopolitanism of individuals and societies as a matter of degree and to ask whether it is increasing.

To speak in these terms is to move from ultra-cosmopolitan idealism to cosmopolitan realism and to shift from the free-floating ideal to the situated reality. The work of Ulrich Beck (2002; 2006) on cosmopolitan vision and society and the writings of Beck and Edgar Grande on cosmopolitan Europe (2007a; 2007b) offer one way forward. Beck and Grande (2007b) endorse cosmopolitan realism as a principle and a practice discoverable in, and applicable to, every level of social and political activity from international organisations to neighbourhoods and families. Cosmopolitan realism respects *both* otherness, difference and diversity, *and* universal norms and unity. It rejects the zero sum of either/or and advocates the positive sum of both/and. Beck and Grande's argument starts with the definition of cosmopolitanism put forward by the German philosopher, Christoph Martin Wieland, in 1788: '[the cosmopolitan] means his own country well; but he means other countries well too, and he cannot wish to establish the prosperity, fame and greatness of his own nation on the outsmarting or oppression of other states' (Beck & Grande, 2007b: 70). We do not have to disown or disdain our interests or local attachments, but we do have to recognise that others have interests and attachments of their own. Beck and Grande do not speak of irony but they do call for recognition of others and, crucially, for more than just tolerance: 'Whatever is strange should be regarded and evaluated not as a threat, as something that brings disintegration and fragmentation in its train, but as enriching in the first place' (2007b: 71). 'One's own interests', moreover, 'should be pursued without "the outsmarting or oppression of others", whether individuals or states. Thus, cosmopolitan realism basically means the recognition of the legitimate interests of others and their inclusion in the calculation of one's own interests' (2007b: 71). But for this to be mutual there does have to be a modicum of common values and norms. Beck and Grande do not enlarge on this, but it is not hard to guess what they are getting at. There has to be a common understanding of who the 'we' are within which diversity is to be more than tolerated, and there have to be norms which govern the conduct of 'our' conversation and the decisions 'we' might properly reach and the means by which they might properly be implemented.

Difference and diversity within nations present challenges of mutuality and solidarity. Put simply, at one end of the range there is hostility, conflict and violence, at the other there is appreciation and unconstrained interaction, and in between there are elements of co-existence, accommodation, toleration, more or less limited understanding, and more or less constrained interaction. The cosmopolitan move is a move towards wider mutuality and solidarity. Similarly differences between nations and states pose challenges of mutuality and solidarity. At one end of the range is war, at the other universal cooperation. In between there is all the paraphernalia of trade, cultural exchange, multilateral treaties and alliances, blocs, international organisations and much else. The cosmopolitan move is a move towards mutuality and solidarity within wider alliances and bigger blocs and, crucially, beyond them.

England and Cosmopolitanism

Discussing England and the English as distinct from Britain and the British is complicated by the fact that the five-sixths of the population of Britain who live in England have a greater identification with Britain than those who live in Wales and especially Scotland. About one in five of the people of England consider themselves more British than English, or only British, and roughly a further two in five consider themselves equally English and British; by contrast less than one-twentieth of the people of Scotland consider themselves more British than Scottish or only British, and only about a fifth consider themselves equally Scottish and British. In short the people of England manifest a marked English / British ambiguity with respect to national identity (Bryant, 2010: Table 1). Much of what is said about Britain perforce applies especially to England and much of what the people of England say about themselves and their country refers to the British and Britain. It is also worth noting that the 2001 Census recorded non-white population percentages as follows: 9.0% in England, 2.1% in Wales and 2.0% in Scotland.[1]

I have elsewhere written at length about English England, Anglo-British England and Little England as well as Cosmopolitan England (Bryant, 2003; 2006: Chs 2, 5 & 8). But by comparison with these other constructions, cosmopolitan England is more oriented to Europe, the Commonwealth and the world, and more open to a diversity of peoples and cultures. Outward looking and contemporary in its orientation, it acknowledges not just the diversification of the people – particularly that legacy of Empire, citizens (whose forebears are) of black or Asian origin – but also the significance for its economy and culture of imports from abroad whether carried by immigrants or transmitted by trade or the media. It can only be a civic nation (Bryant, 1997). The following list of types of evidence about England and its people relevant to a comprehensive examination not just of cosmopolitan diversity but also real cosmopolitanism is by no means exhaustive, but it is long enough to indicate the scale of the task.

English and British identity markers
ethnic composition (citizens and other residents)
immigration and emigration and attitudes to both
labour force composition and attitudes to migrant workers
race relations
religious composition and attitudes towards the religious and the secular
housing (tenure, integration and segregation)
schools (integration and segregation)

marriage and cohabitation
friendship and socialising
English and second and multiple language competencies
experience of life, work, study, travel and holidaying abroad
attitudes to devolution
attitudes to 'multiculturalism'
diversity and interaction (sites, occasions, etc.)
diversity and heroes: celebrities and the successful
patterns of consumption
attitudes to the European Union
attitudes and practices with respect to the global and the local
attitudes to 'global citizenship/citizenship of the world'
voting and party political policies in connection with many of the above.

And most difficult of all, evidence of:

open and closed mindedness
irony and distancing
liberalism, pragmatism and the accommodation and appreciation of
    difference
absolutism and fundamentalism
ethics of conviction and of responsibility.

In practice, the evidence relevant to all the items in the above list is currently both dauntingly copious and frustratingly limited. Their systematic examination would require completion of a big research programme by teams of social scientists and several large books. There is scope here only for an introductory discussion of a few germane matters.

Multi- and inter-culturalism

Robert Winder (2004) recalls how Britain, most often England, has for centuries benefited from the rich talents, scarce skills and cheap labour of successive immigrations even though there are typically many English at the time who have deplored them as threats to English culture and to the profits and jobs of English men and women, and there are many immigrants who have met with racist prejudice and discrimination and some who have suffered physical violence. French Huguenots, Germans, Jews, Italians, Irish, Chinese, Poles and others in the past, West Indians, Indians, Pakistanis, Bengalis, East African Asians, West Africans, Eastern Europeans and others since the 1950s are all part of the same story of entry into the fabric of English life whatever the odds. Those who are comfortable with cosmopolitan

England are quite capable of recognising this and will find Winder's title, *Bloody Foreigners* (2004), indiscriminate and anachronistic. Those who are not will find his title only too apt.

Cosmopolitan England acknowledges that it is culturally diverse even if some of its citizens wish it were less so. It also knows that there are necessarily limits to multiculturalism in practice. Accommodation of diversity is not the same as indiscriminate acceptance of difference. At a minimum, everyone must be able to speak English as the common language, must respect the law and must acknowledge the equal rights of men and women. Cultural diversity can only be accommodated within a common culture. Recognising this Bhikhu Parekh refers to Britain as a community of communities in his preface to the report on *The Future of Multi-Ethnic Britain* that bears his name (Parekh, 2000: ix). This implies that everyone is a member of one or more sub-communities of Britain – in which case what Parekh seeks is what Hartmann and Gerteis (2005) call interactive pluralism. In practice, however, the attachment of individuals to the particular cultural and religious communities in which they were more or less tightly brought up varies greatly. Hybridity and cultural exchange are also commonplace. It would thus be better to say simply that Britain is a community of sentiment (to echo Max Weber) within which there are many differences of culture, that these differences are sometimes themselves community based, and that England is more diverse in terms of the recent origins and current cultures of its people than Scotland or Wales.

In 2004 multiculturalism was questioned from the left and from the Commission for Racial Equality as never before. The debate began in late February when David Goodhart argued that progressives want 'plenty of both solidarity (high social cohesion and generous welfare paid out of a progressive tax system) and diversity (equal respect for a wide range of peoples, values and ways of life)' (2004: np) but there comes a point beyond which these are inversely related. The volume of asylum seekers, he thought, threatened to take us beyond that point. Newspapers picked up on Goodhart, for and against, and the gloves were off. Then Trevor Phillips, the co-author of *Windrush* (1998) and the head of the Commission for Racial Equality, who had called Goodhart 'racist', changed sides in an interview in *The Times* (Benton, 2004: np), and argued that multiculturalism was out of date. It encouraged separateness when the need now was to re-emphasise 'common values ... the common currency of the English language, honouring the culture of these islands, like Shakespeare and Dickens'. The view seemed to prevail that multiculturalism could issue in a dangerous separateness though it need not, that all responsible citizens should guard against this, that more attention to common values and practices was overdue, that the problem of the radicalised minority of young Muslims who rejected Britishness could no longer be ignored, that the ceremonies to mark the award of British citizenship introduced by the then home secretary, David Blunkett, were a good idea, and that it was time to take forward a Britain of which all citizens would be proud. A rebalancing was called for.

This has not settled the debate about multiculturalism. In a speech delivered in Manchester shortly after the London tube and bus bombings of July 2005, Phillips gave voice to the fear that there are 'districts on the way to becoming fully fledged ghettoes' and that 'we are sleepwalking our way to segregation' (2005: np). Following inspection of the statistical evidence Nissa Finney and Ludi Simpson (2009) argue that the incidence of residential segregation has been exaggerated and the dynamics of such segregation as there is are more complex than the mythmakers would have us believe. Even so there is a general view that multiculturalism without interaction between bearers of the different cultures is undesirable. Responses to this include the articulation of more sophisticated versions of multiculturalism (for example Modood, 2007), the switch in emphasis to interculturalism (for example James, 2008), and government support for 'community cohesion' understood as respect for differences within a community, those of the majority as well as minorities, allied to the sharing of experiences and the generation of shared values (see Cantle, 2005: 10–11).

Attitudes to diversity

It is instructive to consider attitudes to diversity as revealed by surveys. All the surveys discussed were accessible in June 2009 in the online archives of the polling companies whose web addresses are given in the references section at the end of this book.

Two weeks after the London bombings, a YouGov survey presented respondents throughout Britain with a list of thirty-seven 'phrases which might be used to describe or define Britain and what it is to be British'. Some 41% thought 'Their tolerance of other people and other people's ideas' was very important, and a further 40% thought the sentiment fairly important. Respondents were then given a list of ten 'institutions, symbols and values that are often thought of as embodying the British way of life' and asked which they personally took pride in. The third most favoured was 'British people's tolerance of individuals of all races and faiths' at 54%. And whilst 24% thought the statement 'The beliefs of Western liberal democracy and the beliefs of Islam are fundamentally contradictory' closest [*sic*] to their own view, 52% preferred 'There is no fundamental contradiction between the beliefs of Western liberal democracy and the beliefs of Islam, only between the beliefs of Western liberal democracy and the beliefs of a minority of Islamic extremists and fanatics.' Tolerance is not appreciation but nor is it to be dismissed lightly at a moment of crisis.

A week earlier another YouGov survey had asked Muslim respondents how loyal they personally felt towards Britain. Some 46% answered very loyal and a further 33% fairly loyal. And when asked 'Which of these views comes closest to your own', 1% chose 'Western society is decadent and immoral, and Muslims should seek to bring it to an end, if necessary by violence', 31% chose 'Western society is decadent and immoral, and Muslims should seek to bring it to an end, but only by NON-VIOLENT means' and 56% opted for 'Western society may not be perfect, but Muslims should live with it and not seek to bring it to an end.' At a time of great tension, a third of Muslims said they should seek to bring a society they most definitely did not appreciate to an end, but more than half rejected so damning a judgement and provocative a course of action.

In August 2005, Ipsos-MORI conducted a 'multiculturalism poll' for the BBC which included a boosted supplementary survey of Muslims. National [sic] and Muslim responses were often similar. One month after the 7/7 bombings, 39% of the national and 31% of the Muslim sample thought that 'Britain is becoming less racially tolerant'. But 62% of the national sample and 82% of the Muslim sample still said the view that 'multiculturalism makes Britain a better place to live' came closest [sic] to their own, compared with 32% and 13% respectively who preferred 'Multiculturalism is a threat to the British way of life.' And asked whether they agreed or disagreed that 'the policy of multiculturalism in Britain has been a mistake and should be abandoned?', only 21% of the national and 14% of the Muslim sample agreed. But these results did mask a difference of emphasis; 58% of the national sample but only 29% of Muslim respondents opted for 'People who come to live in Britain should adopt the values and traditions of British culture' compared with 35% and 59% respectively who favoured 'People who come to live in Britain should be free to live their lives by the values and traditions of their own culture.' Only 27% of the national and 18% of the Muslim sample thought that 'Islam is incompatible with the values of British democracy', though there was a difference of emphasis on what to do next. 'Given the threat to Britain from terrorism', 58% of the national sample thought we should be 'More concerned about ensuring the rights of ethnic minorities are protected' compared with 81% of the Muslim sample, while 30% of the national and 9% of the Muslim samples said we should be 'less concerned'. If the London bombers thought they would quickly drive Muslims and non-Muslims apart, they were wrong.

In March / April 2006 GfK NOP surveyed Muslim opinion for a Channel 4 *Dispatches* programme in areas with a 5% or more penetration of Muslims. Asked 'Britain: my country or their country?', 49% said my country compared with 24% saying their country and 12% saying both. As for Britain as an Islamic state, 52% disagreed with such a dream compared with 28% who agreed with it. A year after the bombings a July 2006 YouGov poll offered another slant on the future. Asked whether they agreed or disagreed that 'It will never be possible for Britain's Muslims to integrate fully into British society' 32% of Muslims and 49% of non-Muslims agreed. Only 9% of Muslims and 15% of non-Muslims agreed that 'It is better if Britain's Muslims DON'T integrate fully into British society.'

A poll conducted by Populus in May 2007 asked MPs whether they agreed with the statement 'The diverse mix of races, cultures and religions now found in society has improved Britain'. Some 92% of the seventy Labour MPs asked agreed, as did 100% of the thirteen Liberal Democrats but only 41% of the thirty-nine Conservatives. Some 94% of the Labour MPs agreed that 'One of the things that would most improve life in Britain today is people being more tolerant of different ethnic groups and cultures', as did 100% of Liberal Democrats but only 67% of Conservatives. Most strikingly of all, 83% of Labour MPs agreed that multiculturalism is a good thing, as did 92% of Liberal Democrats but just 20% of Conservatives. David Cameron's new model, but still predominantly English, Conservative party would seem, if its MPs reflect its supporters, less comfortable with diversity than its main rivals.

Finally an under-reported Populus poll for the BBC of *white British only*, completed in March 2008 when economic growth was already slowing but immigration from Eastern Europe was still high, recorded striking ambivalence about immigration – with 88% saying it was not immigration they objected to, but uncontrolled immigration. *On the one hand*: 53% said that the statement 'On the whole immigration into Britain is a good thing for the country' came closer to their view than the opposite; 54% agreed that new immigrants 'have added richness and variety to the culture of Britain and made the country more prosperous'; 74% agreed that 'Most immigrants end up fitting in here if they're given sufficient time to do so'; and 57% agreed that 'in every generation some people make a fuss about immigration when the truth is that each new wave of immigration has always ended up benefiting Britain'. *On the other hand*: 42% thought immigration a 'bad thing'; 61% agreed that 'people who have made a contribution to this society are being ignored or pushed aside by new immigrants who just take what they can and offer nothing in return'; 77% agreed that 'You can't criticise the amount of immigration or how individual immigrants conduct themselves these days without being labelled a racist'; 75% agreed that 'These days the British population is expected to fit in with new immigrants rather than the other way round'; and 67% agreed that 'New immigrants to Britain make less of an effort to fit in than those who arrived in this country a generation ago.'

In recent years polls have also suggested that a majority of respondents, whether English or British, think there have been too many immigrants taking too many jobs from British workers, that some parts of Britain no longer feel British because of immigration, and that Britain is losing its culture as a consequence of both immigration and European Union policies and directives. In sum the survey evidence for acceptance, let alone endorsement, of multiculturalism is mixed, but much more is positive than critics of multiculturalism would have one suppose.

Ethnic diversity in London

There is more to diversity than ethnic difference – religion and language, for example, often figure prominently – but it is ethnic difference that is the most obvious indicator of diversity in London. London is much more diverse in terms of both the non-white British percentage of its population and the sheer number of ethnic groups significantly represented than anywhere else in England.

In 2004 white British constituted only 58.4% of the population of Greater London compared with an all-England figure of 85.3% (National Statistics & Greater London Authority (GLA), 2007: Table 1.9). Some of the rest of the population of London was white Irish or other white but the black and Asian minority ethnic population (BAME) totalled 30.2% compared with 10.5% in England as a whole. And since 2004 there has been a big influx of Eastern Europeans. The BAME population is projected to reach 37.0% by 2016 and 39.1% by 2026 (Table 2.9). In 2006 twenty-three of the twenty-five local authorities with the highest rankings for ethnic diversity were London boroughs (GLA 2008:Table 2.13). By then Brent and Newham had a BAME population of more than half and by 2026 six more boroughs are projected to join them (Table 2.11). In 2006 32% of the population of London (39% in Inner London) were born outside the UK compared with 7% in England as a whole (p. 28). Of these migrants 27% were born in European Union countries, 23% in Africa and 17% in the Indian sub-continent (p. 30). 63% of migrants in 2006 were from BAME groups.

London is a world city (cf. Massey, 2007). The success of its financial heart, at least until the onset of recession in 2008, raised its standing worldwide, but the extremes of wealth and poverty it also generated were greater in London itself than anywhere else in the UK. Diversity alongside inequality might have led to social conflict and urban disorder, but for the most part they have not. The 7/7 bombings by Muslim extremists might have started the unravelling of London, but they did not. The day before 7/7 London had been awarded the 2012 Olympic Games. London's successful bid had emphasised the ethnic diversity of London and Londoners' contentment with it. It is easy to point to examples of Londoners enjoying London's diversity – the crowds at the (West Indians') Notting Hill carnival, for example; and it is easy to cite examples of objections to it, such as the hostility of some white East Enders to what they perceive as an unfair allocation of council housing in Tower Hamlets that favours Bangladeshis (see Dench et al., 2007). Overall, however, it is arguable that what Paul Gilroy calls a 'convivial cosmopolitanism' (2004: 154) increasingly prevails. Gilroy welcomes 'the ludic, cosmopolitan energy and the democratic possibilities so evident in the postcolonial metropolis' such as London (2004: 154). He is also keen 'to explore aspects of Britain's spontaneous, convivial culture and to discover a new value in its ability to live with alterity without becoming anxious, fearful, or violent' (2004: xi). 'The radical openness that brings conviviality alive makes a nonsense', he adds, 'of closed, fixed, and reified identity' (2004: xi). In the big city the spontaneous interaction of diverse people and peoples generates ever new cultural and economic possibilities. But is that how Londoners see it?

The Greater London annual survey in 2007 found that 81% agreed with the statement 'London may not be perfect but I enjoy living here', and 76% agreed with the statement 'I enjoy the cultural diversity of London' (Ipsos MORI, 2008: 18). Asked 'Which of the following [two] statements would you say comes closest to your view?', 68% of respondents opted for 'London's diverse communities make London a better place to live', compared with 25 opting for 'London's diversity threatens the way of life in London' (Ipsos MORI, 2008: 27). The net percentage agreeing that 'London is a city with good relations between different racial, ethnic and religious communities' fell, however, from a high of 61% in 2004 to 48% in 2007, and the net percentage agreeing that 'There is less discrimination on the basis of race or ethnic origin in London than 3 years ago' fell from a high of 31% in 2004 to just 15% in 2007 (Ipsos MORI, 2008: 28). The general conclusion has to be that most Londoners expressed satisfaction in 2007 with London's diversity though anxieties about community relations, and, especially, race and ethnic discrimination, had intensified. All in all, the notion that London enjoys a significant measure of real and convivial cosmopolitanism remains plausible and merits comprehensive future study.

London's diversity is recognised as a huge asset and not just something to be accommodated, but the world-in-one-city character of London is untypical of England as a whole. The 2001 census recorded big variations in the percentages of non-white British in England from 60.6% in the London borough of Newham to 0.7% in Cumbria. So does London lead the way or is it a place apart? The answer may prove to be a bit of both. There are elements of that same vibrancy and conviviality in Birmingham, Manchester, Leeds and other big cities which are reinventing themselves.

Bi- and multilingualism

Can a monoglot be a cosmopolitan? The English are notoriously poor at foreign languages, often consoling themselves that the effort of learning other languages is unnecessary because, thanks to British imperialism and American economic and military domination, English has become so pervasive a world language foreigners of any education and ambition have to learn it. The attitude that we do not have to learn their languages because they have to learn ours is seemingly confirmed by a national curriculum in England that no longer requires secondary school students to learn a foreign language beyond their third year.[2] This immediately prompts the thought that immigrants and their children who speak community languages as well as English might have a better claim to be cosmopolitan than the rest of us – even if we like to think of ourselves as more urbane and sophisticated than fellow citizens whose families have emigrated quite recently from, say, a Bangladeshi village.[3] Beck and Grande (2007a: 101) support the (European Union) goal that Europeans be tri-lingual, speaking their native language, English as the international business language, and a third language as a way of learning to appreciate a culture other than their own – whilst noting the claim that 75% of people alive today speak two or more languages. The dismal implication is that monoglot English men, women and children are less able to appreciate other cultures than their multilingual counterparts in Europe. 'Monolingualism ... means blinkered vision', Beck and Grande warn (2007a: 100). By contrast, the French journalist Agnès Poirier proclaims: 'Multilingualism makes mental and geographical borders disappear, annihilates chauvinism, and educates the world citizens of tomorrow' (2008: 35). Clearly partisans of multilingualism value it greatly, but research evidence that foreign language acquisition generally leads to a greater propensity to accommodate difference, tolerate the other, and appreciate other cultures is elusive. Interestingly Michael Byram (2008), a leading British researcher on foreign language education, discusses it as a likely, but not inevitable, means to intercultural citizenship without ever suggesting that it is also a necessary one. And for him, intercultural citizenship is not about a cosmopolitan *identity* but rather the *competencies* that make up critical cultural awareness and enable those who have acquired them to act sensitively and effectively when engaging with people from other cultures at home and abroad. These include the attitudes of 'curiosity and openness, readiness to suspend disbelief about other cultures and belief about one's own' (Byram, 2008: 163), a combination similar to Turner's cosmopolitan irony. Significantly, Byram writes about interculturalism rather than multiculturalism. It is not the coexistence of different cultures that interests him but rather the quality of relations between them.

Learning the language of the other may open the way not just to appreciating the culture of the Other but also to readiness to appreciate the cultures of countless other Others whose language one will never know – or so the advocates of foreign language education for intercultural citizenship must hope. But other modes of education and experience from studying sociology to inquisitive travel to sensitivity to difference may serve the same end. It is not impossible for the monoglot English to be cosmopolitans, but it may be harder.

Conclusions

Insofar as cosmopolitan England is consistent with developments in the composition of the population of England in general, and the labour force in particular, and in the diversification of its culture and its social practices, it might be thought to carry the endorsement of contemporary history. But it is easy to see that not all difference is accommodatable; that tolerance is less than appreciation; that defining the terms and limits of accommodation, interaction and exchange is urgent, necessary and difficult; and that attitudes towards the cosmopolitan on the part of the citizenry vary from the appreciative to the complaining.

I have argued elsewhere that all constructions and representations of nation have their light side and their dark side and all have normative dimensions (2003; 2006: 13–29). (1) The light side of a cosmopolitan England is more than tolerant; it appreciates its diversity and is as Gilroy says convivial. (2) It has citizens willing and competent to engage with Others and appreciate what they contribute to the economy and culture. Multiculturalism without interaction and engagement between different communities and the individuals more or less loyal to them – separate lives, parallel communities – at best affords co-existence and at worst conflict and violence. The same can be said for engagement without appreciation. (3) A cosmopolitan England at ease with itself respects local attachments. It neither denies its diversity, nor seeks to transcend it. (4) A cosmopolitan England at ease with itself is also at ease with both devolution within Britain and a European Union that values its own diversity. (On cosmopolitanism and Europe see Bauman, 2004, and Delanty and Rumford, 2005, as well as Beck and Grande, 2007a; 2007b). (5) The light side of cosmopolitan England features citizens exemplifying moments of cosmopolitan virtue. The hope is that such moments are on the increase.

The ultra-cosmopolitan end of cosmopolitan theory is enough to give the theory a bad name, but cosmopolitan realism directs attention to the appreciation of difference, constructive interaction and moments of cosmopolitan virtue. A mere essay cannot attempt systematic examination of the evidence for a cosmopolitan England, but the brief discussions of multi- and interculturalism, attitudes to diversity, ethnic diversity in London, and bi- and multilingualism assemble enough evidence to suggest the possibility of a cosmopolitan England in the making. After casting a critical eye on the debates of the preceding two decades, Krishan Kumar, in *The Making of English National Identity*, opts for what I have called a cosmopolitan England as both the likeliest and the most desirable way of regenerating English identity. England has always benefited from the diversity of its people and has, over the centuries, been remarkably open to infusions of new talents and sensibilities. It might yet, in his view, 'show what a truly civic nationalism can look like' (2003: 273). The social historian

Robert Colls, in his book *Identity of England*, expresses a similar hope; 'the English have never only been right, tight little islanders' and have repeatedly shown that 'extraordinary openness to the cultures of other peoples' (2002: 380) that Kumar also lauds. This is also my view and real cosmopolitanism in England is also my hope. It should also, of course, be acknowledged that Scots, Welsh and Irish in England have long been part of the cosmopolitanism of England. A cosmopolitan Englishness fits most easily in what Arthur Aughey calls 'the real and historic multiculture of Britishness' (2007: 212), and cosmopolitan England fits most easily in what I have called 'cosmopolitan Britain' (see Bryant, 2006: Ch. 8). There is support for this England, with particular reference to traditions of dissent and struggles for inclusion, in the singer Billy Bragg's *The Progressive Patriot* (2006). But then, as Bragg says, the English are only ever half-English.

Acknowledgements

I am grateful to Richard Towell for introducing me to the Centre for Information on Language Teaching and Research (CILT) and the work of Michael Byram, and to Arthur Aughey and to participants in the Political Ideologies Conference at the University of Liverpool, July 2008, for their comments on an earlier draft of this chapter.

Notes

1 All 2001 census figures have been obtained via the website of National Statistics (www.statistics.gov.uk/census2001). All polls accessed via websites on 20 June 2009.
2 Numbers taking French at A level (in England, Wales and Northern Ireland) have fallen from 22,718 in 1996 to 12,605 in 2008, and numbers taking German have fallen from 9,306 to 5,560. These big falls are not offset by an increase in those taking Spanish from 4,095 in 1996 to 5,728 in 2008 and an increase in those taking other languages from 3,435 to 5,530 (CILT National Centre for Languages, January 2009; website accessed 9 May 2009).
3 There are no statistics for speakers of community languages but a question on languages spoken will be included in the 2011 census. 40,000 students in the UK obtained a qualification in a community language in 2005 with the largest numbers in Urdu, Chinese, Irish and Arabic (see the CILT website).

Part II

Englishness in politics and institutions

5

Conservatives and Englishness: a conversation between party and nation

Stephen Ingle

The link between Conservatism and Englishness seems both obvious and natural. That popular and acknowledged commentator on national manners and customs, Anthony Aloysius Hancock, remarked in one of his most memorable sketches that he felt moved to 'do something' for his country. That meant either donating blood or joining the Young Conservatives. Labour modernisers from Gaitskell onwards have tried, unsuccessfully on the whole, to wrest patriotism from the grasp of its perceived owner, the Conservative party. Our task here is to explore the nature of this apparently natural relationship, but we must begin with a *caveat emptor*: definitional ambiguities abound.

Conservatives and others have not always thought it necessary to distinguish between Englishness and Britishness, and for investigators to attempt to impose a rigid distinction is unrealistic and a hostage to fortune.[1] In a recent article Julian Baggini wrote: 'The English comprise 85% of Britons, so surveys about the British tell you mainly about the English. Furthermore, I suspect that much of what I found out applies to Wales, Scotland and Northern Ireland too' (2008: 38). He opted to talk about British rather than English values. George Orwell, acknowledging the same problem, chose to write about Englishness, though his intention was to galvanise the *British* patriotic instinct in the war against Hitler's Germany. We shall talk about the English and Englishness here but must bear in mind not only that any generalisations we make might also apply to many among the other constituent nations of the United Kingdom, but that the usage of these words has changed significantly over the years. For example Disraeli signed the Treaty of Berlin in 1873 as the prime minister of England. Before moving on, however, let us reflect on one example of the confusion that can arise from these blurred edges. William Hague

fought the 2001 election in defence of 'British values' against
European encroachment, and made the rejection of the Euro symbolic
of that general struggle. Britons, he said, would never give up having
the monarch's head on their banknotes! But the monarch's head is not
to be found on Scottish or Northern Irish banknotes.[2] Englishness
elides seamlessly into Britishness even when it is inappropriate, but
this elision is particularly confusing for members of a party that has
traditionally proclaimed its Englishness and yet confusingly has championed Britishness and the Union for well over a hundred years. We
shall return to this paradox.

There are other definitional problems. Few mainstream political
ideologies are monolithic and Conservatism is less so than most. At
Robert Owen's New Lanark mill you can reach out and touch
socialism. Subsequently, British socialism wore many masks and took
on many aspects but it retained its core identity for over a hundred
and fifty years. Conservatism, by contrast, is not recognised as an
ideology at all by some of those who champion it. They regard it as an
attitude of mind, not an 'ism'. We can be confident about only one
thing when defining conservatism: it isn't easily defined.

Exploring the relationship between Conservatism and Englishness
then is not easy, but neither is it impossible and it is certainly worth
attempting. Our contention is that notions of Englishness have given
shape and substance to the Conservative tradition and have continued
to exert an influence on the party's thinking. We shall pursue our
investigation thematically, by examining first the origins of
Conservatism, then its historical development, locating in each the
part that Englishness has played. We will then gain a perspective from
which to investigate briefly the apparent paradox of working-class
support for the Conservatives. All this will provide a platform from
which to survey Englishness, or at least its political aspect, more thor-
oughly, and we will need a good understanding of political
Englishness for our final task, examining its relationship to modern
Conservatism.

Englishness and the origins of Conservatism

English Conservatism can be traced back to Restoration Toryism but
the modern party took its shape in the late eighteenth and early nineteenth centuries during a period of profound social change (see
Mandler, 2007; Kumar, 2003). It is indicative of the confusion
outlined in the introduction that when traditional English values were
enlisted in the campaign to contain social change and parliamentary

reform, the key thinker who deployed these values was Irish and a Whig. Edmund Burke was not only a prolific writer on conservative themes but also a practising politician who sat in the House of Commons for almost thirty years. This link between thought and action provides a defining characteristic of English Conservatism, namely its pragmatism. I have alluded elsewhere to the 'working principles' of English Conservatism. In addition to pragmatism they are: limited government, the rule of law and the national interest. I have suggested that together they represent the political manifestation of a set of guiding principles, namely traditionalism, organicism, scepticism and the defence of property rights. For Burke these guiding principles were inextricably bound up with the history and traditions of England, and English politics provided the ground on which they were practised (Ingle, 2008: 22–7). This was why Burke was far more sympathetic to the American revolutionaries (who were, after all, descendants of Englishmen) than the French. For Burke it was unambiguously English traditions and customs that promoted liberty and English pragmatism that incorporated the defence of liberty into its laws.

Burke's Conservatism owed everything to the fact that the traditions and customs that fostered it were organically and specifically English. Marx and Weber might later argue that what shaped British politics were external factors: the early development of capitalism and the impact of Protestantism. Alan Macfarlane, however, dated the emergence of a specifically English political culture much earlier. Since the thirteenth century, he argued, the English enjoyed a 'social, economic and legal system [that] was in essence different not only from that of the peoples of Asia and Eastern Europe, but also in all probability from the Celtic and Continental countries of the same period' (1978: 165). English culture was different 'in almost every aspect' (1978: 165). Macfarlane buttressed his argument with a series of references to commentaries by visiting dignitaries and ambassadors from continental Europe. De Tocqueville may have been amongst the most eloquent of these but he was far from the first. He wrote about England in the seventeenth and eighteenth centuries but noted that its values drew sustenance from 'some relics of the middle ages' (2008: 21). Writing a century or so earlier Montesquieu, too, noted many distinctive features in English political culture. The English were a free people enjoying the benefits of customs and laws that fostered liberty, independence and individualism (Montesquieu, 1989: 307). Earlier still, before the development of capitalism, commentators such as the Duke of Wirtenberg, the German jurist Paul Henzner, the Antwerp merchant van Materen, each writing in the Elizabethan era, had noted this characteristic passion for individual liberty (in Rye, 1865: 7–8, in Macfarlane, 1978: 165). And before the advent of Protestantism, the Venetian ambassador to the court of Henry VII also noted the same characteristics, linking independent spirit specifically to the wealth of the yeomanry and small traders (in Rye, 1865: 28, in Macfarlane, 1978: 170). English commentators writing about continental Europe made the same kinds of comparison: England was not a kingdom of subjects like France, said one, but 'a society of a multitude of free men ... united by common accord ... for the conservation of themselves' (Harrison, 1968: 10, in Macfarlane, 1978: 178). All these characteristics differentiated the English not only from continental Europe but also from the Celtic nations of these islands (see Anderson, 1979: 130–6).

Burke had reason to ground his principles in history and customs that were specifically English and this Conservatism constituted the shaping of these traditional English values into a political doctrine emphasising the virtues of tradition, liberty and social stability. Such a doctrine commended itself to a landed aristocracy whose interests it clearly favoured. The essence of this Conservatism was that it represented what Auden, in his tirade against aristocratic privilege, 'A Communist to Others', dismissed as 'a completed thing' (1964: 55).

For Auden this completed thing represented a detestable Englishness, one that stood opposed to any move towards enlarging economic and social justice that might be called progress. Though Auden did not favour us with any alternative form of Englishness encompassing the values of the more economically and socially just world for which he hungered, George Orwell did. He specifically rejected the Conservative doctrine of England as a completed thing, concluding: 'we must add to our heritage or lose it, we must grow greater or grow less, we must go forward or backward. I believe in England, and I believe that we shall go forward' (Orwell, 1994: 188). We will return to this important essay on English values later, but back now to Burke.

Large-scale change, let alone revolutionary change, was portrayed in Burke's writing as specifically un-English. He was not opposed to change as such. 'A state without the means of some change is without the means of its conservation. Without such means it might even risk the loss of that part of the constitution which it wishes the most religiously to conserve' (Burke, 1790: 108–9). Burke's idea of a correct balance between 'conservation and correction' was not the same as Orwell's. The use of the word 'correction' is the key here: when turned it reveals that for Burke change was primarily a response to a perceived departure from what he called England's 'entailed inheritance derived to us from our forefathers' (Burke, 1790: 122).

Maintaining England's inheritance did not exclude the 'principle of improvement' (Burke, 1790: 122) but it is difficult to see in what a theory of improvement might be grounded if not in those very principles of 'entailed inheritance' (Burke, 1790: 121). Here, improvement means going backward not forward. Nevertheless improvement may be just as ambitious as progress but it is not the same thing. As we shall shortly see, Margaret Thatcher's ministries were criticised by some of her parliamentary colleagues for their reforming zeal but her intention was to undermine the structure of what she took to be a collectivist state only to restore individual liberty: in other words to correct unwarranted departures from the traditional model of government. This is not how her critics saw things, and many of those critics would have called themselves the natural guardians of the 'entailed inheritance' of Englishness, and have seen Thatcher as the champion of a radicalism which was destructive of that inheritance.

Englishness and the developing Conservative party

But we are getting ahead of ourselves. The nineteenth century, we know, gave birth to the industrial revolution, a social change as dramatic as any that had gone before, and with it the advent of a new elite of industrial capitalists. Strange to relate, this elite left no stamp upon English values. There was no bourgeois cultural revolution but the traditional aristocracy, through its political agent the Conservative party, retained its cultural hegemony thereby bestowing what Martin Wiener referred to as 'legitimacy to antimodern sentiments' (Wiener, 1981a: 7). The openness of the landed aristocracy to advances from individual members of the bourgeoisie led to its being importuned rather than, in Peregrine Worsthorne's dramatic phrase, 'raped by its suitors' (in Wiener, 1981a: 8) and this, in turn, bestowed respectability on the process. Corelli Barnett observed that this accommodation represented an unlikely but important triumph for the landed aristocracy and its values (1963: 81).

The philosopher and mathematician Bertrand Russell, brought up by his grandfather (the same Earl Russell who had passed the Great Reform Act of 1832) claimed that the concept of the English gentleman was invented by the aristocracy precisely to cement the bourgeoisie into an extended ruling class (Russell, in Wiener, 1981a: 8). All this signalled a commitment on the part of the bourgeoisie itself to traditional English values and to the Conservative party and they were accepted by the nobility and its party more readily than their French counterparts.[3] Hence the landed aristocracy, which had originally perceived its political influence as having been eclipsed by Russell's Reform Act and destroyed by Corn Law reform, continued to be a dominant force in British politics (see Wiener, 1981b). Who could have guessed that 130 years later one of their own would renounce his peerage and take up the office of Leader of Her Majesty's Government at the head of a Conservative administration?[4] And how was this managed?

> It was the very soul of the old aristocratic polity that even a tyrant must never appear as a tyrant. He may break down everybody's fences and steal everybody's land but he must do it by Act of Parliament ... and if he meets the people he has dispossessed, he must be very polite to them and enquire after their rheumatism. That's what's kept the British constitution going. (Chesterton, 1917a: 262)

So when the Conservative party 'shifted its base from the land to property in all in forms' (Wiener, 1981a: 98), the traditional values of Englishness were not discarded. According to Nigel Harris when the Whigs allied themselves to the Tories through Unionism, they formally took on the 'aristocratic defence' (1972: 66) of traditional Conservative values.

Englishness and working-class Conservatism

We have substantiated the symbiosis between Conservative doctrine and established English values and seen that the advent of a powerful new economic and social class, the bourgeoisie, only cemented that relationship. In the third quarter of the nineteenth century, however, the industrial proletariat began to be enfranchised and most political commentators believed that a party system based upon social class would ensue, and that on arithmetical grounds alone this would disadvantage the Conservative party. This turned out not to be so, partly as a consequence of Disraeli's tactical *nous* but more crucially because Conservatism struck a chord with a significant number of the industrial and agricultural working class. Numerous commentators have shown how party strategists sought to construct policies that would persuade at least enough working-class voters of the affinity between their interests and the party's to enable it to win elections under the new dispensation (Norton & Aughey, 1981). That it managed this so frequently since universal male suffrage was first granted has been described as 'one grand historical paradox' (Butler & Stokes, 1974: 181).

It might appear heretical to ask why this should be considered a paradox; after all the relationship between class and voting has been proven: Labour is the workers' party. Actually we cannot say that class determines vote, only that class and vote tend to be related. Moreover, even that generalisation has seldom been more than 70% accurate, offering the same degree of probability as a long-range weather forecast. For reasons that need not be elaborated here a significant number of working-class voters have always perceived their interests and the nation's as best served by voting Conservative. Why should that be considered paradoxical?

But where does Englishness fit in? Working-class conservatives, those 'angels in marble' (McKenzie & Silver, 1968, in Ingle, 2008: 106), responded to claims on their loyalty by a party that emphasised its ability to rule in the interests of all. As well as perceiving their material interests to be protected by that party, working-class Conservatives also responded to its values, judging them to reflect their own. George Gissing, one-time socialist and always a passionate supporter of the working class noted in the 1880s that the English were not much moved by concepts, even by ideals such as the 'Rights of Man'. But 'if you talk to them (long enough) about the rights of the shopman, or the ploughman ... they will lend ear, and, when the facts of any such case have been examined, they will find a way of dealing with them. This characteristic of theirs they call common sense' (Gissing, 1903: 130). Gissing linked English common sense to traditional Conservatism and was contemptuous of the utopian aspirations of contemporary socialists, as his novel *Demos: The Story of English Socialism* (1886) clearly shows.

Englishness reconsidered

So far we have taken Englishness more or less as a given, much, indeed, as Conservatives themselves have done. It is time to be more analytical. Englishness, we have seen, appears to be embedded in tradition. There will always be an England, said the patriotic song of the Second World War, 'while there's a country lane / Wherever there's a cottage small / Beside a field of grain'.[5] In John Braine's novel *Room at the Top* the Yorkshire working-class hero Joe Lambton and his mistress take a cottage in Dorset for a week and on their first evening find the countryside with its thatched-roofed cottages both quintessentially English and yet 'so different that it's foreign' (Braine, 1957: 181). He instinctively recognises it as a symbol for his heritage though it has played no part whatever in his life (see also Lowenthal, 1991:

205–30). Two Englands, then! Donald Horne wrote about the two kinds of Englishness, embodied in the Northern and Southern Metaphors (1969: 22–3). It is the Southern Metaphor that has traditionally dominated Conservative discourse, speaking of gentlemanly traditions and social hierarchy. It is Anglican, rural – even bucolic – easy-going, and amateur (in the full sense of that word) in its approach to administration and government. This Englishness is compassionate but markedly self-confident.

The Northern Metaphor on the other hand embodies Nonconformity, industry and resilience. In his poem *The South Country* Hilaire Belloc suggests that the southern Englishman is shaped by those soft hills and gentle sunshine that impressed Joe Lambton, whereas the northerners' hearts 'are set on their waste fells / And their skies are fast and grey' (Belloc, 1920). When discussing these metaphors Martin Wiener simply took it for granted that the Southern Metaphor became the dominant one – indeed, that is the major theme of his book (1981a: 96). Samuel Smiles was profoundly wrong when he zealously trumpeted the 'youngness' (in Wiener, 1981a: 96) of England, for the preference amongst all classes was for an old country, careful to maintain its traditions. Indeed the poet Alfred Austin, travelling round England in 1902, entitled the subsequently published narrative of his pilgrimage *Haunts of Ancient Peace*. The preponderant view, even amongst socialists like William Morris, was that industrialisation and mass production, which he dismissively called 'cockneyfication', were anathema. And Morris' hero, the left-leaning progressive John Ruskin, declared, 'I am by nature and instinct conservative, loving old things because they are old, hating new ones merely because they are new' (in Wiener, 1981a: 68). What was bequeathed to us by history was, for these conservatives, not ours to 'improve'; it belonged to those who had created it and those who would inherit it in the future.

Disraeli was widely considered to have been instrumental in the transformation of the party into one that represented not simply the landed aristocracy but also many of the newly enfranchised working class. In passing the Second Reform Act of 1867, he 'stole the Whigs' clothing', a piece of skilful parliamentary strategy. More significant in the long run, however, was his realigning of the party to an inclusiveness that bestowed a duty on privilege and he conjured up the idea of this inclusive Englishness in his popular novel *Sybil* (1845). This was the politics of 'one-nation' conservatism (Schwartz, 2002: 183–217).

Stanley Baldwin, more than any other twentieth-century leader, retuned Englishness to the kind of prominence in Conservative thought that it had enjoyed under Disraeli. 'Farmer Stan' evoked the sights and sounds of England that would endure long after the Empire had been disbanded and English industrial might had become a memory. The historian and Conservative MP R.R. James considered Baldwin's views reactionary, and there can be no doubt that Baldwin associated himself with the kind of world later depicted by Laurie Lee in *Cider with Rosie*, 'before acceleration was regarded as a manifestation of civilization' (Baldwin, 1939: 74). Churchill's political discourse, too, was cast in the mould of traditional Englishness, as his wartime rhetoric shows. And such values would have been natural to him; after all, Churchill was himself a landed gentleman. The post-war Conservative party sustained its links with traditional Englishness. Both Eden and Macmillan distanced themselves from what the former called 'unbridled, brutal capitalism' (Beer, 1965: 185). Traditionally, it seems, the Englishness that Conservatives had championed was predominantly, though not exclusively, representative of the Southern Metaphor.

Are we then simply to ignore the Northern Metaphor? Surely this won't do. In his book on the development of the language, *The Stories of English*, David Crystal faced a similar problem: should he concentrate on the development of Standard English, a complex enough subject, or should he take account of regional dialects that gave expression to forms of cultural consciousness that were not encompassed within Standard English? To do the former, he concluded, would be to deal only with English 'on its best behaviour' (Crystal, 2004: 8–9) and would take no account of those who expressed their sense of belonging differently. We must dwell a while on the Northern Metaphor, flesh it out a little, and see how it interacts with its more significant southern counterpart: Englishness 'on its best bahviour' won't do.

George Orwell was one of the few political commentators to take the Northern Metaphor seriously.[6] Orwell wrote *The Lion and the Unicorn* in 1941 as a patriotic tract in Britain's hour of need (or England's, as he insisted upon putting it). Orwell sought to reconcile the two metaphors within an Englishness that encompassed social change and tradition, the egalitarianism and cohesiveness of the north and feeling for justice and the sense of tradition of the south. Earlier in his writing career he had contrasted these myths. He spoke disparagingly of the cult of northernness, especially of Yorkshireness, and disassociated himself from this branch of Englishness (Orwell, 1968). His comments on northerners, said Philip Toynbee, 'read like a report brought back by some humane anthropologist who has just returned from studying the conditions of an oppressed tribe in Borneo' (in Meyers, 1975: 15). Orwell went on to identify genuine differences between the Southern and Northern Metaphors, for example in *The Road to Wigan Pier* (1937; 1962). He singled out family loyalty in the north; it led to greater class and regional loyalty and hence towards political cohesion. More important, though, was the sense of equality that characterised the Northern Metaphor. 'In a Lancashire cotton town', he wrote, 'you could probably go for months without once hearing an "educated" accent, whereas there can hardly be a town in South of England where you could throw a brick without hitting the niece of a bishop' (Orwell, 1962: 102).

Orwell was only too aware of the potential contradictions between the two metaphors but his task in 1940 was to reconcile them. He did so by depicting England as a large Victorian family with the 'wrong people' in charge. We have our squabbles and we have skeletons in our cupboards that we had rather stayed there, but we are held together as a family by bonds of great strength, and as a nation by an all-encompassing patriotism that transcends, or at least reconciles the two metaphors, and is 'bound up with solid breakfasts and gloomy Sundays, smoky towns and winding roads, green fields and red pillar boxes'. 'This', Orwell tells us all, northerners and southerners, 'is your civilization, it is you. However much you hate it or laugh at it, you will never be happy away from it for any length of time. The suet puddings and the red pillar-boxes have entered into your soul' (1941: 139). The metaphors gain strength from unity and so any political party that sets this reconciliation as its agenda could surely manage it. Orwell's natural preference was for Labour to construct a 'National' Metaphor, but the record of the Conservative party suggested something different.

It is an irony that would have surprised even Orwell, that during the days of the Thatcher administrations the metaphors were almost reversed. At one level the totemic miners' strike of 1984 was a battle between unaccountable trade union power (the north) and the authority of a representative government (the south). At another level however it was a battle between those who sought to safeguard a traditional way of life based upon English values (the north) and an unrepresentative, transforming elite responding only to market forces (the south). At this level the English values that we have hitherto associated with Conservatism were being deployed by the north and the radically transformative and doctrinaire force previously associated with socialism was being wielded by the south. The north was defeated but the story of that defeat, depicted nowhere more sensitively than in the popular films *Brassed Off* (1996) and *The Full Monty* (1997), suggested that the two metaphors were becoming reconciled in the popular mind throughout the country and across the social classes. In the general election of 1992 the victorious Conservative party won not a single seat in Scotland, Wales or the 'People's Republic' of Yorkshire; they owed their victory chiefly to their support in the south of England. In 1997 however a National Metaphor emerged: even the south of England succumbed to New Labour and Thatcherism was widely rejected.[7]

This episode illustrates the complexity of Englishness, but it also shows that Orwell was right; a National Metaphor of Englishness can be constructed. Moreover, its electoral record from the beginnings of mass democracy up to the advent of Thatcher in 1979 shows clearly that the Conservatives managed it, mobilising wide support from all classes. Historically speaking, until Thatcher reconstructed Conservatism only one party could claim to be the natural party of government, only one party could claim to be seen to reflect English values through creating a National Metaphor: the Conservative party (Ingle, 2008: 18–19). In 1997, 2001, and, arguably, 2005 Blair comprehensively managed the same feat for Labour.

Englishness redefined: Thatcherite Conservatism

Back in 1970 Conservative values came under the stewardship of Edward Heath. Though not the first leader from outside the upper class Heath was the first 'man of the people'. The historian of Conservatism John Ramsden quotes a letter from an industrial manager and lifelong Conservative: 'We were sick of the old men dressed in flat caps and bedraggled tweeds strolling about with 12 bores ... The nearest approach to our man is Heath ... He is our age, he is capable, he looks like a director' (Ramsden, 1980: 226). These sentiments represent the rejection of traditional Englishness and the National Metaphor by important sections of the modern Conservative party. The ethos of Heath's government was meritocratic, radical, libertarian and above all managerialist. His overriding concern was for the efficiency and competitiveness of British industry. His style of governing, nicknamed the politics of 'Selsdon Man',[8] was to oppose macro-economic planning and statutory incomes policies and to favour intervention only to limit trade union powers. What Britain needed was resolute business management and the discipline of the market to bring it out of economic stagnation. Concern for anybody's rheumatism could never survive cost–benefit analysis. Heath's whole approach was turned on its head two years later and replaced by tweedy consensus, but he had laid down a marker for change and when he made way for his nemesis, Margaret Thatcher, she picked up that marker.

In 1979 the Conservatives won nearly 80 per cent of the seats in the south of England (south of a line from the Wash to the Severn [excluding inner London and the West Midlands] – what Butler and Kavanagh (1984: App. 2) referred to as Tory Britain) – and exactly the reverse happened in what they refer to as Labour Britain: the north. In 1983 this apparent re-emergence of 'two nations' was reinforced; the Conservatives won no fewer than 183 of the 186 southern seats. Would Thatcher be the new champion of Southern Metaphor Englishness?

Though she came from a market town in Middle England, Thatcher was no believer in traditional English values. Andrew Gamble argues that Thatcher was driven by a firm belief in the efficiency of markets and sound money, and by a Friedmanite faith in deregulation and privatisation (1988: 85). She had nothing but scorn for those traditional institutions that had helped to frame English values in the modern world. The Church of England, the BBC, the House of Lords, the Civil Service, the army, the navy, the universities, the National Health Service (NHS), even the Football League were battered by that infamous handbag. Her philosophy rested upon the assumption of the demonstrable superiority of the market and she was prepared to legislate to create the right domestic framework for market economics without respect to the traditions of her party. Thatcher declared that there was no such thing as 'society',[9] to which the Tory backbencher and defender of traditional English values Sir Ian Gilmour responded: 'there is nothing Tory about a powerful government presiding over a country of atomized individuals, with its intermediate institutions emasculated or abolished' (21 July 1987). Margaret Thatcher lacked the temperament that goes with Conservative Englishness; not for her the modesty that comes from Burke's mistrust of man's 'fallible and feeble' reason.

The journalist Anthony Howard defended her opponents. 'Backbench knightage and baronetage with its roots in the soil', he mused, 'provided the Tory party with its ballast – and some of them at least … were markedly enlightened and modern-minded in their outlook … Their successors have tended to be young, thrusting professional politicians, for whom party, if not faction, means all' (10

February 1985). Tory traditionalist Julian Critchley characterised Thatcher's 1975 leadership campaign as 'the Peasants' Revolt'. Thatcher, he said, changed the Conservative Party from a 'non-political political party', eschewing ideology, tempering belief with scepticism, and 'flying by the seat of [its] pants' (22 May 1983), into a party of conviction and crusade. She also changed a party that largely viewed the world through the prism of traditional English values into one which championed the kind of radical, balance-sheet politics that Conservatives and Englishmen had traditionally despised. Thatcher sought to rid the party of that tradition and those who were wedded to it (and incapacitated by it!).

There is a crucial distinction to be drawn here between values and interests, for though each may be driven by patriotic sentiment and so may be viewed as versions of Englishness, they are not the same. The pursuit of interests focuses upon ends; that of values upon means. For traditional Conservatives Englishness was procedural; for Thatcherite Conservatives it was instrumental. Though no champion of traditional English values Thatcher did champion English interests as she perceived them, most notably in her policies towards the European Union and devolution. Both policies were driven by her ambition to retain optimum leverage for the free-market economic policies that suited British industry. Unlike her successor John Major during the Maastricht debate she did not present herself as the guardian of English values as Europe inched to integration. She signed the Single European Act in 1986 because she believed it would facilitate the growth of a free market favourable to English interests but in her Bruges Speech only a year later she deplored the centralising and harmonising policies that went with it. Her opposition to devolution was equally unremitting but was never paraded as a campaign to save Englishness or Britishness.[10] In short her Englishness was instrumental, concerned only with favourable outcomes. The wartime Tory Reform group had offered a critique of 'Thatcherism' almost forty years before it manifested itself: 'True Conservative opinion is horrified at the damages done to this country ... by "individualist" business-men, financiers and speculators ranging freely ... [the party] would wish nothing better than that these men should collect their baggage and depart' (Lord Hinchinbrooke, 1943, in Wiener, 1981a: 110–11).

John Gray pointed out that Thatcher wrought havoc amongst the party's traditional supporters (15 May 1995), but her policy stance struck a chord with popular sentiment including sections of the working class, more particularly in the south of England. In an astute analysis Stuart Hall characterised this stance as 'authoritarian populism' (Hall, 1980: 305–45). Thatcherism responded to the populist-authoritarian issues which concerned 'Essex man', as the consequent slump in support for far-right parties at the time suggested. Commentators claimed that middle-class leaders such as Tebbitt and Major were intent upon dismantling the 'old boy' network in the party and were 'insidiously destructive' of its values (Ingle, 2008: 95–8). If all this constituted a new metaphor for Englishness it was a narrow-minded and aggressively nationalistic one focusing on interests not values. These new advocates of Englishness, if that is what they were, took pride in Thatcher's confrontational style especially at the international level. Their Englishness found its natural expression in the tabloid press, especially the *Sun*, which greeted the sinking of the Argentine battle cruiser *ARA General Belgrano* during the Falkland's War with great loss of life with the single-word headline: 'GOTCHA' (the *Sun*, 4 May 1982) and celebrated Thatcher's rebuff of the President of the European Commission's attempts to accelerate the drive towards European unity with the headline 'UP YOURS DELORS' (the *Sun*, 1 November 1990), sensitively embellished with a two-fingered salute. Thatcher was not responsible for the growth of authoritarian populism but she helped to make respectable a brand of jingoism that sought to optimise perceived English interests usually at the expense of traditional Englishness – and foreigners.

We should not forget, however, that a very substantial number of Conservative voters of all classes – no fewer than 49% in 1983 for example – were motivated primarily by fear of Labour; in that election only 40% of those who voted for the party actually 'liked the Conservatives' (Butler & Kavanagh, 1984: 293). Thatcher failed to win over the majority even of southern English voters to her version of Englishness.

Englishness, Conservatism, and the struggle between modernisation and tradition

The most striking social feature of the modern Conservative leadership has been the fact that six of the seven most recent Conservative leaders have been meritocrats of modest social origins. Only the present incumbent, old Etonian David Cameron, son of a wealthy stockbroker whose mother is the daughter of a baronet, breaks the mould. Though Cameron might claim to be the standard-bearer of a new kind of Conservatism he is, or appears to be, the embodiment of the very tradition that Thatcher all but destroyed. Cameron's first shadow cabinet, selected in 2006, was of a similar cut: predominantly well-educated (60 per cent Oxbridge), middle-aged, predominantly male, well-to-do suburbanite southern English. It resembled neither the meritocratic Thatcher cabinets (where Estonians were said to outnumber Etonians) nor the traditional, Olympian kind. What are the new politics that they champion?

Since 1997 the Conservative party has had five leaders and each has sought to 'modernise' the party and search for a narrative that would prove relevant to the modern voter.[11] In 2003 Oliver Letwin indicated the need to portray the party as being concerned more with social justice than the operation of the free market but it was Ian Duncan Smith at the party conference that year who first gave currency in Britain to the key term in the new narrative: a compassionate Conservatism to recast a broken society.[12] In his leadership campaign of 2005, Cameron too argued for a greater sense of cultural identity, a new vision of society, declaring that Conservatism must champion 'compassion and aspiration in equal measure' and added significantly 'there *is* such a thing as society' (Norman & Ganesh, 2006: 1).[13] Cameron believed further that in seeking to limit the power of the state he was not motivated solely by ideological principles but by experience: the state was not working, in fact it was undermining national productivity. Moreover the dominance of the state led to the public 'looking ever more expectantly at government, and more often at Whitehall than the town hall' (Norman & Ganesh, 2006: 23) to tackle social problems. Cameron's objective was not simply to confine the state but to replace it wherever possible by municipal and voluntary agencies – by civic society. Civic society would be much more amenable to compassion and aspiration than either Labour's central state or Thatcher's liberal state. Cameron's emphasis on compassion may initially have been strategic, reflecting the need to confront the Thatcherite stance of David Davis, his opponent in the 2005 leadership run-off. However as he established himself as leader it became increasingly clear that the perceived electoral necessity of modernising the party suited Cameron's disposition. He called himself a compassionate Conservative. But what does compassionate Conservatism actually signify?

There are two things to be said about Cameron's compassionate Conservatism: it is not new and it hardly amounts to a string of beans. To take the first point, our history of Conservatism has shown very clearly that from its earliest days, one strand of Conservative philosophy was paternalistic and charitable – hence compassionate. Disraeli skillfully embroidered exactly these themes into the banner of one-nation Conservatism. Compassionate Conservatism is new only in the sense that it flatly contradicts the accepted wisdom of Thatcherite Conservatism. As for the second point, when Norman and Ganesh try to give life to the concept as deployed by Cameron they find its origin – incredibly – in Thomas Hobbes. Their journey leading from the *Leviathan* to 'Dave' (Cameron) stretches incredulity no less than any fable from *The Arabian Nights*. Having established (to their own satisfaction) its lineage, the writers finally identify Friedrich Hayek, a representative (they say) of the 'Old Whig' tradition, as the father of Cameron's compassionate Conservatism.

This is an unsatisfactory base from which to consider 'compassionate' policy preferences, especially since Cameron is said to have adopted the phrase precisely to eschew specific policy pledges (Denham & Dorey, 2006: 35–42). The authors elicit three principles which should govern compassionate policy-making: freedom, decentralisation and accountability. These principles would inform an 'audit of government' whose task would be to 'reconsider the limits of personal freedom and local responsibility' (Denham & Dorey, 2006: 64–6). This would entail, for example, assessing how families rather than the state might bear responsibility for the care of the elderly; introducing greater competition into the NHS; 'empowering' universities to become independent, and so on. Last but not least, compassion is to be globalised for it implies 'a self-conscious re-commitment to Britain's civilizing mission around the world' (Denham & Dorey, 2006: 57). On the showing of this, the most detailed account of it, compassionate Conservatism is vacuous, inchoate and potentially dangerous; no wonder that, in a recent article on the future of Conservatism, Philip Norton (2008) did not use the phrase.

Cameron himself spoke of his new politics as being reasonable, decent, sensible, practical and non-judgemental (Fielding, 2009: 168–71) and though this hardly helps us get a hold on compassionate Conservatism it should be noted that the party, through the imposition of its A-List of candidates selected by the leadership and imposed upon often reluctant constituencies, took steps to include more female and ethnic minority candidates in the 2010 election. All the same the idea of a central clique overriding constituency autonomy hardly gels with the three principles advanced by Norman and Ganesh. In his recent book, Tim Bale (2010) argues that Cameron's concern was not at all with hazy policy concepts but with a clear strategy for making his party electable. Simon Jenkins (2010) disagrees, suggesting that what the party gained in Cameron and his compassion was not a viable policy framework so much as a potentially electable leader. Many trees were wasted in works seeking to analyse Blair's 'ethical socialism', later 'stake-holder society' and finally 'third way', only to prove the vacuity of these terms. We might have hoped for the sake of the environment that such attempts would not be duplicated in respect of similarly chimerical Conservative slogans. But another emerged during the 2010 election campaign, the 'Big Society'. Not noticeably different from compassionate conservatism in its broad aims, the Big Society palpably failed to galvanise the electorate, but as Blair and New Labour acquired a philosopher in Tony Giddens so Cameron and the Big Society have a champion in Phillip Blond (2010), who has fleshed the concept out.

If it is accepted that the current Conservative leadership shows signs of wishing to return to a more central ideological stance more in line with traditional English values, what of the party it leads? In the 2005–10 parliament the parliamentary Conservative party comprised only 195 MPs, who *ipso facto* represented the bedrock of modern Conservatism. Some 90% of the party represented southern constituencies (as defined earlier), with almost all the remainder representing wealthier parts of the north, such as Wilmslow and Macclesfield in Cheshire and Skipton and Beverley in Yorkshire. Some 71% were born and brought up in the South, the remainder comprising 7% Scots, just under 6% Yorkshiremen and slightly fewer Welshmen and Lancastrians. (There were, in addition, two self-identified Asians, a Tanzanian, a South African, a New Zealander, a Pole and a Newcastle United supporter.) Women made up only 8% of the party. In terms of education this cohort reflected its geographical and social origins. Some 60% were privately educated, with an additional 8% being educated at Eton. The vast majority went on to higher education, 46% to Oxbridge, but only 6% to the 'new' universities. The great majority of this cohort had a background in business and finance. This, then, represents the bedrock of the Conservative party that Cameron seeks to modernise.

In the 2010 general election the party returned 297 MPs and increased its vote in England by nearly 4%, but it remained predominantly a southern English party. It won 83% of the 197 seats in the south. In the south-east region (outside greater London) it gained approximately 50% of the vote compared to Labour's 16% whereas across the north it won 31% compared to Labour's 39%. In Scotland the contrast was even greater: the Conservatives won 16% of the vote compared to Labour's 41%, retaining its single seat. These statistics offer little comfort to a Unionist party.

In brief, Cameron's parliamentary party predominantly comprises well educated, well-to-do southern businessmen. No doubt each is loved for his or her (overwhelmingly his) individual traits and eccentricities but as a group they are remarkably homogenous. Theirs is not an inclusive, broadly representative Englishness, but an Englishness that is narrowly defined geographically, socially and educationally, and is fundamentally instrumentalist in tone. If they participate in any relationship between Conservatism and Englishness that may be characterised as a conversation, it is hard to avoid the conclusion that these people are talking to themselves and about themselves. It is not easy to imagine this party warming to the idea of the Big Society.

Can Cameron modernise this party, and in what sense would his victory constitute a return to English values? In a perceptive essay Wendell Steavenson pictured Cameron as an heir not to Blair but to Harold Macmillan (2010: 43–9). She sought to discover whether Cameron was a traditional shire Tory or a liberal moderniser and concluded that the key to understanding his mixture of 'traditional gentry and urban organic' was to grasp that he was motivated primarily by a Tory 'need to serve' (Steavenson, 2010; 47). Conservatives she spoke to argued that he was not a visionary à la Thatcher nor even a strategist à la Blair but a supreme tactician. Perhaps he *can* out-manoeuvre his right-wing opponents.

A change in 2010 potentially far more consequential to his chances than the underwhelming 4% increase in the national vote, however, was the fact that the party formed a government in coalition with the Liberal Democrats. It is doubtful if Cameron and his close colleagues wished hard for this particular Fairy Godmother but her unexpected appearance transforms their chances of liberalising the party and moving it decisively towards the ideological centre, where it has traditionally thrived. Counter-intuitively, perhaps, Liberal Democrat policy successes in this new government could strengthen Cameron's position vis-à-vis his party and the electorate – to the ultimate detriment of the Liberal Democrats. But would this transformation – for that is what it would amount to – represent a return to English values?

Conclusion

In the introduction to this chapter it was suggested that our study of Conservatism and Englishness would take us into a world of indistinct grey shapes with blurred edges. Nevertheless some features stand out clearly enough to be identified. The first is that a party that represented the landed aristocracy survived the advent of an industrial bourgeoisie that was economically more powerful, and a proletariat that was politically more powerful (by virtue of the potential size of its voting base). It did so largely because, through the perspicacity of leaders like Disraeli, Baldwin and Macmillan, it successfully appealed to a broad spectrum of the population. It skilfully deployed a metaphor for undoctrinaire 'common-sense' Englishness that included elements of both the Southern and Northern Metaphors. Englishness was seen to be much more a way of doing things than a prescription of what was to be done, reflecting our distinction between English values and interests (Cunningham, 1986: 283–307). One backbencher, complaining of the actions of a Labour government claimed that he was not so much against what the government was doing, just that it was Labour who was doing it.

A second visible feature of this grey landscape is Thatcherism, a form of Conservatism that for all its electoral success was never widely popular (Thatcher confronted a Labour opposition that was fighting a protracted civil war). Thatcher reshaped her party and its traditions and in doing so fostered a narrow, jingoistic Englishness that its critics believed spoke to the values of the better-off and 'aspirational' voters especially in the south of England. No leader since has managed to rebuild the traditional values that gave the party its political and electoral resilience. Even in the most propitious circumstances, Cameron conspicuously failed to do this in 2010.

Though Margaret Thatcher is often seen as the nemesis of traditional Conservative Englishness, it was already dying. Those great symbols of Englishness, before which traditional Conservatives of all classes genuflected, had clearly lost their potency. The Empire, the Crown, the Church of England, the many institutions that Thatcher reformed (and then with the MPs' allowances scandals, the one major institution she did not reform!), and even – perhaps most important of all – the traditional family, have palpably declined in influence. At their healthiest these institutions inspired widespread deference and the Conservative party deployed that deference with considerable skill primarily to serve its own ends. But the days of deference are gone.

The modern Conservative party has lost a tradition and has yet to

find a theme. Traditional Burkean Englishness, an organic inheritance already fully achieved, has no place in today's world. Even
when deployed in the apparently propitious territory of opposition to
greater European cooperation the tropes of traditional Englishness
have become inappropriate, as the historian and Conservative
polemicist Andrew Roberts managed to illustrate inadvertently with
his 1995 Europhobic fantasy *The Aachen Memorandum* (Wright,
1996.).[14]

Moreover, in domestic politics the relevance of emblematic
Englishness is questionable. One of the paradoxes of modern
Conservatism is that the party is perceived of as both an essentially
English party and the party of the Union.[15] Ironically, what chiefly
deters Scots from voting Conservative today is the perception of the
party as quintessentially English. Indeed, Andrew Neill and others
advised Scottish Conservatives that to survive they would need to
emphasise their autonomy and sense of Scottishness (Lynch, 2004:
386–91). Whilst Conservative leaders since Thatcher have expressed a
willingness to govern within the spirit of the devolution settlement, the
'West Lothian' question (posed by MPs representing Scottish
constituencies voting at Westminster on issues that do not affect their
constituents) remains a problem. William Hague's solution was to call
for 'English votes on English laws' and this was understood to be
Cameron's position too. The issue is important. In 2003 the Labour
government won a narrow vote to promote foundation hospitals in
England. In 2004 it won an even narrower vote on differential tuition
fees in English universities. In both cases the votes of MPs representing Scottish constituencies, unaffected directly by either measure,
were decisive. Scots enacting legislation that the English (or at least
the majority of their parliamentarians) did not want seemed to be
constitutionally indefensible – and ironic, given Scotland's justifiable
claim throughout the 1980s and much of the 1990s that it was being
governed by a party that it had wholeheartedly rejected at the polls. A
Conservative-dominated government pledged to defend the Union,
might, even so, prove to be the instrument of its demise, by restricting
Scottish voting rights at Westminster and/or by addressing the long-
simmering issue of funding by granting full fiscal autonomy to
Edinburgh. It might then truly become what some already think it is
in part: an inward-looking English national party. Simon Lee (2010)
has demonstrated just how divided in terms of party allegiance the
United Kingdom became in the 2010 election.

It is not certain where Cameron will take the modern Conservative party. We have observed that elements of the Conservative tradition found favour with many ordinary people and we have argued that this should not be seen as paradoxical. Nevertheless the party came into existence primarily to secure the interests of the landed aristocracy and later those of the wealthy generally. It did so by attending to the grievances of ordinary people too, but never to the extent of jeopardising its own privileged position. Whilst still a Liberal, Joseph Chamberlain told his lover Beatrice Webb that the rich had always ruled in their own interests and had, over the decades, made a very good fist of it. Nowadays, deprived by social change of its old inclusive Englishness – one nation, rich and poor, north and south – the newly compassionate Conservative gentleman, unconvinced as yet by the attractions of the Big Society, must resist the temptation to transmogrify into a modern John Tanner, the Shavian hero. On being ambushed by a brigand who boasted that he lived by robbing the rich, Tanner replied; 'Shake hands. I am a gentleman. I live by robbing the poor' (Shaw, 1937: 364). Cameron must persuade the modern Conservative party that such partisanship would represent the way back to the electoral desert.

Notes

1 It is worth observing, however, that most spell checks recognise Englishness but not Britishness.
2 In fact it was not be found on *any* banknote before 1960.
3 Though their tastes may have been ridiculed by painters like Hogarth they did not excite the kind of scorn we see in Molière's earlier *Le Bourgeois Gentilhomme*.
4 Lord Home was persuaded to renounce his peerage to become Prime Minister in 1963 as Sir Alec Douglas-Home.
5 Composed by Ross Parker and Hugh Charles in 1939 this was to become a major wartime hit for Dame Vera Lynn.
6 For a more recent and thorough examination of what we have called the Northern Metaphor see Russell (2004), *Looking North*.
7 The (then) editor of the *Evening Standard*, the Conservative Max Hastings, wrote in 1997 that had his party been a dog it would have been put down out of kindness. The BBC reported that Conservative voters stayed at home rather than vote because their party had become so 'discredited and tainted' (quoted in Ingle, 2008: 109).
8 Selsdon Man because Heath's general approach was formulated at a conference at Selsdon Park in 1970.
9 There are individual men and women, and there are families, said

Margaret Thatcher in an interview with *Women's Own* magazine on 31 October 1987, but there is no such thing as society.

10 The challenges posed by devolution to traditional Englishness are addressed by Aughey (2006). See also Hayton, English & Kenny (2009).

11 Richard Hayton dealt in detail with each in a paper entitled 'Conservative Party Strategy in Opposition', delivered to the PSA Conference, Reading 2006.

12 It had first been used by George W. Bush in the USA.

13 Policy Exchange, which published this pamphlet, is a Centre Right Think Tank based in London.

14 Roberts goes on to tell us that in 'real life' (!) a group calling itself English Array sought to save Englishness by promoting deep breathing through the nose, eating fresh fruit and vegetables and avoiding artificial laxatives. They despised unfettered capitalism and modern inventions, railing against 'the menace of electric light'.

15 Since the defection of Chamberlain and the Unionists to the Conservatives in the 1880s the party has championed first the union with Ireland and then with Scotland. The party supported Carson's revolt against Home Rule in 1910–14 and stood out (alone amongst major parties) against devolution from 1979 to 1999.

6

The left and Englishness

Matt Beech

Introduction: the English left in context

> Until August 1914 a sensible law-abiding Englishman could pass through life and hardly notice the existence of the state, beyond the post office and the policeman ... The Englishman paid taxes on a modest scale: nearly £200 million in 1913–14, or rather less than 8 per cent of the national income ... Still, broadly speaking, the state acted only to help those who could not help themselves. It left the adult citizen alone. (Taylor, 1965: 25)

> The post-war golden age, we can now see, was a short-lived aberration from the norm of the preceding 200 years. It had a variegated ancestry. Its intellectual progenitors included social imperialists, social Christians and social Liberals as well as democratic socialists. (Marquand, 1997: 2)

The English left has always been inferior in number, influence and potency to the English right because England remains the most conservative of the four nations of the United Kingdom. In this sense its politics owe more to the right than the left. England is dominated by the South and the South-East in particular; it is in the South-East of England that approximately one-third of the English live, work and vote, and it is in the South of England that the Conservative Party has its spiritual home. Because England is in large measure conservative in culture, attitude and politics, one's religious practice and public behaviour, the nuances of one's class, and the influence and frame of reference provided by one's education are often contingent factors of the *political mind*. This is not to say that there is a single *English political mind* but that it is probable that there are *English political minds* or intellectual dispositions that may manifest themselves in distinctive allegiances, creeds or ideologies. These are evident in a characteristic political culture, one of conversational disagreement which may be said to be the instinctive *modus operandi* of English politics, left, right or centre. It is a tendency that is given expression in parliamentarianism and in the traditions of political satire and this political culture is conservative mainly in its sense of history; the value it places on the traditions of custom and practice; the understanding of English class difference, and at the same time, the value ascribed to the idea of the English nation. Similarly, liberalism or socialism are living forces to the extent to which they are 'traditional', particular and historically rooted in English practice.

The English left, it can be argued, is a weaker notion than the British left. The preponderance of Tory England remains generally true and has been largely accurate in the post-Second World War era due, perhaps ironically, to factors such as the impact of the Welfare State and education policies based on notions of equality of opportunity which led to greater social mobility and growth in size of the English middle class; the de-industrialisation of England; and the concomitant decline of mass membership trade unions which in turn resulted in partisan de-alignment. Yet also, as David Marquand has noted, there may be a very English ideational factor:

> One reason why Conservative working class voters exist is that a succession of Conservative politicians tried, quite consciously, to bring them into existence. One reason why the death of Liberal England was not followed by the birth of Labour England is that Labour politicians have been less good at 'shaping' values than their rivals. (1992: 11)

According to Marquand, the Labour Party, as the main vehicle of the left, has not been sufficiently successful at political education and at transmitting their values as the Conservative Party. This is a peculiarly English failing because the people and their traditions; the churches and chapels; the ideas and attitudes communicated by the elite of Scotland, Wales and, to a lesser extent, Northern Ireland when combined with the heritage of the English left transform it in to a more formidable political movement: the *British* left. One could argue that the British left in the twentieth century was disproportionately influenced by Scottish and Welsh figures such as Keir Hardie, David Lloyd George, Ramsay MacDonald, James Maxton, Aneurin Bevan, Roy Jenkins, Neil Kinnock and John Smith but the contribution of English radicals is also of major significance and the focus of this chapter is on the contribution of the English left, particularly in the twentieth century. Certainly the English Left has produced many gifted politicians (Clement Attlee, Ernest Bevin, Hugh Gaitskell, Harold Wilson and Tony Benn), scholars (G.D.H. Cole, Harold Laski,

Evan Durbin, John Strachey, Richard Crossman and Stuart Holland) and social reformers (Sylvia Pankhurst, William Beveridge and Michael Young). It is undoubtedly true that the English left reaches beyond Westminster to the universities, non-profit organisations; it stretches into the realms of art and literature, and can be found in England's (former) industrial cities and towns and, perhaps somewhat surprisingly, finds some support in its countryside, too. Historically, the English left was embedded in the trade union movement and, whilst their influence has somewhat diminished, the social democratic English left remains in partnership with the trade unions. Evidence of this is the role their members played in supporting the candidacy of the Labour leader Ed Miliband. When recollecting the social and political divide in twentieth-century England one often talks of 'the urban' and 'the rural' and the received wisdom is that the cities and large industrial towns were strongholds of the Labour Party whilst the countryside was ubiquitously the domain of the Conservative Party, and this unsophisticated rule of thumb is broadly correct. The first quarter of the twentieth century was notably different from the remainder because the Labour Party was still in its relative infancy and the Liberal Party was the main party of reform until 1924. The Liberal Party was an enormously broad and diverse organisation whose members held to different values depending on their geography, their religion and their occupation. This meant that radical or Social Liberals could stand on platforms and side with the interests of the industrial worker whilst a colleague could be returned as the Member of Parliament for a wealthy market town in some part of the English shires. Thus, when the Liberals were still a leading party, the Conservatives did not have a monopoly on rural England. Depending how one defines it, the English left could include Marxist socialists and Communists. But, in this essay, the English left is understood as emanating from the democratic and representative traditions of public life, much more particular in kind than the universal claims of Marxism. One could include all English Liberals as these individuals and their forebears have stood as the anti-Conservative force in English politics before the emergence of the Labour Party but this chapter takes the democratic English left to be advocates of social democracy and radical (or New or Social) liberalism. Currents of thought in this English left have included Christian socialism, Fabianism, the suffrage movement, Guild socialism, republicanism, internationalism, anti-imperialism, the New left, environmentalism, the Campaign for Nuclear Disarmament and anti-war movements.

Electorally, the English left (so defined) was a secondary political movement in England throughout the twentieth century. During that hundred year period, the English left was in power for approximately thirty years whereas Conservatives governed for approximately seventy years. The English left exists because of concerns about the injustice, inegalitarianism and individualism of capitalism in England and, of course, it is not a fixed or programmatic notion since it exhibits tensions regarding social theory, economic methods, constitutional issues, social justice, and Britain's relationship with Europe and the United States. The English left has been divided too along party lines, with radical liberals in the Liberal Party, social democrats in the Labour Party and sometimes vice versa. In periods of Conservative dominance, most recently in the 1990s, there have been dreams of a broad front between them which have foundered on electoral practicalities. Taken as a broad democratic tendency, however, it can be claimed that the English left tradition exists.

Of course, in the space of a single essay one cannot evaluate fully the variety of this tradition. Nevertheless I will comment upon the distinctively English but – importantly – politically representative contributions to radical liberal and social democratic thought by R.H. Tawney, John Maynard Keynes and Tony Crosland. There are a number of reasons for choosing these three thinkers. Firstly, because social democracy has been the dominant aspect of the English left in the twentieth century I have chosen two of its key contributors (Tawney and Crosland) and only one Social Liberal (Keynes). Secondly, Tawney's contribution is the most penetrating, distinctive and lasting in terms of supplying the English left with an ethical basis and I contend that, historically, the moral basis of social democracy is best understood through an appreciation of Tawney's Christian socialism. Thirdly, Keynesian demand management replaced neo-classical economics and was adopted as the West's economic orthodoxy from the 1940s until the 1970s, and aspects of Keynesianism are still utilised today. Therefore, Keynes is the great radical economist bar none. Fourthly, Crosland's political economy was the pre-eminent approach to English left politics from the mid-1950s until the end of the 1970s and furthermore, although markedly different in some areas, contemporary social democrats owe a notable debt to Croslandite social democracy in terms of the idea of welfare capitalism.

The English left's moral philosopher: R.H. Tawney

R.H. Tawney is representative of a particular type of English socialism, namely Christian socialism. In the English left during the twentieth century no person surpassed Tawney in articulating an ethically socialist critique of capitalist society in England. Morgan Phillips' sentiment on the greater role Christianity played in the ideological development of Labour, compared to Marxism, was interpreted and popularised by Harold Wilson when he wrote: 'It was the late Mr Morgan Phillips, who said that Socialism in Britain owed far more to Methodism than to Marx' (1964: 1). Interestingly, it is often forgotten that the sentence that follows the above quotation from Wilson highlights the contribution to British socialism made by Christians in Protestant non-conformity more broadly, and Anglicanism (Wilson, 1964: 1). Thus, Christian socialism also has strong roots in the Church of England. Tawney was an Anglican communicant, and together with his boyhood friend William Temple (who was Archbishop of Canterbury from 1942 to 1945) conveyed a political and economic moralism which emanated from their Protestant understanding of Christianity.

Religion, class and education are usually the most instructive factors in the development of the politics and worldview of people but this is especially the case in the late nineteenth and first half of the twentieth century when religion (and by this I mean the Christian faith) was still a notable aspect of the lives of many individuals and Christian denominations spoke with authority in public life. Class was more rigid and more obvious and class prejudice affected social relations and community interaction. Education was largely determined by the religion and class of one's parents much more so than it is the case today. Religion, class and education were and are factors for thinkers of the British left but they seem to become heightened components for the English left. This, I believe, tells us much about recent English history. Stefan Collini alludes to this when discussing the class and education of Tawney:

> Tawney's impact was also bound up with the kind of social authority he could draw upon, and this, too, is something that makes us feel our distance from him today. For all his genuine sympathy and engagement with ordinary working people, it must not be forgotten that Tawney was Rugby and Balliol at a time when this mattered. (1999: 192)

Michael Postan in his appreciation of D.M. Joslin – one of the editors of Tawney's *Commonplace Book* – notes the contrast between the subject (Tawney) and the author (Joslin) and importantly illustrates Tawney's Englishness in terms of his religion, class and education:

> In age, upbringing and character, as well as in the nature of their studies, David Joslin and R.H. Tawney were very different men ... For all his

socialist views and humble personal tastes Tawney preserved throughout his life the outward manners – not only the tone of voice, but also the *façon d'agir* – of an Edwardian and even Victorian gentleman with family roots in the English countryside, the Church, and the Indian Civil Service. (Postan, 1972: ix)

The following passage written by Tawney on 2 December 1912 in his *Commonplace Book* further reveals a distinctive English disposition, simultaneously demonstrating that Tawney's worldview is English not British, that this is more than the verbal colloquialism of time and place and that this Englishness pervades his attitude of mind, his frame of reference and his political outlook (and, as Lee observes in Chapter 7, this volume, these English references returned in the speeches of Gordon Brown):

> We in England ought to sympathise with the world-wide movement of Labour, because it is aiming at the very objects which we used to boast that we had attained. We look back with pride, at our dealings with the Stuarts. We forget the dogmatism of Pym, the brutality of Cromwell, the intolerance of nearly all of that great time, because behind it all we see that men were striving for freedom, for the right of men to live their own lives and express their own personalities which is what freedom means … The way in which it seeks to attain it is the old English way of the rule of law, that there shall be a settled constitution, that thousands shall not be dependent on the caprices of a few, like slaves, but that they shall have a voice in settling conditions under which they may live. This is what the appeal to the State, the Socialism which frightens so many means. (Winter & Joslin, 1972: 47)

With regard to Tawney's socialist beliefs, J.M. Winter notes how he felt that the English were obliged by history to speak out for economic liberty in the face of capitalism:

> Indeed, since England had led the world 'into the moral labyrinth of capitalist industry', it was incumbent upon Englishmen to teach the world the meaning of economic liberty in the twentieth century, just as they had 'upheld constitutional liberty when all other nations were passing under absolutism … '. Tawney did not underestimate the difficulties of the task. As a student of the Reformation, he drew the following comparison: 'It took men one hundred and fifty years and two revolutions to arrive as [*sic*] some working conception of religious liberty. It may take us as long to work out our idea of economic liberty.' (Winter, 1970: 93)

Tawney notes that Liberalism, the idea of the absolute liberty of the individual coupled with meritocracy, was once a force which assaulted

Tory England and all it held dear but that now this new creed had become the new enemy: 'The motive and inspiration of the Liberal Movement of the eighteenth century had been the attack on Privilege. But the creed which had exorcised the spectre of agrarian feudalism haunting village and chateau in France, was impotent to disarm the new ogre of industrialism which was stretching its limbs in the north of England' (Tawney, 1921; 2004: 18). Tawney's Christian socialism is not sanguine about Liberalism and unlike some contemporary 'social democrats' he does not acquiesce in liberal assumptions. Tawney argues that classical Liberalism gave birth to both the means to create the acquisitive society (industrial capitalism), and the ends for such a society (individualism, acquisitiveness and a robust sense of the justice of such endeavours). The acquisitive society, for Tawney, 'assures men that there are no ends other than their ends, no law other than their desires, no limit other than that which they think advisable. Thus it makes the individual the center of his own universe, and dissolves moral principles into a choice of expediencies' (2004: 30–1). Here is captured the kernel of English Christian Socialism's critique of capitalism. The sociological observation that one's own interests ought to be considered ahead of the interests of others in society and the economic observation that all material gain and material consumption is inherently just under free market capitalism to this day inform the social democratic critique of modern capitalism. Tawney's sociological and economic observations are contingent upon a moral conception of the good society. As a Christian socialist Tawney proposed that such a moral conception requires a belief in God and an understanding of how God wants humanity to behave and to treat one another (Winter & Joslin, 1972: 53–5). The atheist / humanist socialist will maintain that one can endorse Tawney's political critique of Liberalism and capitalism without believing in the fairies at the bottom of his metaphysical garden. While that may well be true it is not fully satisfactory because the full potency of Tawney's politics stem from the foundational assertion that English society has continued to debase itself and is guilty of sinning against itself, others and God (see also Stapleton, Chapter 10, this volume). Through liberal thought, the acquisitive society has been born, nurtured and taken root in English institutions and the *English mind*. The Christian socialist critique suggests that the English as individuals, families, and as a nation must correct this political and economic misadventure. Tawney's corrective is a prescription of service to others and the 'functionality' of property and wealth. In essence, he is calling for English society to copy Christ-like principles of service, compassion and sacrifice. Atheist / humanist socialists would endorse Tawney's critique of the acquisitive society in that his prescription would be beneficial for social cohesion not only because inequality is wasteful and inefficient but also because it is in one's own interest to have a welfare society where the community provides public services. However, I suggest that the moral outrage cannot be replicated and neither can the force of Tawney's argument and his rhetoric be harnessed without the religious element of Tawney's moral philosophy. Tawney is the prophet of English Christian socialism in the twentieth century; a prophet bringing forth a message to the English left in particular and to England in general. He wrote not for a Christian audience but with heart-felt Christian convictions in his critique of laissez-faire, Conservative England but the entirety of his thought, and therefore the deeply radical nature of his diagnosis and prescriptions, have seldom been endorsed by the English left. According to Stefan Collini: 'For Tawney, and perhaps for the first couple of generations of his readers in Britain "morality" had talismanic power, warding off demons of all kinds. It can no longer be confidently expected to play this role, nor do we really feel we would want it to' (1999: 194). This observation speaks volumes of the England that made Tawney and what England has become. If moralism has become displaced by materialism in English public conversation then perhaps Keynes is the person who charts that transformation.

John Maynard Keynes: the English left's economic theorist

If Tawney represents English Christian socialism then John Maynard Keynes is representative of the left-Liberalism prevalent for most of the twentieth century. Keynes was the foremost economist of the age and his contribution to the English left came in the form of his theory of demand management which is most forcefully presented in *The General Theory of Employment, Interest and Money* (1949). Keynes designed a theory of demand management as a counter-argument to what he understood as the flawed assumptions of classical economics. Keynesianism, as his theory became known, asserts that unemployment is a complex phenomenon which can be categorised as involuntary and voluntary. Keynes argued that both types of unemployment were the result of macro-economic shortcomings, that insufficient demand for goods and services necessitates these forms of unemployment. That in turn causes a fall in the level of investment in industries and manufacture, a diminution of consumer demand and a reduction of output and profit which increases the overall level of unemployment and poverty. In addition, Keynes thought the behaviour of private investors was crucial because their choice to invest or not to invest in large measure determines the health and stability of given industries and has a significant influence on the level of demand in the economy. Keynes' prescription therefore was for government, by utilising the levers of the state, to intervene in macro-economic policy and at given times either to stimulate or dampen consumer demand. He proposed that fiscal and monetary policy be used to achieve wherever possible a stable level of demand. According to James Meade:

> It is now universally recognised by governments, at least throughout the industrialised free-enterprise world, that it is one of the primary duties to control the level of total effective demand for goods and services. If demand is insufficient to provide full employment, it is the government's duty to raise it by stimulating the injections (investment, government expenditure, and / or exports) and / or by discouraging the leakages (by reducing the proportions of income saved, paid in taxes, or spent on imports). If demand is excessive, then it is the government's duty to restrain the injections and to encourage the leakages. (Meade, 1975: 87–8)

Keynes was an academic, a rationalist, agnostic and represents a particular strand of the English left which is very different from Tawney. Both were born during Queen Victoria's reign; both were Edwardian Englishmen; and because of their parents' social class, both men were 'gentlemen' (see Berberich, 2007). Keynes' post-Victorian outlook is present in his departure from the Christian worldview and in his affinity with a rationalistic humanism although, as Peter Clarke noted, 'in licensing personal judgement, he implicitly assumed, that it would have been formed and constrained by the same conventional morality which he refused to accept as an infallible commandment – a post-Victorian attitude in more ways than one' (1994: 177). Clarke cites an extract from *The Diary of Virginia Woolf* which records a conversation that she had with Keynes on the topic of the impact of their parents' faith on their generation: 'I begin to see that our generation – yours and mine V., owed a great deal to our fathers' religion. And the young, like Julian [Bell], who are brought up without it, will never get so much out of life. They're trivial: like dogs in their lusts. We had the best of both worlds. We destroyed Xty & yet had its benefits' (in Clarke, 1994: 177).

In terms of Keynes' politics, his first biographer R.F. Harrod concisely summarises his standpoint – 'By temperament and conviction he was certainly a Liberal throughout his life' (1966: 331) – though he was theoretically closer to social democracy than his classically Liberal friends. 'He believed that Liberals should turn their backs on the old doctrine of laissez-faire which had served them in good stead in different circumstance. The state would have to intervene at many points. Yet the structure of a free economy with its scope for individual initiative must be preserved. Keynes remained essentially an individualist' (Harrod, 1966: 334). Harrod also points out that Keynes was hostile to what he understood as state socialism, even democratic state socialism with its parliamentarianism and gradualism: 'During the twenties he hoped to see a working agreement between the Liberal Party and the Labour Party; in the thirties he may have nourished the hope that, when he had achieved the culminating expression of his own views, the cogency of his arguments would wean the Labour Party from State Socialism and make its members his own disciples' (1966: 331). Moreover, Robert Skidelsky comments that 'Keynes's scepticism about the Labour Party as an engine either of Keynesianism or of any radical change hardly seems exaggerated. Intellectually, the Labour Party at the time saw the issue largely in terms of capitalism versus socialism which, as Keynes pointed out, "misses the significance of what is actually happening"' (1975: 95). It is here that one of the most interesting aspects of Keynes can be understood. Namely, that as an English gentleman Keynes was essentially bourgeois and he would therefore remain in the Liberal Party despite the Labour Party adopting his doctrine of demand management during the 1940s. The peculiarities of the English class system defined the English and Keynes here is an object lesson for his class whereas Tawney is the rebel and the outcast. Keynes, in spite of his economic radicalism, illustrates the tradition of upper-middle-class, benevolent ameliorators. Despite being educated at Balliol College, Tawney never took up a permanent position at Oxford; he tutored at Glasgow University and, when the Great War came, enlisted as a private in the Manchester Regiment of the British Army to fight alongside the type of working-class men he tutored in Lancashire and Staffordshire through the Workers' Educational Association between 1912–14. Whereas Tawney's life after the Great War fused a Protestant simplicity and lack of ostentation with social duty to the have-nots, his institutions being the Church of England, the Workers' Educational Association, the Labour Party and the London School of Economics, Keynes lived as his class and as his professional status dictated. Keynes loved rural England and believed he had at least 'done his bit' for the less fortunate of his countrymen whose lot it was to live in the urban centres of England:

The pleasant ways of life of the English countryside could go on; in the harsh setting of the towns employment could at least be assured now, and little by little things of beauty, the drama and music, and possibly even – perhaps through his Arts Council – visual arts would percolate in and enrich the lives of those who dwelt there. (Harrod, 1966: 643)

This was a reflection towards the end of his life, a life dedicated to public service and the common good but despite his effort and hard work, his ideal *England* was still out of reach for most Englishmen. This is probably the wistful realisation of an English social liberal for whom amelioration only remedies immediate ills rather than long-term, structural social inequalities. Keynes had done more than most but even his politics eschewed a robust social democratic state. Both Tawney and Keynes were cut from similar English cloth but they were quite different sorts of radicals, illustrating those two distinctive tendencies, the moral and the material, on the English left in the twentieth century.

Anthony Crosland: the English left's political economist

Crosland is the most important English social democrat of the second half of the twentieth century and he provides a very modern attempt to reconcile the moral tradition of Tawney and the material tradition of Keynes. His 1956 book, *The Future of Socialism*, represents a key contribution to the intellectual debates on the English Left during the 1950s and it was this thesis which was significant through the 1960s until it was countered and critiqued by the new right and the new left in the 1970s. Yet to this day many Labour Party activists and support-ers regard their social democracy as 'Croslandite social democracy'. Crosland was a trained economist but his *magnum opus The Future of Socialism* is not a work of pure economics in the way that Keynes' *The General Theory of Employment, Interest and Money* (1949) clearly is but, to be more precise, it is a work of social democratic political economy in which social conscience becomes applied to questions of how indi-vidual and collective welfare is to be *enjoyed*.

Crosland was a member of a golden generation of English left thinkers who were also politicians; he formed, along with Evan Durbin, Douglas Jay and Hugh Gaitskell, a formidable cluster. These men were friends and, with the exception of Durbin who died in 1948, were advocates of what became known as revisionist social democracy. Crosland was the main intellectual driving force and Gaitskell was their captain who succeeded Clement Attlee as Leader of the Labour

Party in 1955 and led it until his death in 1963. Crosland's thesis was that a combination of the Welfare State, nationalisation of certain industries, the mixed economy (with a large public as well as private sector), the adoption by the governing class of Keynesian demand management (legitimising an active, interventionist role for the state in economic affairs), the growth and robustness of trade unions and most importantly the change in the *modus operandi* of capitalism from owners to professional managers had significantly modified and humanised society in Britain. Therefore, the Labour Party did not need to argue for further nationalisation as the Bevanites maintained or central planning of the like that Durbin had advocated before the war in his influential book *The Politics of Democratic Socialism* (1940: 96). This desire for a diverse economy with varieties of ownership and responsibility is well noted by Crosland's wife, Susan: 'He was a pluralist. He wanted state ownership, private ownership, the co-operative principle to co-exist' (S. Crosland, 1982: 69). Crosland maintained that Labour's focus ought to be on securing economic growth because with growth comes fuller employment and disposable incomes that can purchase manufactured goods, which keep people in jobs and aids the profitability of firms, who in turn pay taxes to the Treasury, enabling the state to deliver the public goods of the Welfare State. Growth sustains the consumption function of the economy and is central to a mixed economy which has a large and diverse manufacturing base. Through this model of welfare capitalism, values of equality of opportunity, positive liberty, social solidarity and social cohesion can be reasonably expected to flourish. But Crosland was at heart an egalitarian and perhaps his most valuable contribution to English social democratic thought lies in his practical understanding of the value of equality:

> I feel clear that we need large egalitarian changes in our educational system, the distribution of property, the distribution of resources in periods of need, social measures and style of life, and the location of power within industry and perhaps, some but certainly a smaller change in respect of incomes from work. I think that these changes, taken together, will amount to a considerable social revolution. (C.A.R. Crosland, 1956: 148)

The extent and level of egalitarianism is one of the central fault-lines between Social democracy and Social liberalism. One of the other fault-lines is the extent to which the democratic state intervenes to engineer such outcomes. Crosland's instinct towards egalitarianism was influenced by his family's Exclusive Brethrenism. The egalitarian and democratic ethos and practices of Protestant non-conformity views each brother and sister in Christ as inherently equal and though, as his wife makes clear, Crosland did not hold to his parent's faith – 'When he rejected the Exclusive Brethren's obsession with the next world, he didn't go to the other extreme of atheism: he was a religious agnostic' (S. Crosland, 1982: 8) – he was shaped by their theological standpoint about the intrinsic equity of all people: 'They were known by their initials, all men being equal – at any rate in the sight of God' (S. Crosland, 1982: 4). It is because of his commitment to a robust conception of equality that Crosland entitled a section in *The Future of Socialism*, 'Why Equal Opportunity is Not Enough'. He was concerned with reforming the education system with the aim of reducing social and economic inequalities between the classes:

> It stems from the danger that under certain circumstances the creation of equal opportunities may merely serve to replace one remote elite (based on lineage) by a new one (based on ability and intelligence) ... Yet this might easily be the case in Britain even with equal opportunities – generally on account of our traditional and deeply-embedded class stratification, which, although no doubt jolted, might not be sufficiently disturbed by the greater mobility: and particularly because we have a segregated, privileged systems of schools. (C.A.R. Crosland, 1956: 165)

Therefore, Crosland's religious inheritance was both a blessing and a burden. On the one hand it seems likely that his English non-conformist upbringing shaped his egalitarianism but that his rejection of the Brethren's puritanism prompted his libertarianism. This led to an inherent tension in Crosland's politics. As Jeremy Nuttall argues:

> His embrace of the excesses of the twentieth-century Bloomsburyesque reaction against Victorian moralism is one example. Crosland, partly in rebellion against his own strict puritan upbringing, and partly against post-war austerity and the apparently drab life prescribed by some within Labour's own puritan tradition, had noted some years before *The Future of Socialism* that it was 'non-sense to say people can't be perfectly happy on sex, gin and Bogart – and if that is what they want under Soc.[ialism], well and good. I know many cultured people who want just that (e.g. me)'. (2004: 58)

This libertarianism was woven into Crosland's socialism. He felt that increasing individual liberty and the liberty for pleasure was part of the merit of a socialist society. This is apparent in a section of the conclusion of *The Future of Socialism* which is entitled 'Liberty and Gaiety in Private Life; the Need for a Reaction against the Fabian Tradition':

We need not only higher exports and old-aged pensions, but more open-air cafes, brighter and gayer streets at night, later closing hours for public houses, more local repertory theatres, better and more hospitable hoteliers and restaurateurs, brighter and cleaner eating-houses, more riverside cafés, more pleasure-gardens on the Battersea model, more murals and pictures in public places ... The enemy in all this will often be in unexpected guise; it is not only dark Satanic things and people that now bar the road to the new Jerusalem but also, if not mainly, hygienic, respectable, virtuous things and people, lacking only in grace and gaiety. (1956: 355)

Crosland is deliberately referring to reforms of the British social and public sphere but his prescriptions are quite clearly indicative of his class and his nationality. Some may say it is the espousal of a cosmopolitan critique of England, anticipating the sort of vision of café society England which informed the early years of New Labour, and one can see how that can be interpreted from the text but that is to assume that England is bereft of the qualities and experiences that Crosland is suggesting for the public sphere. It is rather the case that Crosland wishes to see a considered, deliberate focus on the social and public sphere in order to increase common wellbeing and enjoyment of one's environment and one can say that Crosland's view is fairly typical of his class during the 1950s. His experiences as a tutor at Trinity College, Oxford, and then as a reasonably well-off Member of Parliament with a flat in London naturally meant that he wished to see an England with a richer, more elegant public sphere than the restrictive, austere, battle-scarred one common to the towns and cities of the immediate post-war period. It is interesting that Crosland's critique only seems to apply to a vision of urban England. Just as today, most people lived in cities and towns but perhaps it suggests the deep-seated, English cultural outlook that regards the countryside with its quiet market towns, hamlets, farms, country pubs, village greens, cricket fields and beautiful churches surrounded by acres of barley as somehow purer and better; an England that suffers no want or squalor and has none of the depredation and depravity of city life. Urban England is the problem and thus is in need of remedy. The imagined England of many English people for generations is a place of beauty, peacefulness and simple virtues. It looms largely in the minds of the English middle classes who have known both *Englands* but treasure one above the other. Crosland was also aware of both *Englands* and as Member of Parliament for Grimsby he saw at first hand the hardship faced by many of his constituents. Yet his England was a world away from this since Crosland was an urban dweller with the liberty to spend time in the country. A man born in

Sussex and brought up in a family of the London establishment, as an adult he sat firmly within the social milieu of the English left intelligentsia. Though his politics were radical and compassionate to the have-nots, his essential vision of England was similar to countless others whether Conservative, Liberal or Social democrat, middle, upper-middle or upper class. For all their differences, it is an England that Tawney or Keynes would have recognised.

Conclusion: England's effect

All nations and people-groups are to a significant extent defined by the collective impact of historical events, habits, culture and the like which constitute a 'conversational' history, of 'books not read' but assumed. It is often stated that the English gaze into their past to fully understand who they are, what they believe and why or, as George Orwell puts it in *The Lion and the Unicorn*: 'England will still be England, an everlasting animal stretching into the future and the past, and like all living things, having the power to change out of all recognition and yet to remain the same' (1941; 1988: 70). This does not sound like a negative attitude of mind or a bad habit. If the English and especially English thinkers, artists, poets, writers and scholars, demonstrate a critical evaluation of their historical roots, norms and values then it may well lead to a more open and honest appreciation of the virtues and the vices of Englishness. However, a preoccupation with the past and simultaneously a misguided idea that the best days have been had and that England is in decline might, at best, be overly pessimistic and, at worst, potentially calamitous to the nation's sense of place, community and national identity. The possible reasons why the English are prone to backwards looking are many. They include popular legends of a thousand-year history as an unconquered nation; the development through the period of Reformation of a distinctive English Christian religion (Anglicanism and its non-conformist offshoot, Methodism); the good fortune of a rich and widely respected literary and scientific heritage; the underlying idea that the nation once 'ruled the waves'; and that its experience had been exceptional and exemplary. Those conversational legends are contested today. Arthur Aughey characterises this as a distinct English anxiety:

> Other countries have experienced similar disturbance so why should this English anxiety be felt so acutely? Its English particularity may be traced to the assumption that Englishness has been of universal, not just local significance. Here is a double English tragedy, it seems: although the sense of world-historical significance has been lost, the inheritance

remains as a crippling cultural absence. The other side of being everything is being nothing. (2010: 4)

The Conservative Party has and does still invest much intellectual and cultural energy in reminiscence of a better England (see also Ingle, Chapter 5 this volume). Moreover, social conservatives lament virtues now lost amid a sea of individualism, social fragmentation and extreme pluralism. However, egalitarians of the English left are not free from this state of mind either because they blame the New Right for England's inequalities and ambivalence towards redistributionism. Social liberals too posit the idea that England's traditions are being eroded in the wake of the terror attacks in the early 2000s, arguing that the age-old tradition of *Habeas Corpus* is under siege from ever-increasing anti-libertarian legislation, especially detention without trial.

In this chapter I have looked at the contributions of three figures from the English left; but have Tawney, Keynes and Crosland had a bearing on the contemporary left? This is a difficult question to answer with any degree of certainty. What can be said is that Tawney, Keynes and Crosland are still read and regarded as important thinkers by many social democrats and social liberals. Tawney's work, like those of Keynes and Crosland, appears on undergraduate and postgraduate reading lists. The ethical socialism of Tawney has been discussed by New Labour politicians in terms of the themes of responsibility, social obligation and community, and certainly informs the public discourse of all political parties. In this regard Tawney is arguably *en vogue* in a way that he was not in the 1960s and 1970s. Communitarian social democrats, some of whom share his robust egalitarianism, cite his ideals of the moral obligation of each citizen and of the state to its citizens as a corrective to the 'rights-based' approach of the liberal left and the individualism of the liberal right. Keynes was a thinker discounted by New Labour until the recent past. The financial crash of 2008 and the global recession that followed have forced Western governments to revisit Keynes and to redeploy Keynesian economic measures. Gordon Brown's stimulus package that the United Kingdom government implemented and that was widely followed across Europe was clearly Keynesian. Debates on the left are now full of suggestions to reform the political economy of contemporary social democracy and the ideas of Keynes are once again being hotly discussed. The case of Crosland is more curious. Many academics who regard themselves as social democrats continue to discuss the relevance of Crosland's ideas and insist that their students read his work carefully. However, New Labour appears to believe that

Crosland, though a great Labour thinker, is frankly old hat. He seems to be too closely associated with a world which globalisation generally and Mrs Thatcher particularly consigned to the dustbin of history along with its political economy and culture of a large industrial working class employed in heavy industry and manufacture. This is a curious fate because it is also arguable that there is something enduring because the basis of contemporary social democracy is still a belief in welfare capitalism: a welfare state and public services funded through progressive taxation. This is Crosland's social democratic model. A clear departure can be seen in the fact that Crosland was much more egalitarian than New Labour. Some in New Labour resemble social liberals in their attitude towards inequality; they are less critical of finance capitalism and less worried about the inequalities that markets produce. Crosland was a social democrat and an uncompromising one at that and his scepticism towards finance capitalism and markets and his robust egalitarianism set him apart from many of the Labour Party elite today. Insofar as all political thought expresses a tradition, then, it is important to return to such texts not as mere historical curiosities but as notes of guidance in the margins of our own experience

The work of these three figures affected England's radical, democratic tradition. They did not consciously try to bring the English left and Englishness together but, as evident and obvious Englishmen, their individual contributions pertain to a peculiarly English rendering of social democracy and radical liberalism. But what in turn is England's effect upon these notable twentieth-century figures of the left? What if anything makes the contributions of Tawney, Keynes and Crosland peculiarly English? The answer, I believe, is two-fold; firstly, Tawney, Keynes and Crosland were English gentlemen, sharing a common set of political expectation. This is a self-evident point yet it opens the door to the second part of the answer, namely that in their Englishness one finds the relationships, experiences, events, institutions as well as a plethora of socio-cultural factors that combine to produce Tawney, Keynes and Crosland. In essence, England has helped to fashion the thought of these individuals; England's history, politics, culture and society is their sociology. What English similarities do all three share? Tawney and Keynes were contemporaries both of them born to upper-middle-class families whereas Crosland's parents were professional middle class. Educationally, all three were privately schooled (Rugby, Eton and Highgate respectively) and all were Oxbridge men, Tawney an undergraduate at Balliol College, Crosland a student and later tutor at Trinity College, Oxford, and

Keynes first a student and then a fellow of King's College, Cambridge. All three were culturally Southern (despite Tawney being born in Calcutta and Keynes in East Anglia) and they all had particular ties with Oxford, Cambridge and London. Theirs was the England of the intellectual elite and the political centre. Theirs was an England that was still officially informed by Christian ideals of service, compassion and dignity. It is the claim of this chapter that their radicalism, however idiosyncratic, was tempered by those ideals and by the overwhelming importance given to the value of democracy and, in particular, to the rule of law and the English parliamentary tradition. Although politics in England may be the public outworking of fierce disagreement and opposition, it is at root understood by many – including in their day by Tawney, Keynes and Crosland – as a form of conversation, a free exchange of ideas and not a (literal) call to take up arms and fight. Historically, this has been of the utmost salience to the left, because it is due to the absence of such potential fervour and political violence that the English political tradition has survived for so long and in which, to return to my starting point, conservative England can also at times be radical. Because the conversation has been open, because there has been a culture of adjustment, the tradition has remained dynamic.

7

Gordon Brown and the negation of England

Simon Lee

Introduction

In his landmark study of *The Politics of Englishness*, Arthur Aughey proposed that 'to be English was to participate in a conversation, an imaginative rather than a purely functional engagement, about the country's history, culture and society' (Aughey, 2007: 213). Despite the enactment of devolution to the other constituent nations of the United Kingdom, until recently the conversation had rarely addressed the question of the relationship between politics and Englishness. Those who had explored the impact of constitutional change upon the United Kingdom (e.g. Freedland, 1998; Hitchens, 1999; Redwood, 1999) had preferred to regard England and Britain, and Englishness and Britishness, as synonyms, capable of being conflated and confused. Consequently, the long-standing tendency to conceptualise the politics of England narrowly, in terms of changes to the functional management of England's territory, by and for the convenience of the institutions of the centralised British state at Westminster and Whitehall, to the exclusion of questions of England as a political community, had been maintained.

Fortunately, in recent years, there has been a very welcome broadening and enrichment of the conversation about politics and Englishness. In addition to Aughey's (2007) exhaustive analysis of the politics of Englishness, edited collections have explored the English Question, and imagined both England after Britain, and the implications of breaking up the United Kingdom for its constituent nations (e.g. Perryman, 2009). This largely academic contribution has been accompanied by attempts both to set out a progressive English patriotism (Bragg, 2006) and to chart the loss of quintessentially English institutions (Kingsnorth, 2008). The broader historical, democratic and constitutional British context for this English conversation has been expertly laid out by two important studies (Bogdanor, 2009; Marquand, 2008a). However, as Hazell has noted, given that this is 'a political question, about the governance of England' (2006: 220), it cannot be answered by academics alone. Ultimately, it is a conversation that must be joined by politicians, and the people of England themselves.

In his analysis of British democracy, Marquand has noted how, at the time when Gordon Brown was succeeding Tony Blair as Prime Minister, 'For the first time, since the Act of Union, England's constitutional future was coming into contention, and with it the fundamental assumptions underpinning the multinational British state' (2008a: 399). The process of devolution in the non-English nations of the Union had fashioned 'new sites for civic engagement and fostered new, pluralistic forms of democracy, closer to the rest of Europe than to the Westminster model' (Marquand, 2008a: 406), from which England had been excluded. But any national conversation about Britishness and British values could not fail 'to touch on the English Question, in all its rich complexity, and thereby on the future of the Union' (Marquand, 2008a: 406).

This chapter therefore focuses upon Gordon Brown's engagement with the conversation about England and Englishness. First, it seeks to demonstrate how Brown throughout his tenure as Chancellor of the Exchequer and, latterly, as Prime Minister, sought to advance a modernisation project for British renewal – the British Way – which negated the idea of England as a political community, and created a postcode lottery in citizenship and accountability. Second, the chapter explores how this negation continued during Brown's tenure as Prime Minister through his government's agenda for *The Governance of Britain* (Ministry of Justice, 2009a), proposals for a British Bill of Rights and Duties, and *Building Britain's Future* (HM Government, 2009), Brown's attempt to set out a vision for a fourth term Labour Government. The chapter concludes by evaluating Brown's legacy as Chancellor and Prime Minister for the conversation about the politics of Englishness.[1] Throughout the chapter, the focus is upon questions of statecraft, public policy, political power and political economy, rather than questions of national character or the particular individual or peculiar personal qualities that may, rightly or wrongly, be deemed to be those of the English.

New Labour and England: earned autonomy and constrained discretion

The nature of contemporary politics in England was neatly summarised in a parliamentary select committee report:

> England is one of the developed world's most centralised democracies. The centre controls virtually all taxation, and power has followed money. Over the period since 1945 power and authority have moved upwards within the English political system, as expectations of government responsibilities for improving individual lives have risen with the advent of the welfare state, and as parliamentary and governmental attention has turned from governing overseas territories to directing domestic policy. (HCCLGC, 2009: 7)

Since 1945, England (along with the other nations of the United Kingdom) has experienced four state-led modernisation projects for British renewal. However, throughout the social democratic First Way of Keynesian social democracy, the neo-liberal Second Way of Thatcherism, the Third Way of New Labour and the Fourth or British Way implemented by the Brown government (Lee, 2007; 2009a), one essential continuity has been the negation of local democracy, participation and accountability in England. In terms of policy and services, local government has been stripped of its responsibility for education, health, housing, planning and regeneration. In terms of taxation, the non-domestic rate has been nationalised and local taxation capped (HCCLGC, 2009: 7). This has meant that, when compared with other patterns of governance across Europe, 'by most measures the English model appears at the far centralist end of the spectrum' (HCCLGC, 2009: 15).

From the very outset, any prospect of the advancement of the principles of decentralisation, democratic autonomy or active citizenship in England was dashed by New Labour's nationalisation of the control of policy-making and resource allocation in England. This was engineered by a top-down statecraft, enshrined in Tony Blair's principle of 'earned autonomy', but given greater weight by Gordon Brown's doctrine of 'constrained discretion', and institutionalised in the Treasury's biennial Spending Reviews and accompanying Public Service Agreements. Thus, while Blair was prepared to sanction devolution to Scotland, Wales and Northern Ireland, to enable 'locally-elected representatives to adopt approaches to public services reflecting their own national priorities and concerns', in England alone devolved delivery could 'only operate with national standards and accountability' (Office of Public Service Reform, 2002: 17, 28). Since Blair offered no explanation as to why locally elected representatives in England should not also enjoy devolved power to establish service provision in accordance with England's own 'national priorities and concerns', it appeared Blair was simply the latest British Prime Minister to be strengthening and deepening centralised English governance for the political convenience of the British state, in pursuit of its third great post-war modernisation programme (Lee, 2007).

For his part, while in opposition, and in the face of four successive general election defeats for the Labour Party, Gordon Brown had proposed a decentralist 'politics of potential' which threatened to challenge the relentless drive towards ever greater centralisation. This would have entailed not only a redistribution of power and an enabling role for the state, but also a new constitutional settlement incorporating devolved power 'wherever possible', and the reconstruction of the idea of community (Brown, 1994: 114). By the time that he became Chancellor of the Exchequer, Brown had long since abandoned any thought of a decentralist 'politics of potential' in favour of the centralised prescriptions of the Treasury statecraft of 'constrained discretion'. The principal characteristics of this approach to policy-making for England were a focus upon outcomes as 'the central aim of policy'; an increase in 'operational freedoms and flexibilities' together with 'appropriate minimum standards and regular performance monitoring'; and improved governance via 'clear objectives, appropriate incentives and good performance information in the achievement of higher productivity' (Balls et al., 2004: 346).

Constrained discretion was claimed to be an improvement upon the previous model of 'command and control' public services which had led potentially 'to the delivery of one-size-fits-all, poor-quality services to diverse communities' (Balls et al., 2004: 17, 346). However, the reality for England was that constrained discretion was actually itself a prime example of a command and control system of governance, which was inherently top-down and centralising, and which delivered 'one-size-fits-all' approaches to policy design and resource allocation.[2] Above all, the impact of Brown's 'constrained discretion', in combination with Blair's 'earned autonomy' was to negate any possibility of the extension of democratic citizenship made possible by the implementation of devolution elsewhere in the United Kingdom.

The British way for England

One of the most conspicuous features of Gordon Brown's tenure as Chancellor of the Exchequer was that he did not confine his attention or speech-making to narrow questions of macro-economic stability or fiscal prudence. His preferred topic was the subject of Britain and Britishness, and how what he held to be a lost shared sense of national patriotic purpose could be restored to Britain and the British people. Among the proposals he floated for achieving this objective were the establishment of a British Day, a national celebration of Britishness; the creation of a British youth national community service; the reclamation of the Union flag, to be honoured, and not ignored, 'as a flag for Britain, not the BNP'; English language and British history lessons for immigrants; and the introduction of a biometric British national identity card (Brown, 2004; 2006a; 2006b).

Rather than developing his narrative on Britain and Britishness within the ideological framework of the modernised social democracy espoused by Tony Blair, Brown chose to present his vision within the framework of a 'British Way' of politics and statecraft. This vision was first set out in Brown's November 1997 Spectator / Allied Dunbar Lecture, in which three tenets of the British Way were specified.[3] First, a commitment to liberty through the protection of the individual against the arbitrary power of the state, which the British Way had achieved through the exercise of mutual responsibility and duty rather than the pursuit of crude individualism. Ironically, Brown later chose to develop this theme by references to a series of English liberal thinkers, and key events in England's history, notably the signing of the Magna Carta in 1215 and the 1689 English Bill of Rights. Second, the British Way had been characterised by adaptability, a willingness 'to embrace, not fear, constitutional reform', and the breaking up of 'centralized institutions that are too remote and insensitive and so devolve power' (Brown, 1997: 15). This pointed towards an agenda for England of devolution and decentralisation, the very opposite of what Brown's 'constrained discretion' would actually deliver. Third, the British Way had embraced an outward looking and internationalist patriotism. This was Brown's attempt to put a positive gloss on the fact that Britishness had largely been fashioned overseas during the forging of the British Empire.

The rationale for Brown's British Way reflected his understanding of the longer-term implications of devolution, and England's omission from that process, for his ambitions to succeed Tony Blair as Prime Minister of the United Kingdom. The British Way would provide a means of answering both the pre-devolution West Lothian Question (Dalyell, 1977; 1999), and the post-devolution Kirkcaldy and Cowdenbeath Question. The latter, named after Brown's constituency, asked why Brown, as a representative of a Scottish seat (although the Question would have been equally applicable had Brown represented a Welsh or Ulster seat), should be able not only to vote on policy matters affecting England alone, but also design and control the policy agenda for England. Devolution to Scotland of responsibility for major areas of policy such as health, education and housing, meant that Brown's own constituents would not experience policies developed for England, unless such choices were voted for by the Scottish Parliament.

The British Way would serve a dual purpose. First, by constantly reminding the English of the importance of Britain and Britishness, as the focal point for their own patriotic purpose, it would perpetuate the mindset that had long conflated and confused the identity and interests of England with those of the United Kingdom, and Englishness with Britishness. Second, by subordinating England and Englishness to Britain and Britishness, the British Way might divert the attention of English voters away from the fact that they had been bypassed by New Labour's most important constitutional reform, and thereby denied the parallel extension of democratic citizenship and accountability which had been extended to the people of Wales, Scotland and Northern Ireland.

Seventeen months after his initial definition of the British Way, Brown delivered a major speech about the modernisation of Britain in which he appeared to offer the possibility of a more democratic future for England. Brown's thesis was that, with the rediscovery of the shared values of 'a special and unifying identity', it would be possible for Britain to move 'from an over centralized and uniform state – the old Britain of subjects – to a pluralist and decentralized democracy – the new Britain of citizens' (Brown, 1999). Furthermore, this 'new Britain of citizens' would be characterised by 'the birth of new centres of power and initiative', encompassing a 'commitment to participatory democracy' and 'a unifying and inclusive idea of citizenship' (Brown, 1999).

It seemed inconceivable that Brown's vision of a 'new Britain of citizens', founded upon 'a pluralist and decentralized democracy', could be implemented without rolling forward the frontiers of devolution and citizenship rights in England. However, it soon became apparent that Brown's vision would observe in the breach two of the three tenets of the British Way, namely the willingness to embrace rather than fear constitutional change, and the devolution of power to break up remote and centralised institutions. Brown's 'new Britain of citizens' would also be 'a Britain of regions and nations' in which the regions would be those of England, and the nations would be Scotland, Wales and Britain. England's identity as a discrete nation and source of political identity and citizenship in its own right would be negated on all occasions.

By the time that Brown succeeded Tony Blair as Prime Minister in June 2007, it was apparent that the British Way, as a means of negating both England as a political community and Englishness as a source of political identity, was fundamentally flawed in at least two important respects. First and foremost, Brown had constructed the British Way from a plethora of historical examples and literary quotations whose common denominator was that they were specifically English, or about England and Englishness, but had been presented by Brown as being about Britain and Britishness. In historical terms, Brown had fashioned what he depicted as the 'British desire for liberty' (Brown, 2006a) from a series of examples drawn from English history. These included the Magna Carta, the Peasants' Revolt, the Putney Debates during the English Civil War, and the Bill of Rights of 1689, all of which had predated the Act of Union and the creation of the United Kingdom. In literary terms, Brown had cited Voltaire, Montesquieu, Burke, Gray, Wordsworth, Hazlitt, Lord Henry Grattan, de Tocqueville, Churchill and Orwell to elegise Britain and Britishness, when his sources had been writing about England and Englishness (Lee, 2007).

The second major flaw in Brown's British Way was that it was unable to offer a credible defence for the omission of England from the process of devolution, especially when the justification for the rein-stitution of the Scottish Parliament was recalled. When Donald Dewar, the Secretary of State for Scotland, had introduced the Blair government's White Paper, *Scotland's Parliament*, in July 1997, he had asserted that the consequence of 'Entrusting Scotland with control over her own domestic affairs' would be 'a fair and just settlement for Scotland'. Not only would devolution 'strengthen democratic control and make government more accountable to the people of Scotland', but it would also 'better allow the people of Scotland to benefit from, and contribute to, the unity of the United Kingdom' (Dewar, 1997). Brown could not identify a legitimate reason why England should not also be entrusted to exercise democratic control over its own domestic affairs, and thereby receive 'a fair and just settlement'.

A missed opportunity: *The Governance of Britain*

When Gordon Brown succeeded Tony Blair as Prime Minister on the 27 June 2007, he was faced with the major strategic dilemma of how to distance himself from Blair and the declining popularity of New Labour, especially when Brown himself had been one of the twin architects of the whole project in government. He immediately promised 'a new government with new priorities' (Brown, 2007a), to reinforce his earlier commitment to 'a new kind of politics' and 'new style of government', to be implemented by 'a servant state' (British Broadcasting Corporation, 2007). This commitment might not have sounded so hollow had Blair not promised precisely the same new politics more than a decade earlier. The Brown government's credentials for being able to claim to have fashioned 'a new kind of politics' were embodied in its early publication of a draft legislative programme and Green Paper on constitutional reform, both of which were entitled *The Governance of Britain* (Her Majesty's Government, 2007; Ministry of Justice, 2007). This in itself was indicative of a certain political, legal and historical confusion that was to characterise the Brown government's agenda, in that both the legislative programme and constitutional reform agenda were addressed to the wider United Kingdom, rather than Britain per se. It was soon evident that *The Governance of Britain* agenda would strengthen and deepen, rather than redress the constitutional asymmetries bequeathed by the Blair decade.

Rather than providing a final blueprint for a constitutional settlement, the Green Paper was to serve as 'the first step in a national conversation' (Brown and Straw, 2007: 5). This would include 'an inclusive process of national debate to develop a British statement of values' (Ministry of Justice, 2007: 8). Where England would fit into this broader picture was not entirely certain. The Green Paper conceded that, despite New Labour's previous constitutional changes, 'power remains too centralised and too concentrated in government' and that it was 'not sufficiently clear what power government should and should not have'. Furthermore, people had become 'cynical about, and increasingly disengaged from, the political process' (Ministry of Justice, 2007: 10). To redress this cynicism and disengagement, the Brown government intended 'to reform the institutions central to our political system-government and Parliament', because 'Citizens value the right to choose the people that make the law' (Ministry of Justice, 2007: 58). However, its proposals did not include any measures that would enable the citizens of England, as a democratic community in their own right, to choose the people that made their laws.

While the Green Paper intended to 'invigorate our democracy, with people proud to participate in decision-making at every level' and 'to clarify the role of government, both central and local', it would not entail English devolution (Ministry of Justice, 2007: 11). What the Green Paper offered England instead was a variety of proposals, none of which had been included in the Labour Party's 2005 general election manifesto. To make the executive more accountable, the Green Paper offered a reminder that 'In Scotland, Wales and Northern Ireland devolution has put power closer to the people and the Government has now created Regional Ministers in England. Proposals for regional select committees seek the same aim' (Ministry of Justice, 2007: 31). The Regional Ministers had been appointed by the Prime Minister the day after he became Prime Minister. Their purpose was to 'give citizens a voice in central government', and to make 'central government more visible in the regions' (Ministry of Justice, 2007: 37). Nine regional select committees would be established, to make them more accountable to parliament. Nothing was stated about how these committees would function or be financed. The more direct democratic alternative, as had been implemented elsewhere in the United Kingdom, would have been to have given English citizens a voice in their own regional or local government.[4] This would not have been so much for the purpose of making those localities more visible to central government, because only a centralist, top-down mentality, as institutionalised in Brown's British Way, could conceive of democratic accountability and citizenship in such terms. It would have been for the purpose of institutionalising checks and balances in England's government, by holding it to account more directly and more locally.

The Green Paper could not have provided a clearer statement of Brown's colonialist approach to the governance of England, and its negation of local accountability and participation. The mindset was still one shaped by the need to administer English territory in the manner most likely to deliver efficiently central government's priorities for policy and resources. In the very same sentence, the Green Paper had juxtaposed how moving power closer to the people had meant devolution, in the form of directly elected representatives, for three parts of the United Kingdom, but the extension of Prime Ministerial patronage in England, through the appointment of nine more ministers. The government's wish 'to ensure that decision-making is done at the right level: whether national, regional or in the local community' (Ministry of Justice, 2007: 40), had meant 'the right level' for the Cabinet and Whitehall. Thus, the Green Paper had proudly proclaimed that the nine regional Government Offices in England were there to provide '"central government in the regions"', and to implement the policies devised by no fewer than eleven Whitehall Departments (Ministry of Justice, 2007: 37). They were definitely not there to serve or implement regional or local interests and priorities, or to articulate those interests and priorities to their masters in London.

The Governance of Britain Green Paper was a missed opportunity. As one learned critique asserted, its diagnosis of the problem of political disaffection had lacked 'a depth and thoroughness in its analysis'. It had also failed to provide 'convincing evidence' that some of its partic- ular prescriptions for reform would have the desired effect, and, by the way it had framed the debate, the Green Paper had marginalised some 'substantial and significant areas where reform could and should be considered' (Russell & Stoker, 2007: 2). In short, the Green Paper had demonstrated 'The futility of "moving deckchairs around on the Titanic"' (Hay & Stoker, 2007: 8). It had not only underestimate the role that local government could play in reinvigorating democracy in England but also failed to address 'the need to find a robust response to the compatibility of devolution with perceived fairness to English representation' (Gains et al., 2007: 33). In so doing, *The Governance of Britain* had contributed little to the question of the relationship between politics and Englishness, and how England might be governed both more democratically and effectively.

A British Bill of Rights?

One of the means suggested by *The Governance of Britain* to strengthen the relationship between the citizen and the state was the possibility of a British Bill of Rights and Duties. It might provide people with 'a clearer idea of what we can expect from public author- ities, and from each other, and a framework for giving practical effect to our common values' (Ministry of Justice, 2007: 61). Gordon Brown asserted that the debate about a Bill of Rights and Duties would be of 'fundamental importance to our liberties and to our constitutional settlement and opens a new chapter in the British story of liberty' (Brown, 2007a). The intention was to identify 'the principles which bind all parts of the United Kingdom together and which have the potential to strengthen and enhance them' (Ministry of Justice, 2009a:

3). However, the political, legal and constitutional conversation which developed about rights and responsibilities soon served to highlight the very different legal traditions in different parts of the United Kingdom. It also highlighted the unintended political, legal and constitutional consequences of Brown's continual conflation and confusion of England, English history and Englishness, with Britain, British history and Britishness.

The problems which a Bill of Rights and Duties might create in a devolved United Kingdom were illustrated in the oral and written evidence submitted to the House of Commons and House of Lords' Joint Committee on Human Rights. For example, one English witness furnished a guide to the loss of liberty and rights which had occurred under the Blair and Brown governments since May 1997, describing it as 'the most serious attack on personal freedom and privacy ever mounted during peacetime in this country' (Porter, 2008: Ev 162). However, greater embarrassment was generated by the evidence given by Brown's own countrymen and women, in the form of representatives of the Scottish Parliament, Scottish Government, and Law Society of Scotland.

In the year before the publication of the Green Paper, *Rights and Responsibilities: Developing Our Constitutional Framework*, in a series of major speeches at home and abroad, Jack Straw had couched the Brown government's proposals in terms of 'Modernising the Magna Carta' (Straw, 2008a). Straw had noted how both the United Kingdom (through New Labour's 'Quiet Revolution' of constitutional reforms) and the United States had modernised the Magna Carta, and shared a legal culture thanks, not least, to the role played by the Englishman Thomas Paine, who had created the very name '"The United States of America"' (Straw, 2008a). He noted how the United Nations' Universal Declaration of Human Rights had been described as the '"Magna Carta of mankind"' (Straw, 2008b). Straw also drew attention to 'the vagaries of the English constitution' and noted how the new United Kingdom Supreme Court would 'stand proudly in one corner of Parliament Square, surrounded by, and in the sight of, the other distinctive pillars of our constitution – the Houses of Parliament opposite, the Treasury on one side, and Westminster Abbey, where every King and Queen of England has been crowned since 1066' (Straw, 2008a).

Not surprisingly, given this conflation of English legal and political history with that of the United Kingdom, it was soon pointed out during evidence to the Joint Committee that clarification was needed about the meaning of 'British' in a British Bill of Rights. Given that, in the United Kingdom, 'The citizen's rights differ in each of the constituent parts due to the different legal regimes which apply in each jurisdiction', did 'British' relate to the United Kingdom, Great Britain or the constituent parts thereof (Law Society of Scotland, 2008: Ev 147)? It was stressed that different strands of constitutionality had been created by 'The separate constitutional and rights structures of England and Scotland prior to the Treaty of Union in 1707' (Law Society of Scotland, 2008: Ev 148). Neither the Magna Carta nor the 1628 Petition of Right nor the 1689 Bill of Rights had applied to Scotland. 'British' rights had emanated, 'at the very best, from the Treaty of Union in 1707 and probably more properly from 1801', and even then certain rights had applied in each jurisdiction separately, notably the right to trial by jury-which applied in England, but not in Scotland (Law Society of Scotland, 2008: Ev 148).

Any British Bill of Rights would have to be viewed 'through the different perspectives of the various legal systems' (Clancy & O'Neill, 2008: Ev 69). Moreover, a British Bill of Rights was proposing to extend to economic and social rights, it would have to take account of the devolution of important aspects of healthcare. This now meant that the right to free personal care applied to Scotland, but not to England and Wales, while the right to free prescriptions applied to Wales, but not to England (Clancy & O'Neill, 2008: Ev 72). Rather than emphasising the rights which bound the United Kingdom together, a Bill of Rights might very well highlight divergences in rights which could be the source of politically centrifugal rather than centripetal forces.

This point was made more forcibly in evidence to the Joint Committee given by Kenny MacAskill, a Scottish National Party Member of the Scottish Parliament, and the Cabinet Secretary for Justice in the Scottish government. When asked about the fact that mention of devolution was 'pretty well missing' from *The Governance of Britain*, he reminded the Committee that Scotland had a distinctive legal system predating the Act of Union, and therefore neither the Magna Carta nor the 1689 Bill of Rights was of 'any great relevance to Scotland' (MacAskill, 2008: Ev 59). In relation to the Britishness dimension of a Bill of Rights, MacAskill stated that he and the Scottish National Party government perceived themselves as 'citizens or subjects of the United Kingdom but our nationality is Scottish' (MacAskill, 2008: Ev 60). Indeed, in answer to the question 'Are we British?', his retort was 'No, we are not. We are Scottish, not British and we consider those south of the border to be English. That is perfectly legitimate' (MacAskill, 2008: Ev 60). MacAskill regarded the concept of Britishness as 'rather arbitrary', 'founded for an empire and to some extent it has begun to fragment', and 'something we really do not buy into' (MacAskill, 2008: Ev 60). Furthermore, MacAskill claimed that the belief, south of the border, in the sovereignty of parliament, and north of the border in the sovereignty of the people, meant that 'We are almost operating in a parallel universe', in the face of 'a fundamental schism' about rights (MacAskill, 2008: Ev 61).

Despite the attendant danger that more 'fundamental schisms' might be opened up by the very process designed 'to foster a stronger sense of shared citizenship' (Straw, 2007) and shared Britishness, when the Joint Committee published its report, *A Bill of Rights for the UK?*, it concluded that 'the United Kingdom should adopt a Bill of Rights and Freedoms' (HLHCJCHR, 2008: 5). However, the Committee did note some of the difficulties arising from attempts to define 'British' in a devolved polity. It noted that a 'British Bill of Rights' could not, by definition, apply to Northern Ireland, preferring it to apply to '"people in the UK"' (HLHCJCHR, 2008: 25). The Joint Committee also departed from Jack Straw in identifying the 'difficulties associated with establishing a Bill of Rights on the basis of a statement of "British" values which may or may not be accepted by the people who consider themselves to be, for example, "English", "Scottish", "Irish" or "Welsh", but not "British"' (HLHCJCHR, 2008: 29). The Committee did not consider that the devolution settlement had created 'an insuperable obstacle' to a Bill of Rights (HLHCJCHR, 2008: 32). Nevertheless, the very process of drawing up the report had highlighted the manifold difficulties arising from the conflation of Britishness with Englishness, in relation to political and legal institutions and traditions. It had also demonstrated that a Bill of Rights, while by no means straightforward, would be much easier to fashion if its remit was confined to England and English law, and the English political traditions of liberty which had been usurped by Brown and Straw for their 'British story of liberty'.

On the 23 March 2009, when the Brown government published its Green Paper, *Rights and Responsibilities: developing our constitutional framework* (Ministry of Justice, 2009a), Jack Straw claimed that people's knowledge of their rights and responsibilities helped 'bind us together as a nation' (Ministry of Justice, 2009b). This statement in itself served only to revisit the confusion about national identity that had characterised *The Governance of Britain*, wherein plural interpretations of 'Britain' as a nation, a nation of nations, and (correctly) as a multi-national state (and not a nation) had reflected 'a lack of surety as to its definitive articulation' (Mycock and Tonge, 2007: 18).

The Green Paper sought to sidestep the diversity in legal traditions identified by the Law Society of Scotland and Kenny MacAskill by weaving the Magna Carta, the 1320 Declaration of Arbroath, the 1689 Bill of Rights and Scottish Claim of Right into a single historical narrative. It talked about the United Kingdom's 'proud traditions of liberty' upon which democratic rights and responsibilities had been built, but then had to acknowledge major differences in those traditions, rights and responsibilities (Ministry of Justice, 2009a: 8). One prescient example was the Green Paper's mention of the legal writ of '"Habeas corpus" ("may you produce the body")', first used in England in 1305 and codified in the Habeas Corpus Act of 1689. Habeas corpus had provided 'a fundamental guarantee of individual freedom against arbitrary state interference' in English Law, and yet, as the Green Paper readily acknowledged, it was 'unknown in Scots law' (Ministry of Justice, 2009a: 35).

In relation to rights pertaining to social justice and the welfare state, the Green Paper claimed that a Bill of Rights and Responsibilities would be able to recognise and accommodate, for example, 'the distinctive ways in which healthcare is provided in different parts of the UK' (Ministry of Justice, 2009a: 44). After all, the National Health Service (NHS) was 'the largest health service in the world and a potent embodiment of values that this country holds dear' (Ministry of Justice, 2009a: 44). However, this was to seriously underestimate the degree to which devolution had led to a very different set of values (e.g. choice, competition, personalisation) informing reform of health, education and other public services in England, when these values had been explicitly rejected in the reforms implemented by the devolved administrations in the other parts of the United Kingdom.[5] Indeed, the Green Paper itself repeatedly drew upon examples of policy initiatives which applied to England alone. This was particularly notable in relation to the NHS Constitution for England which had set out 'the enduring values and principles of the NHS in England' (Ministry of Justice, 2009a: 45). In the face of what the Green Paper dramatically described as 'a new age of anxiety and uncertainty' (Ministry of Justice, 2009a: 13), it was unlikely that people would be bound together more closely by their daily experience of welfare rights and responsibilities. The onset of recession, mass unemployment and planned cuts of 0.1% in real terms in public spending from April 2011 until March 2014 would more likely make them even more sensitive to the postcode lottery in service provision and the iniquities of the Barnett Formula.

Building Britain's future, ignoring England's present

Gordon Brown paid a considerable political price for the consequences of the transition from economic boom to bust, and the public anger over the scandal of MPs' parliamentary expenses. A series of embarrassing by-election defeats, and disastrous English local council and European Parliament election results, accompanied opinion poll trends showing the Conservative Party to be enjoying a lead sufficient to give David Cameron a comfortable Westminster majority at the next general election. In *Building Britain's Future*, in which his government set out its final legislative programme for this parliament, and its prospectus for a fourth term Labour government, Gordon Brown made one final attempt to restore the Labour Party's and his own political fortunes.

For Brown, England remained the nation and focal point for political identity whose name he dare not speak. Thus, in his Foreword to *Building Britain's Future*, Brown referred to 'Britain' or 'British' on no fewer than twenty-one occasions in less than two and a half pages. He also mentioned Scotland, Wales and Northern Ireland. However, not for the first time in a major policy statement from the Brown government, mention of England was conspicuous by its absence. When referring to the government's 'next generation' of public service reform, Brown could not bring himself to acknowledge such reforms would apply to England alone. Instead, as when noting his government's plans for 'devolving and decentralising power even further', Brown chose to use the term 'our country' rather than resorting to the dreaded 'E' word (Brown, 2009: 8–9). This obfuscation was despite his government's stated intent to rebuild trust through 'a radical programme of further democratic and constitutional reform' which would enshrine the principles of openness and transparency (HM Government, 2009: 13).

Brown's reticence to acknowledge the specifically English aspects of his government's programme was reflected throughout the document. For example, in relation to the promise to commence 'a radical programme of further democratic and constitutional reform', the government contended that 'The challenges that communities face cannot be tackled by a one-size-fits-all approach to governance. Greater devolution from central government is necessary' (HM government, 2009: 13–14). Therefore, stronger and clearer powers would be offered to local and city-regional government. No mention was made that 'This new era of devolution and local accountability' would apply to England alone (HM Government, 2009: 14).

The same criticism, however, could be applied to the government's commitment to building new homes, local Sure Start Children's Centres, its Planning Act 2008, the NHS Constitution, Trust and Academy Schools, low-carbon eco-towns, Comprehensive Area Assessments for local services, its Local Democracy, Economic Development and Construction Bill, universal access to activities at school from 8 a.m. to 6 p.m. and, above all, its proposals for building 'the next generation of public services', including a guarantee to parents of access to 'an education that is individually tailored for their child' (HM Government, 2009: 17, 61). None of these commitments had appeared in the 2005 Labour Party general election manifesto. Despite the promise of transparency and openness, and the commitment to 'delivering personalised services, establishing rights to minimum levels of entitlement and giving people new ways to shape their local services', there was no departure from the British narrative (HM Government, 2009: 17–18). Although the government claimed 'Across the country the next generation of public services will be central to Britain's future', at no point did the unbroken British narrative make the reader aware that such reforms applied to England alone. Only a single footnote acknowledged 'While much of the work set out here applies across the UK, aspects of public services are devolved in Northern Ireland, Scotland and Wales' (HM Government, 2009: 125). These 'aspects' included determining a policy agenda, based upon a set of values markedly different from that applicable to the personalisation of public services in England.

The Brown government continued to offer nothing to address any of the various English questions identified by select committee reports, even though it conceded 'it is clear that the democratic deficit in Britain is deeper and wider than the expenses scandal' (HM Government, 2009: 27). Indeed, it was symptomatic of Brown's approach to the governance of England that his idea of rebuilding trust and democratic renewal was to establish and chair a Democratic Renewal Council (DRC) to 'ensure a sustained focus at a senior ministerial level on the task of democratic and constitutional renewal'(HM Government, 2009: 29). It was hard to envisage how such a top-down, centralised institution could be reconciled with the guiding principle of 'the redistribution of power from the hands of the few, to the hands of the many' that his government claimed to espouse (HM Government, 2009: 30).

In terms of devolution, the Brown government noted that in England it had created Regional Development Agencies (RDAs), devolved powers to local council and to cities and sub-regions, and introduced and extended the powers of the directly elected mayor of London. It also claimed to be making 'steady progress on a bottom-up approach, culminating in the Budget announcement of two City-Regions in Greater Manchester and Leeds'. By the same token, there was 'improved scrutiny and accountability in regions through the intro-duction of both Regional Ministers and Regional Select Committees; through the establishment of Leaders' Boards representing local government interests at regional level; and through a new responsibil-ity for RDAs to develop strategies in partnership with local authori-ties' (HM Government, 2009: 32). The common denominator of all of these reforms was that none had been mentioned in the Labour Party's 2005 general election manifesto. They were also not 'bottom-up' in the sense that there had been any popular demand for the creation of such institutions. Only in an overly centralised polity like England could a government boast of having reduced 'the number of targets for local authorities from over 1000 performance indicators to just 35 agree priorities for each area' (HM Government, 2009: 63). Indeed, only a centralised state could have imposed more than a thousand performance indicators upon a single nation in the first place.

Conclusion: Brown's legacy for England and Englishness

During his tenure both as Chancellor of the Exchequer and Prime Minister, Gordon Brown shied away from any possibility of a new politics of democracy and participation for the citizens of England. Indeed, as this chapter has sought to demonstrate, Brown's statecraft and political rhetoric need to be understood as part of a wider strategy that led to the negation of England as a political community. The Brown government claimed: 'Our radical drive toward devolution in the last 10 years means that power is already more dispersed than at any time in our nation's modern history' (HM Government, 2009: 31). Successive parliamentary select committee reports identified a very different political and constitutional legacy.

One such report concluded: 'there needs to be substantial change in the balance of power between central and local government. The power to govern in England remains too heavily centralised to be efficient or effective. Put simply, the balance of power between central and local government in England is currently in need of a tilt towards localities' (HCCLGC, 2009: 60). Another select committee report discounted the impact of devolution elsewhere in the United

Kingdom, noting 'no such change has taken place in the way England is governed' (HCJC, 2009: 50). However, the same report also acknowledged: 'The governance of England is seen by many as the "unfinished business" of devolution, but this perception is not accompanied by any widespread agreement on what should be done' (HCJC, 2009: 50).

In the absence of a stronger English political consciousness, leading academic commentators have continued to discount the possibility that the negation of England as a political identity might lead to demands for constitutional reform. Bogdanor has claimed 'none of the three responses to the West Lothian Question – an English Parliament, "English votes for English laws' and English regional assemblies – can provide a satisfactory answer. For the time being, therefore, the West Lothian Question will have to remain unanswered' (Bogdanor, 2009: 105). This need not matter. Bogdanor's thesis is that critics of Britishness 'have underestimated the deep organic ties that hold the country together', and, in the absence of an English backlash against devolution, 'The English have adjusted to the new status quo, but are uninterested in further constitutional change' (Bogdanor, 2009: 106). In a similar vein, Hazell has concluded: 'The English Question does not have to be answered. It is not an examination question which the English are required to answer. It can remain unresolved for as long as the English want. Ultimately only the English can decide if they want to seek an answer to the English Question' (Hazell, 2006: 240).

For English voters who found themselves angered by Gordon Brown's negation of England, the simplest and most immediate remedy was to use their vote in the May 2010 General Election to bring to an end Brown's British Way. In the event, the Brown government secured only a 28% share of the vote and 286 MPs or 36% of the seats in England, compared to the Conservative / Liberal Democrat coalition's 64% share of the votes and 341 MPs or 64% of the seats in England (Lee, 2010). However, this simply ushered in David Cameron and Nick Clegg's fifth-generation British modernisation project. In its genesis, this programme for government equally had demonstrated little interest in giving greater political identity to England and Englishness (Lee, 2009b).

Notes

1 Earlier and lengthier versions of the ideas developed in this chapter are available in Lee (2007; 2009a).
2 For a more detailed analysis of constrained discretion, and impact upon public services in England, see Lee (2007: 103–31).
3 William Hague was later to put forward his own vision of 'the British Way'. Hague identified its four characteristics as individualism, expressed through 'a nation of individuals and small, close-knit families'; a spirit of enterprise; an open and mobile society; and a loyalty to local institutions, expressed through 'the little platoons' of voluntary associations and charities (Hague, 1999).
5 One of Gordon Brown earliest acts as Prime Minister was to abolish the English regional assemblies, the institutions composed of local councillors which had the sole claim, among the structures of English regional governance, to any form of democratic representation (albeit indirect) of the people of England.
6 For an analysis of the reform of public services in England, see Lee (2009a: 102–33).

8

The Englishness of Westminster

Philip Norton

The United Kingdom has exhibited a parliamentary system of government, but one premised essentially on English political dominance and English constitutional norms. As England has joined with other nations to create a United Kingdom with one parliament, that parliament has inherited and maintained the constitutional status and norms of the predecessor English Parliament.

The relationship of the UK Parliament to the component parts of the Union has been determined largely by constitutional and political considerations. In constitutional terms, the UK has been united under one Crown and parliament, the Queen-in-Parliament enjoying legal supremacy. The doctrine of parliamentary sovereignty was asserted before the Glorious Revolution, but it was the events of 1688–89 that were to confirm it. If the Crown was bound by the will of parliament, then so too were the Crown's courts. The Further Act for the Union with Scotland (1707) declared that, the union of two kingdoms having been achieved, the whole island 'is thereby subject to One Sovereignty and represented by One Parliament' (Costin & Watson, 1961: 110). Within parliament, members have been drawn from territorial constituencies and, as members, have enjoyed the same rights.

Politically, the nation has, for much of the past century, been dominated by two British political parties, each necessarily drawing its principal strength from the dominant element of the kingdom – that is, England – and the procedures of the House of Commons have largely reflected this reality. The parties have competed with one another in parliamentary elections, with one usually achieving a majority in the House of Commons and able to enact policy that applies throughout the United Kingdom. Parliamentary procedure has largely been premised on the axiom that the government is entitled to get its business but the opposition is entitled to be heard. There has been what has been termed the 'equilibrium of legitimacy' (Norton, 2001: 13–33) within the House. That, and the prospect of the parties alternating in office, has underpinned the stability of the parliamentary process and that stability has long been an aspect of English political self-understanding.

Though there have been tensions in the system, these have not undermined – or rather have not been allowed to undermine – the doctrine of parliamentary supremacy or the workings of the parliamentary system. English hegemony has ensured that the system has been maintained and protected. However, the growth of nationalist parties and the devolving of powers to elected bodies in Scotland, Wales and Northern Ireland has challenged both the dominance of English parties and those norms underpinning parliamentary procedure. Tensions have come to the fore, have challenged traditional English norms, and have not been resolved.

An English system

A Parliament of Great Britain was created in 1707 from the parliaments of England and Scotland. The two parliaments demised and were succeeded by a new entity. Article III of the Act for the Union with Scotland 1707 provided 'That the United Kingdom of Great Britain be represented by One and the Same Parliament to be stiled The Parliament of Great Britain'. There has been a difference of views as to whether the new parliament was legislatively supreme or constrained by the Treaty of Union.

The orthodox, or *English*, view is that with the Union of the two countries, the two parliaments extinguished themselves with their powers being acquired by the new Parliament, 'and it is assumed that the Parliament of Great Britain inherited and developed the characteristics of the English Parliament, including sovereignty' (Hood Phillips & Jackson, 1978: 68). This view is exemplified by A.V. Dicey in 1885, in his classic work on the constitution, in which he asserted that parliament 'has, under the English constitution, the right to make or unmake any law whatever; and, further, that no person or body is recognised by the law of England as having a right to override or set aside the legislation of Parliament' (1885; 1959: 39–40). The doctrine, as we have seen, was intimated by the Glorious Revolution, in other words *prior* to the Act of Union. It is equally noteworthy that Walter Bagehot's classic work on the constitution, first published in 1867, was titled *The English Constitution*. 'The English Constitution', declared Bagehot, 'is framed on the principle of choosing a single sovereign authority, and making it good' (1867; 1963: 220).

Scottish jurists have not necessarily accepted this English view of parliamentary supremacy. In *MacCormick v Lord Advocate* in 1953, Lord President Cooper in his *obiter dictum* declared

> The principle of the unlimited sovereignty of Parliament is a distinctively English principle which has no counterpart in Scottish constitutional law ... I have difficulty seeing why it should have been supposed that the new Parliament of Great Britain must inherit all the peculiar characteristics of the English Parliament but none of the Scottish Parliament, as if all that happened in 1707 was that Scottish representatives were admitted to the Parliament of England. (Hood Phillips & Jackson, 1978: 69)

However, it was the English principle that prevailed. It may have been a new parliament, but it was largely indistinguishable from the preceding English Parliament. As Bradley and Ewing recorded, 'after the Union the Westminster Parliament continued to conduct its affairs exactly as before, subject only to its enlargement by members from Scotland' (2007: 75–6). It was difficult to see how it could in practical terms be anything different, certainly in terms of the basic constitutional principle. If the Act of Union was to form a higher constitutional law, what was to happen if it was infringed? Who but parliament could alter the Act of 1707? Arguably, the Treaty of Union was spent once Scotland and England ceased to exist as independent countries.

Similarly, Union with Ireland had basically the same consequences as the Act of Union with Scotland. The Act for the Union with Ireland (1800) merged the two kingdoms and under the third article provided that the United Kingdom 'be represented in one and the same Parliament, to be stiled *The Parliament of the United Kingdom of Great Britain and Ireland*' (Costin & Watson, 1961: 21). Again, the principal change was the addition of members to the House of Commons, this time representing Irish seats.

The merging of the parliaments, creating an enlarged parliament but one premised on English constitutionalism and the norms of the English parliamentary practice, proved more successful in respect of Scotland than it did in respect of Ireland. According to McLean and McMillan, the treaty commitments to Scotland were largely honoured, whereas those made to Ireland were not (2010: 47–85). Though the union was not popular in Scotland, the treaty nonetheless embodied concessions that appeared sufficient for Scotland to become part of a union. 'The Union made the Empire possible. It seemed to swallow Scottish politics up into English politics to make British politics' (McLean & McMillan, 2010: 75). Though McLean and McMillan argue that it never actually did that, English parties in the nineteenth century did become primarily British parties, but British parties had difficulty in becoming dominant UK parties. Tensions within Ireland, and the failure to deliver Catholic emancipation, militated against Ireland being absorbed into a stable United Kingdom parliamentary system of government.

Irish nationalism was a significant force and Irish Nationalist MPs were returned to Westminster. Demands for home rule or independence for Ireland were a feature of the nineteenth century and created two problems for parliament at Westminster. The first arose from the existence of a UK Parliament. So long as Irish Nationalist MPs were elected to Westminster, how was their failure to accept the norms of Westminster to be dealt with? Towards the end of the century, Irish Nationalist Members sought to obstruct parliamentary proceedings. The second arose in the context of attempts to meet the demands made for home rule. If home rule was to be conceded, how was Westminster going to cope with the existence of two parliaments – a sovereign parliament at Westminster and a devolved legislature in Ireland? The problems were to be resolved in favour of existing English norms, either by adaptation or by studied ambiguity.

In 1881, Irish nationalist MPs led by Charles Parnell sough to obstruct parliamentary proceedings. Debate on the motion for leave to bring in a Protection of Person and Property (Ireland) Bill lasted several days. As Josef Redlich was to observe, Parnell 'overlooked the fact that the Government, and both English parties, must now in self-defence break the power of obstruction' (1908: 154). That is what they did. The Speaker took it upon himself to bring obstruction to an end and the rules of procedure were then changed in order to protect what were seen as the basic principles underpinning parliamentary government – 'British parliamentary government' as Redlich (1908: 155) put it.

Attempts to provide for Home Rule generated another major question. How was parliament to adapt to the existence of a body that could pass laws for Ireland while MPs from Irish constituencies were also returned to the Westminster Parliament? Various solutions were pursued. One was to exclude Irish members from the Westminster Parliament. Another was to prevent Irish MPs from voting on anything other than UK-wide legislation. A third was to reduce the number of seats in Ireland. The alternative was to permit Irish MPs to vote on the same basis as other MPs, thus maintaining the convention that all Members, as Members, were equal. There was a principled case for the *status quo* as well as it constituting the obvious default option. A variant on the second option was later to be suggested by the

Speaker's Conference on Devolution in 1919, which proposed Grand Councils comprising MPs from England, Scotland and Wales considering Bills that affected their particular part of the United Kingdom.

The Home Rule Bill in 1886 went for the most radical option: that is, excluding Irish MPs from Westminster. Prime Minister William Gladstone told the House of Commons, 'That Irish Members and Irish Peers cannot, if a domestic Legislature be given to Ireland, justly retain a seat in the Parliament at Westminster' (8 April 1886; in Costin & Watson, 1961: 200). As John Morley argued, removing the Irish MPs would also relieve parliament of a particular burden, 'who weakened our policy, upset ministries, and rejected Bills for reasons which British opinion could not recognise as patriotic in any English sense' (in O'Donnell, 1910: 207). There was the obvious objection that this was not appropriate in the context of home rule – as opposed to independence – in that Westminster would still be taking decisions for the whole of the kingdom, including Ireland, not least on issues of taxation. The Bill failed in the Commons. The exclusion of Irish members, according to Joseph Chamberlain, was 'not a technical point, but the symbol and flag of the controversy' (in Bogdanor, 1999: 29).

The Government of Ireland Bill introduced in 1893 pursued the second and third options: it provided for a reduction in the number of Irish MPs (to eighty) who would vote only on 'imperial' legislation, though they were not excluded from voting on votes of confidence. The problems inherent in this proposal were apparent at the time. As one Irish MP observed, 'Thus a ministry, though possessing a normal majority of fifty or sixty votes on questions of British interest, might be summarily overthrown by a division on some question relating to Ireland which would authorise the eighty Irish representatives to cast their votes for the opposition. The Bill was popularly named the In-and-Out Bill, in consequence of this delightful provision' (O'Donnell, 1910: 335–6). The Bill ran into opposition from Liberal Unionists as well as Conservatives and in committee in the Commons the 'in-and-out' provision was removed (see Shannon, 1999: 541). The Bill failed in the House of Lords.

The provision to reduce the number of MPs was also included in the Home Rule Bill introduced in 1912 and enacted in 1914 under the provisions of the Parliament Act. However, the Act was accompanied by another suspending its implementation because of the outbreak of the First World War and was never put into effect. The issue of the numbers to be returned to Westminster was, in any event, overshadowed by the Irish uprising and Unionist determination to preserve Ulster as part of the United Kingdom.

The provision to reduce the number of MPs returned from Ireland also featured in the Government of Ireland Act 1920, which provided for parliaments in Southern and Northern Ireland, but in the event with only the provisions relating to Northern Ireland, which remained part of the United Kingdom, taking effect. A Northern Ireland Parliament came into existence in 1922. Instead of the seventeen seats to which its population would otherwise entitle it, it had thirteen seats, later reduced to twelve with the loss of a University seat under the Representation of the People Act 1948.

The implementation of the 1920 Act as it affected Northern Ireland thus finally created the anomaly that had been debated and fought over in the earlier Home Rule Bills. The UK had two parliaments, a sovereign parliament at Westminster and a devolved parliament in Northern Ireland (Stormont). Matters relating to the province were left to the Stormont Parliament. However, with the exception of one short period, this did not generate controversy or prompt challenges that MPs returned from Northern Ireland constituencies were voting on matters affecting the rest of the UK whereas other MPs could not vote on issues affecting only Northern Ireland. The exception was the period of Labour government from 1964 to 1966, when Labour had a minuscule parliamentary majority and was keen to ensure the passage of its legislation to nationalise the steel industry. Prime Minister Harold Wilson put the point succinctly in the House of Commons:

> I am sure the House will agree that there is an apparent lack of logic, for example about steel, when Northern Ireland members can, and presumably will, swell the Tory ranks tonight, when we have no power to vote on questions about steel in Northern Ireland because of the fact that the Stormont Parliament has concurrent jurisdiction in these matters. (in Bogdanor, 1999: 70–1)

For the Conservatives, Shadow Home Secretary Peter Thorneycroft argued that 'every Member of the House of Commons is equal with every other Member of the House of Commons, and that all of us will speak on all subjects' (House of Commons Debates, 26 October 1965).

Wilson asked the Attorney General, Sir Elwyn Jones, to devise an 'in-and-out' solution, but Jones concluded that it was too complex. In any event, the issue lost its prominence when Labour was returned to office with a large majority in the 1966 general election. The issue of the status of Northern Ireland MPs receded into obscurity.

Why was the anomaly inherent in the representation of Northern Ireland at Westminster not more prominent during the fifty-year existence of the Stormont Parliament? There are three explanations. The first was the fact that, other than the parliament of 1964–66, a government usually had a reasonable parliamentary majority, which meant that the votes of Ulster Unionists would not make a difference to the outcome of votes. The second was unwillingness on the part of government and parliament to take an interest in what was happening within the province. A dominant feature of the period, as Bridget Hadfield noted, was 'a desire for non-involvement on the part of Westminster in "internal" Northern Ireland affairs' (1992: 4). The third was the small number and activity of MPs returned from Northern Ireland. Given that there was a parliament at Stormont, the number of MPs returned to Westminster was, as we have noted, smaller than would be justified by its population. Most were Ulster Unionists who formed part of the parliamentary Conservative Party. They had a low profile at Westminster. They tended not to have long parliamentary careers, had a poor attendance record, and rarely achieved prominence: the more talented politicians operated in Stormont (Norton, 1996a: 130). The result was an era of 'dual politics' (see Bulpitt, 1983: 134–63). Westminster and Stormont operated largely independent of one another. The era of dual politics came to an end in the 1960s and in 1972 the Stormont Parliament was suspended, and later abolished. Direct rule meant that the equality of members at Westminster was restored. Procedures were devised to deal with orders specific to Northern Ireland. Otherwise, the change made little difference in practice to what happened in the House of Commons. Moreover, devolution in Northern Ireland was understood as the exception which confirmed the British rule. 'Real politics', as opposed to Northern Ireland's sectarian version, meant the continuation of politics according to the Westminster model as the residual Irish problem was quarantined.

In contrast, recent constitutional changes cannot be so easily quarantined. The rise of nationalist parties and the devolution of powers to elected bodies in the different parts of the United Kingdom have affected what happens in parliament. Those essentially English norms underpinning the parliamentary system have been challenged, generating instability and uncertainty. The system is challenged both in respect of what happens in the House of Commons and in the relationship between Westminster and the devolved assemblies. What we are witnessing is a reversion to some of the issues and debates of the nineteenth and early twentieth centuries.

Within parliament

The challenges within the House of Commons are essentially twofold. One is adapting to the existence of parties drawn exclusively from specific parts of the United Kingdom, essentially an administrative problem. The other is coping with what amounts to a two-tier membership, a more intractable political problem which affects England directly. What was generally ignored during the Stormont period could no longer be ignored given the sheer number, and influence, of the MPs returned from Scotland and Wales.

Accommodating third parties

England has been used primarily to two-party conflict. The nature of the parties involved has changed – Labour replacing the Liberal party as the main challenger to the Conservatives – but the fundamentals of what Giovanni Sartori termed 'two-partism' (1976: 185) have characterised the English system and, for much of the twentieth century, extended to the rest of Great Britain. The procedures of the House of Commons have largely been premised on the existence of two parties, one forming the government and the other the opposition. 'Third parties are for all intents and purposes an embarrassment. They do not fit in with the normal adversary relationship between the two largest parties and the organisation and behaviour with which it is associated' (Norton, 1983: 143).

In the immediate post-war decades, there was not a problem. Two parties dominated the House of Commons. Between 1951 and 1966, the Conservative and Labour parties accounted for over 98 per cent of the membership. Not until 1966 was the number of Liberal MPs elected to reach double figures. The return of some nationalist MPs in the 1960s and, more especially, the 1970s, coupled with the split between the Conservative parliamentary party and the Ulster Unionists – and the divide in the 1970s between the Ulster Unionist (UU) party and the Democratic Unionist Party (DUP) – increased notably the number of parties in the House. Northern Ireland also began to see members of the Social Democratic and Labour Party (SDLP) and, later, Sinn Fein (SF) elected. The two main parties continued to dominate the House, but the number of parties achieving parliamentary representation at a general election sometimes reached double figures, courtesy of the Northern Ireland parties (though Sinn Fein members declined to take their seats). In the 2005 general elections, ten parties had candidates elected to the House, six of them (Scottish National, Plaid Cymru, Ulster Unionist, Democratic

Unionist, Sinn Fein, and SDLP) operating exclusively in a particular part of the United Kingdom. With the exception of Sinn Fein and the lone Ulster Unionist, each had some organisation, with the SNP and PC holding a weekly joint meeting.

The principal problem arising from their existence is not primarily that they challenge the rules and norms of the House, though on occasion they have proved willing to test them. Sinn Fein MPs have challenged the legitimacy of the House by refusing to take their seats. Scottish National MP Alex Salmond on occasion proved disruptive, not least during the budget speech of the Chancellor of the Exchequer, Nigel Lawson, in 1988 (see Lawson, 1992: 816). (He was suspended for five days.) However, the principal problem has been a practical one for the House, not least the Speaker.

Incorporating third parties into proceedings has been problematic. As Robert Rogers and Rhodri Walters – both senior parliamentary clerks – recorded in the latest edition of *How Parliament Works*, problems remain for small parties – 'business is arranged principally between the two major parties' (2006: 110). Only in recent years have the Liberal Democrats attempted to emulate the official opposition and designate spokespersons as Shadow Secretaries of State. Deciding when to call members of third parties to speak, especially members of nationalist parties, has been an issue for the chair, and the member-ship of select committees has been an issue for the House. The chair has sought to ensure that third parties get heard, but the occasions they can be called are limited by their numbers. As a result, the chair may recognise one nationalist, in effect as the voice of all nationalists, rather than calling a Scottish Nationalist MP *and* a Plaid Cymru Member.

Under the rules for calculating membership of the select commit-tees – designed to replicate party strength in the chamber – individual nationalist parties have not qualified for membership. Instead, third parties have tended to be grouped together and a third-party member appointed. There has also been a specific problem in respect of the Select Committee on Northern Ireland, given that no Labour or Conservative MPs are returned from the province. The principal select committees covering government departments were established in 1979, followed shortly by select committees covering Scotland and Wales. A Northern Ireland Select Committee was not established until 1994 (see Wilford & Elliott, 1999: 23–42). The committee was appointed with thirteen members, larger than most other departmen-tal select committees, in order that it could comprise MPs from the province, along with members from the government and opposition parties. In the 2005–10 parliament, there were seven Labour Members, two Conservative Members, two Democratic Unionist Members, one Ulster Unionist Member, and one Social Democratic and Labour Member.

The standing orders of the House of Commons also prescribe twenty opposition days for debate each parliamentary session. Of these, the subject for debate is to be determined on seventeen of them by the leader of the opposition and the remaining three by the leader of the second largest opposition party in the House (until 2010 the Liberal Democrats). This again tends to leave out all other parties. The parliamentary authorities have sought to adapt by finding an additional day for use by third parties. In the 2008–09 session, for example, an un-allotted half-day was given to the Scottish National Party (SNP) and Plaid Cymru (PC) for a debate on the topic of the dissolution of parliament and another un-allotted half-day given to the Democratic Unionist Party (DUP) for a debate on parading in Northern Ireland.

The West Lothian question

However, the main problem has arisen as a result of devolution. The core problem that was debated in the home rule debates in the nineteenth century, and surfaced briefly in the 1964–66 parliament, has now returned to become an issue on the political agenda. It has been encapsulated in the term 'the West Lothian question', coined by Ulster Unionist MP Enoch Powell and named after the constituency of the then MP for West Lothian, Tam Dalyell, who raised it. The term was novel but the substance of the issue well established in parliamentary discourse. What has been witnessed since the 1970s, with debate on and implementation of devolution, has been precisely the same questions debated by Gladstone and other parliamentarians in the Victorian era.

Dalyell posed the question, essentially echoing Wilson's comments of 1965, during Second Reading of the Scotland Bill in 1977:

> For how long will English constituencies and English honourable Members tolerate … at least 119 Honourable Members from Scotland, Wales and Northern Ireland exercising an important and probably often decisive, effect on English politics while they themselves have no say in the same matters in Scotland, Wales and Northern Ireland? (House of Commons Debates, 14 November 1977, cols 122–3)

He argued that the measure did not provide the remotest chance of a lasting settlement between Scotland and England and if it was passed they would be on 'a motorway without exit roads to a separate Scottish state'. He was one of eleven Labour MPs to vote against the Bill (Norton, 1980: 274–6). Whereas Irish home rule in the nineteenth century had been scuppered by Liberal Unionists, a number of Labour unionists sought to scupper Scottish – and Welsh (Norton, 1980: 277–8) – home rule in the twentieth. Initially, they succeeded.

The solutions to the conundrum posed by Dalyell were the same as those advanced in the nineteenth century (Harding et al., 2008: 73–89; Scottish Affairs Committee, 2006: paragraph 50). The main options advanced were those of a reduction in a number of MPs returned from the devolved parts of the UK and some form of 'in-and-out' provision. The stance taken by the political parties was the reverse of that taken in 1965. Labour now adhered to the principle of the equality of membership and the Conservatives favoured some form of 'in-and-out' provision.

When the Scotland Bill was before the House of Lords, Conservative peer Earl Ferrers achieved the inclusion of a clause covering Bills that did not affect Scotland. If the votes of MPs representing Scottish constituencies made the difference to the outcome of the vote on the Third Reading of such a Bill – that is, it would have been defeated had it not been for the votes of these Members – then the Bill would not be deemed to have been read a third time unless the House confirmed its decision after fourteen days. The clause was initially rejected in the Commons (on the casting vote of the Speaker) (Norton, 1980: 364–5), put back in by the Lords (though replacing Third Reading with Second Reading) and then – courtesy of dissenting votes cast by five Labour MPs – accepted by the Commons by a majority of one (Norton, 1980: 373–4). The provision became section 66 of the Scotland Act 1978. However, it never took effect as the Commons also agreed the provision, moved by Labour MP George Cunningham, to provide for a threshold in referendums in Scotland and Wales of 40% of eligible voters voting yes. The yes vote in Scotland in 1979 just fell short of the threshold, while voters in Wales decisively voted no.

Two decades later, the Labour government under Tony Blair did achieve passage of devolution legislation. Secure in its parliamentary majority, the government was able to ensure that the devolution Acts embodied its preferred model. There was to be no 'in-and-out' provision, partial or otherwise, but there was acceptance of the case for a reduction in the number of Scottish seats in the House of Commons. Initially, Scottish representation at Westminster was less than its population justified, but this changed in the early twentieth century. Following the disappearance of most Irish seats, Scotland become marginally over-represented, and this over-representation became more marked following the Speaker's Conference of 1944 and the creation of a permanent Boundary Commission. The over-representation of Scotland and Wales became, in effect, institutionalised and, according to Iain McLean, gave rise to the belief that the Union *guaranteed* Scottish over-representation (1995: 250–68). The over-representation was more by accident than design and the case for the over-representation was difficult to sustain in the face of Scotland having its own parliament. As a result, the Scotland Act 1998 provided that Rule 1(2) of the Rules for the Redistribution of Seats – which guaranteed that the number of Scottish seats at Westminster would be at least 71 – was no longer to apply and that the electoral quota for Scotland (the number of seats divided by the total electorate) was to be the same as that for England. The effect of this was to considerably reduce the number of Scottish seats, from 72 to 59, and the change took effect at the 2005 general election.

The reduction failed to still demands for further change. There were three principal reasons for this. The first was that the reduction in the number of seats simply cancelled out the over-representation of Scotland at Westminster. It brought it into line with England, which had no parliament of its own. It did not follow the logic applied to Stormont between 1922 and 1972, namely that the number of seats from the province should be less than its population justified, in other words that there should be an under-representation – not an equal representation – relative to those parts of the UK that did not have parliaments of their own. After Stormont was abolished, Unionist MPs were effective in persuading the Labour government of James Callaghan to increase the number of Northern Ireland seats at Westminster to bring it into line with what its population size justified (Callaghan, 1987: 454–5). To follow the Stormont precedent, Scotland would have fewer than 59 seats at Westminster.

The second reason, though attracting relatively little attention, is the fact that Wales and Northern Ireland remain over-represented at Westminster. Wales has not been subject to any reduction in the number of seats at Westminster. The justification for this – that devolution to Wales in 1998 was administrative but not legislative – was undermined by the enactment of the Government of Wales Act 2006, providing for the gradual transfer of powers to the National Assembly for Wales. Following the creation of a Northern Ireland Assembly, there has been no attempt by government to revert to the reduced representation that existed during the previous Stormont era. If seats from Scotland, Wales and Northern Ireland were to be reduced in line with the Stormont model, the Constitution Unit has estimated that Scotland would have 40 MPs, Wales 22 and Northern Ireland 12. 'This', it noted, 'is politically explosive, and might be a gift to nationalist parties in all three parts of the country' (Constitution Unit, 2010: 36). In short, it could be protrayed as the anglicisation of the House of Commons.

The third and most fundamental problem remains the failure to answer the West Lothian question. As Gladstone and others discovered, it is a question that is largely unanswerable. When he was Lord Chancellor, Lord Irvine of Lairg is reported to have said that the best way to deal with the West Lothian question is not to ask it (in *The Economist*, 8 July 2006: 36). However, so long as it has been asked, there are only two logical answers to it. One is to revert to the pre-devolution era, with no devolved assemblies, thus ensuring equity of representation in the House of Commons. This is not seen as a politically viable option. The other, as Vernon Bogdanor observed, is to 'implement legislative devolution all round, so becoming a thorough-going federal state', which is not politically viable either: 'there is no demand for legislative federalism in England' (1999: 228). It is also not clear that it would be practical, even if politically acceptable. In a federal UK, England – with more than 80 per cent of the population and of the wealth – would remain dominant. The alternative would be to break up England into regions with a form of home rule akin to that of Scotland, but in a context where in some parts of England there would be no clearly accepted boundaries or affinity with that area. Moreover, there is no demand for regionalism in England either.

The compromise solution, as in the nineteenth century, is some form of in-and-out option, though critics contest the claim that it would be a solution, arguing instead that it would become part of the problem, making it difficult if not impossible for a Labour government, dependent on seats from Scotland, to govern. The in-and-out option has been advanced in different forms and by different bodies, including the Commission to Strengthen Parliament, established by Conservative leader William Hague (Commission to Strengthen Parliament, 2000: 52–4), by former Scottish Secretary and Foreign Secretary, Malcolm Rifkind (BBC News Online, 28 October 2007) and by the Conservative Party's Democracy Task Force (2008).

Conservative party leader David Cameron has embraced the principle of English votes for English measures. The proposals have essentially taken two forms. One has been to exclude MPs representing Scottish seats from voting on any issue that is certified by the Speaker as applying exclusively to England or to England and Wales. The other, designed to maintain the principle of equality of membership, is that forwarded by the Democracy Task Force, namely to permit all MPs to vote on the Second and Third Readings of all Bills, but to refer Bills dealing solely with England to committees comprising English MPs; the House thus determines the principle of the measure but MPs from English seats have to agree the detail. 'In this respect the Task Force sought to modify previous party policy, and to address the criticism that full strength English votes on English laws would be unworkable' (Constitution Unit, 2010: 37).

The problem with the in-and-out option remains the one identified in the nineteenth century. Applied in the contemporary context, it would limit especially a Labour government. The Conservative Party is now essentially the party of England. For electoral success, the Labour Party relies normally on success in Scotland to deliver a parliamentary majority. An in-and-out option would thus have the potential to create a Labour government for UK issues but a Conservative majority for English issues, which would make coherent government almost impossible and threaten the integrity of the UK. The issue, of course, would be less significant in the case of a Conservative Government but also irrelevant.

It would also create two tiers of MPs, destroying the constitutional convention that all MPs are equal. Though in practice devolution has created two types of MP – those from the devolved party of the UK having fewer responsibilities, given that matters previously within their constituency remit have passed to MSPs – MPs remain equal in terms of their position within the House: one MP's vote is as good as another's. An in-and-out solution would rid them of that equality.

The in-and-out option may also be impractical, not least because of the problems attached to identifying measures that affect exclusively England or England and Wales (since most will have some conse-quences for the rest of the UK) (see Hadfield, 2005: 286–305) but the issue it addresses remains highly salient in England. Devolution was designed to address a sense of political alienation in Scotland and Wales, but its implementation has only served to generate political resentment in England. Surveys have tapped the degree of resentment. The Hansard Society's *Audit of Political Engagement 5* found that on a range of constitutional issues, the highest level of dissatisfaction was with Scottish MPs being able to vote on English issues in the House of Commons and with how political parties are funded (2008: 28). The West Lothian question has in consequence undergone a change of name: it is now referred to as the *English* question. Polls show not only that a majority of those in England believe that Scottish MPs should not be allowed to vote on English laws, but also that a majority of Scots support limiting the rights of Scottish MPs to vote on English issues (Harding et al., 2008: 78).

In constitutional terms, the House of Commons is thus between a rock and a hard place in seeking to address the English question. The status quo is unpopular in England, and especially with the dominant party of England, the Conservative Party, but the proffered solutions generate significant problems of their own, challenging the basis on which an English-constructed parliament has been traditionally built. The point was well put by the then young Welsh MP, Neil Kinnock, in opposing Welsh devolution in 1977 when he said his feelings were summed up in the words of Bevin: 'If you open that Pandora's Box, you will find it full of Trojan horses' (15 November 1977; see also Norton, 1980: 278).

Relations with devolved assemblies

The English question is thus new in name but not in content. However, the reality of devolution has created a new problem for Westminster. That is, how to deal with the devolved bodies? Westminster, with its English norms, is used to operating as a single entity for the whole of the United Kingdom. The period of the Stormont Parliament was, as we have seen, marked by studied neglect of what went on in Northern Ireland. Although MPs are precluded from discussing issues that fall within the remit of the Scottish legislature, maintaining a form of 'dual politics' is now not feasible given the extent of devolution to the different parts of the United Kingdom and the fact that what goes on in Westminster still has significant consequences for Scotland, Wales and Northern Ireland. The Scottish Parliament can legislate in areas that are not reserved to Westminster, but the Westminster Parliament can also – and does – legislate in areas that are not reserved. It does so by invitation. The Scottish Parliament can pass a legislative consent motion (previously known as a Sewel motion) that invites the Westminster Parliament to extend to Scotland the provisions of a measure that it is considering. The Northern Ireland Assembly can do likewise. Measures passed by the Westminster Parliament in reserved areas, therefore, can have significant implications for Scotland, Wales and Northern Ireland.

As a result, the issue has arisen of how the different legislatures can communicate and as necessary cooperate with one another. There has been a perception in Scotland and Wales that Westminster has tended to maintain its old (English) ways and neglect the particular needs and views of the different parts of the United Kingdom. The National Assembly for Wales, in particular, had reason to feel particularly aggrieved in that measures passed at Westminster extended to Wales but the National Assembly had no established method of making its views known to Westminster and having them considered during deliberations on a Bill. There have been problems with ensuring coordination between the UK government and the executives of the devolved parts of the UK, but at least there are formal mechanisms in place (Constitution Committee, House of Lords, 2002–03: HL Paper 28). The legislatures have lacked the equivalent mechanisms. Contact between Westminster, Holyrood, Cardiff Bay and Stormont has tended to be very much at the governmental level rather than the legislative. Though legislative consent motions are passed by the Scottish Parliament, the preliminary discussion as to their introduction takes place between the UK and Scottish governments and not between the Westminster and Holyrood Parliaments.

The Westminster Parliament has made efforts to improve relationships, but the problem still remains. One danger is that, by default rather than design, the Scots, Welsh and Northern Irish voters may come to think of Westminster as an exclusively English rather than a UK Parliament. The Constitution Committee of the House of Lords, in its 2003 report on inter-institutional relations in the UK, described the neglect of inter-parliamentary relations as 'regrettable' (paragraph 137). A number of steps were taken to improve communication, including alerting parliament to decisions on legislative consent motions by including them ('tagging') on the Order Paper. However, communication has remained an issue and various bodies have since sought to address what more could be done. The Commission on Scottish Devolution (the Calman Commission), set up by the Scottish Parliament, issued a final report (2009) and among the issues it addressed was co-operation between the UK and Scottish Parliaments. The Commission recommended among other things that there should be detailed communication about legislative consent motions, the inclusion of one or more Scottish MPs on public bill committees where legislative consent motions applied (with the MPs then being invited to meet the relevant Scottish parliament committee), the ending of Westminster's self-denying ordinance in respect of issues devolved to Holyrood (with a regular 'State of Scotland' debate), co-operation between Holyrood and Westminster committees, improved access for members of one parliament to the other, and for ministers from one executive to be willing to appear before a committee of the other parliament.

These recommendations were considered by the Scottish Affairs Committee of the House of Commons which organised a seminar with Scottish MPs and heard from various invited speakers, including Sir Kenneth Calman. The Committee reported in March 2010 and largely endorsed the Calman Commission recommendations (Scottish Affairs Committee, 2010). It was not persuaded of the case for a standing joint liaison committee of the UK and Scottish Parliaments to oversee relations and consider appointing committees – it was wary of the complexities involved – but it did revert to a previous proposal of its own, namely a 'super' Scottish Grand Committee composed of MPs, MSPs and Scottish MEPs that could meet to discuss matters of mutual interest. 'This option would not only be more practical in procedural terms but would also include Scottish MEPs, providing a broader political canvas to debate Scotland's future' (Scottish Affairs Committee, 2010: paragraph 31). Among the Calman proposals it endorsed was enabling improved access arrangements to Westminster for Scottish MSPs and for similar arrangements for Westminster MPs visiting Holyrood.

The need for such consideration reflected the fact that, a decade after devolution, the Westminster Parliament had still not quite adapted fully to the realities of the existence of other legislatures within the United Kingdom. The number of MPs representing seats from Scotland, Wales and Northern Ireland meant that the devolved parts of the United Kingdom could not be ignored, even though for many purposes they could not be discussed. The Scottish Affairs Committee recognised the need for improved co-operation but added 'we would also warn that although the Commission looked at the necessary structures to facilitate this co-operation, it is political will that will drive forward real change' (2010: 3). One can grasp the dilemma. On the one hand, there are those who believe the lack of separate consideration for English matters means that Westminster is not English enough. On the other hand, there are those who believe that devolution has made Westminster even more Anglo-centric in its norms and assumptions than it has ever been before.

Conclusion

Devolution has created particular problems for the Westminster Parliament, primarily the House of Commons. An English Parliament ceased formally to exist in 1707 but in practice merely expanded and absorbed members from other parts of the United Kingdom, constituting the sole legislature for the kingdom. Demands for home rule for Ireland and later other parts of the UK created problems of how to accommodate (or not accommodate) members from devolved parts of the United Kingdom in Westminster, an inherent conundrum in the context of asymmetrical devolution and parliamentary sovereignty. There was no neat or logical solution in the nineteenth century and the same problems arose in the twentieth. Attempts have been made to find an answer to the 'English question' and, given the reality of devolved assemblies, to improve co-operation between the legislatures of the United Kingdom. The English question, however, permits of no logical or agreed solution.

What will happen in the future is far from clear. It was once said in respect of House of Lords reform that if you put four people in a room to discuss reform they will produce five different solutions. A survey of MPs' opinions on devolution suggests a similar observation may be appropriate in respect of devolution and the 'English question'. When 114 MPs were surveyed by the IPPR, few favoured the status quo (only 10% favoured the proposition that 'England should be governed as it is now') but there was no consensus on what should happen or what was likely to happen (Kenny & Lodge, 2009). Opinions were spread over 'English votes for English laws', regional devolution, more powers for local government, and (the least popular) a parliament for England. Conservative MPs tended to favour 'English votes for English laws' and Labour MPs favoured regional devolution. Though most Conservative MPs thought 'English votes for English laws' would be introduced, only a minority of Labour MPs thought regional devolution was likely to be implemented in the next twenty years.

It is possible that the House of Commons may end up with a twin-track approach to devolution, somewhat akin to how it deals with the issue of European integration: that is, a high level and adversarial debate on the broad issue while a less visible and more regular scrutiny is undertaken through dedicated committees in the two Houses (see Norton, 1996b: 92–109). MPs may continue to debate how to resolve relations between Westminster and the devolved parts of the UK – given that it remains a contested and largely insoluble issue – while at the same time developing greater co-operation with devolved legislatures and making greater use of its committees for such contact. If so, it will be something of an English solution to the problem: the basic issue may remain unresolved, but parliament will get on and adapt to the political reality.

9

Englishness and local government: reflecting a nation's past or merely an administrative convenience?

Colin Copus

Introduction

In Britain central government decides the shape, population, responsibilities, powers and functions of councils in England. It is central government which can, and does, abolish councils, or entire layers of local government which lacks even the most basic constitutional protection, including the right to continued existence. While central government will consult with councils and communities about the nature of local government, it is not bound by such consultation, nor are citizens given the final say over what happens to their councils via a referendum. The British unitary system is based on top-down parliamentary sovereignty, not a bottom-up citizen democracy. English local government then must look to the British Parliament and government, unlike local government in Scotland and Wales which looks firstly and directly to their respective devolved regional chambers.

The devolved institutions of Scotland and Wales have created a democratic intermediary body between local and central government which is lacking in England, excluded as it was from the Celto-centric constitutional devolution arrangements. Current constitutional arrangements make it increasingly difficult to refer to 'British' education policy, 'British' health policy, 'British' transport policy, or 'British' policy on local government, or much else for that matter. This chapter explores the factors and debates that influence the nature of local government in England. It sets out a case for a new constitutional settlement for the UK; one which develops from the localities upwards and which sees political power and democracy, governance, and representation, emanating not from the centre but from the localities. It also considers why the three main parties' policy is not to grant England the same constitutional privileges granted to Scotland and Wales over ten years ago.

The demise of an English approach to local government

Loyn comments that 'the history of government in Anglo-Saxon England is the history of local government'; in this period governing rested in 'the lord's hall, the hundred court and ... the shire court' (1991: 78) rather than with the monarch at the centre. Moreover, 'the shire court and hundred court provide the most enduring testimonial ... to positive Anglo-Saxon success in the art of government' (Loyn, 1991: 79). Anglo-Saxon England, for administrative, governing and military purposes, was divided into shires, hundreds (a sub-division of a shire large enough to sustain 100 households, headed by a hundred-man or hundred eolder) and burhs, which rested within the original Anglo-Saxon kingdoms. Loyn (1991: 80) shows how East Anglia fell naturally into Suffolk and Norfolk (to which we shall return). The word 'shire' comes from the early English 'scir', referring to an administrative unit but after the Norman Conquest it was replaced by 'county', deriving from comte or count because the Normans did not understand the concept of a 'shire' (perhaps English people today should refer not to the county council but to the shire hall). The defensive burhs were initially a military initiative inspired by Alfred the Great as a way of defending England. Indeed, no place in Wessex was to be more than 20 miles from a town. Burhs were also centres of commerce and local government. Rex notes that not all burhs, were defensible units, some where enclosed but not fortified land. He calculates that a burh occupied a 'median area of about 25 acres, or some 380,000 square yards' (2004: 57).

In the words 'shire' and 'burhs' we see the toponymic origins of English local government and also how much of those origins have been lost, particularly with the use of the bland and ahistorical term 'district' council. We also see the importance, for local government, of clearly identifiable communities and that recognisable geographic areas should have some degree of self-government. The burhs were not, of course, elected representative bodies as we expect from democratic and representative local government; rather they were a coming together of the freemen of the area in a way which provided for regular, fixed and accessible settings where the local common interest could be debated and decided upon – often by a vote of those present (Toulmin Smith, 2005). The early Anglo-Saxon system, while not representing local government as it would now be understood, did lay the foundations of a common-law system of local self-government which could act as a counter-balance to central authority and provide for self-government rather than representative government. It was for this reason that the Norman-French ruthlessly set about destroying any vestige of Anglo-Saxon England after the conquest of 1066. The centralising tendencies of British government can be traced to Norman despotism and has its roots in the need to control a conquered nation (England) from the centre (Redlich and Hirst, 1958).

In distinguishing local government and local self-government we see how far from its roots English local government has moved. Toulmin Smith (2005) uses Anglo-Saxon governing of the localities in his case against the centralisers of the Victorian age. He distinguishes between local self-government, where the *folk* would meet together to decide upon local issues; and local government, where elected representatives would meet and do the people's business on their behalf. Toulmin Smith emphasises the key characteristics of the Anglo-Saxon (English) approach to the localities, primarily small territorial units, governing themselves; for him, representative government is not local self-government but local government. He derides representative assemblies as having only secondary powers because they exist by derived authority (2005: 137): the English are a sovereign people that should govern themselves locally.

One could add the judge-made doctrine of *ultra vires* to the factors Toulmin Smith identified as undermining the Anglo-Saxon base of English local government. *Ultra vires* challenges the political and governing legitimacy of localities, binding them ever more tightly to statute. Councils can take no action without a specific statutory source on which to base that action. Moreover, councils are creatures of statute and exist at the whim of the central state. Yet, English distinctiveness displays itself through the centrality of the 'Common Law' from which the division of England into its local units stems (Redlich & Hirst, 1958: 5). It was the common law which Toulimin Smith so vigorously defended against statute law and common law which laid the foundations of local self-government, arguing 'All law must spring from the people and be administered by the people' (2005: 26). Indeed, it is the

> universal law and practice of this country [England], of old time, for the folk and people to meet in frequent, fixed, regular and conveniently arranged assemblies, for the purpose of understanding, and discussing

together, and determining upon, all those matters which have regard to the welfare of the separate associated bodies and to the common interest of the whole realm. (2005: 33)

Toulmin Smith provides a different formulation for local (self-) government to that of local representative government. But centralisers such as Bentham and Chadwick were suspicious of any local government and democracy (Hill, 1974). Such thinkers saw the best solution to social and political problems as coming from central boards and *ad hoc* agencies not from local government – a theme still resonant today. Hill reminds us of the primacy of 'localness' which persisted though social and economic change, noting that 'the definition of localness and the idea of collections of local people responsible to themselves in their community, remains a continuing part of English thinking on democracy' (1974: 27). Even today the main parties battle with differing versions of 'localness'; ironic for a country with the largest units of local government in Europe.

What has happened to England and its local government must be carefully examined to address a common misconception: that the development of Britain as an imperial power relied on the supremacy of parliament to prevent Scottish, Welsh and Irish localism fraying the Union. Far from it, rather, the success of Britain as a supranational state rested on subjugating England and Englishness to the British project and in preventing English distinctiveness maintaining itself and emerging from under the cloak of the British project. The continued existence of a separate Scottish legal system and the development of Scottish local government through separate Acts of Parliament ensured that Scottish localism survived, while at the same time submerging English self-government under the blanket of Britain. The gradual enlargement of local government (see below) and the undermining of Anglo-Saxon common law based self-government through centralising statute law, served to diminish the localities as meaningful political institutions.

Yet, painting too romantic a vision of local government would be a mistake. Local self-government had been extinguished long before the arrival of representative local democracy and corporations often degenerated into self-serving clubs of the local elite with little useful purpose and no democratic pretentions (see Chandler, 2007). Representative local government began with the 1835 Municipal Corporations Act. However, the Act did not introduce elected councils across England. Rather, it gave the right to petition parliament to be allowed to apply the conditions of the Act; and it applied to existing borough councils. Parliament, in other words, gave permission for communities to form corporations, thus emphasising its supremacy, establishing the subordinate nature of local government. An Act of 1888 democratised the county councils with a London reorganisation following in 1899, confirming central government regulation of the localities.

The representative nature of local government took time to establish itself from the notion of representing ratepayers' financial interest to a more modern conception of representation (see Gyford, 1986: 128; Hennock, 1973: 10; Keith-Lucas, 1952; Young, 1989). Moreover, the political role of local government has been far less well articulated than its role in the provision and management of public services. There are notable exceptions to this, with thinkers such as J.S. Mill laying the theoretical foundations for local government to develop as a locus of alternative political loyalty to that of the centre. Palmerston and Gladstone both expressed some sympathy with the view that local government should be left, as far as possible, alone (Chandler, 2007: 109). Yet, they did so against the firm understanding that local government should not compete with the centre, and that councillors, while they may oversee the expenditure of public funds, could only do so within a framework imposed by the centre. From this it follows that something can easily be left alone when it can do no harm. But what of contemporary local government in England?

English local government: no longer local and certainly not government

A defining characteristic of English local government is its grand scale, compared to local government elsewhere in Europe and overseas, and we see a continual shift from the idea that localities have geographical meaning. England has some of the largest councils in Europe (Stewart, 2003: 181). Economies of scale, efficiency and effectiveness have driven the demand for larger and larger units of local government and have underpinned the debate about the unitary or tiered nature of local government. Evidence suggests that the link between size and efficiency / effectiveness is inconsistent and inconclusive. What becomes clear – and often ignored in the English debate – is that a number of democratic criteria are damaged as the size of a local government increases (see Laamanen & Haveri, 2003; Ladner, 2002; Larsen, 2002; Muzzio & Tompkins 1989: 95; Rose, 2002; Travers, et al, 1993). Nielsen concludes that 'local distrust, local lack of efficacy, and local lack of saliency are systematically higher in medium – large municipalities than in smaller one' (1981: 57). He warns against far-reaching amalgamations.

The Labour government's aim of enhancing trust between citizens and councils, increasing voter turn-out and improving satisfaction with local services are all aspects (Department of Transport, Environment and the Regions, 1998; 1999; ODPM, 2004; 2005) adversely affected as council size increases (see Baglioni, 2003; Denters, 2002; Kelleher & Lowery, 2004; Ladner, 2002; Mouritzen, 1989; Oliver, 2000). Yet, some have found that citizen involvement initially went up as the population size increased – only to then decline again (Cusack, 1997; Frandsen, 2002; Keating 1995; Rose, 2002).

Key government commissions on local government have grappled with the complexity of the size question, but have been constrained in their thinking by government preferences for bigger councils. Redcliffe-Maud (1969) recognised the deleterious effect on democratic engagement by increases in size: if councils became too large and remote councillors would find it difficult to maintain contact with constituents, monitor and hold council officials to account, comprehend the problems of the area, and determine priorities and take policy decisions, while citizens would fail to identify with large units of local government and have any sense of belonging to it. Yet, Maud also argued that effective local democracy meant authorities should cover areas within which they can provide efficient services and contain populations large enough for effective use of resources – populations of 'about 250,000 to not much above 1,000,000' (1969: para. 456), with a maximum of 75 councillors. But with such population size it is almost impossible to retain the word 'local' to describe what is left.

The Widdicombe Committee (Committee of Inquiry into the Conduct of Local Authority Business, 1986) was aware of how larger councils exacerbate the tension between the management and representative roles of the councillor and saw these more easily reconciled in smaller authorities. But the committee made no recommendations about council size other than to say that the matter should be reviewed in the light of developments in local democracy. Arguments about increasing the size of English councils go hand-in-hand with a barely hidden agenda to reduce the number of councillors. Indeed, the English councillor already has the largest representative ratio across Europe (Wilson & Game, 2006: 263).

Newton maintained that 'the search for optimum size . . . has proved to be as successful as the search for the philosophers' stone, since optimality varies according to service and type of authority' (1982: 193). We are left with one conclusion: council size is a matter of ideology, how local government can serve ideology, and how it can promote and protect political interests (Keating, 1995). Today, most English councils cannot claim to represent clearly identifiable communities, located in historically and traditionally relevant local territories. What passes for 'local' councils are often artificially created administrative conveniences, rather than communities of place. Consequently, and most disturbingly, for many citizens their council may not even bear the name of a recognisable place. Table 9.1 sets out the major Acts of Parliament since 1835 that have affected the scale and number of English councils (other Acts also altered boundaries and numbers of councils but were substantively dealing with other matters).

The high point for number of councils was in the 1920s, with over 1,700, but this gradually declined to the current low-point of 352. Table 9.2 sets out by type of English council the largest and the smallest population size. Birmingham City Council is the unitary council with the largest population of 1,329,700. The Greater London Authority, which is not a traditional council but a local government administrative area with its own elected authority, dwarfs Birmingham's population, with over 7 million (almost as big as Scotland and Wales combined).

The Local Government Act 1972 set the shape of English local government; it reduced county councils from 47 to 39; replaced 1,086 urban and rural districts with 296 district councils; abolished 79 county borough councils and created 6 metropolitan county councils. The Act replaced 1,212 councils with 378. Subsequent legislation reduced county councils to 27 (excluding county-based unitaries) and the number of district councils to 202. The 1972 Act created six metropolitan counties which, along with the Greater London Council (GLC), were subsequently abolished by the Local Government Act, 1985. The GLC was replaced by the 25-member London Assembly and directly elected mayor of London, by the Greater London Act 1999. In addition to the two-tier structure of local government which covers most of England there are 55 unitary authorities created under the Local Government Act 1992. Unitary councils can be created by a statutory instrument without the process of parliamentary legislation and, as we will see, by ignoring local people.

Table 9.1 The legislative journey of English local government

Act	Effect of the Act
Municipal Corporations1835	The right to petition for an elected council
Local Government Act 1888	51 County Councils; 62 County Boroughs (and the London County Council)
London Government Act 1899	28 Metropolitan Boroughs within the LCC
Local Government Act 1894	688 Urban District Councils; 692 Rural District Councils
Local Government Act 1926	83 County Boroughs; by 1927, 785 Urban District Councils and 787 Rural District Councils created
Local Government Act 1929	206 Urban Districts abolished and 49 created (a net decrease of 159); 236 Rural Districts abolished and 67 created (a net decrease of 169)
London Government Act 1963	Greater London Council and 32 London Boroughs
Local Government Act 1972	46 Counties and 296 Districts (excludes London)
Local Government Act 1985	Abolishes 6 Metropolitan Councils and the GLC
Local Government Act 1992	34 County Councils; 36 Metropolitan Borough Councils; 238 Districts; 46 Unitary Councils
Local Government and Public Involvement in Health Act 2007	Loss of 44 Councils replaced by 9 new Unitary Councils
	Current proposals for 4 new Unitary Councils to replace 23 Councils

Source: Copus, compiled from 2001 census data and based on NSO 2008 mid-year estimates.

Table 9.2 Largest and smallest English council populations,
by council type, 2009

Council Type	Largest population	Smallest Population
County	Kent: 1,382,700	Dorset: 406,800
District	Northampton: 202,800	Christchurch Borough: 45,400
Unitary (Excluding Birmingham)	Cornwall: 529,500	Rutland: 38,400 (Next largest, Hartlepool: 91,400)
London Boroughs	Croydon: 339,000	Kingston upon Thames: 157,900
Metropolitan Boroughs	Leeds: 761,100	South Tyneside: 151,000

Source: Copus, compiled from 2001 census data and based on NSO 2008 mid-year estimates

Two-tier, one-tier or floods of tiers?

The map of local government which the 1972 Act swept away included county borough councils which were an early recognition of the perceived benefits of separating town and country in unitary local governing arrangements. What such separation did was also share out the party political spoils with the Conservatives being stronger in county councils and Labour in the urban areas. The 1888 Local Government Act created 72 county borough councils, with populations of 50,000 (raised to 75,000 in 1926 and 100,000 in 1958) as a minimum requirement (see Chandler, 2007). The 1972 Act abolished over 80 county boroughs and one can say that unitary local government is part of the *British* adjustment of *English* local government for 120 years.

The creation of new unitary councils has been supported by both the Conservative and Labour Party. Indeed, John Major's Conservative government's guidance to the 1992 Local Government Commission favoured unitary local government and stressed the importance of efficiency, accountability, responsiveness and localness, criteria that display the contradictions inherent in the technocratic-democratic arguments played out since 1945 (Young & Rao, 1997). Yet the commission rejected the production of a national unitary blueprint for local government and recommended a mix of unitary and two-tier councils. The commission justified its recommendations on the basis of cost, community identity and local geography, and the degree of local support for change.

The Blair and Brown Labour governments favoured unitary local government, the introduction of which would have been mandatory for areas voting 'Yes' in a referendum for an elected regional assembly. Despite suggesting it had no plans for unitary reorganisation (ODPM, 2004: 20), in October 2006 the government announced it was seeking proposals from councils that wished to re-organise on a unitary basis. By January 2007, 16 proposals were received. In July 2007, the government, under the new Prime Minister Gordon Brown, announced a reduction of 44 councils to 9 new unitaries (Chisholm & Leach, 2008). Table 9.3 sets out the successful proposals and the basis of the new council.

Table 9.3 New English Unitary Councils created in 2007

County area unitary proposal (number of districts in brackets)	New unitary structure	Change in number of councils
Bedford (3)	2 Unitary Bedford	4 reduced to 2
Chester (6)	2 Unitary Cheshire	7 reduced to 2
Cornwall (6)	County unitary	7 reduced to 1
Durham (7)	County unitary	8 reduced to 1
Northumberland (6)	County unitary	7 reduced to 1
Shropshire (5)	County unitary	6 reduced to 1
Wiltshire (4)	County unitary	5 reduced to 1

Source: Game and Copus, 2009.

The Labour government's preference for larger, upper-tier county-based unitaries is clear from figure three; in only two applications – Cheshire and Bedford – was a sub-county proposal successful, but still resulted in merging district councils into larger units. The councils came into existence on April Fools Day 2009, which was appropriate as it revealed the trick that had been played. The 3.2 million residents in these counties, hitherto governed, served, and allegedly confused by 7 county and 37 district councils and 2,065 councillors, now have 9 unitary councils and a mere 744 councillors.

In Norfolk and Suffolk, a cavalier disregard for locality and history, often displayed in the amalgamation process, was evident with the boundary commission's 'preferred options'. The Commission suggested that Lowestoft, currently in the county of Suffolk, be transferred to a new unitary council based on Norfolk County Council. That proposal led to demonstrations in the streets of Lowestoft and an outpouring of public anger. The two areas concerned were on different sides during the War of the Roses from 1455 to 1487 and fought on opposite sides during the English Civil War from 1642–51. Central government simply ignores such local loyalties. The Brown government decided to pursue a unitary option for Suffolk, but could not decide on which one, so Suffolk councils and MPs were asked to convene a county constitutional convention to come up with a unitary solution – a two-tier system had been ruled out. Unitary councils for the *whole* of Norfolk and of Devon were ruled out as they could not command local support; sub-county unitaries were then still a possibility. Yet, help was at hand in the shape of the coalition government elected in May 2010, which swiftly revoked the orders to create new unitary councils for Exeter and Norwich and have also halted further consideration of unitary councils in Devon, Norfolk and Suffolk.

Prior to the creation of the new Durham Unitary Council seven district councils organised a referendum. A total of 76.4% of voters said 'no' to a single unitary council, each district returned a majority vote to keep the existing two-tier system. In Shropshire, three of the five district councils that faced abolition and replacement by a Shropshire unitary council held referendums. In each case a majority of voters opposed that proposal. Yet the government's decision was to create a single county based unitary authority. Local government boundaries, in the government's view, are nothing to do with local people.

The unitary authorities created in 2009 have average populations of nearly 350,000 and it is questionable whether they are left with anything seriously recognisable as *local* government at all. Cornwall heads the population table with well over 500,000; Northumberland with its 1,942 square miles is nearly twice the size of Luxembourg – which, for its population of 486,000, has three districts comprising 12 cantons and 118 communes. Luxembourg's population is smaller than unitary Cornwall and Durham.

Since the reorganisation of the 1970s English local government has operated on a population scale completely out of line with most of Europe and Table 9.4 emphasises just how out of line. Along with the issue of scale, we find that local government now cannot be guaranteed to reflect a geographical locality. A widespread mismatch has been created between the places in which people live and the artificial boundaries of the council within which they find themselves. Typically, place names tell us about a place, its culture and history, traditions and the people connected with it. English local government has been

Table 9.4 The scale of European local government

	Pop. (mill.)	Number of lower tier (most local) principal councils	Average population per council	Total councillors (000s)	Persons per councillor
France	59	36,700 Communes	1,600	515	120
Spain	40	8,100 Municipios	4,900	65	620
Germany	83	12,400 Gemeinden	6,600	200	420
Italy	57	8,000 Comuni	7,200	100	600
Belgium	10	589 Gemeenten	18,000	13	800
Sweden	9	290 Kommuner	31,300	46	200
Netherlands	16	443 Gemeenten	36,000	10	1,700
Denmark	5	98 Kommuner	51,000	5	1,200
UK (1974)	56	520 (all authorities)	108,000	26	2,150
UK (2008)	60	468 (all authorities)	128,000	22	2,730
UK (2009)	61	433 (all authorities)	140,000	21	2,900
England (2010)	51	352 (all English councils)	144,900	18	2,800

Source: Game & Copus 2009, developed from Wilson & Game, 2006. The figures have been rounded.

stripped of any connection to past, place or people as part of a gradual process of de-Angloification by successive British governments.

When councils are merged and a new, larger council formed, a new name must be found as it is not possible for the successor entity to take the name of an abolished council; any name, using any point of reference, will be found to avoid upsetting the residents of smaller communities being merged with a bigger neighbouring town in a new council. A good example here is the council of Kirklees, founded in 1974, and merging Batley, Cleckheaton, Dewsbury and Holmfirth with the much larger neighbouring Huddersfield. The name 'Kirklees' from Kirklees Priory where Robin Hood is rumoured to be buried – at least some connection to an English past. England has many councils which do not exist as areas with traditions, histories and a past and which have names that do not reflect a place. Councils have become too large to match the 'real places with which people identify – hence the necessity for so many to construct an identity (Game & Copus, 2009). Many English councils must engage citizens within artificially constructed boundaries which do not reflect any sense of place, people or past. Indeed, if the de-Angloification of England is to be successful, such links must be broken completely and this can be achieved by creating councils with no roots in a shared community and heritage.

As well as made-up names, approximately one-sixth of district and unitary councils bear 'compass point' names: North West

Leicestershire, South Northamptonshire, East Staffordshire, North East Derbyshire, South Norfolk, West Berkshire, West Lindsey, Mid Suffolk, and the 2009 creations: Central Bedfordshire and the clumsily named Cheshire West and Chester. Finally, laziness can creep into naming new councils, which luckily results in real place names being retained by the 'and' councils. Here two names are simply brought together and an 'and' placed between them, so we have: Redcar and Cleveland, Kings Lynn and West Norfolk, Basingstoke and Deane, Brighton and Hove, Bath and North East Somerset, Shrewsbury and Atcham (abolished in 2009 when Shropshire County became the unitary authority), Oadby and Wigston, as well as the curiously named Blackburn 'with' Darwen (warning: when you visit the area – never say 'and').

We have seen with re-organisations of English local government more than a careless disregard for past, place and culture. Rather, there has been a systematic and deliberate policy designed to increase the size of local government and subordinate it within the UK constitutional arrangements. The treatment of local government is linked to a broader British attempt at the de-Angloification of England and a policy of smothering England and Englishness in a way that the Normans would have recognised. Does the new government elected in May 2010 offer a glimmer of hope for a reversal of the decline of local government? The Coalition Agreement (Cabinet Office, 2010) raises some interesting prospects. Point 15 of 28 bullet points dealing with local government suggests that the 12 major cities of England will hold referendums on the introduction of directly elected mayors. Voters in Birmingham, Bradford, Bristol, Coventry, Leeds, Leicester, Liverpool, Manchester, Newcastle, Nottingham, Sheffield and Southampton may get the chance to decide on the governing arrangements for their cities. The Agreement, however, does not set out any new powers for the mayors or their councils, which has been previously identified as a failing of the current mayoral system (Copus, 2006).

Hidden away at bullet point 16 of the Agreement are these nine words which propose a fundamental shift in the nature of the relationship between local and central government and the courts and which herald the potential for a major constitutional repositioning and reshaping of the governing arrangements in England: 'we will give councils a general power of competence' (Cabinet Office, 2010: 12): a promise also included in the Conservative Party's policy green paper (Conservative Party, 2009: 14). The devil, of course, is in the detail of any legislation promoting such a change and in the reaction of a civil service (not just in the DCLG, but in other more powerful departments that deal with local government), not known for its love of local freedom. On the other hand, such a move may only provide councils with no more than the legal ability to do things not permitted by other legislation, rather than lead to a fundamental re-appraisal of the centre-localities governing relationship. The Coalition government also proposes an injection of direct democracy into the localities; this time under the heading of 'Political Reform' it is suggested that: 'We will give residents the power to instigate local referendums on any local issue' (Cabinet Office, 2010: 27). All this sounds radical enough, but, there is little need to get too excited about at this stage as the British way of dealing with English local government is not steeped in localism. So, given what has gone before set alongside the new government's plans, what possible solutions exist for English governance? And what are the implications for local government?

Federation, confederation or goodbye?

The first Blair government quickly moved to introduce devolution to three of the four nations of the UK, a process from which England as a nation was excluded (see Lee, Chapter 7, this volume). Within a unitary state, powers of any sub-national body are either granted because the central authority wishes to recognise something distinctive about the area, usually claims to some form of nationhood; or some political arrangement for representation is granted to geographically distinct areas to ease the burden on central government. Such governmental off-loading was recognised by the Kilbrandon Commission on the Constitution, which commented: 'Any arrangement which fell short of the devolution of executive powers would do nothing to lighten the load on Parliament and the central government' (Royal Commission on the Constitution, 1973: para. 1192). Devolution is not a sharing of governmental authority. Rather is it lent by the centre in a political-governmental mortgage; a mortgage on which any future government can foreclose. In theory, the UK government could abolish any or all of the devolved chambers or alter their powers, responsibilities and duties. Indeed extra powers are being considered for the Scottish and Welsh devolved bodies and the Northern Ireland Assembly has been suspended in the past.

On the other hand, Bogdanor (2009: 116–18), citing Hadfield (2004), has argued that devolution rests *not* on parliamentary supremacy but on the *will* of the Scottish and Northern Irish (and presumably Welsh) people. Moreover, should Scotland decide to separate from the Union, then a British government is unlikely to resist. The 'will of the people' sets up a competing constitutional principle in a unitary state where there is no notion of 'we the people'. Parliament decides to accede or not to any expressions of the will of the people and may change its mind at any later point. Bogdanor emphasises that devolution 'expresses the belief that the non-English parts [of the UK] represent separate nations' which choose to remain within the British 'multi-national framework' (2009: 118). By omission, then, England is denied even the faintest recognition of nationhood by the British state and has been prevented from choosing its own governing arrangements, or whether or not it wishes to remain in the UK. Those that like to point to the lack of interest of the English in constitutional reform or argue that the English question does not need to be answered (Hazell, 2006) show what is really at the bottom of such a position: the fear that the English will give the wrong answer: Goodbye to the Union.

Prior to the 2010 election the Conservative Party's policy on the English question was 'English Votes on English Matters' but EVoEM is little more than parliamentary tinkering where only second readings of Bills would be reserved for MPs from English seats. As a unionist party the Conservatives are just as worried as Labour about England developing a separatist agenda or demanding to govern itself in the same way as Scotland and Wales. The Conservative-Liberal Democrat Coalition Agreement promises to implement the recommendations of the Calman Commission, which proposed greater powers for the Scottish Parliament (the report also repeated the British view that asymmetrical devolution was appropriate for the UK and that 'the tidy solutions that work where every part of a larger country can be governed in the same way cannot simply be applied here' (Commission on Scottish Devolution, 2009). In other words: England is the problem because it is too big, not Scotland and Wales because they are too small. But, tidy solutions do work: Belgium manages to survive with 60% of its population in the wealthier Flanders region. The UK devolution solution is a Belgium model, where eventual separation is the likely outcome; but isn't it strange that 'big' is a problem when it comes to England, but not where local government is concerned? Moreover, the new government has promised Wales a referendum on further devolution and a review of powers (Cabinet Office / Coalition, 2010: 28); and Scotland has been promised more money and the likelihood of more powers as a result of Calman. The

English, on the other hand, have been promised 'a commission to consider the West Lothian Question' (2010: 27) – not the English Question – with a foregone conclusion no doubt that nothing more than parliamentary tinkering is required. The new British government therefore displays the usual accession to Celtic demands and deflection of English nationhood and self-government.

Devolution by the last Labour government opened up a gigantic democratic deficit of its own creation and left a vital piece missing in the UK constitutional and governing jigsaw: an English Parliament. The need for each of the nations of the UK to have their own distinct representative institutions is not one solely of fairness. Rather, an English Parliament is necessary to formally recognise the reality that the British unitary state is a 'political-cultural construct' and one which is a 'top-down official national identity, not a popular democratic national identity' (Preston, 2004: 71), as well as to present the separate nations of the UK with an opportunity to develop their own cultural and national directions.

An English Parliament could rebalance the constitutional settlement and make a federal UK possible; can any federation exist without all of the federated having their own governing institutions? Hazell (2006) has argued that an English Parliament should not be formed because of the size and power of England in relation to the rest of the UK. He suggests that because the German post-war constitution dismantled Prussia into distinct states to prevent it from dominating the new Germany, England should be regionalised. But, the purpose of the 1949 German constitution was to bind western Germany together and secure its existence as a political unit; this would not be the purpose of an English Parliament in a federal UK; nor of a Belgium-style solution. On the contrary, each nation, including England, having its own parliament is designed to loosen the ties between the centre and the UK nations and between the nations themselves, giving each more power over its own affairs. Scotland has a population of just over 5 million (smaller than London) and has its own parliament; Wales has a population of just under 3 million and its own Assembly; Northern Ireland, has a population of just over 1.5 million and has its own Assembly. England has a population of over 50 million and no representatives or government of its own to pursue and protect its interests: just as the British government and Celtic nations like it. The population figures alone are a sufficient enough argument for the formation of an English Parliament.

Most federal states balance, in a second chamber, the smallest with the most populous states. The Coalition's proposals for elections to the upper-house (Cabinet Office, 2010: 27) would produce a newly legitimised second chamber with a manadate of its own. The revised upper chamber could be constructed in such a way as to provide the regional (or rather national) balance which seems to so trouble those desperately opposed to an English Parliament. The upper-chamber would then play a similar role to the US Senate. Or, using the German Länder model, the upper house, rather than directly elected, could be made up of representatives appointed by councils across the UK. The USA, for example, functions quite adequately with Wyoming's population of 509,000 against California's 36 million. Rhineland Westphalia with 18 million and Bremen with 700,000 still enables Germany to survive; Flanders 6 million, Wallonia's 3 million and Brussels 1 million populations function as an imbalanced three-state union moving towards federation. Yet, the English are expected to think of Scotland or Wales and to resist the temptation to govern themselves. The Scots and Welsh were not asked to 'think of England' during their referendum campaigns. Why, then, should England put Scotland, Wales or Northern Ireland before considering its own democratic interest? If England did dominate a federal system, that would simply be a democratic recognition of its size. Consequently, trying to ignore England, or, worse still, to regionalise it is anti-democratic and further evidence – were it required – that the success of Britain, as a multi-national state, has always relied on the sacrificing of England.

As it appears that Government off-loading is now a requirement for the formation of national parliaments in the UK (Bogdanor, 2009), not something widely trumpeted during the creation of the devolved regional chambers for Scotland and Wales, then a more radical solution presents itself. The UK could move to a staged uni-cameral system, where the House of Commons acts as a second chamber for the English, Scottish and Welsh parliaments, with the latter having identical powers of tax, spend and primarily legislation. The Commons would retain a UK perspective and power on defence, economy, and international affairs, with most other responsibilities devolved to the parliaments, thus certainly off-loading responsibilities from Westminster and Whitehall. Thus, equity, fairness and national self-determination, for all the nations of the UK, are possible, only Anglophobia and the British parties' obsession with maintaining the Union at any cost to England prevent such developments.

But federation is only one option; there is also confederation, where the consistent nations retain the right to cede from any governing arrangements; or, of course, dissolution of the Union. This option was raised in November 2009 when the First Minister of Scotland, the SNP's Alex Salmond, launched a White Paper setting out plans for a separation referendum in Scotland. It would mean the end of Scottish representation at Westminster. But why should Scotland lead the way? England also has the right to demand its independence, regain its freedom and leave a form of Celtic Union behind it. This may seem fanciful but the letters' pages of national and local newspapers, websites, blogs and English public discourse show that the slumbering giant that is England is beginning to awake. It is not likely that England would consider secession first but if Scotland did leave the UK it would provide the opportunity for England to reconnect with its own history, tradition, culture, and to recognise its own economic, social, and political needs. Impassioned and detailed arguments can be made for both separation and for Union, but the key factor is one of democratic right. In short, the English have the same right to decide their own future as the Scots, the Welsh and Northern Irish.

Quite clearly the Union which the Conservative, Labour and Liberal Democrat parties defend is under pressure and the parties are responsible for that pressure. The exclusion of England from nation-based devolution in the UK rests on the fact that the three British unionist parties made their own accommodation with nationalism in Scotland, Northern Ireland and Wales. No such accommodation was made with English nationalism. On the contrary, prominent politicians in the three parties have spoken out vociferously and often insultingly against the English, in ways they have not about Scottish and Welsh nationalism. Some examples include Jack Straw's and William Hague's comments about the dangerous and violent nature of English nationalism (and the English) (BBC Radio 4, 9 January 2000); or David Cameron's repeated comments about 'sour little Englanders' and the 'ignorance of the English about their Celtic neighbours' at the Conservative Party Conference in 2006. England, with no representative institutions of its own, with none of the major parties prepared to address and promote the interests of England in the way they do the other nations of the UK, and with no nationalist party in England currently gaining the type of support as those in Scotland and Wales, the only question that remains to be answered is: how long will English tolerance of such an imbalanced Union last?

The possible shape of local government under English home rule

What might local government be like if England had home rule? It would be local and it would be government. It is possible to envisage a model of small, multi-tiered councils that matched the boundaries of identifiable communities of place. The shape, size and boundaries of councils could be set by local people themselves. Indeed, if a group of citizens wished to secede from a larger authority and create a new council – and convince sufficient of their fellow citizens to support such an idea – then a new council could be formed.

Councils could have powers to co-operate with other councils and with other public and private agencies to provide services and they could have legislative powers. Indeed, many of those issues which are dealt with centrally could be dealt with locally, thus adding to Government off-loading that would occur with the formation of an English Parliament. There is no test in a unitary state for what can be legislated about: everything is legislatable. For example, there were three groups of people concerned about the abolition of fox-hunting: those that wanted it banned everywhere; those that wanted it allowed everywhere; and, those – the biggest group – who didn't really mind. So, why was a nationally imposed solution thought to be the only answer? Councils should have the right to deal with a raft of devolved legislative issues. There is rarely one national debate about any issue; rather many local debates coming to different solutions for different localities.

Self-government – of the Toulmin Smith kind – can be balanced in representative local democracy by introducing political checks and balances. These could include the right of citizens to petition for re-call elections for any councillor or elected mayor and a right to recall an entire council for new council elections to be held. Shorter terms of office for councillors would provide the electorate with opportunities to cast a judgement on council policies and term limits would bind councillors to the communities they represent. The Coalition government's proposals for local referendum (Cabinet Office 2010, p.27) are a necessary component of local political accountability, as direct democracy plays a vital part in allowing citizens to control the local political agenda.

Local government systems are not ideologically free and the British left and right would find much to fear in such a model. The left require large councils to capture sufficient wealth for redistributive local welfare services and could not countenance areas being able to cede from a council; it would be, the left would argue, the wealthier affluent areas that would cede to free themselves from taxation for services to poorer areas. The right would argue that too many small councils would lead to duplication, inefficiency, too many councillors and bureaucrats and too much taxation. Thus right and left in the British tradition agree about large councils if not the reasons for it. But, that is an admission that a local government system must be designed to suit an overarching political ideology rather than provide a forum where local citizens and representatives can deal with issues that matter to them in a way they find acceptable.

What if some councils fail and the poor and disadvantaged are left in areas with no resources to tackle their needs? That already happens under the current system and what is central government for, in a federal, confederal or independent state, if not to equalise to some degree. In the present system, however, local government has beome one thing only: an integral part of the welfare state and of service provision. That is not the only role it has, and conceived as a representative institution in its own right, ideological arguments about large local government fall away. Much of Europe and the United States manage quite well with local government operating on a smaller scale than in England and in a much more politically connected fashion (see John & Copus, 2011).

If the 'will of the people' is to prevail then the direction of travel should be from the bottom up, with strong, politically powerful representative and governing institutions growing from communities upwards to an English Parliament, within whatever arrangements for Britain. If public services are demanded on the basis of national standards, the scope for local initiative need not be eroded. Indeed, without the constant demands of centrally-directed service and welfare management, councillors and councils are freed to govern and respond to political initiatives and the needs of local citizens. In this case a distinctive English localism can develop that fits within the framework of English nationhood represented through an English Parliament.

Conclusion

With the largest size in Europe and very few real political powers, English local government is neither local nor government. Interventions and reorganisations from successive British governments have taken English local government away from any notion of tradition, history, people, place or past and created artificial conglomerations. Such a process cannot be an accidental or haphazard occurrence. Rather, the de-localisation of English local government has been a systematic, if gradual process, designed to undermine it as a meaningful and powerful governmental institution. Government, aided by local political elites, have colluded in creating a belief that larger is more efficient, indicating that local government is not a political, but a welfare institution and so not a body which can genuinely govern an area or present an alternative politics to that demanded by the centre.

The nationalisation of local politics and the domination of councils by the three main British parties occurred because local government was seen as a way of implementing national party and government policies, rather than as an independent political voice of the localities. It eases the implementation of national government policy if the local and national governing parties are the same; if the local and national governing parties are different, then an appearance of political plurality is presented, while the lack of local political power does not effectively impede the implementation of central policy or provide a barrier to a dominant political ideology. The future of English local government does not look healthy. The lack of engagement between councils and citizens is generally bemoaned but this has been exacerbated by creating even larger councils. There are no signs that the main parties have grasped the problem of council size, the disconnection of councils from people, places and past, or the lack of powers resting in localities. What is required is a major reversal in thinking about the role, purpose and very nature of governing processes in the English localities centre. The gradual destruction of English local government is all but complete.

England sits uncomfortably within a union that is probably unraveling, certainly in its old centralist form. It is the exception in this process. Devolution gave national representation to Scotland, Northern Ireland and Wales, but England was excluded. England is unable to develop economically, politically, socially and culturally in a way it chooses because it does not have a representative chamber of its own. This makes English alienation more acute and separation more likely. Unionists have to offer England far more than bland and unprovable statements that 'we are stronger together'. Indeed, England as a nation has most to gain from exercising national self-governance in an English Parliament not least an opportunity to ensure that is local government reflects its Anglo-Saxon roots. These are not alternatives but complementary political objectives.

Part III
Englishness in history and imagination

10

Faith, people, and place: the English union in the writings of Arthur Mee and G.K. Chesterton

Julia Stapleton

Introduction

The nature and strength of the ties of English nationhood has been the subject of much scholarly discussion recently, particularly following Krishan Kumar's *The Making of English Identity* (2003). Kumar identifies England's key nationalist 'moment' as the four decades between 1880 and 1920. In his view, this was triggered by the erosion of *British* industrial and imperial hegemony and the space it created for a national identity distinct from that of Britain. However, he maintains that the enhanced sense of Englishness in this period was confined to the realm of culture and was 'highly selective, partly nostalgic, and backward-looking' at that. For Kumar, the failure of English nationalism to develop at a political level left the English vulnerable to the snares of 'ethnic' nationalism. This is nowhere more evident than in recent times following the end of empire and the uncertain future of Britain after devolution (Kumar, 2003: 269, 238–9, 251).

However, as the editors of this book make clear in their introduction, and as Kumar himself concedes, the English contribution to the art of civic inclusion has hardly been negligible (Kumar, 2003: 272–3). Moreover, in focusing on the absence of 'political nationalism' within a narrative of British decline, Kumar misses much of the richness and complexity in the expression of Englishness and the wealth of persuasive uses to which it has been put. Vibrant conversations concerning English habits of thought, action and belief have established powerful markers of loyalty and affinity, and at other levels than that of 'ethnicity'. This is despite stopping short of demands for national self-government and despite variations in the distance that has been placed between England and Britain.

One such focus of identity is the idea of England as a spiritual whole, bound together by ties of religion. As Stuart Jones has pointed out, the origins of Englishness in this mould lie in the Liberal Anglican interpretation of history of the first half of the nineteenth century. Through the work of Matthew Arnold, F.D. Maurice and J.R. Seeley, Liberal Anglicanism was shaped into a wider stream of thought and pitted against the crisis of faith associated with the legacy of evangelicalism in mid-Victorian Britain, among the political and cultural elite, especially. It went on to become a touchstone of social and political reform in the closing decades of the nineteenth century (Jones, 2006: 19; Hilton, 2006: 236). In much the same way as Jones, Matthew Grimley has shown how Christian readings of *English*, not just *British* national identity persisted in the years between the two world wars, and from a variety of denominational perspectives (Grimley, 2007).

The present chapter seeks to build on this research. It does so by examining the work of two journalists and writers who came to prominence in the Edwardian years: Arthur Mee (1875–1943) and G.K. Chesterton (1874–1936). On the surface, at least, they offer unlikely material for comparison. The subtlety and originality of Chesterton's mind could not be further removed from the shallowness and sentimentalism of Mee's. Further, while Chesterton rapidly lost faith in Liberalism at the same time as he moved closer to Roman Catholicism, Mee remained a stalwart Liberal and Nonconformist. They also occupied different positions on the Fleet Street spectrum, Chesterton as a leading columnist for the Liberal newspaper *The Daily News* before his resignation in 1913, and Mee as a protégé of Alfred Harmsworth. Chesterton loathed Harmsworth's 'Yellow Press' empire, along with that of Arthur Pearson (Chesterton, 1905: 97–105).

Yet despite these differences, Chesterton and Mee regarded English religion and patriotism as a seamless whole. This was grounded in three beliefs: first, in the existence of a distinctively English union forged by a common Christian faith; second, in the virtue of the English people against their *elites*; and third, in place as the focus of a wider attachment to England. These three aspects of English nationhood run counter to what Kumar regards as 'true' nationalism marked by an elite-mass symbiosis, secularism, and the effacement of subnational identities (Kumar, 2007: 196, 200, 198). Nevertheless, England in the cultural imagination of Mee and Chesterton was inextricably tied to political and cultural critique in ways that invite closer inquiry.

Arthur Mee

Apart from Dennis Smith's brief comparison with Neville Chamberlain to illuminate different aspects of the relationship between Englishness and Liberalism at the turn of the nineteenth century, Mee has generated little scholarly interest (Smith, 1986). This is despite the fame he achieved as a journalist, writer, popular educator, teetotal campaigner, and motoring enthusiast, before his sudden death in 1943.

Mee was born in 1875 in Stapleford, Nottinghamshire, to staunch Baptist parents; his father was an engineer of the artisan class and Deacon of the local Baptist chapel (Hammerton, 1946: 22–3). His work was fired by a spirit of wonder and improvement that owed much to the Nonconformist Liberalism of northern cities in which he grew up. In particular, he absorbed the great store which that creed set by science, on the one hand, and a religion based on biblical truth, on the other.

Advanced thinkers from this milieu, for example Herbert Spencer, John Tyndall, and Thomas Archer Hirst, resolved the tensions between these two forces in agnosticism. This became the basis of a 'new spiritualism' distinct from Christianity (Francis, 2007: 127–31, 148–52).

Mee cited Spencer, Darwin and Tyndall with much approval as supporters of the view that evolution is propelled by a higher force. However, he added, 'and the mind that is balanced in reason ... sees in it all the controlling Hand of God' (Mee, 1935: 19–20). In this he reflected the sustained strength of evangelical Christianity in Britain, on the ground at least, if not among elites, throughout the third quarter of the nineteenth century. John Coffey has underlined the success of revivalist preachers such as the American evangelists D.L. Moody and Ira D. Sankey in drawing large urban audiences in the 1870s, enhancing populist politics as well as religion (Coffey, 1996). Unsurprisingly, Mee hailed indigenous popular preachers such as his fellow Baptist C.H. Spurgeon, delighting in the phenomenal sales of his sermons both before and after his death throughout the world and, he claimed, among all religious denominations (Mee, 1899). At the same time, Mee perpetuated the legacy of Victorian popularisers of science, those who rejected the scientific naturalism of professional scientists like T.H. Huxley and Tyndall and who returned to an older tradition of natural theology in interpreting scientific truth (Lightman, 1997).

Mee rose quickly through the ranks of provincial journalism. In this he had much in common with W.D. Stead, whose crusading style he admired and with whom he compared his employer, Alfred Harmsworth, in making 'modern journalism a powerful personal force' (Mee, 1920a: 217–18; Mee, 1936b: 145). He worked first for the *Nottingham Daily Express* – then under the editorship of John Derry – at the age of sixteen, becoming editor of its evening offshoot, the *Nottingham Evening Post* at the age of twenty. As a key figure in the Harmsworth press subsequently, Mee took great pride in his success, not least because of his lack of 'the old school tie' (Letter Mee to Frank Salisbury, 23 May 1943).

Mee was especially fortunate in the support he received from two associates during his early days as a provincial journalist: John (later, Sir John) Hammerton (1871–1949) and John Derry (1854–1937). Hammerton was to become Mee's biographer. He succeeded Derry to the editorship of the *Nottingham Daily Express* in 1895, and helped to smooth Mee's path to Fleet Street the following year. Encouraged by Hammerton, Mee worked for George Newnes and then Alfred Harmsworth, despite initial opposition to Harmsworth by both men (Hammerton, 1946: 75). Mee's association with Harmsworth enterprises was to prove enduring following his appointment as literary editor of the *Daily Mail* in 1903 in succession to Philip Gibbs. Mee became one of Harmsworth's most trusted employees, although his attempt to stamp his religious convictions on the *Mail* caused Harmsworth some grief; the latter also had to restrain Mee's anti-militarist convictions (see letters Alfred Harmsworth to Mee, 26 January 1909; 22 August 1908; 28 August 1908).

Hammerton and Mee shared a passionate commitment to the spread of knowledge. In addition, they were of one mind in politics: Liberal (Hammerton, 1946: 62). However, these shared interests did not extend to religion (Hammerton, 1946; Robson, 2003: 17), unlike his friendship with Derry. Derry was an older man who, Mee recalled in a letter to Derry in 1908, 'first encouraged me in the work which today I would not give up for the Empire of India or for all the shares in the *Nottingham Daily Express*'. In the same letter, he recalled his delight in accompanying Derry to the Woodborough Road Baptist Chapel in Nottingham on Sunday afternoons; also, his memory of Derry picking up a new book in the *Express* offices and 'marching with it like a king who [had] annexed a new territory across to the mechanics [Institute]' (letter Mee to John Derry, 7 December 1908).

This letter marked the beginning of a lively correspondence between Mee and Derry that lasted until Derry's death. Derry had just become a freelance journalist after relinquishing his editorship (and part-proprietorship) of the *Sheffield Daily Independent*, the newspaper for which he had left the *Nottingham Daily Express*. His editorship had complemented a number of civic responsibilities he had assumed in Sheffield, especially centring on education (*Who Was Who*, 1941). Retiring from all civic duties in 1913, he devoted himself to assisting Mee with his numerous pedagogical projects.

Another formative influence on Mee was George Byford, the headmaster of his school in Stapleford, Nottinghamshire, in the 1880s. A Tory in politics, Byford ensured that Mee's radicalism was balanced by a love of his native land (which for Mee was inseparable from its people) and a belief in the British Empire as the greatest force for good in the world (Hammerton, 1946: 27). On both these accounts Mee distanced himself from another fellow Baptist and one-time leader of Radicalism, Joseph Chamberlain. He contributed a popular biography to a series entitled 'New Century Leaders Series' edited by Hammerton in 1901 in which he attempted to place Chamberlain in 'national' rather than party perspective. He could not disguise his disappointment at Chamberlain's desertion of Liberalism after 1886. It was not so much the abandonment of his commitment to Home Rule that weighed against Chamberlain in Mee's eyes as the prominence he gave to England's material and commercial greatness. This was to the detriment of her moral reputation in the world (Mee, 1901a: 149–50). Such crassness was all of a piece with the questionable standards of personal honour and probity that Chamberlain brought to public life, unlike the Prime Minister, Lord Salisbury, whom he served as Colonial Secretary (Mee, 1901a: 151). Also against Chamberlain was his growing contempt for the people – 'the people with a capital "P"', as Chamberlain referred to them sneeringly in 1889 – who had once captured his political imagination (Mee, 1901a: 125–6). At least Salisbury's contempt for all things popular was 'honest', Mee wrote, in a parallel biography for Hammerton's series, however 'un-English' was his professed belief in the priority of 'rank' over the demos (Mee, 1901b: 132–3).

For all the wealth he was to acquire, Mee took care never to distance himself from his compatriots in the same way as Chamberlain; on the contrary, he strove to bring their English consciousness up to the same level as his own. He did so through the reputation he quickly gained as a popular educator of the first rank. He edited the *Harmsworth Self-Educator* between 1905 and 1907 in 48 parts. He followed up its success with the *Harmsworth History of the World* (1907–09), famously parodied by E.L. Lucas and C.L. Graves as one of several skits aimed at the flourishing encyclopaedia industry of the early twentieth century (1908). In turn, Mee built on the success of the *History* the work for which he became best known throughout his life, *The Children's Encyclopaedia* (1908–10). The latter was published in fifty fortnightly parts, inspired by Herbert Spencer's belief in spontaneous learning as essential to success in the education of children (Mee, 1908: 3). It continued for another twenty-five years as a monthly entitled *My Magazine*, complemented by Mee's equally pioneering *Children's Newspaper*, which ran from 1919 to 1965.

All these works were informed by Mee's sense of the mystery and wonder of a 'fathomless' universe. He conceived the cosmos as held together by humankind, God's 'conscious partner' in evolution and servants of righteousness when formed into nations (Mee, 1936a: 5–7, 89–90). Evolution was no dry abstract science but extended to the furthest reaches of everyday life. For example, he wrote of the invention of radio at the time of the General Strike as a 'Providential blessing', a 'wonderful example of the working of Evolution'; as such, it helped to offset the dispiriting prospect of living at the 'bidding of the TUC' (letter Mee to John Derry, 7 May 1926).

Mee's work as an encyclopaedist greatly enhanced his standing and earning power, enabling him to purchase a substantial property within easy commuting distance of London. He settled in Hextable, Kent in 1905, a county that was to become the focus of his English patriotism for the remainder of his life. Initially, it became the focus of his civic spirit, too; this was before Harmsworth, worried about the extent of his local commitments and their adverse effect on Mee's work, insisted that they be scaled back. With this Mee duly complied (see letter Mee to Alfred Harmsworth, 30 October 1910). However, he allowed himself one last fling as a celebrity turned local activist, campaigning for the Liberal candidate at Dartford, James Rowlands, in the election of December 1910. In doing so he helped to reverse Rowlands's defeat in the January election of that year. He was given a plaque by the local party in gratitude for his services in June of the following year, a week before the Coronation of George V. In thanking party members, he expressed his sense of pride in his country and his confidence in its future, guided by a party that had put peers in their place. While he 'cared little' for kings, nevertheless 'it is a moving thing to think of this scene in Westminster next week, when a peer without a veto will crown the king, and turn to north and south and east and west and find facing him at every turn a Liberal minister of a Liberal Empire. The stars in their courses are with us, leading this happy England of St George to our promised land' (appendix to letter Mee to John Derry, 17 January 1930).[1]

This vision of a nation – clearly English rather than British – that had fulfilled its populist destiny pervaded Mee's vast literary output. For example, in persuading Derry to contribute to *My Magazine*, he emphasised the importance of 'not writing down to a child'. 'Remember', he urged in December 1909, 'that in doing this sort of thing you are training up a generation that will know quite well what to do with Lord Lansdowne' (letter Mee to John Derry, 8 December 1908).[2] The diffusion of knowledge free from establishment control and anti-establishment in spirit was at the forefront of the Radical agenda after 1867, primarily, as Eugenio Biagini has emphasised, as a constituent element of democracy (Biagini, 1992: 198). But with Mee, popular education acquired an additional end: reinforcing the idea of a providential national inheritance centred on the extension of freedom to all classes in society. While this had always been a feature of his work as an encyclopaedist, it became especially apparent when he turned to writing books inscribed with his own personal philosophy.

His first such venture was *Little Treasure Island: Her Story and Her Glory* published in 1920. This was a product of the Great War, together with the inspiration provided by the impressive hilltop house which Mee had built for himself in Eynsford, Kent in 1914. From its grounds he could see troop trains heading for Dover through fields that had witnessed some of the earliest battles to defend England against invasion. He expressed his heightened sense of connection to the English past in a chapter entitled 'The Gateway of the Island'. There, he reflected that 'that spirit of the English people which has guarded these islands and kept them free' was born when Caesar's army was turned back by the ancient Britons. But it was not the latter who were the English people proper; true to the Whig historiography of Edward Freeman's protégé, J.R. Green, Mee reserved that honour for the Anglo-Saxons. Following the triumph of Horsa's forces at Aylesford in 449, the Anglo-Saxons had quelled internal conflict among the tribes and ensured that the English fulfilled their mission as standard-bearers of liberty and Christianity. These thoughts were all the more poignant to Mee as 'the Island' embarked on yet another 'great adventure' in 'driv[ing] back the enemy of mankind'. Again, Kent played a pivotal role (Mee, 1920b: 97, 99, 209; 1941: 42–3).

However, Mee's narrative of English history was not wholly one of celebration. What he called 'ignorance and superstition, and the prejudice against new things' often dragged England down; for example, it had produced a deep-seated resistance to scientific innovation in the nineteenth century (Mee, 1920b: 56–7). This claim was central to his radicalism, an extension of his contempt for those who had tried to keep learning from the people, first in persecuting the

English translators of the Bible, and second in scorning the idea of national education throughout the first half of the nineteenth century (Mee, 1920b: 57). His concern about the 'other' England than that which had led the world in advancing 'liberty, humanity and government' (Mee, 1935: 91) only increased with the passage of time. The focus of his anxiety also widened; his book *God Knows* of 1935 drew a wide, censorial arc across vast swathes of English history since the time of Shakespeare, itself sunk in an abyss of immorality. While the brutality of the eighteenth century was bad enough, the exploitation of the poor and vulnerable in the nineteenth century was far worse; it produced casualties on the scale of the Great War, Mee calculated. Much of the pride of the flag belonged to its achievements abroad: 'from the Tower of Parliament it flies over things that would disgrace Dahomey' (Mee, 1935: 91, 142–3).

At the root of the problem was 'private interests'; they had been allowed to 'grow up like a millstone around the neck of those who fought to give these islands a happier and healthier and wiser race' (Mee, 1935: 140). Foremost among such would-be redeemers was Gladstone. In Mee's view the decay of Gladstonian Liberalism was responsible for the even darker predicament of the world after the war than before. Here he aligned himself with other pre-war English liberals, Gilbert Murray and Norman Angell especially, who believed that salvation from the ills of the inter-war period lay in a revival of Gladstone's legacy (Mee, 1935: 169). Not least, this entailed a conception of Liberalism as acting primarily through the 'few', whose role it was to 'urge on' the 'average' of the people. Often, added Mee, 'the weight is too great for them to drag along' (Mee, 1935: 91).

More clearly than these other figures, however, Mee hitched Liberalism firmly to religious faith, the kind of faith that he believed was uniquely English. It was essentially a faith that was self-taught for, as he expressed it in his *Book of the Flag* in 1941, 'it was deep in every English heart that none need be a slave to pope or priest; the breath of the English spirit was communion with God' (Mee, 1941: 355). In celebrating the English people as religious autodidacts Mee was writing especially of the legacy of Puritan England. Here, he recycled the political and cultural ideals of Puritanism that had been expressed in the work of nineteenth-century historians such as T.B. Macaulay and J.R. Green. However, he did so for new audiences of limited education. Far from being 'gloomy fanatics', he wrote in his *Hero Book* of 1920, 'Puritan gentlemen' such as the regicide Colonel Hutchinson were noble and accomplished. Their anti-hero was James I, who 'ushered in that dark chapter of our nation's history which covered the reign of the Stuarts'

(Mee, 1920a: 86). But Puritanism proved resilient, even in the face of the dissolute values and persecution of Dissent associated with the Stuart Restoration (Mee, 1941: 354). In this way, Mee reinforced a wider revival of Puritanism within English national consciousness in the twentieth century, emphasising its role as a vehicle of national liberty rather than religious sectarianism (Grimley, 2007: 896). He upheld the Protestant Reformation more widely as the key to England's global reach. In 1920 he quoted the remark of the contemporary historian A.F. Pollard that 'a race that sticks like a limpet to the soil may be happy but cannot be great' (Mee, 1920b: 7). Pollard was castigating the monastic estates as impediments to trade in land and hence national progress (Pollard, 1911: 102–3).

All of Mee's work in the interwar period was written against a background of anxiety pertaining not only to the fragile state of world peace and the threat of rearmament but also the uncertainty of England's role in the world. In a letter to Derry in August 1925, on his fiftieth birthday, he expressed his fear that shadows were gathering around 'the setting sun of the only decent country on the face of the earth'. He thought that he remained an optimist, if only because he felt strongly that 'if England goes there is nothing left [so] that I cannot believe God will let us go down' (letter Mee to John Derry, 7 August 1925). But while – unlike Derry[3] – he supported federal solutions to world problems, this was not at the expense of his English patriotism. He wrote to Derry in 1931 of his ambition to 'make everybody realise the uniqueness of England's contribution to the world. If we are dying let it be known what we have done; it we are going to live let it be told to inspire us on' (letter Mee to John Derry, 5 January 1931).

Mee had been corresponding with Derry for some time about a large project, initially entitled 'Motherland', which would fulfil this ambition. The original plan was to produce what Hammerton recalled as 'a vast descriptive and pictorial survey of the British Isles' (Hammerton 1946: 203). However, Mee seized the opportunity afforded by the death of George V in 1935 to confine the work to England. As *The King's England*, it removed the sense of constraint he had felt previously in including England in the title. This was because of suspicion elsewhere in the United Kingdom that Britain had been effaced by England.[4] In Mee's view, however, it was the other way round: England had been effaced by Britain. The original venture, 'Motherland', was intended to teach the Scots, especially, a lesson. As he wrote to Derry in 1931:

[t]here is too much sinking of England at the bidding of these northern tribes beyond the Tweed, and I think it a capital stroke to call this book

Motherland because it enables us to centre it on *England*, putting
Ireland and Scotland and Wales in their places with Fiji and Jersey and
Australia . . .

   It pleases me as a dig at these Johnnies who have worried me for
twenty years if ever I dared to say England, but it is, of course essentially
right. England is the mother of them all. (letter Mee to John Derry, 5
January 1931)

With a team of assistants, he had 'motored' throughout England,
gathering information, forming impressions, and enjoying the novel
and exhilarating experience of door-to-door travel, for example from
York Minister to Peterborough Cathedral and to Ely cathedral (see
letter Mee to John Derry, 3 October 1927). *The King's England* was to
be the crowning achievement of his life's work, a county guide to the
country in forty-one volumes. It would be a history of England
centred on place where Mee believed the past was most concentrated
and alive. The opening volume, *Enchanted Land*, published in 1936,
offered the reader a tour of the country as a whole. Nonetheless, the
account was heavily skewed towards a countryside that was made up
of 'ten thousand villages'. At their heart was the church, 'the village
treasure house'. English churches represented more than just
buildings for Mee; he believed that uniquely among places of worship,
they combined the eternal and earthly elements of human life. They
were certainly the places where the English most wanted to be remem-
bered (Mee, 1936a: 21, 48, 49).

   It was on the basis of a patriotism much strengthened by the experience of researching and writing *The King's England* that Mee
supported Britain's entrance into the war. This was despite the perils
of the first year of the war and despite the stance he had taken against
the build-up of national armaments before the First and Second World
Wars. In the summer of 1940 he exclaimed to a contemporary, the
artist and fellow Nonconformist Frank Salisbury: 'what a great great
glory [it is] to be fighting alone, all the rats and traitors gone! Never
was I so proud to be an Englishman' (letter Mee to Frank Salisbury,
23 July 1940).[5] He expressed his sense of England's inordinate significance in a letter of thanks to Salisbury's wife after a visit to the
Salisburys' Hampstead home around the same time: 'I think the
English spirit is the greatest thing in the world today and how much it
means when there is added to it something from the depths of the
universe which we can only call the love of God' (letter Mee to Alice
Salisbury, nd). It was in much the same vein that he engaged fiercely
in the *Children's Newspaper* with the Duke of Bedford, an advocate of
peace with Hitler on pacifist grounds. The duke had pleaded in the

House of Lords for something to be done to honour conscientious objectors, or in Mee's words, 'those few citizens who would willingly see their country perish' (Mee, 1943). In private correspondence, he urged the duke to heed the words of Oliver Cromwell, 'there is no liberty for us when the house is on fire', and to recognise that 'every man must lend a hand to save this country which is trying so hard to save the world' (letter Mee to the 12th Duke of Bedford, 20 April 1943).

Mee became a leading chronicler of the nation's wartime travails before his sudden death in 1943. His celebratory book, *Nineteen Forty* (1941) inspired by Churchill's 'finest hour' speech was followed by *Immortal Dawn* a year later. This reflected on the sharp moral differences between the English-speaking nations and their enemy. The 'secret' of the former, he noted, in keeping with all his previous writings on England, was the secret of Christianity itself, 'the recognition of the immortal soul within a man. We leave him free to choose his path, to chain his mind or to let his spirit soar into infinity. It is that that we mean when we say we fight for liberty' (Mee, 1942: 15).

Mee contrasted the 'enduring' element among humankind that England represented with Hitler's rootedness in the present. After quoting Robert Browning's poem 'A Grammarian's Funeral', he commented: 'For [Hitler] there is no future; he has only Today. But for us there is Tomorrow, and for Man, as Browning says, there is Forever' (Mee, 1942: 18).

G.K. Chesterton

This appeal to Browning – it is by no means the only one in Mee's *oeuvre*, and extended to Elizabeth Barrett Browning too (Mee, 1935: 194, 199–200) – is significant. For Browning formed a crucial point of intersection between literature, poetry, Christianity, patriotism, and English and British identity for the generation born into the last quarter of the nineteenth century. The influence is apparent in the life and thought of the British prime minister Clement Attlee (Field, 2009: xxxi, 15–16). But it can be seen most clearly in the writings of G.K. Chesterton.

Born in 1874 into a comfortable middle-class home in West Kensington, Chesterton concentrated much of his early fire on the movement in art and literature that developed in the 1880s known as the decadence. This was associated with the work of Oscar Wilde, Walter Pater, Aubrey Beardsley, George Moore, Max Beerbohm, and the infamous 'Yellow Book'. The decadence injected a new freshness

into the *fin de siècle* after the earlier phase of Aestheticism began to flag
(Denisoff, 2007: 39). To the aesthetic emphasis upon beauty as its own
end, the decadents explored and vindicated new depths of sensuality
and sexuality in human behaviour. But Chesterton came to view the
decadence as a symbol of a society in which the springs of religion had
dried up. He claimed that England's spiritual vitality and its concomitant sense of fraternity had declined at the same time (Chesterton,
1913: 96).

Central to this insight was the complex transition that Chesterton
underwent during his youth from a Unitarian belief in the divinity of
humankind to a more 'mainstream' Christian belief in the divinity of
Christ (Oddie, 2008: 156). In this transition Browning played a key
role. Browning, Chesterton wrote in his book on the mid-Victorian
poet, excelled in bringing out the 'energy and joy' (1903: 148–9) at the
heart of the natural world no less than that of the human mind.
Chesterton linked these qualities directly to the boundless creativity of
a transcendental God, while recognising that Browning himself could
not get beyond the notion of an impersonal Absolute Good in the
world. Browning's conception of the dynamism of the world was the
source of his fascination with grotesque forms and images, gargoyles
especially; like them, the world was driven by an energy which 'takes
its own form and goes its own way' (Chesterton, 1903: 148–9).
Browning's optimism was fuelled in turn, not so much by a belief that
all was right with the world but a passionate attachment to existence
and an associated sense of 'strangeness' and wonder that was best
expressed poetically. He was essentially a romantic: 'he offered the
cosmos as an adventure rather than a scheme' (Chesterton, 1913:
175).

But to Chesterton the appeal of Browning's poetry would have been
heightened by its Englishness, as well as what he took to be its strong
religious symbolism. He had already identified a penchant for extrav-
agance and exuberance as the distinguishing feature of English
balladry. In a review of selections from that genre in the Liberal
weekly, *The Speaker*, in 1901 he argued that the English ballad was
marked by a 'fierce and humorous energy in things', '[a] defiant
wholesomeness of courage and experience'. This was because of the
centrality it gave to the grotesque. In contrast, Irish mythology and
poetry was driven by a yearning for beauty and rest and a 'search for
perfection' (Chesterton, 1901: 574).

Chesterton was enthusiastic about the various expressions of
cultural nationalism in England at the turn of the twentieth century,
for example pageants and fairs as well as the revival of interest in

native ballads (Stapleton, 2009: 23–4). In the opening of his review of English balladry, he emphasised the secret existence England was made to endure as a 'remote and secluded' outpost of the British Empire. Yet although it was often confused with Britain, it was not so much an island as a 'peninsula'. Moreover, it was one to which, 'in spite of its insignificance, its own inhabitants are deeply and mysteriously attached' (Chesterton, 1901: 573).

This protest against England's invisibility within the United Kingdom made no such claims as Mee for the derivative status of the other British nations. Nevertheless, Chesterton's resentment is equally apparent. Why had England become obscured thus? The most extended of all Chesterton's narratives on the subject can be found in his 1913 book *The Victorian Age in Literature* for the Home University Library. Its starting point was a conception of nineteenth-century Radicalism as having lost its way. As a result, 'towards the end of the eighteenth century the most important event in English history happened in France'. Gone was the basis of Radicalism in 'rural republicanism ... [and] English and patriotic democracy' associated with eighteenth-century Radicals such as Wilkes, the Luddites and above all, William Cobbett. The flame of Radicalism had been extinguished by the Enclosure movement. In driving forward that movement the aristocracy secured its position, strengthened by the alliance it forged simultaneously with the middle class to exclude the working class from power (Chesterton, 1913: 17–19).

But the 'Victorian compromise' that resulted from this pact ran parallel with an opposing sensibility in thought and culture, sometimes in the same person. The historian T.B. Macaulay was a case in point. On the one hand, Macaulay extolled the virtues of constitutional repair and at the same time admired England's industrial wealth; this was in keeping with the 'conscious formulae' at the heart of the Victorian age. On the other hand, he epitomised the 'richness and humanity' of what Chesterton called the age's 'unconscious tradition' (Chesterton, 1913: 31). It was in the subterranean depths of Victorian literature that Chesterton located the 'real England', the England that had missed its revolutionary moment thanks to the deft action of the ruling class. Dickens, in particular, ensured that Cobbett's legacy endured, albeit in the spiritual rather than in the political realm. In Dickens' novels (although not those of female writers who dominated the Victorian novel and merely shored up the Victorian compromise (Chesterton, 1913: 106)) ordinary humanity, or 'the mob', reigned supreme.

The work of Dickens was reinforced by two other sets of rebels:

those associated with the Oxford Movement on the one hand, and what Chesterton called – in terms that suggest his clear sense of distance from it – 'a sort of new romantic Protestantism' (1913: 83) on the other. Among protagonists of the latter were Thomas Carlyle, John Ruskin, Charles Kingsley and F.D. Maurice. A noticeable omission on this side of Chesterton's Victorian battle-lines was English Nonconformity. In his view, that religious current was merely a prop to the Establishment, particularly in its Puritan incarnation. He took much pleasure in rehearsing Dickens's condemnation of the Little Bethel attended by Kit's mother in *The Old Curiosity Shop* as 'hateful'. Chesterton attributed its 'hatefulness' to its lack of roots in a religious tradition. Adding insult to injury, he continued, 'it was not even a sapling sprung of the seed of some great human and heathen tree' (1913: 83).

For Chesterton, Dickens's death in 1870 marked the end of the Victorian era, certainly the end of the Victorian compromise and the spirited opposition it had encountered in turn. Just as the Revolution was crushed in France, so the *fin de siècle* dealt fatal blows to both Christianity and Republicanism in England. In his view these often antagonistic strands of thought and belief had been instrumental in keeping the Victorian 'compromise' in check. The chief victim of their decline was Liberalism, now the servant of plutocracy rather than democracy (Stapleton, 2009: 79–126). In this part of his narrative Chesterton chided Oscar Wilde for his narrowness in taking art and civilisation as his 'only gods' and for the ironical way in which he distanced himself from popular revolt in his Sonnet to Liberty (Chesterton, 1913: 221–4; Wilde, 1890: 440–1). But it was not only decadent thinkers such as Wilde whom Chesterton held responsible for the corruption of Liberalism; he also targeted the two social movements at the centre of the *fin de siècle*, socialism and imperialism. Especially in the form of Fabianism, not least that of his friend George Bernard Shaw, socialism brought the rebellion against Victorianism to a halt. This was because Shaw's socialism was rooted in 'common sense' divorced from sentiment and the attachments it bred (Chesterton, 1907; 1913: 235). In this way socialism reinforced imperialism. While socialism emptied the English nation into an ideal of efficiency, imperialism abandoned it to an ideal of greatness defined by colonial adventure. With Kipling as its mouthpiece, it was moved not by the idealism that had tempered the effects of the Victorian compromise but what Chesterton called 'a sort of cynical romanticism' (1913: 250).

At no point were Mee and Chesterton further apart than in their assessment of the British Empire. Nevertheless, in striving to connect Christianity with nationhood in general and English patriotism in particular, they shared much common ground. In Chesterton's early poetry, as in Mee's account of the cosmos, nations were appointed by God to assist His work, not least the search for Him beyond, rather than within individuals; nations 'marched on' relentlessly towards the light, shunning men who 'stayeth in darkness' (Chesterton, 1892: 107). This emphasis upon movement as signifying humanity's separation from God – and the sharp distinction between good and evil it represented – pervades Chesterton's poetry and prose. In *Orthodoxy*, he castigated the passivity resulting from worship of a pantheist God in both Eastern religions and Christian heterodox circles. It was 'only we of Christendom [who] have said that we should hunt God like an eagle upon the mountains: and [that] we have killed all monsters in the chase' (Chesterton, 1908: 339).

In his recent study of Chesterton's thought, William Oddie relates Chesterton's feel for lines, divisions and edges to his keen sense of the passage from the seen to the unseen on a number of fronts: from man to God, individual to nation, nation to humanity. For Oddie, an emergent 'orthodoxy' in religion was chiefly responsible for this cast of mind (2008: 22, 193–4). However, it can be argued that Liberal discourses of Englishness were equally important in sensitising Chesterton to boundaries. The influence is apparent in his understanding of the distinctively English characteristics of his home; also of England as something separate from the empire, located instead in the land and its people (Readman, 2008: 137–60, 212; Stapleton, 2009: 19–22).

Like Mee, Chesterton identified the English people primarily with their religious faith; but increasingly, it was Roman Catholicism that for him represented the quintessence of both cultural and religious Englishness. In his *Short History of England* of 1917, published five years before his reception into the Roman Catholic Church, Chesterton engaged fiercely with Protestant and Whig narratives of English history. He projected the English people as never more certain of their national purpose as when winning their spurs for Christendom in the Crusades under the inspiration of their new national saint, St George. But the Reformation led to the displacement of their religious life, so profane had English Christianity become and so grasping the rich on the spoils of monastic wealth (Chesterton, 1917b: 463–4, 518).

The influence of his friend Hilaire Belloc is evident in this rewriting of the English past (Lothian, 2009: 127); yet Chesterton was more alive than Belloc to the complexity of English identity after the Reformation. Writing towards the end of his life in a pamphlet for the British Council, he emphasised that the strength of literature and patriotism in England was relative to the weakness of religion. On the one hand, literature, poetry and the humour they expressed became the main connecting threads of the English people once the rich public life of the Church had been destroyed (Chesterton, 1935: 623–4). On the other hand, a sense of nationhood was sublimated by a 'religion of patriotism'. This was epitomised in Kipling's reference to Westminster Abbey in the poem, 'The Native-Born', when toasting 'the hush of our dread high-altars, / Where the Abbey makes us We' (1896: 52). Chesterton remarked on how perplexing the pre-Reformation English buried in the Abbey would have found these lines. Chaucer would have regarded the Abbey as a place in which his dust *was sanctified*, not a place which his dust *sanctified* (Chesterton, 1964: 111). But although the sublimation of English nationhood in this way spelt the death-knell of democratic nationalism, it provided the basis of a purer ideal of the nation that came into its own in the interwar period. To Chesterton, it seemed that the English alone would withstand the corruption of the nation by spurious doctrines of the master race, and 'may yet live to be the last of the old nations' (Stapleton, 2009: 189).

As well as literature and patriotism, the collective identity of the English was sealed by a heightened attachment to place. In this respect, England provided a good example of the human search for the universal in the particular, in contrast with the levelling effect of cosmopolitanism (McCleary, 2009: 39). The importance of locality for Chesterton is especially apparent in his novels. Many of these – like *The Napoleon of Notting Hill* (1904) – are set in an urban context. But it was in the English countryside that he found the most powerful sense of place. It was also where the sense of place was most threatened, not least by the English themselves; in the interwar period, they seemed bent on a course of rural despoliation (Chesterton, 1931b). As with Mee, the village assumed special importance for Chesterton. In an address to the Council for the Preservation of Rural England in April 1931, he emphasised the supernatural aspect of the English village as all of a piece with its natural and national face: 'The English village was a relic: it was even a miraculous relic, like the relic of a great saint.' It was not something to be taken for granted, even in Christian parts of the world, as his recent travels in the United States underlined; the absence of any equivalent to the village inn, especially, told heavily against its American counterpart (Chesterton, 1931a: 11c).

In *Enchanted Land*, Mee quoted from Chesterton's address, while studiously omitting the centrality of the English inn to his analysis (Mee, 1936a: 11). In turn, Chesterton recognised Nonconformist places of worship as sites of special national interest and as providing testimony to the spiritual value of place. In 1931 he supported a campaign to save Jordans Meeting House near his home in Beaconsfield from the intrusion of road traffic following plans for a local road-widening scheme. His response to the head of the 'Penn Country' branch of the Campaign for the Preservation of Rural England (Buckinghamshire) is worth quoting in full.

> I am most warmly in favour of the effort ... which aims at preserving Jordans and its setting from the operation of this dull mania for driving ugly roads through places, and past places, to the disadvantage of those who still possess the intelligence to go to places. Jordans is not only a historic place; it is one of the few examples of such a place that has contrived to remain a place, and has not been turned by tourists into a totally different sort of place. It is a shrine of pilgrimage which does still to some extent exist for pilgrims, and not only for touts and trippers. The shrine is not one of my religion, but it is one of enormous significance in the history of my country. What many people will not understand is that what should remain sacred in such a place is the place; the approach, the surroundings, the background; not detached and dead objects that might be put in a museum. The effect of Stonehenge is the effect of Salisbury Plain. If you wire in Stonehenge like a beast at the zoo, you are really making it a fetish, and idolatrously worshipping the mere stones; instead of seeing the large vision of the beginnings of Britain. Anybody who would leave Jordans must leave it looking like Jordans. And Stonehenge marks only a dead religion. Whereas the other is historic in the living sense that its history is not ended, for no one knows what may come at last of that revival of a purer mysticism in spite of the storms of Puritanism; of the beginnings of a Reformation of the Reformation, and of the greatness of William Penn. (letter Chesterton to G. Langley Taylor, 15 July 1931)

He elevated the Quakers, particularly Penn, high above the Puritans, particularly the Pilgrim Fathers, in his pantheon of Englishness (Chesterton, 1932: 148–52). In his low estimation of the Puritans, he differed radically from Mee.

Chesterton was acutely sensitive to the influence of place on poetry and literature, particularly the poetry and literature of England. In 1904 he compared unfavourably the 'alien landscape with a stretch of dry places, palms, and a floor of fire' that formed the backdrop of Kipling's poetry with the 'great uplands and huge pale dawns' of Yorkshire that had inspired the poetry of William Watson (1858–1935). He argued that the two environments reflected wholly different moralities and political temperaments (Chesterton, 1904: 765–6). Watson was much admired by Chesterton for his patriotic poetry; this was principally directed against the wrong imperialist turn that foreign policy in England had taken since the 1880s. He praised Watson's critique of the decadence in what has been termed his finest poem, 'Wordsworth's Grave' (1887), and also in *Lachrymae Musarum* written on the death of Tennyson in 1892 (Nelson, 2004: 681; Stapleton, 2009: 19). His admiration for Watson was shared by Mee, who often quoted Watson's poetry, for example 'Restored Allegiance' (1885) (Mee, 1903: xiii).[6] In this poem Watson expressed his sadness at the wrongs committed in his country's name in such far-flung places as the Sudan. In quoting from it, Mee recognised that the record of the British Empire was not wholly unstained.

Conclusion

This chapter has explored a strand of Englishness that defies categorisation in simple cultural or civic terms, one that is not lightly dismissed as an inferior or deformed expression of nationhood, or as the thin end of the 'ethnic' nationalist wedge. It has shown that, for all the disparity in the religious and political persuasions of Mee and Chesterton, the two writers were unified by a common English patriotism soldered by Christianity and Liberalism. If they differed widely in their choice of English exemplars, they shared an unquestioning belief in the reality of England as a nation and its significance as a focus of pride and attachment. Both men embraced patriotism as a means of revitalising Christianity in the wake of the scientific rationalism and philosophic scepticism of the late nineteenth century. In this they built upon – but gave a strong English twist to – the enhanced patriotism of different religious denominations in Britain since the third quarter of the nineteenth century (Williamson, 2008: 168). Through their journalism and books, they reached large audiences whose religious and national identities they shaped in distinctively English ways. In doing so, they underline the distance between historical ideals of faith and nationhood in Britain and those that are cultivated today. The ideals of the twenty-first century in this regard often spring from a progressive, multiculturalist agenda that values religion largely for its role in enhancing 'social capital' (Kenny, 2008: 67). By contrast, those explored here emphasise the constitutive relationship between faith and the nation, English as much as British. Yet, they do not belong entirely to the past: echoes, however faint, can still be heard (Nazir-Ali, 2008; 2009; Sentamu, 2008: 23).

Notes

1 'On receiving Illuminated Address from Dartford Liberal Council', copy attached to a letter from Mee to Derry, 17 January 1930. Such was Mee's confidence in the Liberal government, he anticipated the passage of the Parliament Bill in August 1911 as a foregone conclusion.

2 Henry Charles Keith Petty-Fitzmaurice, 5th Marquess of Lansdowne, was the leader of the Unionist opposition in the House of Lords. He had moved the rejection of Lloyd George's budget in November 1909.

3 He protested against Derry's rejection of a 'United States of Europe', a rejection founded upon the 'unlikeness of Europeans'. See letter Mee to John Derry, 11 January 1926.

4 Letter Mee to John Derry, undated, beginning 'It is a breaking if not broken heart today.' The occasion of his grief was the decision of Amalgamated Press – once part of Harmsworth's publishing empire and which was to have published the work in serial form – to pull out of the venture on commercial grounds. However, he had no difficulty in persuading Hodder & Stoughton – the publisher of all his books to date – to issue the work in single volumes.

5 Salisbury was also an English patriot, as is clear from his membership of the Royal Society of St George (*Who Was Who*, 1972: 995).

6 Mee praised Watson in a letter to Derry. In the course of lamenting Robert Bridge's elevation to the Laureateship, he asked, despairingly, 'Was there anything quite like this boosting of Bridges? If you have [Watson's] Elegiac Poems to Tennyson, Burns, Wordsworth and Arnold, sit down and read them straightaway. I did so on Sunday after reading some modern stuff, and I sat down and wrote to him that it was like a trumpet from the Heavens after ten penny whistles' (letter Mee to John Derry, 17 January 1930).

11

The changing face of Englishness: history, culture and character

Gary Day

In his *The Making of English National Identity* (2003), Krishan Kumar distinguishes between the political and the cultural nation. Applying this to England, we can say the former refers principally to Parliament and the organs of state, while the latter refers to a range of phenomena from cricket to queuing, from language to the last night of the Proms. The distinction between the two is not absolute. As Patrick Parrinder points out, the novel, while belonging to the cultural nation, never-theless performs what could be considered a political function by setting up 'a hierarchy of discourses' which parallel the social hierarchy and privilege 'the written, the more elaborate and the more educated linguistic registers over the spoken, the familiar, and the parochial' (2006: 15). This observation could be applied to the three novels discussed in this chapter: Julian Barnes' *England, England* (1998), Monica Ali's *Brick Lane* (2003) and Philip Hensher's *The Northern Clemency* (2008a).

However, our focus will be on how each of these novels registers the growth of the free market and its effect on Englishness. This can only be a very broad analysis but I hope it is a suggestive one. The free market has produced two basic effects on the novel. First, it has weakened the link between language and place, which was a feature of Parrinder's hierarchy of discourses. We can see this most clearly in *England, England* where commerce manipulates language and where English history is transported from the mainland to the Isle of Wight. The second effect of the free market is on the portrayal of 'character', one of the staples of English fiction, and this is discussed in connec-tion with *The Northern Clemency*. Neither of these effects are particu-larly apparent in *Brick Lane*, but what is interesting about that novel is the way it juxtaposes two ideas of the 'cultural nation', the immigrant one that confers meaning and significance on life and the indigenous one that does not. But, as we shall see, this too, is down to economic change.

England, England: history and the construction of 'Englishness'

An understanding of history is essential to an understanding of Englishness. As Barnes puts it in *England, England*, 'Old England had lost its history, and therefore – since memory is identity – had lost all sense of itself' (Barnes, 1998: 251). But can we trust memory? Barnes thinks not. Martha, the novel's protagonist, thinks that our first memory is always an invention – and this means that what comes after is always built on a fiction or, more harshly, a 'lie' (Barnes, 1998: 4).

Martha's first made-up memory is of doing a Counties of England jigsaw puzzle but it is mixed up with a true memory of her never being able to complete the puzzle until her father has given her the last piece. One day, he does not come home – he has deserted his wife for another woman – and so Martha is unable to complete the jigsaw. This episode is important for two reasons. First it helps shape Martha's character and her relations with men and, second, it introduces the idea that England is always an incomplete construct.

It also establishes a parallel between how Martha remembers her own history and how England remembers its history because the way in which she shapes her past anticipates how Sir Jack Pitman will reshape England's past. But there is a difference. The more Martha reflects upon her own past, as in the chapter 'A Brief History of Sexuality' (Barnes, 1998: 48–52), the more she grows and changes. Sir Jack's reshaping of the English past, by contrast, is merely a re-enactment of the country's most mythic moments. There is no analysis, no interrogation, just constant repetition – and consequently re-enforcement – of familiar stories.

But it is with Barnes' more general notion of history that we are concerned at present. The shape of the story suggests that history is a cycle. Both at the beginning and end Martha attends an agricultural fête and, at the end of the novel, England has itself returned to its pre-industrial past. These personal and public histories frame the wider dramatisations and speculations about history in the novel.

At school Martha learns to chant the key dates of English history from the Roman Invasion (55 BC) to the Treaty of Rome (1973). Her relation to history, like that of the other children, is one of passive acceptance rather than active engagement (Barnes, 1998: 11). But the chanting does create the sense of a shared past which is the basis of community. That past is seen largely in terms of individual liberty (Magna Carta), the assertion of national identity (the Reformation), and heroism (the Battle of Britain). It is a narrative of progress, self-expression and triumph against the odds.

A little later in the novel, Jerry Batson, a brand consultant, presents the contrary and more familiar story, that of England's decline from a mighty empire to a country struggling to survive in the new global order (Barnes, 1998: 37–9). The very fact that these accounts are opposed to one another suggests that history can be told from different points of view: it depends on where you start and what you want to say. History, in other words, is not just the relation of what happened, or even why it happened. It is about persuading people to believe one particular version of events because that suits the needs of the present. And it is those in power who define what those needs are. A good example is Sir Jack's manipulation of history in order to acquire the Isle of Wight for his replica England; for example, he argues that the Isle of Wight had been acquired illegally by Edward I. (Barnes, 1998: 126, 168–73).

This, indeed, brings us to the main use of history in the novel: to create an 'authentic' experience of England. Tourists who visit the Isle of Wight can watch enactments of major episodes of the nation's history and enjoy aspects of its culture – Stonehenge, Big Ben, the White Cliffs of Dover, and so on. This is history as commodity. Sir Jack Pitman, who seems partly modelled on Josiah Bounderby in Dickens' *Hard Times* (1854),[1] is the driving force behind the project, turning the past into a theme park or, as he would have it 'the thing itself' (Barnes, 1998: 59). The idea that there is no difference between reality and representation (see Baudrillard, 2001: 169–87) is part of Barnes' attack on the heritage industry, which sprang up in the mid to late 1980s, partly as a response to the loss of Britain's manufacturing base.

History as heritage is opposed to history as, if not fact, at least competing interpretations over the available evidence. Jeff, the project's 'concept developer' (Barnes, 1998: 58), represents the first position and the nearest we get to the second is Dr Max, the project's 'official historian'. But he is more a TV personality (Barnes, 1998: 68–9) than a scholarly historian, that is one who spends his time searching archives, comparing sources and checking records. Even so, Dr Max despairs that very few people know anything about 'the origins and forging [of England]' (Barnes, 1998: 82) while Jeff merely thinks 'the point of our history [is to make people] *feel better*' or, as he also puts it, to make them 'feel less ignorant' (Barnes, 1998: 70; italics in original).[2]

Jeff contrasts the history written by experts with history as entertainment. The one is specialised, cautious and exclusive (Barnes, 1998: 71), the other has drama, passion and most of all a sense of the grand sweep of events. What Jeff and Sir Jack plan to provide in their newly developed theme park is the comfort of a familiar narrative: history as heritage. Events are chosen mostly on the basis of how enjoyable they prove, not for the light they shed on the past. I say 'mostly' because history is also shaped to reflect current orthodoxies: for example, Robin Hood's men must include women, the disabled and gays (Barnes, 1998: 146–52).

History as heritage abolishes history. This is apparent in the way that the key episodes of English history, for example the Battle of Hastings and the Battle of Britain, all occur at the same time. There is no sense of how the past relates to the present, just the juxtaposition of disparate historical phenomena, the execution of King Charles, the trial of Oscar Wilde and so on. This is history as spectacle. It creates the sense that history is complete and all we have to do is contemplate or rather consume it.

As part of the preparation for making the Isle of Wight a miniature England, Sir Jack asks Jeff to conduct a survey of potential purchasers of 'Quality Leisure' (Barnes, 1998: 83), the name of the company overseeing the project. They are invited to list six characteristics which the word 'England' suggests to them. The fifty most popular include the Royal Family, Manchester United and Gardening (Barnes, 1998: 83–4). Surprisingly, that staple of English conversation, the weather, does not appear on the list. But of course there is no definitive list of English characteristics. No matter how comprehensive, something will always be missing. And if by chance there were such a list, it would be so huge as to be meaningless. We would not be able to organise its numerous characteristics into a coherent vision of Englishness.

Jeff's survey, then, is necessarily limited and indeed arbitrary. Why should London taxis appear on the list but not London buses? The random character of his survey – which is perhaps an element of all surveys – is accentuated by the fact that the respondents were from twenty-five different countries (Barnes, 1998: 82), none of them England. Englishness, then, is not how the English see themselves but how they are perceived by others, a theme we will take up in the next section.

But we can also note that both Englishness and history are presented in the form of a list. Martha, incidentally, finds lists satisfying because of their 'calm organisation' (Barnes, 1998: 9). But lists do not conjoin the items that appear on them. Paul, Martha's young lover, makes the same point about history. It too can seem nothing more than a succession of unrelated happenings. Paul tells the story about a Soviet composer who is ordered by Stalin to go and collect folk music which would inspire the people (Barnes, 1998: 66–8). But the composer discovers that Stalin has wiped out the villages and scattered the peasants who made the music. Fearing to go back empty handed, he invents some new folk music. Martha asks what reaction the composer's music produced and Paul's reply is 'History doesn't relate' (Barnes, 1998: 68). This story serves two purposes in the novel. The first is that it captures some of the main themes of the book, using the past to help define the present, the creation of *ersatz* traditions, portraying them as authentic and the divergence between 'fact' and 'fiction' in the narration of history, and more generally Barnes' interest in the nature of story-telling.

But it is the second purpose which is concerns us here and it centres on the word 'relate'. It is important because that is precisely what lists do not do. They don't 'relate', they itemise. But it is only by bringing things into relation that we can understand them. For example, the term 'class system' occurs on Jeff's list as one of the characteristics of Englishness. But since class is what divides the English along the lines of wealth, power, status, occupation, education and culture it suggests that there can be no common experience of Englishness.

All lists are nothing more than a collection of items falling under a particular heading. As a result, 'class system', like 'Marks and Spencer' and 'marmalade' becomes just one more instance of Englishness instead of an interrogation of it. The list is the written equivalent of history as heritage because it juxtaposes its items in the same way that Quality Leisure juxtaposes different historical events as if they all existed separately from one another and were all of equal value.

But events are connected. History is not, as Henry Ford is reputed to have claimed, one damn thing after another,[3] but one thing in relation to another. But history is not just about understanding what happened in the past and why – Marx puts it down to class conflict – it is also about establishing its relation to the present. If King John had not been compelled by his Barons to sign the Magna Carta (1215), would parliamentary democracy have developed differently? Ideally, we should study history so that we can understand who we are, where we have come from and where we may be going; questions whose relevance to Englishness are self-evident.

History will always contain an element of invention if only because our knowledge of the past is incomplete. This does not make it untrue

– even the story of Betsey, a woman blown over the cliff but whose umbrella and crinoline dress ensure she parachutes gently down to safety (Barnes, 1998: 121), has its roots in an actual event – but merely incomplete and open to revision in the light of new information. At the same time, Barnes is careful to remind us that there is a distinction between truth and fiction. The real Nell Gwynn, Charles II's most famous mistress, was fifteen when she began her affair with the king but her age is increased to twenty-three on the island in order to avoid accusations of pedophilia. (Barnes, 1998: 163).

Barnes also asks whether we can really tell the difference between the real and the represented. A good example of the latter is the actor who plays Dr Johnson, himself an emblem of a certain kind of Englishness, bullish yet melancholy, literary yet an exponent of common sense. The actor becomes Johnson, changing his name and speaking Johnson's words as if they were his own with the result that the distinction between his own character and that of Johnson disappears (Barnes, 1998: 207–12). This suggests that the identity is a matter of imitation, it is modelled on another with whom there is an eventual fusion.

If we apply this process to national identity, as Barnes seems to imply we should, then just as the actor loses himself in identifying with the part he plays, so too does a nation lose its identity by identifying with caricatured versions of its own past. The paradox is that the very things which express national identity are also the very things that limit, distort and stifle it. By becoming fixated on one or two stories from its past, a nation not only misses out on alternative accounts of its history,[4] it is also prevented from developing freely and fully in the future.

Barnes' play with Baudrillard's theory of simulation as well as Guy de Bord's claim that "'All that was once directly lived has become mere representation'" (de Bord, 1994: 12 and cited in Barnes, 1998: 54) is part of his exploration of what we mean by history and identity, and how they come together in 'Englishness'. We have seen that national identity, like the history on which it is based, is largely a construct and can be presented in different ways.

Barnes' speculations about these matters are part of a postmodern self-consciousness about fiction and truth but there is more to them than that. We have to place such debates in the context of late twentieth-century society. Briefly, arguments about authenticity, about what is real, cannot be divorced from the operation of big business that leaves nothing untouched. Even a jay is seen as 'advertising the new season's car colours' (Barnes, 1998: 43). It is corporate power that purchases the Isle of Wight and corporate power that chooses which aspects of English history will be staged there.

To put this another way, big business has the means to elide the difference between truth and fiction, to substitute the replica for the original and to resurrect the past. A pub, for example, is 'returned to authenticity by the brewers' (Barnes, 1998: 43). The market achieves all this by transforming use value into exchange value; that is the value of an object, say a pen, lies not in what it does but in how much it is worth compared to other objects from a pound of oranges to a foreign holiday. The transformation of use value into exchange value turns an object into a commodity which has value only in relation to other commodities. But whoever bought the pen would use it to write with, whoever bought the oranges would eat them, and whoever bought the foreign holiday would enjoy the pleasures of whatever facilities were on offer at their destination. This means that, say, the pen has a dual identity, as an instrument for writing and as a commodity, but it is only as the latter that it has value in the marketplace. Being caught between use value and exchange value means the pen is really neither one thing nor the other and this gives it an unreal quality. It is true that, as a commodity, the pen appears to have substance but, since all commodities are nothing more than manifestations of monetary value, value which is constantly shifting then, even as a commodity, the pen has no real foundation or continuity of being.

The debate about artifice and authenticity in the novel, which is closely connected to notions of personal and national identity is, then, not simply a matter of philosophic speculation or advanced technology, but arises out of the economic operations of capitalism. Or so a Marxist would say. Barnes, though, is no Marxist. For him, corporate power is a matter of individual character, Sir Jack's to be precise, rather than an integral part of the capitalist system. But his novel does show that only those with power can shape our perception of the past, making sure that we only see those parts of it that do not contradict the favoured narrative of political progress and individual freedom. They can also cut us from that past by turning it into a spectacle and if we become fixated on that spectacle, we will find it very hard to move into the future.

But having just said that Barnes is no Marxist, *England, England* does provide an illustration of one of Marx's most famous sayings which I paraphrase. History occurs twice, the first time as tragedy, the second time as farce. Or, to give this saying a little twist, the second time as tourism.[5]

Brick Lane: two cultures

As the title implies, the characters live in and around Brick Lane, which offers a very different idea of England from that found in Barnes' novel. Tower Hamlets, the district in which Brick Lane is located, has one of the highest ethnic minority populations in London. They are mostly Bengali and it is their perceptions of one small part of England that we see in the novel. Another difference is that Ali's characters live their history and identity, they do not commodify them or treat them as ideas for discussion in a seminar. That is to say, religion, history and tradition are an integral part of everyday life. There is a strong sense of culture spontaneously lived in food, clothing and forms of behaviour.

The novel tells the story of Nazneen, her marriage to Chanu, and her affair with Karim, a politically conscious Muslim. One of Nazneen's first sights of England is 'the tattoo lady' (Ali, 2003: 17) who lives in the block of flats opposite her own. She spends her days sitting in a chair in a curtainless room smoking and drinking. The tattoo lady suggests that the English are isolated from one another, a point reinforced a little further on when Nazneen reflects that everyone around her lives 'in their boxes, counting their possessions' (Ali, 2003: 24). This is part of what she finds so difficult about being in England. Not only can she not speak the language – and Chanu is reluctant to let her learn it – but for the first time in her life she finds herself alone most of the time.

The communal nature of Bengali culture contrasts with the individualism of English culture. The white people, remarks Mrs Islam, a money lender (which is, incidentally, a practice frowned on in Islam), 'all do what they want, it's nobody's business' (Ali, 2003: 88). The habit of 'minding one's own business' means that people like the tattooed lady can often be marginalised. But Ali is too good a writer to set up such simple oppositions. For example, Chanu's dismissal of the Sylhetis as 'uneducated, illiterate and close-minded' (Ali, 2003: 28) shows that Bengali culture contains divisions, and that it also exerts control over its members, particularly women. As Razia says to Nazneen: 'if you go to the shops, go to Sainsbury's. English people don't look at you twice. But if you go to our shops the Bengali will make things up about you. You know how they talk. Once you get talked about, then that's it. Nothing you can do' (Ali, 2003: 59).

Chanu's view of England is based on an idealisation of its literature and a distaste for the working-class culture that immediately surrounds him. He uses his knowledge of that literature to distinguish between himself and various others, notably other immigrants, the white underclass and his colleagues at work, who know 'nothing of the Brontës or Thackeray' (Ali, 2003: 28, 38–9).[6] But when he fails to gain promotion, he puts it down to racism.

He also says that the English are deceitful, 'they shake your hand with the right, and with the left they stab you in the back' (Ali, 2003: 72). The very similar qualities of 'perfidy' and 'untrustworthiness', incidentally, show up on Jeff's list in *England, England* (Barnes 1998: 84). Ali, however, makes it clear that Chanu's failure is more to do with his character; he is a dreamer rather than a doer. He makes 'a kind of fortress of books around him on the sitting room floor' (Ali, 2003: 208) to keep out the world.

Chanu never understands what the reader does, namely that an appreciation of English literature is not the path to success in English society, dominated as it is by a market economy that has little use for the imaginative exploration of human ends. Once it becomes clear to Chanu that he is not going to rise in English society, and that indeed English literature is probably more of a hindrance than a help in this matter, he begins to take a more active interest in his own history and culture. He is very critical of what the British did to his country. Yes, they brought the railway, he says to his friend Dr Azad, but are we supposed to be grateful? '"Do you think they would have brought the railway if they did not want to sell their steel or locomotives. Do you think they brought us railways from the goodness of their hearts? We needed irrigation systems, not trains"' (Ali, 2003: 249). Here, we get the colonised's view of British rule. Chanu makes it clear that the purpose of Empire was not the spread of civilisation, but the accumulation of wealth. The needs of the native population were overridden by the desire for profit. Chanu's criticism of what the British did to his country is perfectly understandable, but it means he associates Britain with the idea of empire as do those Blimpish[7] figures who look back with pride on to the time when Britain ruled a third of the globe. Chanu is, of course, different to them but they are both trapped by the past, and in Chanu's case the experience of Empire provides a template for his experience in Tower Hamlets: he is still a victim.

He does, however, claim that the West should be grateful to Muslims for keeping the flame of civilisation alive when it threatened to go out in the West. It was Muslims, he tells his daughters Shahana and Bibi, 'who saved the work of Plato and Aristotle for the West during the Dark Ages' (Ali, 2003: 215). And the so-called 'Dark Ages', he fumes, 'was the Golden Age of Islam, the height of civilisation' (Ali, 2003: 215). Chanu also teaches his daughters about the history of

Bangladesh. It may be a place of floods and famine now but, in the sixteenth century, it was called the 'Paradise of Nations' and was 'the home of textiles.' It also has an immensely rich heritage: '"The Qur'an, Hindu philosophy, Buddhist thought, Christian parables."' '"If you have history"', Chanu concludes, '"you have pride"' (Ali, 2003: 185–6, 197, 185).

He contrasts Bengali culture with 'white working class culture' which consists of 'television, pub, throwing darts, kicking a ball' (Ali, 2003: 254). His worry, like that of other parents, is 'our children are copying what they see here, going to the pub, or nightclubs [or] drinking at home in their bedrooms' (Ali, 2003: 34). This is certainly true of Shahana, who does not want to listen to Bengali classical music or even eat dal; instead, she prefers baked beans, wants to wear western clothes and get her lip pierced (Ali, 2003: 280, 292).

Chanu's attitude to history and culture contrasts with the attitude to history and culture that we find in *England, England*. He regards them as substantive entities whereas Jeff, for example, regards them as constructions. Chanu also sees history and culture as repositories of living values, whereas Sir Jack regards them as a money-making resource. Chanu, in short, views his own culture as fuller and more vibrant than the host one, believing it confers a sense of identity and belonging in a way that the other does not. For that reason, it needs to be protected against the forces that appear to have laid waste to the indigenous one.

If Chanu revisits the history of Bangladesh to get some sense of his own identity and to instil pride in their heritage in his children, his fellow Muslims look to religion to articulate their grievances against English society. Karim, Nazneen's lover, is radicalised by the racism his father, a bus driver, had to endure. His motto was 'Don't make trouble' but Karim points out that the prophet Muhammad 'was a warrior' (Ali, 2003: 233). Karim plays a leading role in the Bengal Tigers, a Muslim group active on the estate. They are for 'Muslim rights and culture [and for] protecting our local ummah and supporting the global ummah' (Ali, 2003: 241).

Until the Oldham Riots (May 2001) and particularly 9/11, the Bengal Tigers are mostly engaged in a war of words with a rival English group called the Lionhearts. The groups clash over posters of topless women displayed in the community hall. The Bengal Tigers tear them down, with the Lionhearts responding that this is an attempt to impose Islamic values on the community. 'KEEP YOUR BREASTS TO YOURSELF' comes the reply from the Bengal Tigers who believe such display degrades women (Ali, 2003: 257–8). The difference between the 'two cultures' is here expressed in their attitudes to women, and neither come out very well. The English appear to have a one-dimensional view of women as sex-objects, but the Bengalis seem to view women in terms of their ability to cook and clean (Ali, 2003: 23). Moreover, violence towards women almost seems to be institutionalised in some aspects of Bengali culture. Nazneen expects Chanu to beat her but is pleasantly surprised when he doesn't (Ali, 2003: 22). Others are not so lucky. One woman has a split lip and her arm in a sling and there is a suggestion that another is murdered because she failed to provide her husband with children (Ali, 2003: 27, 71).

The main dividing line between the 'two cultures' is religion. The Bengalis are Muslim and the surrounding white society hardly even Christian. It seems strange that Englishness, once partly defined in terms of Protestantism, should now be defined in terms of secularism. Such are the ironies of history.

Islam gives the members of the Bengal Tigers an identity they otherwise lack in white society and a resource for expressing their grievances. It also constructs the English as godless, oppressive, trivial and sex-obsessed. Their only interests, sneers a speaker at a meeting of the Bengal Tigers called to discuss the riots in Oldham, are 'bingo, beer and half naked women'. Later they organise a march to show they will not be intimidated by critics of Islam but it turns into a riot (Ali, 2003: 284, 413, 470–3). Is this Ali's way of saying that there can be no accommodation between at least some of the Bengali community and their white neighbours?[8]

The issue of how to bridge the 'two cultures' is broached early in the novel. Chanu says that it is hard to be part of England and to preserve his identity and heritage largely because England is a racist society. His remarks infuriate Mrs Azad, the wife of Dr Azad, the man whose company Chanu continually seeks. 'Crap' she shouts. First she says that being part of Western society 'is no bad thing' particularly for women as her daughter is 'free to come and go' in a way she was not. Second, she says that it is up to immigrants to adapt. 'When I am in Bangladesh, I put on a sari and cover my head . . . But here I go out to work. I work with white girls and I'm just one of them' (Ali, 2003: 114). In fact, what Ali does, throughout the novel, is draw the 'two cultures' together at the level of the simile. Nazneen, in particular, uses imagery from her background to mediate her experience of living in England. 'She had tamed the machines [life support systems for her baby] that stood guard by talking to them softly like a mahout calms an angry elephant' (Ali, 2003: 124). By doing this Ali implies that we need to look beyond 'national' identities which create tensions, and towards multi-cultural ones which accommodate different traditions. There is a further implication: if the Bengalis are expected to surrender some part of their culture, then so too should the English, which suggests that there can be no such thing as a distinctively 'English' identity in the multi-cultural twenty-first century.

Chanu, inevitably, is shocked by Mrs. Azad's outburst, but Nazneen 'feels something like affection' (Ali, 2003: 114) for her. Mrs. Azad is one of the women who help Nazneen reject the idea that she must always submit to her fate, the main theme of the novel. But the one who most influences her in this respect is her sister, Hasina, who elopes with the nephew of a saw-mill owner back in Bangladesh. He abandons her and she is left to fend for herself. She has a variety of jobs and is badly treated by a succession of men but retains her independence. Hasina writes to Nazneen regularly and her letters are a source of inspiration in helping her to become a person in her own right.

At the end of the novel Nazneen's friend, Razia, takes her ice-skating, something she has wanted to do since first seeing it on television shortly after arriving in England (Ali, 2003: 36). As a symbol of freedom, ice-skating occurs many times throughout the novel. When she finally gets to a rink, Nazneen is worried that she can't skate in a sari. 'This is England,' replies Razia. 'You can do whatever you want' (Ali, 2003: 492). The key characteristic of English culture is not, as Mrs. Islam claims, isolation, but individual self-determination. And this freedom, for which the female characters have striven, is not, as the male characters maintained, a threat to Islamic culture but an enhancement of it. Nazneen steps onto the ice in her traditional dress.

This is the optimistic reading of *Brick Lane*. A more pessimistic interpretation is that the ending is a little too idealistic. If the novel tells us anything, it is that the power to choose and to determine a course of action takes place within the constraints of class, culture and ethnicity. But beyond that is the wider question of the survival of culture as a distinctive way of life. In very general terms, English culture is seen through the eyes of immigrants in one of three ways: as bound up with the British empire; as a source of freedom; or as a moral and spiritual wasteland. But there is little understanding of how it has arrived at that latter condition.

The members of the white working class, or rather underclass, of Tower Hamlets are cut off from their own history and culture. Traditional patterns of work have disappeared along with traditional ways of life. They are marooned in a mass culture that does not acknowledge, never mind address, the conditions in which they find themselves. This may explain the broken people Nazneen sees, not just the 'tattooed lady' but the 'apoplectic man', and the 'hunched men and gesticulating women' (Ali, 2003: 47, 117). But if the underclass are severed from their past so too are the Bengalis. They try to hold on to their customs and beliefs but the sense is that these will fade with each new generation. The rural existence which sustained their traditions has been exchanged for the hope of a better life in a new country. But, as we saw in *England, England*, commercial forces erode customs, culture and history which are ultimately seen as barriers to economic progress. The damaged and distraught members of the white underclass that haunt the margins of *Brick Lane* are a sign of what may be in store for the Bengali immigrants.

The Northern Clemency: the problem of character

The Northern Clemency is set in Sheffield so, like *Brick Lane*, it has a strong sense of place, a characteristic that sets both novels apart from *England, England*.[9] But, like Barnes, Hensher is interested in history. His timescale, though, is not the entire span of English history but the recent past, specifically 1974–96. Unlike Barnes, though, he is not concerned with the nature of history, how true it is, and to which uses it is put. Key events of the period, the Miners' Strike of 1984–85, for example, are just part of the backdrop of ordinary life for most of the characters of *The Northern Clemency*.

Hensher has written what he himself calls a 'state of the nation novel' (2008b: 32?) and has reached back to the nineteenth century in order to do so. His depiction of working-class characters, of whom there are very few in the novel, is reminiscent of Dickens. The furniture removal man, for example, is called Mr Jolly and he, like those who work with him, is a source of comedy. Philip Cavan, a miner, is similar to Dickens' Stephen Blackpool in *Hard Times*. Neither man supports strike action and both dislike left-wing politics. Hensher also uses the same device, marriage, that Mrs. Gaskell does in *North and South* to reconcile the classes: Philip's daughter, Helen, marries the middle-class Daniel Glover.

Hensher distinguishes *The Northern Clemency* from other state of the nation novels by its emphasis on 'character'. He argues that other novels, for example Hanif Kureishi's *Something to Tell You* (2008), rely too heavily on public events, or popular culture – particularly music – or radical politics to convey a sense of the past. The most convincing way to conjure a period, Hensher asserts, is by showing how a character develops over time, how their own conflicts and those of the wider world gradually shape them (Hensher, 2008b: 29).

Perry Anderson famously claimed that the problems of society could only get an airing in novels where they appeared as conflicts between characters. This was part of his larger thesis that debates about literature served as a substitute for a thorough going analysis of English / British society. After the French Revolution, he argued, the middle class, 'had learnt to fear general ideas' (1992: 93) and so actively discouraged discussion of them. One of the characteristics of English culture, he claimed, is to treat literature as a substitute for politics because understanding a character is less threatening than understanding society.

But this is a false opposition. To adapt an old phrase, 'character is political'.[10] As a largely middle-class form, the novel often endorses the middle-class ideology of the self-reliant individual, the one who makes his or her own way in the world. Furthermore, the novel's interest in character coincides with the search for a national character, a feature of English writing particularly from the nineteenth to the mid-twentieth century (Mandler, 2006). We can see the political aspect of character if we look a little more closely at the brothers Daniel and Tim Glover.

Tim was an unplanned baby, his parents never warmed to him and, in the most notorious episode in the book, Katherine, his mother, stamps his pet snake to death in the street (Hensher, 2008a: 150–1). Despite Tim's lack of love, and the cruel treatment he receives from his mother and, indeed, his siblings, the reader finds it very hard to sympathise with him. He is just unpleasant. He visits a boy in hospital, for example, asking him what it is like to die (Hensher, 2008a: 301). Tim grows up to be a left-wing lecturer whose politics are seen to be an extension of his embittered personality. By damning Tim, Hensher effectively damns unions, welfare and the struggle for a better society. Or, to put this another way, Hensher seems to reject the radical tradition which is another component of English identity.[11]

Daniel, by contrast, is a businessman who, with the help of Helen, opens his own restaurant. Daniel, too, has his faults chief of which is narcissism. 'He greeted his own face like his best friend' (Hensher, 2008a: 422). But they pale into insignificance beside Tim's. We first see Daniel at his mother's party, aged sixteen, draped over the sofa, thinking about sex. Daniel is very popular with women and his escapades symbolise the hedonistic 1970s and 1980s. But he is also portrayed as 'the ringmaster of the festivities' for, when he leaves, 'the party was decisively over' (Hensher, 2008a: 8, 13). This quality is evident later on. At his restaurant Daniel wanders round, making sure everyone has a good time. 'He liked to keep up the appearance of a favoured guest at the party, perhaps some kind of favoured client, rather than the *patron*' (Hensher, 2008a: 619, 655).

The contrast between Daniel and Tim is one way in which the novel captures the changes in Britain from particularly the 1980s to the 1990s. Daniel represents the successful small businessman; Tim, who eventually commits suicide, the failure of radical politics. To that extent the novel seems to endorse the Thatcherite revolution. What could be more innovative, dynamic and entrepreneurial than Daniel's conversion of a disused forge, in its day used for making steel, into a restaurant (Hensher, 2008a: 547)? In blunt terms Daniel's character represents the free market, Tim's the planned economy, two poles between which not just English but British political life has swung since the eighteenth century.

Daniel and Tim may be very different, but in one respect they are the same; neither has any close friends. This is true of all the children we see growing up in *The Northern Clemency* which suggests the disintegration of social and even family ties. But this may be something the Thatcherite revolution intensified rather than initiated. At the beginning of the novel, for instance, none of the neighbours attending the party really know each other. But the true significance of Katherine's party, which she hosts in the hope that Nick, her employer and the man with whom she is infatuated, will appear, lies in its relation to Daniel's restaurant.

The novel starts at the house in Rayfield Avenue and finishes in the converted forge. Its trajectory is from the home as a place of social gathering where food is offered freely, to the social space of the restaurant where it must be paid for. But the decline of industry and the rise of the service economy, with its access to easy credit, does something more than transform the character of hospitality from spontaneous generosity to a financial transaction: it transforms the workplace into a domestic setting. Daniel wants to make the restaurant more 'homey' (Hensher, 2008a: 733) and does so by buying a case of books that look as if they are from someone's house. In the nineteenth century an Englishman's home was his castle, but in the late twentieth, the boundary between home and work is blurred and so that particular expression of Englishness falls into abeyance.

Hensher may be hostile to Marxism but *The Northern Clemency* demonstrates Marx's assertion that the bourgeoisie has removed all ties between people leaving no other nexus between man and man but 'callous cash payment' (Marx & Engels, 1848; 1973: 38). It has even, he continues 'reduced the family relation to a mere money relation' (Marx & Engels, 1848, 1973: 38). And we may recall here that Daniel does not even give his mother a discount at the restaurant (Hensher, 2008a: 589). Money, it seems, has now insinuated itself into the most intimate of bonds.

Money also affects notions of Englishness. In *England, England*, it turns history into a commodity; no longer a subtly shifting narrative nourishing a distinctive culture, history is now a form of entertainment. Money, in fact, is intrinsically opposed to the notion of identity whether at an individual or, indeed, a national level. We saw this earlier when we analysed how money converts use value into exchange value. That is to say, money takes no account of the fact that a pen is used to write or an axe is used to chop, it is simply a measure of the amount of labour used to produce them. Money measures what things have in common, not what makes them different. Money, in other words, eliminates what is individual.

And the logic of money insinuates itself ever further into human relations. Sir Jack Pitman, for example, calls all his personal assistants 'Susie' and tells his staff that he could have them all replaced with substitutes, with ... simulacra' (Barnes, 1998: 31, 34). To put this bluntly, we all are all regarded by business and government as interchangeable units of production and consumption. If Englishness is to survive in such an environment it must, like history, be turned into a spectacle, its many, perhaps mythic layers, from humour to class, from eccentricity to support for the underdog must be separated out, flattened and turned into either heritage or a form of coercion.

This is not what happens in *The Northern Clemency*. What we see here is an association between money and the gradual loss of 'character' the term on which Hensher places so much weight. 'The curious thing about all the novels I read' writes Hensher, 'is that none of them seems to understand that people change over the decades, that though there is a single unchanging quality to any human being, he will not look or sound the same at 30 as he did at 10. Every character in every book here is just the same at the end as at the beginning' (Hensher, 2008b: 31). Strong words. Yet they could be turned on him. For Daniel's character is, in one sense the same at the end of *The Northern Clemency* as it was at the beginning. He began as a host and ends as one.

But Daniel is also an actor. What was it we quoted earlier? 'He liked to keep up the appearance of a favoured guest at the party' (Hensher, 2008a: 655). Helen tells him that he spends too much time in front of a mirror, no doubt practising his 'special smile' (Hensher, 2008a: 417, 466). Daniel's reality as a 'character' is always in question, no more so at the end of the novel when he picks up one of the books he has bought for the restaurant and that turns out to be 'about people like us' (Hensher, 2008a: 737). The book, in fact, is *The Northern Clemency*. Daniel is reading the same novel as we are.

Why does a book that begins as a state of the nation novel, a book that invests heavily in the notion of character, end in this fashion? In fact, the last few pages only come as a surprise if the reader has failed to notice that an awareness of literary artifice runs right through the novel; 'characters' make up stories, episodes parallel one another and there is a studied use of symbolism as well as a series of often bizarre similes. But there need be no contradiction between trying to write a realistic and character driven history of England's recent past and fictional self-consciousness. Not if we take into account Richard Sennett's thesis in *The Corrosion of Character* (1998). Briefly, he argues that changes in the nature of work have affected our idea of character. Previously, a person could expect to join a firm when they were young and rise up through the ranks remaining there until they retired, a description that matches the career of Bernie, one of the main characters in *The Northern Clemency*. Staying in one place meant 'character' was understood in terms of depth, complexity, strong bonds, trust and loyalty. But the new economy, where there is no job for life, means that people have to be prepared to move, to network, to take on new roles and learn new skills. Consequently, the idea of a stable and continuous character is replaced by a series of provisional identities.

What is fascinating is that Hensher stops his novel in 1996, just before Sennett publishes his study. Did he sense that his 'return to character' could not be sustained beyond that point? That, in fact, the notion of 'character' was highly problematic and that is hollowed out by the rise of a service economy and the plentiful supply of credit? The key word of this economy is not 'be' but 'perform' a term that has a strong connection with acting.

Conclusion

Each of the novels we have discussed presents England and Englishness in different ways. Although Barnes makes England his explicit focus, both Ali and Hensher are pre-occupied, in their different ways, with questions of history, identity and belonging. Their work is part of a much larger concern with Englishness that has been apparent not just in fiction but in numerous radio and television programmes as well as newspaper and magazine articles.

There are many reasons for this anxiety: loss of empire, the spread of mass culture, the blurring of class boundaries, globalization, immigration, and devolution among them. But as this chapter has hopefully shown, another reason is the expansion and elevation of commercial values by which all others will be judged.

This might appear to be a rather simplistic way of stating the matter but each of these novels pose problems about England, Englishness and the nature of culture which cannot be divorced from the economic transformation of Britain generally, and England in particular since the 1970s. These changes are most apparent in Hensher's novel where the characters dissolve and where the private space of the home begins to merge with the public space of business. *Northern Clemency* is a warning that a cultural identity is slowly being replaced by a corporate one. Already the language of commerce determines public discourse, defining the parameters of what can and cannot be said and now it seems its associated concepts are beginning to shape notions of history and identity in fiction in ways of which Hensher, at least, seems unaware.

Notes

1 Both, for example, are bullying entrepreneurs who hide their origins. It is not inconceivable that Barnes may also be making a sly reference to Lord Alan Sugar.

2 Perhaps we might detect in this exchange one of the deepest shifts in English culture that occurred in the 1990s precipitated by the death of Diana, Princess of Wales, and that is a move away from the traditional 'stiff upper lip' to a demand that feelings should be not just be openly expressed, but also respected and not questioned.

3 If Ford did say this, he adapted the remark from the American writer Elbert Hubbard who stated that 'Life is just one damned thing after another' (*The Philistine: A Periodical of Protest*, December 1909).

4 See Vallance (2009) for an example of one such alternative history.

5 For a recent study on how global capitalism is eradicating traditional aspects of English identity, see Kingsnorth (2008).

6 There is a similar idea in Roma Tearne's *Bone China* (2008) where the image of England in its literature is shown to be very different to England in reality. But, ironically, this point is made in a literary work that is itself about England, or rather some immigrants' experience of it.

7 Colonel Blimp was the creation of cartoonist of David Low. Pompous, irascible and aggressively patriotic, he was intended as a satire on the reactionary opinions of the British establishment in the 1930s and 1940s.

8 For a provocative account of the 'problems' of multi-culturalism, see Goodhart (2004).

9 Kingsnorth (2008: 10) argues that a sense of place, an attachment to the local, is a constitutive part of national identity though he does not specify quite how the local relates to the national.

10 The old phrase is 'the personal is political'. It is credited to Carol Hanisch who used it as the title for her contribution (1970) to the anthology *Notes from the Second Year Women's Liberation in 1970*. Ed. S. Firestone and A. Koedt. New York: Radical Feminists, 11–16.

11 See, for example, Thompson (1963), or, for a more quirky view, Ashe (2007).

12

From Hardy to Larkin: poets and novelists in national conversation

Patrick Parrinder

Donald Davie and Philip Larkin

In 1963 Donald Davie, poet, critic and lecturer in English at Cambridge, published an article on 'Poetry and Landscape in Present England' in the 19 October issue of *Granta* (then a humble student magazine). Writing a year before the publication of Larkin's collection *The Whitsun Weddings*, Davie began with the arresting claim that 'I think everyone knows, really, that Philip Larkin is the effective laureate of our England' (1963: 2). Ten years later, reprinting this essay almost verbatim in Chapter 3 of his influential study of *Thomas Hardy and British Poetry*, Davie rephrased his opening sentence, making it noticeably less conversational but at the same time betraying a certain satisfaction that Larkin's standing was now almost universally accepted: 'in fact there has been the widest possible agreement, over most of this period, that Philip Larkin is for good or ill the effective unofficial laureate of post-1945 England' (1973: 64). In this chapter I shall explore the literary genealogy of the notion of post-1945 England sketched out in Davie's essay, with its assumptions about agriculture and industry, about suburbanisation and national decline. The result will be to look more sympathetically at Larkin's position as national poet than, for example, David Gervais does in his *Literary Englands* (1993). Above all, I shall ask how Larkin's 'England' may be able to speak to our own twenty-first century England.

It would, of course, be absurd to attribute Larkin's canonisation among later twentieth-century English poets to a single essay by Donald Davie. Nevertheless, to return Davie's essay to its original time(s) and place(s) is very revealing. By 1973, when he qualified Larkin's effective laureateship with the word 'unofficial', Davie had moved from Cambridge via the troubled new University of Essex to a

professorship at Stanford University in the United States. He may
have felt a need to remind his much expanded audience that England,
or rather the United Kingdom, still had an official Poet Laureate. Ten
years earlier that post had been occupied by the ineffective if not poetically defunct John Masefield, appointed in 1930, but in the interven-
ing time Cecil Day-Lewis's brief tenure had been succeeded by that of
John Betjeman, a much more formidable contender for the title of
'England's' effective laureate. Betjeman crops up as the subject of an
unfavourable comparison in Davie's essay: 'It's in this that Larkin
differs from Betjeman, whom he admires; Betjeman is the most
nostalgic of poets, Larkin the least' (1963: 2). Gervais in *Literary
Englands* shows at length how much Larkin may have owed to
Betjeman, but his detailed contrast of the two poets (in many ways a
sustained polemic against Davie) is very much on Betjeman's side.
According to Gervais, 'Betjeman came just in time to do something
the younger poet was too late for … One may not share his idea of
England … but it remains an England that is credibly there … and
not just a poetical England' (1993: 189).

The dismissal of Larkin's England as merely 'poetical' would not
have been credible thirty years earlier, when, in Davie's view, Larkin
was above all a recorder of 'the congested England that we inhabit day
by day', an industrialised England in which hedges and cattle survive
in a polluted landscape of 'industrial froth and dismantled cars' (1963:
2): the images are taken directly from Larkin's poem 'The Whitsun
Weddings', which had just been published in Robert Conquest's
anthology *New Lines 2*. Far from writing a protest or an elegy, Larkin
offers a 'level-toned acceptance of that England as the only one we
have, violated and subtopianized and poisoned as it is', in Davie's
words (1963: 2). His England is set against that of Ted Hughes, of
whom Davie writes disparagingly that 'we all know that England still
has bullfrogs and otters and tramps asleep in ditches' (1963: 2). These
statements were all repeated in *Thomas Hardy and British Poetry*, but
their meaning was now subtly different. In a kind of diplomatic shuffle
Davie had changed 'our England', as we have already seen, to 'post-
1945 England', an objectified, socio-historical phenomenon which
might well be best observed from his newly acquired Californian eyrie.
While hardly comparable to the transatlantic migrations of W.H.
Auden and Christopher Isherwood in the late 1930s, Davie's retreat to
Stanford after a disastrous period of confrontation with revolutionary
students at Essex in 1968 had more than merely personal significance.
He had fallen out with most of his English disciples, including
younger poets who had appeared in the same 1963 issue of *Granta*. In

fact, the opening sentence of 'Poetry and Landscape in Present England' was already an attempt to exert his authority over a potentially restive and sceptical new generation. The fraught teacher–student relationship is evident in the final pages of the magazine, where the late Andrew Crozier (at the time very much in awe of Davie) contributes a scathing review of *New Lines 2*. Crozier's conclusion is that (apart from Davie, Larkin, and Thom Gunn) 'the "New Lines" poets have closed their poetry to most experience; they have little to say to us. What they give us in place of their experience is a dilute poeticism, so many words slotted into a pattern' (1963: 28). For Crozier the 'pattern' is imposed by the iambic pentameter rather than by a particular sociological perspective; but his words seem to anticipate Gervais's imputation that Larkin's is 'just a poetical England' (1993: 189).

There is more to this fifty-year-old spat than its reminder that the poetic world is sometimes given over to intimate and intense infighting. Manifestly, Davie's endorsement of Larkin's England is as much an argument about modern England as about Larkin. Yet his description of Larkin's attitude as one of 'level-toned acceptance' (1963: 2) would soon become disconcertingly unstuck. Davie makes Larkin sound like an unsentimental social democrat in contrast to Betjeman the Tory romantic, but the actions of Harold Wilson's Labour government from 1964 onwards pushed both Larkin and Davie himself towards the reactionary posturing summed up in the former's 1969 poem 'Homage to a Government'. Larkin is responding to the long-overdue withdrawal of British troops from former imperial outposts east of Suez:

> Next year we shall be living in a country
> That brought its soldiers home for lack of money ...
> Our children will not know it's a different country.
> All we can hope to leave them now is money. (1988: 171)

Larkin was now self-consciously out of touch with the temper of his times, and out of touch with the young. In 1972 he would publish 'Going, Going', a poem that, he tells us, was 'commissioned by the Department of the Environment' (1974: 8), predicting a future for congested England as the 'First slum of Europe':

> And that will be England gone,
> The shadows, the meadows, the lanes,
> The guildhalls, the carved choirs ...
>   all that remains
> For us will be concrete and tyres. (1988: 190)

The mood here is more 'Disgusted of Tunbridge Wells' than one of level-toned acceptance. To look more deeply into Larkin as a poet of Englishness, however, we shall need to begin with David Gervais's judgement that 'the best writing about England is that which avoids rolling the word "England" around its mouth. Larkin wrote most deeply about it when he did not need to write about it literally' (Gervais, 1993: 218). Moreover, early in his career Larkin had been a novelist of great promise as well as a poet, and his 'England' is something that is also defined in his novels.

Donald Davie's evolution as poet and critic is complex, tortuous and beyond the scope of this essay, though it should be said that the poets whom he influentially championed included Ezra Pound and Boris Pasternak as well as Hardy and Larkin. His oeuvre, though remarkably cosmopolitan, wrestled with the question of 'our England' in ways that suggest that – flinging down his gauntlet in 1963 – he was, as much as anything, arguing with himself. In *Under Briggflatts* (1989), the cross-grained 'History of Poetry in Great Britain 1960–1988' that functions as a kind of sequel to *Thomas Hardy and British Poetry*, he virtually disowned his earlier enthusiasm for Larkin. Behind his *Granta* essay is an echo of another opening gambit by a writer much given to arguing with himself, D.H. Lawrence's 'England my England! But which is *my* England?' from his long-banned novel *Lady Chatterley's Lover*, which had at last reached a huge readership in the early 1960s (1961a: 162).

Conflicting genres and conflicting Englands

In poetry – at least in modern lyrical poetry – Englishness is not normally argued about; it is celebrated, lamented, or tacitly embodied, but it is not discussed as it would be in an essay or a novel, especially – as in *Lady Chatterley's Lover* – in a novel with long discursive inter-ludes. No novelist is more doggedly argumentative than the later Lawrence:

> England my England! But which is *my* England? The stately homes of England make good photographs, and create the illusion of a connexion with the Elizabethans. The handsome old halls are there, from the days of Good Queen Anne and Tom Jones. But smuts fall and blacken on the drab stucco, that has long ceased to be golden. And one by one, like the stately homes, they were abandoned. Now they are being pulled down. As for the cottages of England – there they are – great plasterings of brick dwellings on the hopeless countryside ...
>
> This is history. One England blots out another. The mines had made

the halls wealthy. Now they were blotting them out, as they had already blotted out the cottages. The industrial England blots out the agricultural England. One meaning blots out another. The new England blots out the old England. And the continuity is not organic, but mechanical. (1961a: 162–3)

Lawrence's view is of a class-divided England seen from the top down, so that his distinction between the 'stately homes' and the lesser 'halls' is no longer easy for most readers to grasp. Although a miner's son, he writes in *Lady Chatterley's Lover* and elsewhere from the viewpoint of the 'aristocracy', in this case Constance Chatterley who is married to the mine-owner and war veteran Sir Clifford. The two Englands in contention in the quoted passage are, ostensibly, agricultural and industrial England, but Lawrence's stridency hints that this is not quite what is at issue. Industrial England has already 'blotted out' most, if not all, of what came before it. A few pages earlier we have seen the ugliness of Teovershall, the mining village, through Connie's eyes. The 'England of today', she realises, is 'producing a new race of mankind, over-conscious in the money and social and political side, on the spontaneous, intuitive side dead, but dead' (1961a: 159). Against this broken England the novel can only set a lingering redoubt, the area of unfelled woodland on the Chatterley estate which, we are told, is the last remnant of the ancient Sherwood Forest. This is the province of Mellors the gamekeeper, a kind of latter-day Robin Hood. At the end of the novel Mellors is preparing to rejoin the modern world by working as a farmer and raising a family with Connie, but he has few illusions about the future. The farm will be a utilitarian business to help feed the great industrial population. Lawrence understandably terminates *Lady Chatterley's Lover* before his protagonists' new life can get started, so the reality of modern agricultural England is never shown directly. We are left with the euphoria of the sexual connection between Mellors and Connie and a few hints that the ugliness of industrial life might somehow come to be filled with beauty and joy; otherwise, the contrast of different Englands leads to near-despair.

Philip Larkin once said that 'novels are about other people and poems are about yourself' (1983: 49). As a basis for the distinction between genres this is highly arguable to say the least, but it is a reminder that Lawrence, as a poet-novelist, was adept at writing about himself through a veil of fictional characterisation. He rejected level-toned acceptance and saw no need to try to reconcile the conflicting Englands. This is sharply summed up in his difference with his contemporary E.M. Forster, who was a novelist but not a poet and longed for some kind of reconciliation between different social groupings. On 20 September 1922 Lawrence wrote to Forster to admonish him as follows: 'But think you *did* make a nearly deadly mistake glorifying those *business* people in *Howard's End* [sic]. Business is no good' (1961b: 139). Lawrence presents himself as a radical critic of Englishness, with Forster as the temporising reformer whose error lies in trying to bring together opposing social castes – the businessmen (the Wilcoxes) and the cultured intellectuals (the Schlegels). Within certain confessed limitations, Forster was aiming at a panoramic and inclusive view of society, but this is far from being the anodyne project at which Lawrence hints. Indeed, it is no accident that prose fiction, and above all the realist novel which was Forster's medium, has often been regarded as a more subversive and questioning form of expression than poetry. This is true of the anxiously fair-minded, liberal novelists – Forster, George Eliot, Elizabeth Gaskell – as well as their more romantic and belligerent rivals such as Dickens, the Brontës and Lawrence.

Historically it is poets, not novelists, who have enjoyed court and government patronage, since poetry is a performative and comparatively public art. British poets have not only aspired to the Laureateship but have long been considered suitable recipients of titles and honours, whereas the only novelist to be knighted before the twentieth century was Walter Scott, who made his name as a poet. In general, poetry is more authoritarian, the novel more democratic, in outlook and origins; and partly this is a matter of language, with the traditional high literary language of verse set against the multi-voiced, dialogic character of prose fiction. It is the poets who have done more to shape a recognised public discourse about Englishness, whether as cheerleaders or as outspoken critics of the monarchy and the government. National poets – from Tennyson's 'Someone had blundered' (1845) to Rupert Brooke's 'corner of a foreign field / That is forever England' (1914) – are much concerned with overseas, military matters, while the panoramic realism of a 'Condition of England' novel such as *Howards End* is largely, though not entirely, civil and domestic.

'The South Country': Thomas Hardy and Edward Thomas

These contrasts may be overstated, and we should not assume the generic difference between poetry and the novel to be inevitable and permanent. However, there is no equivalent in the novel to the rash of patriotic verse by prominent poets at the turn of the twentieth century when Forster and Lawrence were serving their literary apprenticeship. The year 1898, for example, saw the publication of Henry Newbolt's *The Island Race* and Alfred Austin's *Songs for England*. Austin had been appointed Poet Laureate (to some derision) two years earlier, while Newbolt was later knighted. Another titled poet, Sir William Watson, named his 1904 collection *For England*. W.E. Henley's *For England's Sake* appeared in 1900, and Laurence Binyon's *England and Other Poems* in 1909.[1] But these were also the years of Thomas Hardy's abandonment of fiction for poetry in the wake of the scandals caused by *Tess of the d'Urbervilles* (1891) and *Jude the Obscure* (1895). His first verse collection, *Wessex Poems*, appeared in 1898. It is Hardy rather than the patriotic poets who has come to be seen as a major spokesman for Englishness (or, sometimes, 'little Englandism') during this period, although this was to some extent foisted upon him by his later readers: his own concerns are almost obsessively regional and bounded, as it were, by the map of 'Wessex' printed in later editions of his novels. The frequent references to prehistory in his fiction take us back to a British past before the birth of the English nation, and Hardy very rarely acknowledges a sense of England as a self-contained whole. For example, even in *Jude*, the most self-consciously modern of his novels, it is Christminster in Upper Wessex rather than London that is the intellectual capital and focus of his hero's aspirations.

Nevertheless there is a remarkable, if somewhat hidden, expression of Englishness in Hardy. Alun Howkins, in an essay on 'The Discovery of Rural England', attributes the stereotyped 'rural and Southern' image of what is typically English to the period from 'the late 1870s through to the early 1900s', when Hardy was in his prime (1987: 63–4); yet Howkins concentrates on three writers from the end of this period, W.H. Hudson, George Sturt and Edward Thomas, rather than such predecessors as Hardy and Richard Jefferies. According to Howkins it was Hudson, Sturt and Thomas who 'created the world of the South Country and fixed it as a part of national ideology', although their ideological effect was 'often unintentional' since it was the popularisers of 'South Country' Englishness who played a greater part than these supposed originators (1987: 74–5). I shall return to the Edwardian rural writers after looking at Hardy's representation, not so much of the Southern countryside (in contrast to the Midland landscapes of George Eliot, Larkin and Lawrence) as of the Southern rural character. This is seen at its clearest in *The Mayor of Casterbridge* (1886), where the Southerner Michael Henchard is contrasted with the Scotsman Donald Farfrae.

Henchard is seen at first as an out-of-work labourer trudging through rural Wessex, where he sells his wife and child at a fair before pledging himself to twenty years' abstinence from strong drink. He moves to Casterbridge and reforms his life, succeeding in business as a corn-factor and becoming Mayor of the town. Eventually, his ex-wife returns to find him lording it over a banquet in Casterbridge's best hotel, with the band playing 'The Roast Beef of Old England' in the street outside. On the same day Farfrae turns up in Casterbridge, and later that evening he enchants a small audience with his haunting songs of Scotland. Music is the first medium of national competition between the two men, who become, briefly, bosom friends and then bitter commercial and personal rivals. Their rivalry comes to a head very much later in the novel on the day of the 'Skimmity-ride', with Henchard engaging Farfrae in man-to-man combat (Henchard with one arm tied behind his back). Earlier on the same day Farfrae, who has now replaced Henchard as Mayor, officially welcomes an unnamed 'Royal Personage' (presumably Prince Albert) who is visiting the town. Henchard has asked the town council for permission to take part in the municipal welcome, but has been refused. Armed with a home-made Union Jack, and already drunk (since the twenty years are at last over), he barges in front of Farfrae and succeeds in buttonholing the royal visitor. It is Farfrae's subsequent criticism of Henchard's actions that leads to their fight. Henchard's response is both truculent and (ostensibly) patriotic: '"Royalty be damned," said Henchard. "I am as loyal as you, come to that!"' (Hardy, 1968: 275). Hardy, as often, stops short of explaining Henchard's feelings, but it seems likely he feels that a native Wessex man rather than an interloper from Scotland has the right to welcome royalty to their town. The narrator has earlier observed that the contest between the two men 'was, in some degree, Northern insight against Southron doggedness – the dirk against the cudgel' (Hardy, 1968: 124). 'Southron' here is a traditional Scots word for the English, while the cudgel was the traditional weapon of the eighteenth and nineteenth centuries' favourite personification of Englishness, John Bull. Henchard too, in these scenes, becomes the embodiment of national character.

In the first part of the novel, once he has taken the pledge, Henchard is John Bull sober; but by the time of the royal visit he displays Bull's legendary qualities in full measure. Here is part of the original characterisation from John Arbuthnot's *The History of John Bull* (1712):

> For the better understanding of the following History, the Reader ought to know, that *Bull*, in the main, was an honest plain-dealing Fellow,

Cholerick, Bold, and of a very unconstant Temper . . . he was very apt to quarrel with his best friends, especially if they pretended to govern him: If you flatter'd him, you might lead him like a Child . . . *John* was quick, and understood his business very well, but no Man alive was more careless, in looking into his Accounts, or more cheated by Partners, Apprentices, and Servants: This was occasioned by his being a Boon-Companion, loving his Bottle and his Diversion; for to say Truth, no Man kept a better *House* than *John*, nor spent his Money more generously. (1976: 9)

Farfrae, in contrast to Henchard, is the modernising, Puritanical Scot who runs his business by cool calculation rather than, as Henchard does, by instinct and a readiness to gamble. Without Henchard's impulsive generosity at the start of their acquaintance, Farfrae would have sung his Scottish ballads and then left the 'Southron' town for ever. Insofar as Henchard is John Bull, he personifies Old England – the rural England that all Hardy's novels show to be slowly dying, to be replaced by new agricultural machinery, new and harder-faced business methods, and new and more impersonal standards of conduct. The obdurate, uncouth 'characters' like Henchard are superseded by a more formal, managerial culture: Farfrae, unlike Henchard, is a good husband and a reliable employer, but as a figure in a novel he is completely overshadowed by his tempestuous, unpredictable rival. Finally the tragedy of Henchard's self-destruction is complete, and he writes his will consigning himself –and, we might feel, Old England too – to utter oblivion.

Hardy is as responsible as any writer for the tone of elegy for a predominantly rural nation that is so prominent in early twentieth-century accounts of Englishness. He was to some extent simply recording the irreversible social changes initiated by the Agricultural Depression of the 1870s, and in scenes such as the famous 'Skimmity-ride' in *The Mayor of Casterbridge* he provides a deliberate ethnography of the traditional country town and village. His portrayal of the conflict between tradition and modernisation in the countryside was taken up by the rural historian and sociologist George Sturt ('George Bourne') in such books as *Change in the Village* (1912). Sturt's writing combines the political – in its angry protests against the effects of enclosure and rural capitalism – with the self-consciously anthropological; he speaks constantly of 'survivals'. There is also a tone of self-critical regret as he blames himself for failing to recognise the glory of Old England until it had virtually disappeared. The people (generally very old people, the dying generation) in his Surrey village were, he says, 'a survival of the England that is dying out now; and I grieve that

I did not realize it sooner. . . . In their odd ways of talk and character I was affected, albeit unawares, by a robust tradition of the English countryside, surviving here when the circumstances which would have explained it had already largely disappeared. After too many years of undiscernment that truth was apparent to me' (Bourne, 1955: 4, 10). The 'robust tradition' in Sturt's village was not, in fact, all that old – it had been, he suggests, '[i]mported into the valley by squatters two centuries ago' (Bourne, 1955: 10–1) – but it is made to stand for an immemorial, national possession which can only be properly appreciated at the moment of its irreparable loss. Thus, while the late Victorian and Edwardian patriotic poets were churning out their 'songs for England', the much more long-lasting convention of Englishness as rural elegy was being born.

Of Howkins's Edwardian trio – Sturt, Hudson and Thomas – I shall discuss the poet-novelist Edward Thomas before returning to E.M. Forster and *Howards End*. Thomas did not turn to verse until after his meeting with the American poet Robert Frost in August 1914; and he was killed by a shell-blast in northern France less than three years later. His prose works include *The Heart of England* (1906), *The South Country* (1909) and *A Literary Pilgrim in England* (1917). He begins *The South Country* by quoting Hilaire Belloc's poem of that name:

> When I am living in the Midlands,
> They are sodden and unkind,
> I light my lamp in the evening,
> My work is left behind;
> And the great hills of the South Country
> Come back into my mind. (in Thomas, 1993: 1)

This has all the picturesque eccentricity of Belloc's verse (which should not be confused with the splenetic, quarrelsome character of some of his prose). Born near Paris in 1870, Belloc moved with his family to England two years later and went to school in Birmingham. The 'great hills of the South Country' suggest an almost childlike vision, since to an adult England's great hills are clearly all north of Birmingham. The same tract of territory between Birmingham and the Sussex downland is present in the opening stanza of one of the most genuinely popular twentieth-century English poems, 'The Rolling English Road' by Belloc's friend and ally G.K. Chesterton:

Before the Roman came to Rye or out to Severn strode,
The rolling English drunkard made the rolling English road.
A reeling road, a rolling road, that rambles round the shire,
And after him the parson ran, the sexton and the squire;
A merry road, a mazy road, and such as we did tread
The night we went to Birmingham by way of Beachy Head.
(1926: 238)

The place-names in Chesterton's later stanzas (Glastonbury, Goodwin Sands, Brighton Pier) reinforce this vision of southern England, with one exception (Bannockburn); but, as Chesterton's imagination was as much suburban as rural, the poem's final line takes us 'to Paradise' by way of the North London cemetery of 'Kensal Green'. The poem first appeared in Chesterton's *The Flying Inn,* a book that Edward Thomas reviewed shortly after its publication in January 1914.[2] (For an in-depth discussion of Chesterton's Englishness, see also Stapleton, Chapter 10.)

Thomas's most famous poem based on southern English place-names is 'Adlestrop', written exactly a year later and beginning with at least a faint echo of Chesterton's rollicking, hail-fellow-well-met style: 'Yes, I remember Adlestrop–'.[3] Thomas is one of the most influential of modern English 'countryside' poets, yet the hills and the woods, the birds and the flowers, and the wind and rain of his poems are very much an internal landscape – a simplified, pastoral world hinting obscurely at a deep personal crisis. During 1915, when he was at his most productive, Thomas was torn between emigrating with his family to join Frost in America and enlisting in the British Army. As a soldier in his late thirties, his decision to serve in the front line was voluntary though scarcely unique; the novelist Ford Madox Ford, five years older than Thomas, went through a similar experience and was able to write of it in the third volume of his *Parade's End* novel-sequence, *A Man Could Stand Up* (1926). But if the rural world of Thomas's poetry seems at times to be hermetically sealed from everyday modern life, in 'Adlestrop' the presumably suburban poet sees and hears the Cotswolds through a train window.

There are other reasons for linking Thomas to suburbia. A prose writer who became a poet, he was also – almost – a novelist. *The Happy-Go-Lucky Morgans* (1913) is more a collection of anecdotes and folktales than a novel, but it is held together by its evocation of a lost childhood domain set in Balham in south London. Here Thomas draws heavily on his Welsh roots, portraying a family who came from Carmarthenshire, and whose older members eventually return there. When the subject of patriotism comes up in the Morgan household, it

is the Welsh national anthem 'Land of my Fathers' that is sung. But
The Happy-Go-Lucky Morgans also contains Thomas's most extended
argument about Englishness, in the comically titled fifteenth chapter,
'Mr Stodham Speaks for England – Fog Supervenes'. Asked if
England is anything more than a geographical expression, Stodham
(who is an intimate friend of the family) launches into a 'sermon'
lasting several pages. The burden is that national identity is an integral
part of the individual self:

> Deny England – wise men have done so – and you may find yourself
> some day denying your father and mother – and this also wise men have
> done. Having denied England and your father and mother, you may
> have to deny your own self, and treat it as nothing, a mere conventional
> boundary, an artifice, by which you are separated from the universe and
> its creator. ... He is a bold man who hopes to do without earth,
> England, family, and self. (Thomas, 1913: 222)

The singing of 'Land of My Fathers' comes immediately after this and
is felt to embody the spirit of patriotism that Stodham was trying to
express: 'It was exulting without self-glorification or any other form of
brutality' (Thomas, 1913: 224). The moment of rapture is cut off not
only by the visible descent of fog outside but, even worse, by its
auditory effects. In the sudden hush the family members can hear 'the
mutter of London', a distant noise resembling 'a brutish yell of agony'
and 'a dying curse' (Thomas, 1913: 227). No doubt this metropolitan
cacophony can be shut out by closing the windows, but in the long
term the Morgans' life at Balham is doomed and their house, with its
three acres of grounds including a garden called the Wilderness, will
give way to suburban streets. The Morgans lived at Abercorran House
in the early 1890s; twenty years later the narrator returns to find that
the house has been demolished and, in a detail that would reappear a
quarter of a century later in George Orwell's novel *Coming Up for Air*,
the carp pond in the Wilderness has been drained and built over. What
is most moving in *The Happy-Go-Lucky Morgans* is its sense of the
false security of childhood and the impermanence of place.

Thomas concluded an essay on 'England', commissioned at the
outbreak of the First World War, with the observation that 'all ideas of
England are developed, spun out, from such a centre [of place] into
something large or infinite, solid or aëry, according to each man's
nature and capacity; that England is a system of circumferences
circling round the minute neighbouring points of home' (1981: 231).

Although he is trying to reconstruct a common experience of Englishness, this statement rings false since the intellectual's perception of national identity is so often centripetal rather than centrifugal – a displaced, disembodied spirit passionately seeking a place it can call home – and Thomas is nothing if not such an intellectual. So too is the Forster of *Howards End* and elsewhere. It is no surprise that so many of Forster's homecomings, including that in *Howards End*, are both rural and southern.

Post-English Englands

There are two famously lyrical set-pieces in *Howards End*, the one opening up a world of cosmopolitan culture, the other of national, geographical identity: the evocation of Beethoven's Fifth Symphony and the vision of England as seen from the Purbeck Hills in Dorset. These hills, Forster's narrator says, are the place to go 'If one wanted to show a foreigner England', the foreigner in question being the Schlegels' German cousin Frieda Mosebach. From Purbeck 'the imagination swells, spreads, and deepens, until it becomes geographic and encircles England' (Forster, 1973: 157), an effect that is registered not by the pedantic Frieda but, perhaps, by the Schlegel sisters to whom (Forster hints) England spiritually 'belongs':

> Does she belong to those who have moulded her and made her feared by other lands, or to those who have added nothing to her power, but have somehow seen her, seen the whole island at once, lying as a jewel in a silver sea, sailing as a ship of souls, with all the brave world's fleet accompanying her towards eternity? (Forster, 1973: 164)

This is Thomas's centrifugal vision, spreading out from the local to the national, but *Howards End* is principally concerned with the Schlegel sisters' quest to find a home. To do so these cosmopolitan intellectuals must compromise with the empire-building business class, represented here by the Wilcox family who own Howards End in Hertfordshire, a house that, we are told, is ambiguously located in the border zone between 'England' and 'suburbia' (Forster, 1973: 24). Suburbia in the shape of 'Bournemouth's ignoble coast' is explicitly included within the visionary South Country England seen from the Purbeck Hills, but the novel's pastoral conclusion, with its scene of haymaking at Howards End, offers a fragile hope that suburbia is only a passing phase, a blot on the nation's green fabric. The 'red rust' of new residential development is just visible from the old house, meaning, as Helen Schlegel points out, that London is 'creeping' towards them,

'And London is only part of something else, I'm afraid. Life's going to be melted down, all over the world.'

Margaret knew that her sister spoke truly. Howards End, Oniton, the Purbeck Downs, the Oderberge, were all survivals, and the melting-pot was being prepared for them. Logically, they had no right to be alive. One's hope was in the weakness of logic. Were they possibly the earth beating time?

'Because a thing is going strong now, it need not go strong for ever', she said ... All the signs are against it now, but I can't help hoping and very early in the morning in the garden I feel that our house is the future as well as the past.' (Forster, 1973: 306)

Against the wistful utopianism of Forster's ending we shall need to set both the fate of Abercorran House in Thomas's novel and, for that matter, Larkin's 'And that will be England gone' (1988: 190). The countryside mourned by all three writers once had the 'Stilled legendary depth' of the fishpond celebrated in 'Pike' by Larkin's contemporary Ted Hughes: 'It was as deep as England' (1960: 57). Hughes's pond with its lurking pike is the last survival of an old monastic settlement, but fishponds, as we know, can be drained and bricked over in no time.

It is not surprising, then, that the England of many recent novels is what could be called a post-English England, a deliberately antiquated parody, as in Julian Barnes's *England, England* (1998) – where it leads back to a version of Forster's pastoral utopia – and James Hawes's *Speak for England* (2005) (see also Day, Chapter 11). There is a long tradition of such parodies, perhaps going back to Evelyn Waugh's *A Handful of Dust* (1934) with its significantly named protagonist Tony Last. Yet from another perspective the 'post-English Englands' can be seen as a simple evasion of Forster's question – to whom does England belong? – and of Lawrence's question, 'which is *my* England?'

From Hull to homelessness – and 'Mr Bleaney'

We cannot assume that the celebrants of literary Englishness are themselves undividedly, let alone stereotypically, English, or that they could readily identify with a particular English home. Margaret Schlegel, who is stimulated to her vision of Englishness by an obdurately German cousin, is half-German herself. For every Philip Larkin, born in Coventry and resident for most of his adult life in Hull, there is a poet or novelist whose experience of national identity is all the more intense for emerging under conditions of greater or lesser geographical displacement. For example, Edward Thomas was born in

London of 'mainly Welsh' parents, and he gave his children Welsh names (Thomas, 2008: 327). The Morgans, 'more Welsh than Balhamitish' (1913: 1), are a strong expression of what, for their author, was at least a wished-for identity. Thomas was a close friend of the nature essayist W.H. Hudson, the third of the literary pioneers of 'South Country' Englishness singled out in Howkins's essay, and between Hudson and Thomas, as Helen Thomas later recalled, the 'love of the English country and its people was the great bond' (1978: 108). Yet Hudson (as Howkins nowhere mentions) was born in Argentina and did not set foot in England until he was in his early thirties. In his foreword to Edward Thomas's posthumous *Cloud Castle and Other Papers*, Hudson comments on the strangeness of the friendship between two writers who, given the disparity in their ages, might have been father and son. Their circumstances were totally different: 'He, an Oxford graduate, and a literary man by profession; I, unschooled and unclassed, born and bred in a semi-barbarous district among the horsemen of the pampas' (1922: v). Hudson is commemorated in Hyde Park not by the figure of one of his Wiltshire shepherds but by Jacob Epstein's sculpture of Rima, the protagonist of his novel *Green Mansions* (1904) set in the Amazon forests. Nor was Hudson alone in the sense of estrangement underlying his vision of Englishness. Among his contemporaries Belloc, as we have seen, was born in France; Ford Madox Ford, author of the prose trilogy *England and the English*, was of German origin; and while Rudyard Kipling spent much of his unhappy childhood in an English boarding school, his marvellous evocation of a boy's life in *Kim* draws on his equally estranged, but far more intense, identification with Anglo-India. Can it be that the contrast between first- and second-generation immigrant writers and those with a longer-term English background is as important as the split between the rural and the suburban in the formulation of Englishness?

At this point a recent poem by Grace Nichols, 'Outward from Hull', can take us back to Larkin. I will quote it in full:

> The gulls of Hull
> the train pulling out –
> a metallic snake
> along the estuary
> leaving behind
> the forceful ghost
> of Wilberforce
> the confluence
> of the Hull and the Humber,

Brough, Selby, Doncaster.
How many times
have I sat this way, England,
gazing out at the leafless
names of trees, at cathedrals
I still haven't seen –
our inter-city boa pushing
through the deepening night –
the wet black roots
of the country.
Suddenly, for some
unearthly reason,
it falters, then stops –
an inexplicable
paralysis of rhythm –
the broach of a small town
gleaming in the distance –
the eels and eels
of branching tracks.

O England –
provincial as Larkin
omnivorous as Shakespeare. (2009: 3)[4]

Grace Nichols is of Guyanese origin, and Guyana provides the setting of her first novel *Whole of a Morning Sky* (1986). 'Outward from Hull' offers a brief reminder that the British Empire was built on the slave trade which Wilberforce did so much to outlaw; and there is a hint of tropical terrain as the train's 'metallic snake' becomes an 'inter-city boa' pushing through the country's 'wet black roots'. The 'eels' of the branching tracks have swum across the Atlantic, as – figuratively, at least – Nichols herself has done. But hers is a very English poem, the evocation of a journey from Hull to (presumably) London recalling both Larkin's 'The Whitsun Weddings' and – when the express train suddenly comes to a halt – Thomas's 'Adlestrop'. In this sense, 'Outward from Hull' is as provincial as both Larkin and Thomas, but it is also separated from the English landscape by the glass of the train window just as their poems were: the epigrammatic last three lines produce a kind of fish-tank effect which has been prepared for by the eel-like tracks. This is England as a place and a culture glimpsed from outside and, as it were, from a different element. Yet this is a technique that Nichols might have learnt from Larkin himself, from 'The Whitsun Weddings' but also from what I see as one of his finest and most characteristic poems, 'Mr Bleaney'.

The 'novel of immigration' to Britain is, by any standard, a major form of post-1945 English fiction, with the contrast between the dream and the reality of England – the fantasised destination and the down-at-heel, disillusioning, sometimes hateful but ultimately often loveable presence – as its stock-in-trade (see also Day, Chapter 11). Novels of immigration have been written both by immigrant authors and by those with more orthodox English origins, in which case they can become a vehicle for somewhat masochistic national self-criticism. A recent novel of this kind is Rose Tremain's prize-winning *The Road Home* (2007), but one of the pioneering examples of the form is *A Girl in Winter* (1947) by that self-critical masochist Philip Larkin. Larkin at this time took his fiction immensely seriously – his ambition was to become a successful novelist, not a poet – and in his first novel, *Jill* (1946), the protagonist undergoes another emblematic late twentieth-century experience, leaving his working-class 'roots' to go to university in a different part of the country. The novel begins with his sense of displacement on an acutely embarrassing (and very funny) train-ride to his posh university city. In *A Girl in Winter* his main character is a wartime refugee from an unnamed Central European country who is serving as a library assistant in a provincial town.

The sense of displacement and of merely temporary settlement is pervasive in Larkin's poetry as well. 'Home' for him is an area of blankness rather than a fixed centre. Thus 'I Remember, I Remember', the poem recalling his Coventry childhood, begins with 'Coming up England by a different line' and ends with his dismissal of a now meaningless past: 'Nothing, like something, happens anywhere' (1988: 81–2). In 'Poetry of Departures', 'We all hate home / And having to be there' (1988: 85), but more often in Larkin's poetry not only are we away from 'home' but we do not know where it is. Thus, in 'Friday Night at the Royal Station Hotel', the hotel's amenities include 'The headed paper, made for writing home / (If home existed) letters of exile' (1988: 163). And in at least one poem, 'The Importance of Elsewhere', Larkin encapsulates the immigrant experience. Here he is 'Lonely in Ireland, since it was not home', but the 'strangeness' offers him a kind of freedom and a feeling of relaxation that he does not find in England. Being 'at home' in one's own country is at once an impoverishment and a kind of entrapment, since 'no elsewhere underwrites my existence' – yet this may not prevent 'Living in England' from being his preferred destination (1988: 104).

If Larkin's turn from fiction to poetry may be seen, in part, as the product of a need to write about himself rather than 'invented' characters, certain of his poems read like compressed or unwritten novels:

notably, 'Dockery and Son' and 'Mr Bleaney'. Bleaney is a fictional character even if the poem's final line concedes that Larkin does not know, and cannot know, anything of his inner life. Despite his Irish-sounding name, he seems to be an epitome of mid-twentieth-century lower-middle class Englishness: a smoker, a keen gardener, a radio listener, a man who does the football pools and spends his summer holidays at Frinton and his Christmases with family in Stoke-on-Trent. He is, like the poet himself, a bachelor who finds temporary quarters in a solitary bedsit, lying on the 'fusty bed' and (perhaps) 'Telling himself that this was home' – but the most sinister-sounding piece of information his landlady supplies is right at the start of the poem:

> 'This was Mr Bleaney's room. He stayed
> The whole time he was at the Bodies, till
> They moved him.' (1988: 102)

'Bodies' is a typically Larkinesque reminder of mortality, as is Mr Bleaney's 'one hired box' in the poem's penultimate line: the box may be simply a portmanteau, or a coffin, or the room he is presumed to have called home (1988: 103). 'Bodies', too, has a literal reference, reminding us that Larkin grew up in Coventry and went to university in Oxford, both centres of the British motor industry. The landlady's odd locution suggests that Mr Bleaney worked in a car factory, apparently as a clerk or junior manager rather than on the assembly line since his employers moved his livelihood to another part of the country rather than laying him off when he was no longer required. Car production involves both body plants and engine plants; and, if we see Mr Bleaney himself as a kind of car, we know exactly where his body lay but can only speculate (along with Larkin himself) about what motivated or 'drove' him. 'I know his habits', the poet tells us (1988: 102), but he can only hope to grasp who Bleaney is or was by analogy with his own experience. (It is possible that Bleaney is either dead or has been moved into hospital, but at the literal level the poem does not say this.) To the extent that Larkin as the next tenant follows in Bleaney's footsteps, it may be that both are reluctantly driven – to continue the motoring metaphor – by what the poet elsewhere calls 'the toad *work*' (1988: 89), the toad that may indeed help us to get through life, as suggested in 'Toads Revisited': 'Give me your arm, old toad; / Help me down Cemetery Road.' (1988: 148).

Larkin's almost comically depressed manner, the 'mustn't grumble' stoicism of his incessant grumbling about life, is what some have seen as the stereotypically English element in his verse.[5] But in Mr Bleaney he has also created a tacit embodiment of Englishness, a successor, in that respect, to Hardy's Michael Henchard. Neither Henchard nor Bleaney, we should note, has a real home. Henchard is a displaced countryman, while Bleaney is a townsman and product of the modern industrial landscape whose only obvious connection with nature is his love of gardening. His room looks out on 'a strip of building land, / Tussocky, littered', and if it is true that, as Larkin asserts with some dread in one of the poem's last lines, 'how we live measures our own nature', then Bleaney's Englishness is a desperately reduced thing compared to Henchard's (1988: 102–3). He is English (we assume), yet he lives in England like a displaced person, an immigrant or refugee who is destined to be moved on by forces outside his control. But Henchard, too, begins and ends as a nomad, his glory as Mayor of Casterbridge only a brief interlude like Bleaney's time at the Bodies. That this is a near-universal fate is suggested by Larkin's poems set in hospitals and old people's homes, a phrase such as 'residential home' revealing that the word 'home' itself takes on a different meaning and resonance as we approach the last stages of our lives. This impermanent, shaken, tawdry but not entirely hopeless England is the country of which Larkin was, in his time – and surely still is – such an effective laureate. How far this is matter for celebration, or anything other than level-toned acceptance, is another matter. One mustn't grumble about Larkin's England; but to speak of or about it is to grumble all the same.

Notes

1   Thanks to Phillip Mallett for some of the information in this paragraph.
2   I am grateful to Edna Longley for this information.
3   The rhythm here strongly depends upon punctuation. The comma after 'Yes' is found in the British Library manuscript version, but sometimes – as in Edna Longley's recent edition – it is replaced by a full stop; see Thomas 2008: 177.
4   Reproduced with permission of Curtis Brown Group Ltd. London, on behalf of Grace Nichols. Copyright © Grace Nichols 2009.
5   *Mustn't Grumble*, as it happens, is the title of a travelogue by Joe Bennett, subtitled in some editions *In Search of England and the English* (2006).

Afterword

Christine Berberich and Arthur Aughey

The popular travel writer H.V. Morton prefaced his *The Call of England* (1928) with lines from G.K. Chesterton's *The Ballad of the White Horse*: 'An island like a little book / Full of a hundred tales'. This book has tried to show how England (if not quite an island) is full of many tales and that to write or speak of the 'identity' of England at any one time is to write or speak of the conversation implied in those tales. Though the conversation is constantly changing it is remarkable how, as Oakeshott remarked and as we discussed in the Introduction, there is also a 'swerving back to recover and make something topical out of even its remotest moments' (1991: 59). For example, Paul Kingsnorth's (2008) lament at the contemporary commercial evisceration of all that is worthwhile in the traditions of England calls to mind William Morris's thought in *Under an Elm Tree* that 'the Battle of Ashdown will be forgotten for the last commercial crisis; Alfred's heraldry will yield to the lions of the half crown' (1889: 212).

This 'yielding' of heritage to the 'top dollar, long yen' (Barnes, 1998: 58) has been perfectly illustrated, as Gary Day demonstrated in Chapter 11, in Julian Barnes' novel *England England* where England's heritage – real or embellished – has been turned into a highly marketable commodity. The fact that England's past has been (ab)used for commercial or political means is one that has preoccupied a host of contemporary novelists, prominent among them Kazuo Ishiguro who, in his 1989 novel *The Remains of the Day*, attempted to show the dangers of looking at the past uncritically and merely through nostalgically tinted glasses. In an interview with Alan Vorda, Ishiguro famously explained that

> the kind of England that I create in *The Remains of the Day* is not an England *that I believe ever existed*. I've not attempted to reproduce, in a historically accurate way, some past period. What I'm trying to do here ... is to actually *rework a particular myth* about a certain kind of England. I think there is this very strong idea that exists in England at the

moment, about an England where people lived in the not-so-distant past, that conformed to various stereotypical images. That is to say an England with sleepy, beautiful villages with very polite people and butlers and people taking tea on the lawn. Now, at the moment, particularly in Britain, there is an enormous nostalgia industry going on ... trying to recapture this kind of old England. The mythical landscape of this sort of England, to a large degree, is harmless nostalgia for a time that didn't exist. The other side of this, however, is that it is used as a political tool. (1993: 14–15)

Ishiguro was critical of the way politicians, mainly but not only Conservatives, tried to manipulate the past to sell a wholesome picture of England domestically and internationally that did not necessarily reflect reality. The England sold to the world in coffee table books and so-called 'white-flannel dramas'[1] produced for TV and cinema consumption (for example the 1981 ITV adaptation of Waugh's *Brideshead Revisited,* or the hugely successful film *Chariots of Fire* of the same year) presented an aesthetically pleasing England – but a predominantly mythical England cleansed of serious political controversy. The danger, as Ishiguro rightly pointed out, lay not only in the fact that politicians would sell this image to their electorate but also that the electorate might buy it.

However, as Patrick Parrinder's chapter has demonstrated, this more critical preoccupation with England is not a contemporary phenomenon. Writers from Hardy onwards have already shown themselves aware of changes in the country and commented on them, sometimes wistfully, sometimes critically, sometimes, as in the case of Larkin, in a unique combination of both attitudes. Larkin is a poet who expresses a sense of being English in the twentieth century, this unique combination of pride in the country, nostalgia for a past that is not always praiseworthy, an awareness of the shortcomings of both past and present and a deep foreboding about its future. His poetry, like all great poetry, is itself a conversation. In a recent series for *The Guardian,* 'roving reporter' Laura Barton 'travels around England, Scotland and Wales to build up a portrait of modern Britain' (Barton, 2009). The result is a series of short films, accessible via *The Guardian* website, that showcase aspects of Britain (mainly England) today. In May 2009, Barton added a short film dedicated to Larkin's 'The Whitsun Weddings', retracing the poet's train journey from Hull to King's Cross Station in London, and commenting on the changes – social, cultural, agricultural, religious – since the first publication of the poem in 1964 (Barton, 2009). Barton's sensitive report avoids nostalgia and calls to mind Paul Cezanne's famous statement that

'Right now a moment of time is passing by. We must become that moment' (quoted in Webster's, 2008). It is a call to be(come) more aware of our surroundings, their past, their history, and their future potential, and not to take them as an unchangeable given, but as something that should be appreciated for the very fact that they *do* change.

To take another example, in an influential study which its publishers claim is 'the book for our times', Phillip Blond returns to 'the analysis of servitude first offered by Chesterton and Belloc early in the twentieth century' (2010: 49) as the basis of a radically *new* political settlement. To claim such an inspiration is to challenge other tales – perhaps conventional wisdoms – about that analysis of Chesterton and Belloc, confirming Oakeshott's other observation that even such swerving back leaves little in the present unmodified. The reference to Chesterton is doubly relevant in this case. As Julia Stapleton has pointed out, Chesterton thought that English patriotism was best approached through consciousness of its weakness and vulnerability rather than through celebration of its strengths. 'Against one critic who mocked him by professing to be baffled by his expression of "fear" for England on account of his "love" of it, he cleared up the confusion thus: "You have never begun to love anything until you have begun to fear for it"' (2009: 7; see also Chapter 10, this volume). Certainly, the chapters in this volume have revealed that relationship too. Anxieties about England, the English and Englishness are intimately connected with concern for the country itself, about its political, civil, social and cultural character as revealed in the concrete references preferred by all those English list-makers.

Stephen Ingle and Matt Beech have shown the importance of the idea of 'conversation' at party-political level. None of the big parties can boast a straightforward history with unanimity on direction and policy. Instead, and as both authors have pointed out, there has always been a process of dialogue and discussion: ideas have been presented, discussed, compromised on and adapted in a process involving past, present and future, a process that has been further explored by Philip Norton. The most prominent contemporary example for this is, as Colin Copus has pointed out, the 2010 Coalition Agreement between David Cameron's Conservatives and Nick Clegg's Liberal Democrats: two parties which, until May 2010, seemed to have little in common but who suddenly found themselves in coalition talks. However, Copus points out the importance of conversation not only at national but, potentially even more importantly, at local level: he emphasises the importance of a form of English local government that allows representatives to engage properly with their electorate, rather than being mere administrators of thousands of centrally devised programmes. Moreover, Susan Condor, John Curtice and Paul Thomas have emphasised a different kind of conversation: research interviews that allow participants to voice their opinion about national identity, its varied expression and institutionalisation. Simon Lee illustrates once again that 'vague mental toothache' noted by Morton, an English disquiet more often based on the feeling that they *should* feel anxious rather than the actual state of *being* anxious. For Lee, this mental toothache has become politically acute and needs to be addressed urgently. The English have become alienated, unsure and displaced, and not by accident but as the result of government policy. Of course, such argument has a long pedigree in both conservative and radical literature about Englishness but its current expression is bound up with the new (devolved) complexity of United Kingdom governance and with the uncertainty of how England fits into it. For most, it would seem, England remains *somewhere* and *home*. If it seems invisible or nowhere that is because most people take England and their Englishness for granted. As the introductory chapter tried to show, to persuade the English of the virtue of nationalist thinking (in the political sense) is to convince the English to think *differently* about themselves and their country. This may be difficult, but it is not, of course, impossible.

The culture of what Bagehot once described as the 'age of discussion' (what we have called 'conversation') required a disposition of 'animated moderation', and he thought that it was this quality 'in which the English – at least so I claim it for them – excel all other nations' (1906: 201). There was, he conceded, 'an infinite deal to be laid' against England and as 'we are unpopular with most others, and as we are always grumbling at ourselves, there is no want of people to say it' (1906: 201). But he also thought that there was enough to show that this spirit of animated moderation – despite questions about who, how and what was said or heard – was more than a mere ideal for it animated the vigorous practice of public affairs. Though many English people could be (and continue to be) coarse, illiterate, stupid, venal and aggressive there remained, despite all the defects, a distinctive union of energy and moderation. It was that other great doyen of reflection on English constitutional thinking, A.V. Dicey, who argued that the 'singular absence in England of all popular tradition causes some natural regret to poets and even to patriots' but he was assured that it had also favoured 'the preservation of English freedom' (2008: 239). It was the very absence of 'historical hatreds' that had delivered England from what Dicey called 'spurious patriotism' (2008: 239). If patriotism was to animate the world of thought it had to be of the moderate kind, one that was the opposite of spurious and dedicated to a conception of material and even moral improvement. And if this sounds eminently Victorian and cut from a faded utilitarian cloth, consider the more recent remarks of Roy Hattersley. Reflecting, as Dicey did a century earlier, on the distinctiveness of English national identity when contrasted with more romantic kinds of nationalism, Hattersley actually makes a similar point. 'We English do not need to behave in those flamboyant ways and we lose something that is essentially English if we start to copy the behavior of less secure nationalities.' The English are not without their pride in nationhood but their pride lies in 'not boasting about being English' (2009: 2–3). Dicey's patriotism is the patriotism of the administrator for whom the supreme value is the value of good government in the (English) tradition of Alexander Pope:

> For forms of government let fools contest
> Whate'er is best administered is best:
> For modes of faith let graceless zealots fight;
> His can't be wrong whose life is in the right. (1733; 2008: 35)

Hattersley's Englishness is, as he admits, cultural, an unapologetic 'fondness' for England without which he thought it impossible to be serious when being critical of things that are wrong with the country (2009: 5). Here, though separated by a century, is the common ground of 'animated moderation'. Which is why, for the moment at least, the fortunes of radical groups on the left and the right have fared so poorly. Christopher Bryant suggests that this 'animated moderation' is alive and well and intimated in a form of cosmopolitanism that is distinctively English.

What the chapters in this volume have done is to show that there is, at present, considerable animated conversation about England, about being English, and about that most elusive of all terms, 'Englishness'. They have addressed the English past and the English present, with some suggestions towards possible futures. This, we believe, provides some guidance if we want to understand that conversational 'flow of sympathy' which connects the various elements of 'These Englands' in their diverse listings.

Note

1 See http://www.museum.tv/eotvsection.php?entrycode=bridesheadre for more information on so-called 'white-flannel dramas', accessed 19 November 2010.

References

All polls cited were accessible via the archives of the following polling companies as of 20 June 2009.
Gfk-NOP: www.gfk.nop.com
Ipsos MORI: www.ipsos-mori.com
Populus: www.populus.co.uk
What England Means to Me: http://whatenglandmeanstome.co.uk
YouGov: www.populus.co.uk

Abbas, T. (ed.) (2005). *Muslim Britain: Communities under pressure*, London: Zed

Abell, J. and G. Myers (2008). Analysing research interviews. In R. Wodak and M. Krzyzanowski (eds). *Qualitative Discourse Analysis in the Social Sciences*. London: Palgrave Macmillan, 145–61

Abell, J., S. Condor and C. Stevenson (2006). 'We are an island': geographical imagery in accounts of citizenship, civil society and national identity in Scotland and in England. *Political Psychology* 27: 191–217

Abell, J., S. Condor and C. Stevenson (2007). Who ate all the pride? English patriotism and national football support. *Nations and Nationalism* 13: 97–116

Abell, J., A. Locke, S. Condor, S. Gibson and S. Stevenson (2006). Trying similarity, doing difference. *Qualitative Research* 6: 221–44

Ackerman, B. (1989). Constitutional Politics/Constitutional Law. *Yale Law Journal* 99. 3: 453–547

Ackroyd, P. (2002). *Albion: The Origins of the English Imagination*. London: Chatto & Windus

Albrecht, T., G.M. Johnson and J.B. Walther (1993). Understanding communication processes in focus groups. In D.L. Morgan (ed.). *Successful Focus Groups*. Newbury Park: Sage, 51–64

Alexander, C. (2004). Imagining the Asian gang: ethnicity, masculinity and youth after 'the riots'. *Critical Social Policy* 24.4: 526–49

Ali, M. (2003). *Brick Lane*. London: Doubleday

Anderson, B. (1991). *Imagined Communities: Reflections on the Origins and Spread of Nationalism*. London: Verso

Anderson, P. (1979). *Lineages of the Absolutist State*. London: Verso

Anderson, P. (1992). *English Questions*. London: Verso

Arbuthnot, J. (1976). *The History of John Bull*, ed. A.W. Bower and R.A. Erickson. Oxford: Clarendon Press

Arendt, H. (1959). *The Human Condition*. Chicago: University of Chicago Press

Arendt, H. (1977). *Between Past and Future*. Harmondsworth: Penguin

Arendt, H. (1990). *On Revolution*. Harmondsworth: Penguin

Ashe, G. (2007). *The Offbeat Radicals: The British Tradition of Alternative Dissent*. London: Methuen

Atkinson, P. and D. Silverman (1997). Kundera's immortality: the interview society and the invention of self. *Qualitative Inquiry* 3.3: 324–45

Auden, W.H. (1964). A communist to others. In R. Skelton (ed.). *Poetry of the Thirties*. Harmondsworth: Penguin Books, 54–8

Aughey, A. (2006). The challenges to English identity. In R. Hazell (ed.). *The English Question*. Manchester: Manchester University Press, 45–63

Aughey, A. (2007). *The Politics of Englishness*. Manchester: Manchester University Press

Aughey, A. (2010). Anxiety and injustice: the anatomy of contemporary English nationalism. *Nations and Nationalisms* 16.10: 506–24

Austin, A. (1902). *Haunts of Ancient Peace*. London: Macmillan

Austin, J.L. (1962). *How to Do Things with Words*. Oxford: Clarendon

Back, L. (1996). *New Ethnicities and Urban Culture*. London: UCL Press

Back, L., M. Keith, A. Khan, K. Shukra and J. Solomos (2002). New Labour's white heart: politics, multiculturalism and the return of assimilationism. *Political Quarterly* 73:4: 445–54

Bagehot, W. (1867; 1963). *The English Constitution*. London: Fontana

Bagehot, W. (1906). *Physics and Politics*. New York: Appleton & Company

Baggini, J. (2007). *Welcome to Everytown: A Journey into the English Mind*. London: Granta Books

Baggini, J. (2008). Across the great divide. *Prospect* (January): 38–41

Bagguley, P. and Y. Hussain (2005). Flying the flag for England? Citizenship, religion and cultural identity among British Pakistani Muslims. In T. Abbas (ed.). *Muslim Britain: Communities under Pressure*. London: Zed, 208–21

Baglioni, S. (2003). The effects of political institutions and city size on political participation: the Swiss case. Paper presented to ECPR

Joint Sessions, Edinburgh, 28 March–2April, 2003

Baldwin, S. Earl (1939). *An Interpreter of England*. London: Hodder and Stoughton

Bale, T. (2010). *The Conservative Party from Thatcher to Cameron*. London: Polity

Balfour, A. (1927). Introduction. In W. Bagehot. *The English Constitution*. London: Oxford University Press, i–xxvi

Balls, E., J. Grice and G. O'Donnell (eds) (2004). *Microeconomic Reform in Britain: Delivering Opportunities for All*. London: Palgrave Macmillan

Barber, M. (2005). *Anthony Powell: A Life*. London: Duckworth

Barker, E. (1947). An attempt at perspective. In E. Barker (ed.). *The Character of England*. Oxford: Clarendon Press, 556–8

Barker, E. (1961). *Principles of Social and Political Theory*. London: Oxford University Press

Barnes, J. (1998). *England England*. London: Jonathan Cape

Barnett, C. (1963). *The Swordbearers*. Bloomington: Indiana University Press

Barton, L. (2009). Barton's Britain: the Whitsun weddings. *The Guardian Online*. Accessible at www.guardian.co.uk/travel/video /2009/may/26/bartons-britain-whitsun-weddings

Barton, L. (2009 to date). Barton's Britain. *The Guardian Online*. Accessible at www.guardian.co.uk/travel/series/bartons-britain

Baudrillard, J. (2001). *Selected Writings*, 2nd edn. Ed. M. Poster. Stanford, MA: Stanford University Press

Bauman, Z. (2004). *Europe: An Unfinished Adventure*. Cambridge: Polity

Bayard, P. (2007). *How to Talk about Books You Haven't Read*. London: Granta

Bechhofer, F. & D. McCrone (2009). National identity, nationalism and constitutional change. In F. Bechhofer and D. McCrone (eds). *National Identity, Nationalism* and Constitutional Change. London: Palgrave Macmillan, 1–15

Bechhofer, F., D. McCrone, R. Kiely and R. Stewart (1999). Constructing national identity: arts and landed elites in Scotland. *Sociology* 33: 515–34

Beck, U. (2002). The cosmopolitan society and its enemies. *Theory, Culture and* Society 19: 17–44

Beck, U. (2006). *Cosmopolitan Vision*. Cambridge: Polity

Beck, U. and E. Grande (2007a). *Cosmopolitan Europe*. Cambridge: Polity

Beck, U. and E. Grande (2007b). Cosmopolitanism: Europe's way out of a crisis. *European Journal of Social Theory* 10: 67–85

Beck. U. and N. Sznaider (eds) 2006). Cosmopolitan sociology. Special issue of *British Journal of Sociology* 57.1

Beech, M. and K. Hickson (2006). *Labour's Thinkers: The Intellectual Roots of Labour from Tawney to Gordon Brown*. London: I.B.Tauris

Beer, S. (1965). *Modern British Politics*. London: Faber & Faber

Bellah, R., R. Madsen, W.M. Sullivan, A. Swidler and S.M. Tipton (1985). *Habits of the Heart*. Berkeley: University of California Press

Belloc, H. (1920). The South Country. In *Modern British Poetry*. Ed. L. Untermeyer. New York: Harcourt, Brace and Howe

Benner, E. (1997). Nationality without nationalism. *Journal of Political Ideologies*. 2.2: 189–206

Bennett, J. (2006). *Mustn't Grumble. In Search of England and the English*. London: Simon Schuster

Benton, T, (2004). I want an integrated society with a difference. Interview with Trevor Phillips. *The Times* (3 April): np

Berberich, C. (2007). *The Image of the English Gentleman in Twentieth-Century Literature. Englishness and Nostalgia*. Aldershot: Ashgate

Berberich, C. (2009). A Peculiarly English Idiosyncrasy? Julian Barnes's Use of Lists in *England England. ABC. American, British and Canadian Studies* 13 (December): 75—87

Betjeman, J. (1943). Oh, to be in England. *The Listener* (29. 739: 295–6

Biagini, E.F. (1992). *Liberty, Retrenchment and Reform: Popular Liberalism in the Age of Gladstone, 1860–1880*. Cambridge: Cambridge University Press

Billig, M. (1995). *Banal Nationalism*. London: Sage

Blake, R. (1998). *The Conservative Party from Peel to Major*. London: Arrow Books

Blattberg, C. (2003). Patriotic, not deliberative, democracy. *Critical Review of International Social and Political Philosophy* 6.1: 155–74

Bogdanor, V. (1999). *Devolution in the United Kingdom*. Oxford: Oxford University Press

Bogdanor, V. (2009). *The New British Constitution*. Oxford and Portland, OR: Hart

Bord, G. de (1994). *The Society of the Spectacle*. Transl. D. Nicholson. New York: Zone Books

Boucher, D. (1991). Politics in a different mode: an appreciation of Michael Oakeshott 1901–1990. *History of Political Thought* 12.4: 717–29

'Bourne, G.' [G. Sturt] (1955). *Change in the Village*. London: Duckworth

Brace, C. (1999). Looking back: the Cotswolds and English national identity, c.1890–1950. *Journal of Historical Geography* 25.4: 502–16

Brack, D., R. Grayson and D. Howarth (eds) (2007). *Reinventing the State: Social Liberalism for the 21st Century*. London: Politico's

Bradley, A.W. and K.D. Ewing (2007). *Constitutional and Administrative Law*, 14th edn. London: Pearson Longman

Bragg, B. (2006). *The Progressive Patriot: A Search for Belonging*. London: Bantam Press

Brain, J. *Room at the Top* (1957). Harmondsworth: Penguin

British Broadcasting Corporation (2007a). Tories ponder English only voting. *BBC News Online* (28 October)

British Broadcasting Corporation (2007b). Transcript of an interview between Gordon Brown and Andrew Marr for the *Sunday AM*, BBC1 television programme (7 January)

Brown, G. (1994). The politics of potential: a new agenda for labour. In D. Miliband (ed.). *Reinventing the Left*. Cambridge: Polity

Brown, G. (1997). Outward bound. *The Spectator* (8 November): 15–16

Brown, G. (1999). Speech at the Smith Institute, London (15 April), available online: http://webarchive.nationalarchives.gov.uk /20100407010852/http://www.hm-treasury.gov.uk/speech_chex _150499.htm (accessed 12 August 2010)

Brown, G. (2004). Annual British Council Lecture, London (7 July), available online: http://webarchive.nationalarchives.gov.uk /20100407010852/http://www.hm-treasury.gov.uk /speech_chex_070704.htm (accessed 12 August 2010)

Brown, G. (2006a). The future of Britishness. Speech to the Fabian Society, 'Future of Britishness' Conference, London (14 January), available online: http://webarchive.nationalarchives.gov.uk /20100407010852/http://www.hm-treasury.gov.uk /speech_chex_140106.htm (accessed 12 August 2010)

Brown, G. (2006b). Securing our future. Lecture at the Royal Institute of International Affairs, Chatham House, London (13 February), available online: http://webarchive.nationalarchives.gov .uk/20100407010852/http://www.hm-treasury.gov.uk /speech_chex_130206.htm (accessed 12 August 2010)

Brown, G. (2007a). Speech on liberty. University of Westminster, London (25 October), available online: http://news.bbc.co.uk/1/hi /uk_politics/7062237.stm (accessed 12 August 2010)

Brown, G. (2007b). We need a United Kingdom. *Daily Telegraph* (13 January)

Brown, G. (2009). Foreword. In HM Government (2009). *Building*

Britain's Future. London: The Stationery Office

Brown, G. and J. Straw (2007). Foreword. In Ministry of Justice (2007). *The Governance of Britain*. Cm.7170. London: The Stationery Office

Bryant, C.G.A. (1997). Citizenship, national identity and the accommodation of difference: reflections on the German, French, Dutch and British cases. *New Community* 23: 157–72

Bryant, C.G.A. (2003). These Englands, or where does devolution leave the English? *Nations and Nationalism* 9: 393–412

Bryant, C.G.A. (2006). *The Nations of Britain*. Oxford: Oxford University Press

Bryant, C.G.A. (2008). Devolution, equity and the English question. *Nations and Nationalism* 14: 664–83

Bryant, C.G.A. (2010). Reconfiguring Britain. The 2010 O'Donnell Lecture in the University of Wales, Swansea. Deposited in the National Library of Wales, Aberystwyth

Bulpitt, J. (1983). *Territory and Power in the United Kingdom: An Interpretation*. Manchester: Manchester University Press

Bulpitt, J. (1991). The Conservative Party in Britain: a preliminary paradoxical portrait. Paper presented to the PSA Annual Conference, Lancaster

Burdsey, D. (2008). Half of some and half of the other: the racialised (dis)contents of Englishness. In M. Perryman (ed.). *Imagined Nation. England after Britain*. London: Lawrence and Wishart, 207–22

Burke, E. (1790; 1999). *Reflections on the Revolution in France*. In *Select Works of Edmund Burke*, Vol. 2. Ed. F. Canovan. Indianapolis: Liberty Fund

Butler, D. and D. Stokes (1974). *Political Change in Britain*, 2nd edn., London: Macmillan

Butler, D. and Kavanagh, D. (1984). *British General Election of 1983*. London: Macmillan

Butterfield, H. (1944). *The Englishman and his History*. Cambridge: Cambridge University Press

Byram, M. (2008). *From Language Education to International Citizenship: Essays and Reflections*. Clevedon: Multilingual Matters

Byrne, B. (2007). England – whose England? Narratives of nostalgia, emptiness and evasion in imaginations of national identity. *Sociological Review* 55: 509–30

Cabinet Office / Coalition (2010). *Our Programme for Government*. London: Cabinet Office. Also available online at: Available online at www.cabinetoffice.gov.uk/media/409088/pfg_coalition.pdf

Callaghan, J. (1987). *Time and Chance*. London: Collins/Fontana

Cameron, D. (2000). *Good to Talk?* London: Sage

Cantle, T. (2001). *Community Cohesion: A Report of the Independent Review Team*. London: Home Office

Cantle, T. (2005). *Community Cohesion: A New Framework for Race Relations*. Basingstoke: Palgrave

Carrington, B. (2008). Where's the white in the Union Jack? Race, identity and the sporting multicultural. In M. Perryman (ed.). *Imagined Nation. England after Britain*. London: Lawrence and Wishart, 109–33

Carrington, B. and G. Short (1998). Adolescent discourses on national identity. *Educational Studies* 24: 133–52

Chandler, J.A. (2007). *Explaining Local Government: Local Government in Britain Since 1800*. Manchester: Manchester University Press

Chesterton, G.K. (c. 1892). The march of the nations. In D.J. Conlon (ed.). *G.K. Chesterton: Collected Works*, Vol. 10. *Collected Poetry Part II*. San Francisco: Ignatius Press, 107

Chesterton, G.K. (1901). Our English goblins. *The Speaker* (23 February): 573–4

Chesterton, G.K. (1903). *Browning*. London: Macmillan

Chesterton, G.K. (1904). The poetry of Mr. William Watson. *The Fortnightly Review* (December): 761–8

Chesterton, G.K. (1905). *Heretics*. In D. Dooley (ed.). *Collected Works: G.K. Chesterton*, Vol. 1. San Francisco: Ignatius Press, 39–207

Chesterton, G.K. (1907). Common Sense in Politics. *The Daily News* (16 March): 6

Chesterton, G.K. (1908). *Orthodoxy*. In D. Dooley (ed.). *Collected Works: G.K. Chesterton*, Vol. 1. San Francisco: Ignatius Press, 211–366

Chesterton, G.K. (1913). *The Victorian Age in Literature*. London: Williams and Norgate

Chesterton, G.K. (1915). The secret people. In *Poems*. London: Burns & Oates, 243–6

Chesterton, G.K. (1917a). *The Return of Don Quixote*. London: Chatto & Windus

Chesterton, G.K. (1917b). *A Short History of England*. In James V. Schall (ed.). *Collected Works: G.K. Chesterton*, Vol. 20. San Francisco: Ignatius Press

Chesterton, G.K. (1925). French and English. In H. Milford (ed.). *Selected Modern English Essays*. Oxford: Oxford University Press, 286–91

Chesterton, G.K. (1926). *The Flying Inn*, 7th edn. London: Methuen

Chesterton, G.K. (1931a). Preservation of rural England: Mr.

Chesterton on the Village. *The Times* (30 April): 11c

Chesterton, G.K. (1931b). Mr Chesterton on the English countryside. *The Times* (4 December): 12b

Chesterton, G.K. (1932). *Sidelights*. London: Sheed & Ward

Chesterton, G.K. (1935). Explaining the English. In James V. Schall (ed.). *Collected Works: G.K. Chesterton*, Vol. 20. San Francisco: Ignatius Press, 623–30

Chesterton, G.K. (1964). The religious aspect of Westminster Abbey (undated). In D. Collins (ed.). *The Spice of Life*. Beaconsfield: Darwen Finlayson, 103–11

Chisholm, M. and S. Leach (2008). *Botched Business: The Damaging Process of Re-Organising Local Government 2006–2008*. Gloucestershire: Douglas McLean

Clancy, M. and C. O'Neill (2008). Oral evidence. 10 March in House of Lords / House of Commons Joint Committee on Human Rights, *A Bill of Rights for the UK?* Twenty-ninth Report of Session 2007–08, Volume II: Oral and Written Evidence, HL Paper 165–II/HC 150–II. London: The Stationery Office

Clark, H. (1996). *Using Language*. Cambridge: Cambridge University Press

Clark, H. and S. Brennan (1991). Grounding in communication. In L. Resnick, J.M. Levine and S.D. Teasley (eds). *Perspectives on Socially Shared Cognition*. Washington, DC: American Psychological Association, 127–49

Clark, H. and M. Schober (1991). Asking questions and influencing answers. In J. Tanur (ed.). *Questions about Questions: Inquiries into the Cognitive Bases of Surveys* New York: Sage, 15–48

Clarke, P. (1994). J.M. Keynes 1883–1946, 'The Best of Both Worlds'. In S. Pedersen and P. Mandler (eds). *After the Victorians*. London: Routledge, 171–87

Coffey, J. (1996). 'Democracy and popular religion': Moody and Sankey's mission to Britain, 1873–1875. In E.F. Biagini (ed.). *Citizenship and Community: Liberals, radicals and Collective Identities in the British Isles, 1865–1931*. Cambridge: Cambridge University Press, 93–119

Cohen, R. (1994). *Frontiers of Identity: The British and the others*. London: Longman

Coleman, S. (2004). Whose conversation? Engaging the public in authentic polyogue. *Political Quarterly* 75.2: 112–20

Collini, S. (1999). *English Pasts: Essays in History and Culture*. Oxford: Oxford University Press

Colls, R. (2002). *Identity of England*. Oxford: Oxford University Press

Colls, R. (2007a). The making of English national identity, or
Krishan's Kasino. In J. Hutchinson, S. Reynolds, A.D. Smith, R.
Colls and K. Kumar, Debate on Krishan Kumar's *The Making of
English National Identity. Nations and Nationalism* 13.2: 179–203

Colls, R. (2007b). After Bagehot: rethinking the constitution. *Political
Quarterly* 78.4: 518–26

Commission on the Future of Multi-Ethnic Britain (CFMEB) (2000)
The future of Multi-Ethnic Britain: The Parekh Report. London:
Profile Books

Commission on Scottish Devolution (2009). *Serving Scotland Better:
Scotland and the United Kingdom in the 21st Century, Final Report –
June 2009.* Edinburgh: Commission on Scottish Devolution. Also
available online at: www.commissiononscottishdevolution.org.uk
(accessed 19 November 2010)

Commission to Strengthen Parliament (2000). *Strengthening
Parliament.* London: The Conservative Party

Committee of Inquiry into the Conduct of Local Authority Business
(1986). *Report of the Committee into the Conduct of Local Authority
Business.* Cmnd 9797. London: The Stationery Office

Condor, S. (1996). Unimagined community? Some social psycholog-
ical issues concerning English national identity. In G. Breakwell and
E. Lyons (eds). *Changing European Identities.* Oxford: Butterworth
Heinemann, 41–67

Condor, S. (1997). Having history: a social psychological analysis of
Anglo British autostereotypes. In C. Barfoot (ed.). *Beyond Pug's
Tour.* Amsterdam: Rodopi, 213–53

Condor, S. (2000a). Pride and prejudice: identity management in
English people's talk about 'this country'. *Discourse and Society*
11.2: 163–93

Condor, S. (2006b). Temporality and collectivity: images of time and
history in English national representation. *British Journal of Social
Psychology* 45: 657–82

Condor, S. (2010). Devolution and national identity: the rules of
English (dis)engagement. *Nations and Nationalism,* 16: 525–43

Condor, S. and J. Abell (2006a). Vernacular accounts of 'national
identity' in post-devolution Scotland and England. In J. Wilson and
K. Stapleton (eds). *Devolution and Identity.* Aldershot: Ashgate,
51–75

Condor, S. and J. Abell (2006b). Romantic Scotland, tragic England,
ambiguous Britain: versions of 'the Empire' in post-devolution
national accounting. *Nations and Nationalism* 12: 451–70

Condor, S. and S. Gibson (2007). 'Everybody's entitled to their own opinion': ideological dilemmas of liberal individualism and active citizenship. *Journal of Community and Applied Social Psychology* 6: 178–99

Condor, S., S. Gibson and J. Abell (2006). English identity and ethnic diversity in the context of UK constitutional change. *Ethnicities* 6: 123–58

Conservative Party (2009). *Control Shift Returning Power to Local Communities*. London: Conservative Party

Constitution Committee, House of Lords (2003). *Devolution: Inter-Institutional Relations in the United Kingdom*. Session 2002–03, HL Paper 28. London: The Stationery Office

Constitution Unit (2010). *The Conservative Agenda for Constitutional Reform*. London: The Constitution Unit

Copsey, N. (2008). *Contemporary British Fascism: The British National Party and the Quest for Legitimacy*, 2nd edn. Basingstoke: Palgrave

Copus, C. (2006). *Leading the Localities: Executive Mayors in English Local Governance*. Manchester: Manchester University Press

Costin, W.C. and J.S. Watson (eds) (1961). *The Law and Working of the Constitution: Documents 1660–1914*, Vol. 1, 2nd edn. London: Adam and Charles Black

CRE (2005). *Citizenship and Belonging: What Is Britishness?* and *The Decline of Britishness* (surveys conducted by Ethnos). London: CRE

Critchley, J. (1983). In *The Observer* (22 May)

Crosland, C.A.R. (1956). *The Future of Socialism*. London: Jonathan Cape

Crosland, S. (1982). *Tony Crosland*. London: Jonathan Cape

Crozier, A. (1963). Take two. *Granta* 68.1229 (19 October): 27–9

Crystal, D. (2004). *The Stories of English*. London: Penguin Books

Cunningham, H. (1986). The Conservative party and patriotism. In R. Colls and P. Dodd (eds). *Englishness: Politics and Culture 1880–1920*. London: Croom Helm, 283–307

Curtice, J. (1999). Is Scotland a nation and Wales not? In B. Taylor and K. Thomson (eds). *Scotland and Wales: Nations Again?* Cardiff: University of Wales Press, 119–48

Curtice, J. (2009). Is there an English backlash? Reactions to devolution. In A. Park, J. Curtice, K. Thomson, M. Phillips and E. Clery (eds). *British Social Attitudes: The 25th Report*. London: Sage, 1–23

Curtice, J. and A. Heath (2000). Is the English lion about to roar? National identity after devolution. In R. Jowell, J. Curtice, A. Park, K. Thomson, L. Jarvis, C. Bromley and N. Stratford (eds). *British Social Attitudes: The 17th report – Focusing on diversity*. London: Sage, 155–74

Cusack, T.R. (1997). *Social Capital, Institutional Structures, and Democratic Performance: A Comparative Study of German Local Governments.* Publication of the Berlin Social Research Centre's Department 'Institutions and Social Change' (Research Group on Social Change, Institutions, and Mediation Processes)

Dalyell, T. (1977; 1999). *Devolution: The End of Britain?* London: Jonathan Cape

Davie, D. (1963). Poetry and landscape in present England. *Granta* 68.1229: 2–4

Davie, D. (1973). *Thomas Hardy and British Poetry.* London: Routledge

Davie, D. (1989). *Under Briggflats: A History of Poetry in Great Britain 1960–1988.* Manchester: Carcanet

Day, G., H. Davis and A. Drakakis-Smith (2006). Being English in North Wales. *Nationalism and Ethnic Politics* 12: 577–98

DCLG (2007a). *Preventing Violent Extremism: Winning Hearts and Minds.* London: DCLG (Department for Communities and Local Government)

DCLG (2007b). *Preventing Violent Extremism Pathfinder Fund: Guidance Note for Government Offices and Local Authorities in England.* London: DCLG

DCLG (2008a). *PVE Pathfinder Fund: Mapping of Project Activities 2007/08.* London: DCLG

DCLG (2008b). *Local Leadership to Tackle Violent Extremism.* Speech by Rt Hon. Hazel Blears MP to the Prevent Conference, London (10 December)

Delanty, G. (2006). The cosmopolitan imagination: critical cosmopolitanism and social theory. *British Journal of Sociology* 57: 25–47

Delanty, G. and C. Rumford (2005). *Rethinking Europe: Social Theory and the Implications of Europeanization* London: Routledge

Democracy Task Force (2008). *Answering the Question: Devolution, the West Lothian Question and the Future of the Union.* London: Conservative Party Democracy Task Force

Dench, G., K. Gavron and M. Young (2006). *The New East End: Kinship, Race and Conflict.* London: Profile

Denham, J. (2001). *Building Cohesive Communities: A Report of the Inter-Departmental Group on Public Order and Community Cohesion.* London: Home Office

Denham, A. and P. Dorey (2006). A tale of two speeches? The Tory leadership election of 2005. *Political Quarterly* 22.1: 35–42

Denisoff, D. (2007). Decadence and aestheticism. In G. Marshall (ed.). *The Cambridge Companion to the Fin de Siècle*. Cambridge: Cambridge University Press, 31–52

Denters, B. (2002). Size and political trust: evidence from Denmark, the Netherlands, Norway, and the United Kingdom. *Environment and Planning C: Government and Policy* 20.6: 793–812

Devos, T. and D. Ma (2008). Is Kate Winslet more American than Lucy Liu? *British Journal of Social Psychology* 47: 191–215

Dewar, D. (1997). Foreword. In The Scottish Office. *Scotland's Parliament*. Cm. 3658. Edinburgh: The Scottish Office

Dicey, A.V. (1885; 1959). *An Introduction to the Study of the Law of the Constitution*, 10th edn. London: Macmillan

Dicey, A.V. (2008). *Lectures on the Relation between Law and Public Opinion in England during the Nineteenth Century*. Ed. and Intro. R.VandeWetering. Indianapolis: Liberty Fund

Disraeli, B. (1845; 1980). *Sybil.* Harmondsworth: Penguin Books

Dixon, W.M. (1931). *The Englishman*. London: Edward Arnold

Driscoll, L. (2009). *Evading Class in Contemporary British Literature*. Basingstoke: Palgrave

Durbin, E.F.M. (1940). *The Politics of Democratic Socialism*. London: George Routledge & Sons

Edmunds, J. and B.S. Turner (2001). The re-invention of national identity? Women and 'cosmopolitan' Englishness. *Ethnicities* 1: 83–108

Edwards, D. (2000). Extreme case formulations: softeners, investment, and doing nonliteral. *Research on Language and Social Interaction* 33.4: 347–73

Eliot, T.S. (1972). *Notes Towards the Definition of Culture*. London: Faber & Faber

Faas, D. (2008). Constructing identities: the ethno-national and nationalistic identities of white and Turkish students in two English secondary schools. *British Journal of Sociology of Education* 29: 37–48

Fenton, S. (2007). Indifference towards national identity: what young adults think about being English and British. *Nations and Nationalism* 13: 321–39

Fielding, S. (2009). Cameron's Conservatives. *Political Quarterly* 18.2: 168–71

Field, F. (ed.) (2009). *Attlee's Great Contemporaries: The Politics of Character*. London: Continuum

Fine, R. and V. Boon (2007). Cosmopolitanism: between past and future. *European Journal of Social Theory* 10: 5–16

Finney, N. and L. Simpson (2009). *'Sleepwalking to Segregation':*

Challenging Myths about Race and Integration. Bristol: Policy Press

Flint, J. and D. Robinson (eds.) (2008). *Community Cohesion in Crisis?* Bristol: Policy Press

Forster, E.M. (1910; 1973). *Howards End*. London: Folio Society

Fox, K. (2005). *Watching the English: The Hidden Rules of English Behaviour*. London: Hodder & Stoughton

Foucault, M. (1979). *The History of Sexuality*, Vol. 1. London: Allen Lane

Francis, M. (2007). *Herbert Spencer and the Invention of Modern Life*. Stocksfield: Acumen

Frandsen, A.G. (2002). Size and electoral participation in local elections. *Environment and Planning C: Government and Policy* 20.6: 853–69

Freedland, J. (1998). *Bring Home the Revolution: The Case for a British Republic*. London: Fourth Estate

Froud, S. (2006). *The English Year: From May Day to Mischief Night*. Harmondsworth: Penguin

Gains, F., M. Flinders, J. Bradbury, G. Stoker and W. Grant (2007). The constitutional missing pieces? In Political Studies Association. *Failing Politics? A Response to The Governance of Britain Green Paper*. Newcastle: Political Studies Association, 30–6

Gambetta, D. (1998). 'Claro!': an essay on discursive machismo. In J. Elster (ed.), *Deliberative Democracy*. Cambridge: Cambridge University Press, 19–43

Gamble, A. (1988). *The Free Economy and the Strong State*. London: Macmillan

Game, C. and C. Copus (2009). Scale, democracy, toponymy: three measures of the destruction, rather than reinvention, of English local government. Unpublished conference paper, presented to the EGPA conference. Malta, Local Governance and Democracy Study Group

Garfinkel, H. (1967). *Studies in Ethnomethodology*. Englewood Cliffs: Prentice-Hall

Garnett, M. (2008). *From Anger to Apathy: The Story of Politics, Society and Popular Culture in Britain since 1975*. London: Vintage

Gelfert, H.-D. (1992). Picturesque England, or, the part and the whole. *anglistik and englischunterricht* (46/7): 31–48

Gervais, D. (1993). *Literary Englands: Versions of 'Englishness' in Modern Writing*. Cambridge: Cambridge University Press

Gibson, S. and J. Abell (2004). For Queen and country? National frames of reference in the talk of soldiers in England. *Human Relations* 57: 871–91

Gibson, S. and S. Condor (2009). State institutions and social identity: national representation in soldiers' and civilians' interview talk concerning military service. *British Journal of Social Psychology* 48: 313–36

Giddens, A. (1990). *The Consequences of Modernity*. Cambridge: Polity

Gilmour, I. (1987). In *The Independent* (21 July)

Gilroy, P. (2002). *There Ain't No Black in the Union Jack: the Cultural Politics of Race and Nation*. 3rd ed. with new introduction. London: Routledge

Gilroy, P. (2004). *After Empire: Melancholia or Convivial Culture?* Abingdon: Routledge

Gissing, G. (1886). *Demos: The Story of English Socialism*. London: Smith Elder

Gissing, G. (1903). *The Private Papers of Henry Ryecroft*, summer, part XX. London: Archibald, Constable & Co.

Goffman, E. (1955). On face-work: an analysis of ritual elements in social interaction. *Psychiatry* 18: 213–31

Goffman, E. (1983). Felicity's condition. *American Journal of Sociology* 89: 1–53

Goodhart, D. (2004). Too diverse? *Prospect Magazine*, 95.20: 3–7. Also at www.prospect-magazine.co.uk/article_details.php?id=5835 (accessed 10 April 2009)

Gray, J. (1995). In *The Guardian* (15 May)

Greater London Authority (2008). *Focus on London 2008*. www.london.gov.uk/gla/publications/factandfigures/fo12008 (accessed 18 May 2009)

Grice, H. (1975). Logic and conversation. In P. Cole and J. Morgan (eds). *Syntax and Semantics*, Vol 3. New York: Academic Press, 41–58

Grimley, M. (2007). The religion of Englishness: Puritanism, providentialism, and 'national character', 1918–1945. *Journal of British Studies* 46.4: 884–906

Gyford. J. (1986). Diversity, sectionalism and local democracy in the conduct of local authority business. *Research* Vol. IV: *Aspects of Local Democracy*. London: The Stationery Office

Habermas, J. (1990). *Moral Consciousness and Communicative Action*. Cambridge: Polity

Hadfield, B. (1992). The Northern Ireland constitution. In B. Hadfield (ed.). *Northern Ireland: Politics and the Constitution*. Buckingham: Open University

Hadfield, B. (2004). The United Kingdom as a territorial state. In V. Bogdanor (ed.). *The British Constitution in the Twentieth Century*.

Oxford: Oxford University Press, 623–6

Hadfield, B. (2005). Devolution, Westminster, and the English question. *Public Law* (summer): 286–305

Hague, W. (1999). Identity and the British way. Speech delivered to the Centre for Policy Studies, London (19 January)

Hall, S. (1980). Popular democratic versus authoritarian populism. In A. Hunt (ed.). *Marxism and Democracy*. London: Lawrence and Wishart, 157–85

Hall, S. (2000). Conclusion: the multicultural question. In B. Hesse (ed.). *Un/Settled Multicuturalisms*. London: Zed Books, 209–41

Hammerton, J. (1946). *Child of Wonder: An Intimate Biography of Arthur Mee*. London: Hodder & Stoughton

Hansard Society / Ministry of Justice (2008). *Audit of Political Engagement 5*. London: Hansard Society

Harding, R., R. Hazell, M. Burch and J. Rees (2008). Answering the English question. In R. Hazell (ed). *Constitutional Futures Revisited*. London: Palgrave Macmillan, 73–89

Hardy, T. (1886; 1968). *The Mayor of Casterbridge*. London: Folio Society

Harris, N. (1972). *Competition and the Corporate Society: British Conservatism, the State and Industry*. London: Routledge

Harrison, N. (1968). *Description of England*. Ithaca: Cornell University Press

Harrod, R.F. (1966). *The Life of John Maynard Keynes*. London: Macmillan

Hartman, D. and J. Gerteis (2005). Dealing with diversity: mapping multiculturalism in sociological terms. *Sociological Theory* 23: 218–40

Hattersley, R. (2009). *In Search of England*. London: Little, Brown

Hawes, J. (2005). *Speak for England*. London: Jonathan Cape

Hay, C. and G. Stoker (2007). Who's failing whom? Politics, politicians, the public and the sources of political disaffection. In Political Studies Association. *Failing Politics? A Response to The Governance of Britain Green Paper*. Newcastle: Political Studies Association, 4–8

Hayton, R., R. English and M. Kenny (2009). Englishness in contemporary British politics. In A. Gamble, T. Wright and A. Wright (eds). *British Perspectives on the British Question*. London: John Wiley and Sons, 122–36

Hazell, R. (2006). *The English Question*. Manchester: Manchester University Press

Heaney, S. (1975). Whatever you say, say nothing. *North*. London: Faber & Faber, 57–60

HCCLGC (2009). *The Balance of Power: Central and Local Government*. Sixth Report of the House of Commons Communities and Local Government Committee, Session 2008–09, HC 33–I. London: The Stationery Office

HCJC (2009). *Devolution: A Decade On*. Fifth Report of the House of Commons Justice Committee, Session 2008–09, HC 529–I. London: The Stationery Office

Head, D. (2006). Julian Barnes and a Case of English Identity. In P. Tew and R. Mengham (eds). *British Fiction Today*. London: Continuum, 15–27

Heathcoat Amory, E. (2007). The new apartheid. *Daily Mail* (16 June)

Heffer, S. (1999). *Nor Shall My Sword: The Reinvention of England*. London: Weidenfeld & Nicolson

Heffer, S. (2007). The Union of England and Scotland is over. *Daily Telegraph* (14 November)

Hennock, E.P. (1973). *Fit and Proper Persons: Ideal and Reality in Nineteenth-Century Urban Government*. London: Edward Arnold

Hensher, P. (2008a). *The Northern Clemency*. London: Fourth Estate

Hensher, P. (2008b). Writing the Nation. *Prospect* 145 (April): 29–32

Hill, D.M. (1974). *Democratic Theory and Local Government*. London: George Allen and Unwin

Hilton, B. (2006), Moral Disciplines. In P. Mandler (ed.). *Liberty and Authority in Victorian Britain*. Oxford: Oxford University Press, 224–46

Hitchens, P. (1999). *The Abolition of Britain*. London: Quartet Books

Hitchins, H. (2008). *How to Really Talk about Books You Haven't Read*. London: John Murray

HLHCJCHR (2008). *A Bill of Rights for the UK?* Twenty-ninth Report of the House of Lords/House of Commons Joint Committee on Human Rights Session 2007–08, Volume I: Report, HL Paper 165–I/HC 150–I. London: The Stationery Office

HM Government (2007). *The Governance of Britain: The Government's Draft Legislative Programme*, Cm. 7372. London: The Stationery Office

HM Government (2009). *Building Britain's Future*. London: The Stationery Office

Hole, C. (1941). *English Custom and Usage*. London: Batsford

Home Office (2005). *Improving Opportunity, Strengthening Society: The Government's Strategy to Increase Race Equality and Community Cohesion*. London: Home Office

Home Office (2007). *Improving Opportunity, Strengthening Society: A 2 Year Review*. London: Home Office

Hood Phillips, O. and P. Jackson (1978). *O. Hood Phillips' Constitutional and Administrative Law*, 6th edn. London: Sweet & Maxwell

House of Commons Debates: Official Report (Hansard), 5th series, Vol. 178, cols 96–7 [26 October 1965]

Horne, D. (1969). *God Is an Englishman*. Ringwood Victoria: Penguin Books

Horton, J. (2005). A qualified defence of Oakeshott's politics of scepticism. *European Journal of Political Theory* 4.1: 23–36

House of Commons Debates: Official Report (Hansard), Vol. 939, cols 122–3 [14 November 1977]

Howard, A. (1985). In *The Observer* (10 February)

Howkins, A. (1987). The discovery of rural England. In R. Colls and P. Dodd (eds). *Englishness: Politics and Culture 1880–1920*. London: Croom Helm, 62–88

Hubbard, E. (1909). *The Philistine: A Periodical of Protest* 29: 6 (June–December)

Hudson, W.H. (1922). Foreword in E. Thomas, *Cloud Castle and Other Papers*. London: Duckworth, pp. v–vi

Hughes, T. (1960). *Lupercal*. London: Faber & Faber

Ingle, S. (2008). *The British Party System*, 4th edn. London, Routledge

IPPR (1991). *The Constitution of the United Kingdom*. Constitution Paper No.4. London: Institute of Public Policy Research

Ipsos Mori (2007). *Young People and Britishness: Survey for Camelot Foundation*. London: Ipsos Mori

Ipsos MORI (2008). *London in 2008: Ipsos MORI London Briefing Pack*. Download supplied following request to Ipsos MORI

Isaacs, S. (2006). *The Politics and Philosophy of Michael Oakeshott*. Abingdon: Routledge

James, M. (2008). *Interculturalism: Theory and Policy*. London: Baring Foundation (accessed via www.baringfoundation.org.uk 16 February 2009)

James, R.R. (1977). *The British Revolution: British Politics, 1880–1939*. London: Hamilton

Jefferson, G. (2004). Glossary of transcript symbols with an introduction. In G.H. Lerner (ed.). *Conversation Analysis: Studies from the First Generation*. Amsterdam / Philadelphia: John Benjamins, 13–31

Jenkins, S. (2010). The waiting game. *The Guardian* (30 January)

John, P. and C. Copus (2011). The United Kingdom: is there really an Anglo model? In J. Loughlin (ed.). *Handbook on Subnational Democracy in the European Union*. Oxford: Oxford University Press, pp. 27–47

Johnson, R.W. (1985). *Politics of Recession*. London: Macmillan

Jones, H.S (2006). The idea of the national in Victorian political thought. *European Journal of Political Theory* 5.1: 12–21

Kalra, V.S. (2002). Extended view: riots, race and reports: Denham, Cantle, Oldham and Burnley Inquiries. *Sage Race Relations Abstracts* 27.4: 20–30

Keating, M. (1995). Size, efficiency and democracy: consolidation, fragmentation and public choice. In D. Judge and G. Stoker, H. Wolman (eds). *Theories of Urban Politics*. London: Sage, 117–34

Keith-Lucas, B. (1952). *The English Local Government Franchise*. Oxford: Basil Blackwell

Kelleher, C. and D. Lowery (2004). Political participation and metropolitan institutional contexts. *Urban Affairs Review* 39.6: 720–57

Kenny, M. (2008). Conclusion: secular or sacred? Towards a new settlement between faith and the public realm. In A. Cooper and G. Lodge (eds). *Faith in the Nation: Religion, Identity and the Public Realm in Britain Today*. London: Institute for Public Policy Research

Kenny, M. and G. Lodge (2009). *The English Question: The View from Westminster*. London: Institute for Public Policy Research

Keynes, J.M. (1949). *The General Theory of Employment, Interest and Money*. London: Macmillan & Co. Ltd

Keynes, J.M. (1949). *Two Memoirs*. London: Rupert Hart-Davis

Keynes, M. (ed.) (1975). *Essays on John Maynard Keynes*. Cambridge: Cambridge University Press

Kiely, R., D. McCrone, F. Bechhofer and R. Stewart (2000). Debatable land: national and local identity in a border town. *Sociological Research Online* 5: 2, www.socresonline.org.uk/5/2/kiely.html (accessed 12 December 2010)

Kiely, R., D. McCrone and F. Bechhofer (2005a). Whither Britishness? English and Scottish people in Scotland. *Nations and Nationalism* 11: 65–82

Kiely, R., F. Bechhofer and D. McCrone (2005b). Birth, blood and belonging: identity claims in post-devolution Scotland. *The Sociological Review* 53: 150–71

Kingsnorth, P. (2008). *Real England: The Battle against the Bland*. London: Portobello Books

Kipling, R. (1896). The native-born. In *The Seven Seas*. London: Methuen, 48–53

Kumar, K. (2001). 'Englishness' and English national identity. In D. Morley and K. Robins (eds). *British Cultural Studies. Geography, Nationality, and Identity*. Oxford: Oxford University Press, 41–55

Kumar, K. (2003). *The Making of English National Identity*. Cambridge: Cambridge University Press

Kumar, K. (2006). English and British national identity. *History Compass* 4: 428–47

Kumar, K. (2007). Reply. In J. Hutchinson, S. Reynolds, A.D. Smith, R. Colls and K. Kumar, Debate on Krishan Kumar's *The Making of English National Identity. Nations and Nationalism* 13.2: 179–203

Kundnani, A. (2002). *The Death of Multiculturalism.* London: Institute of Race Relations (accessed via: www.irr.org.uk/2002/april /ak000001.html, 14 January 2005)

Kundnani, A. (2007). *The End of Tolerance? Racism in 21st Century Britain.* London: Pluto

Kyriakides, C. and S. Virdee, T. Modood (2009). Racism, Muslims and the national imagination. *Journal of Ethnic and Migration Studies* 35.2: 289–308

Laamanen, E. and A. Haveri (2003). Size, efficiency and democracy: how local government boundaries affect performance. Paper presented at the EGPA Conference on Public Law and the Modernising State, Oerias, Portugal, 3–6 September

Ladner, A. (2002). Size and direct democracy at the local level: the case of Switzerland. *Environment and Planning C: Government and Policy* 20.6: 813–28

Larkin, P. (1946; 1964). *Jill: A Novel.* London: Faber & Faber

Larkin, P. (1947; 1966). *A Girl in Winter: A Novel.* London: Faber & Faber

Larkin, P. (1974). *High Windows.* London: Faber & Faber

Larkin, P. (1983). *Required Writing: Miscellaneous Pieces 1955–82.* London: Faber & Faber

Larkin, P. (1988). *Collected Poems.* Ed. A. Thwaite. London: Faber & Faber

Larsen, C.A. (2002). Municipal size and democracy: a critical analysis of the argument of proximity based on the case of Denmark. *Scandinavian Political Studies* 25.4: 317–32

Latour, B. (1987). *Science in Action.* Cambridge, MA: Harvard University Press

Lawrence, D.H. (1928; 1961a). *Lady Chatterley's Lover.* Harmondsworth: Penguin

Lawrence, D.H. (1961b). *Selected Literary Criticism.* Ed. A. Beal. London: Mercury

Law Society of Scotland (2008). *Memorandum from the Law Society of Scotland* in the House of Lords/House of Commons Joint Committee on Human Rights, *A Bill of Rights for the UK?* Twenty-ninth Report of Session 2007–08, Volume II: Oral and Written Evidence, HL Paper 165–II/HC 150–II. London: The Stationery Office

Lawson, N. (1992). *The View from No. 11.* London: Bantam Press

Lee, S. (2007; 2009a). *Boom and Bust: The Politics and Legacy of Gordon Brown.* Oxford: Oneworld

Lee, S. (2009b). David Cameron and the renewal of policy. In S. Lee and M. Beech (eds). *The Conservatives under David Cameron: Built to Last?* London: Palgrave Macmillan, 44–59

Lee, S. (2010). Cameron Scotched. *Parliamentary Brief* (May): 9–10. Also available online at: www.parliamentarybrief.com/2010/05/cameron-scotched (accessed 20 May 2010)

Letter Arthur Mee to the (12th) Duke of Bedford (Hastings William Sackville Russell), 20 April 1943, The Papers of Francis (Frank) O. Salisbury, Methodist Archives (MA), University of Manchester, Fos. 1.4.1

Letter Arthur Mee to Mrs Alice Salisbury, undated, The Papers of Francis (Frank) O. Salisbury, Methodist Archives (MA), University of Manchester, Fos. 1.4.16

Letter Arthur Mee to Frank Salisbury, 23 May 1943, The Papers of Francis (Frank) O. Salisbury, Methodist Archives (MA), University of Manchester, Fos. 1.4.11.

Letter Arthur Mee to Frank Salisbury, 23 July 'Year of Deep Water' 1940, The Papers of Francis (Frank) O. Salisbury, Methodist Archives (MA), University of Manchester, Fos. 1.4.14

Letter Arthur Mee to John Derry, 7 December 1908, Arthur Mee Papers, University of Reading, MS 4057, File One

Letter from Arthur Mee to John Derry, 8 December 1909, Arthur Mee Papers, University of Reading, MS 4057, File One

Letter Arthur Mee to John Derry, 7 August 1925, Arthur Mee Papers, University of Reading, MS 4057, File One

Letter Arthur Mee to John Derry, 11 January 1926, Arthur Mee Papers, University of Reading, MS 4057 File One

Letter Arthur Mee to John Derry, 7 May 1926, Arthur Mee Papers, University of Reading, MS 4057, File One

Letter Arthur Mee to John Derry, 3 October 1927, Arthur Mee Papers, University of Reading, MS 4057, File One

Letter from Arthur Mee to John Derry, 17 January 1930, Arthur Mee Papers, University of Reading, MP, MS 4057, File One

Letter Arthur Mee to John Derry, 5 January 1931, Arthur Mee Papers, University of Reading, MS 4057, File Two

Letter Arthur Mee to John Derry, undated, Arthur Mee Papers, University of Reading, MS 4057 File One

Letter Arthur Mee to Alfred Harmsworth, 30 October 1910, Northcliffe Papers, British Library, BL Add. Mss. 62183 (129)

Letter Alfred Harmsworth to Arthur Mee, 22 August 1908 and 28 August 1908, Northcliffe Papers, British Library BL Add. Ms 62183 (114, 117)

Letter Alfred Harmsworth to Arthur Mee, 26 January 1909, Northcliffe Papers, British Library, BL Add. Ms 62183 (119)

Letter G.K. Chesterton to Mr G. Langley Taylor, 15 July 1931, British Library, The Chesterton Papers, BL Add MS 73240 folios 98–99

Letwin, O. (2003). *The Neighbourly Society: Collected Speeches 2001–3.* London: Centre for Policy Studies

Levitas, R. (2005). *The Inclusive Society? Social Exclusion and New Labour,* 2nd edn. Basingstoke: Palgrave

Levy, A. (2004). *Small Island.* London: Headline Review.

Lightman, B. (1997; 2009). 'The voices of nature': popularizing Victorian science. In B. Lightman. *Evolutionary Naturalism in Victorian Britain.* Aldershot: Ashgate, 187–211

Local Government Association (2002). *Guidance on Community Cohesion.* London: LGA

Lothian, J.R. (2009). *The Making and Unmaking of the English Catholic Intellectual Community, 1910–1950.* Notre Dame, IN: University of Notre Dame Press

Lowenthal, D. (1991). British national identity and the English national landscape. *Rural History* 2: 205–30

Loyn, H.R. (1991). *The Making of the English Nation: From the Anglo-Saxons to Edward I.* London: Thames and Hudson

Lucas, E.V. and C.L. Graves (1908). *Hustled History, Or: As It Might Have Been.* London: Pitman

Lynch, P. (2004). Saving the Union. *The Political Quarterly* 75.4: 386–91

MacAskill, K. (2008). Oral Evidence, 10 March, in House of Lords/House of Commons Joint Committee on Human Rights, *A Bill of Rights for the UK?* Twenty-ninth Report of Session 2007–08, Volume II: Oral and Written Evidence, HL Paper 165–II/HC 150–II. London: The Stationery Office

Macfarlane, A. (1978). *The Origins of English Individualism.* Oxford: Blackwell

Malik, K. (2009). *From Fatwa to Jihad: The Rushdie Affair and Its Legacy.* London: Atlantic

Mandler, P. (2006a). The *English National Character: The History of an Idea from Edmund Burke to Tony Blair.* New Haven: Yale University Press

Mandler, P. (2006b). What is 'National Identity'? Definitions and applications in modern British historiography. *Modern Intellectual History* 3.2: 271–97

Mandler, P. (2007). *The English National Character*. Princeton: Yale University Press

Mann, R. (2006). Reflexivity and researching national identity. *Sociological Research Online* 11.4, www.socresonline.org.uk/11/4 /mann.html

Mann, R. and S. Fenton (2009). The personal contexts of national sentiments. *Journal of Ethnic and Migration Studies* 35: 517–34

Manzoor, S. (2009). Bradford reflects on many shades of Englishness. *The Observer* (5 July) Review section: 5–6

Mapel, D. (1992). Purpose and politics: can there be a non-instrumental civil association. *The Political Science Reviewer* 21 (spring): 63–80

Marquand, D. (1992). *The Progressive Dilemma*. London: William Heineman

Marquand, D. (1997). *The New Reckoning: Capitalism, States and Citizens*. Cambridge: Polity Press

Marquand, D. (2008a). *Britain Since 1918: The Strange Case of British Democracy*. London: Weidenfeld & Nicolson

Marquand, D. (2008b). Give us a moral vision for England. *Open Democracy* website, www.opendemocracy.net/node/43935 (accessed 16 February 2009)

Marquand, D. (2008c). Come on England: vision or barbarism. *Open Democracy* website, www.opendemocracy.net/node/43968 (accessed 16 February 2009)

Marr, A. (2000). *The Day Britain Died*. London: Profile Books

Marshall, P. and D. Laws (eds) (2004). *The Orange Book: Reclaiming Liberalism*. London: Profile Books

Marx, K. and F. Engels (1973). Manifesto of the Communist Party. In *Marx and Engels: Selected Works* (1973). Ed. C.J. Arthur. London: Lawrence & Wishart, 31–63

Massey, D. (2007). *World City*. Cambridge: Polity

May, S. (ed.) (1999). *Critical Multiculturalism: Rethinking Multicultural and Anti-Racist Education*. London: Falmer

McCleary, J.R. (2009). *The Historical Imagination of G.K. Chesterton: Locality, Patriotism, and Nationalism*. New York: Routledge

McCrone, D. (2002). Who do you say you are? *Ethnicities* 2: 301–20

McCrone, D. (2006). A nation that dares not speak its name? *Ethnicities* 6: 267–78

McCrone, D., R. Stewart, R. Kiely and F. Bechhofer (1998), Who are we? Problematising national identity. *The Sociological Review* 46: 631–52

McGhee, D. (2006). The new Commission for Equality and Human

Rights: building community cohesion and revitalising citizenship in contemporary britain. *Ethnopolitics* 5.2: 145–66

McKenzie, R. and N. Silver (1968). *Angels in Marble*. London: Heinemann

McLean, I. (1995). Are Scotland and Wales over-represented in the House of Commons. *Political Quarterly* 66: 250–68

McLean, I. (2005). *The Fiscal Crisis of the United Kingdom*. London: Palgrave Macmillan

McLean, I. and A. McMillan (2010). 1707 and 1800: a treaty (mostly) honoured and a treaty broken. In I. McLean (ed.). *What's Wrong with the British Constitution?* Oxford: Oxford University Press, 47–85

McLean, I., G. Lodge and K. Schmuecker (2008). *Fair Shares? Barnett and the Politics of Public Expenditure*. London: Institute for Public Policy Research

Meade, J. (1975). The Keynesian Revolution. In M. Keynes (ed.). *Essays on John Maynard Keynes*. Cambridge: Cambridge University Press, 82–8

Mee, A. (1899). C.H. Spurgeon's sermons: the story of their marvellous popularity. *The Puritan*: 605–10

Mee, A. (1901a). *Joseph Chamberlain: A Romance of Modern Politics*. London: New Century Leaders Series

Mee, A. (1901b). *Lord Salisbury: The Record Premiership of Modern Times*. London: New Century Leaders Series

Mee, A. (1903). *England's Mission by England's Statesmen*. London: Grant Richards

Mee, A. (1908). *The Children's Encyclopaedia*. London: Amalgamated Press

Mee, A. (1920a). *Arthur Mee's Hero Book*. London: Hodder & Stoughton

Mee, A. (1920b). *Little Treasure Island: Her Story and Her Glory*. London: Hodder & Stoughton

Mee, A. (1935). *God Knows: A Faith for Youth*. London: Hodder and Stoughton

Mee, A. (1936a). *Enchanted Land: Half-a-Million Miles in the King's England*. London: Hodder & Stoughton

Mee, A. (1936b). *Heroes of Freedom: Stories for Children*. London: Hodder & Stoughton

Mee, A. (1941). *Arthur Mee's Book of the Flag*. London: Hodder & Stoughton

Mee, A. (1942). *Immortal Dawn*. London: Hodder & Stoughton

Mee, A. (1943). Christ or Hitler. *The Children's Newspaper* (27 March): 9

Meyers, J. (1975). *George Orwell: The Critical Heritage*. London: Routlege & Kegan Paul

Miller, D. (1995). *On Nationality*. Oxford: Clarendon Press

Ministry of Justice (2007). *The Governance of Britain*, Cm. 7170. London: The Stationery Office

Ministry of Justice (2009a). *Rights and Responsibilities: Developing our Constitutional Framework*, Cm. 7577. London: The Stationery Office

Ministry of Justice (2009b). *Rights and Responsibilities*. Ministry of Justice Press Release (23 March)

Minogue, K. (2003). Rationalism Revisited. Presidential Address, Michael Oakeshott Association Conference, Colorado (25 September)

Minogue, K. (2004). Oakeshott and political science. *Annual Review of Political Science* 7: 227–46

Mizen, P. (2004). *The Changing State of Youth*. Basingstoke: Palgrave

Modood, T. (2007). *Multiculturalism*. Cambridge: Polity

Modood, T., Berthoud, R., Lakey, J., Smith, P., Virdee, S. and Beishon, S. (1977). *Ethnic Minorities in Britain: Diversity and Disadvantage*. London: Policy Studies Institute

Montesquieu, C. de (1989). *Spirit of the Law*. Cambridge: Cambridge University Press

Moore, C. and S. Heffer (eds) (1989). *A Tory Seer: The Selected Journalism of T.E. Utley*, London: Hamish Hamilton

Moreno. L. (1988). Scotland and Catalonia: the path to home rule. In D. McCrone and A. Brown (eds.). *The Scottish Government Yearbook 1988*. Edinburgh: Unit for the Study of Government in Scotland

Morton H.V. (1928). *The Call of England*. London: Methuen

Morris, W. (1889). Under an elm-tree; or, thoughts in the country-side. *Commonweal* 5.182: 212–13

Mouffe, C. (2005). *The Return of the Political*. London: Verso

Mouritzen, P.E. (1989). City size and citizens' satisfaction: two competing theories revisited. *European Journal of Political Research* 17.6: 661–88

Mueller, J.-W. (2010). Re-imagining Leviathan: Schmitt and Oakeshott on Hobbes and the problem of political order. *Critical Review of International Social and Political Philosophy* 13.2–3: 317–36

Muzzio, D. and T. Tompkins (1989). On the size of the city council: finding the mean. *Proceedings of the Academy of Political Science* 37.3: 83–96

Mycock, A. and J. Tonge (2007). The future of citizenship. In Political Studies Association. *Failing Politics? A Response to The Governance of Britain Green Paper*. Newcastle: Political Studies Association, 18–21

Nairn, T. (1981) [1977]. *The Break-up of Britain: Crisis and Neo-Nationalism*. London: Verso

Nairn, T. (2000). *After Britain: New Labour and the Return of Scotland*. London: Granta Books

National Statistics and Greater London Authority (2007). *Focus on London 2007*. Basingstoke: PalgraveMacmillan. Also at www.statistics.gov.uk/statbase/product.asp?vlnk=10527 (accessed 18 May 2009)

Nazir-Ali, M. (2008). Breaking faith with Britain. *Standpoint* (June), available at: www.standpointmag.co.uk/node/85 (accessed 3 July 2009)

Nazir-Ali, M. (2009). Ignore our Christian values and the nation will drift apart. *The Sunday Telegraph* (5 April): np

Nelson, J.G. (2004). Sir (John) William Watson. In H.C.G. Matthew and B. Harrison (eds). *Oxford Dictionary of National Biography*, Vol. 57. Oxford: Oxford University Press, 2004, 681–2

Newton, K. (1982). Is small really so beautiful? Is big really so ugly? Size, effectiveness and democracy in local government. *Political Studies* 30.2: 190–206

Nichols, G. (2009). Outward from Hull. *Guardian* (2 May): Review, 3

Nielsen, H.J. (1981). Size and evaluation of government: Danish attitudes towards politics at multiple levels of government. *European Journal of Political Research* 9.1: 47–60

Norman, J. and J. Ganesh (2006). *Compassionate Conservatism*. London: Policy Exchange

Norton, P. (1980). *Dissension in the House of Commons 1974–1979*. Oxford: Clarendon Press

Norton, P. (1983). The Liberal Party in parliament. In V. Bogdanor (ed). *Liberal Party Politics*. Oxford: Clarendon Press, 143–71

Norton, P. (1996a), Conservative politics and the abolition of Stormont. In P. Catterall and S. McDougall (eds). *The Northern Ireland Question in British Politics*. London: Macmillan, 129–42

Norton, P. (1996b). The United Kingdom: political conflict, parliamentary scrutiny. In P. Norton (ed). *National Parliaments and the European Union*. London: Frank Cass, 92–109

Norton, P. (2001). Playing by the rules: the constraining hand of parliamentary procedure. *Journal of Legislative Studies* 7.3: 13–33

Norton, P. (2008). The future of Conservatism. *Political Quarterly* 79.3: 324–32

Norton, P. and A. Aughey (1981). *Conservatives and Conservatism*. London: Temple Smith

Nünning, V. (2001). The invention of cultural traditions: the construction and deconstruction of Englishness and authenticity in Julian Barnes's *England, England. Anglia* 119: 58–76

Nünning, V. (2004). The importance of being English: European perspectives on Englishness. *European Journal of English Studies* 8.2: 145–58

Nuttall, J. (2004). Tony Crosland and the many falls and rises of British social democracy. *Contemporary British History* 18.4: 52–79

O'Brien, C.C. (1994). *Ancestral Voices: Religion and Nationalism in Ireland.* Dublin: Poolbeg Press

O'Donnell, F.H. (1910). *A History of the Irish Parliamentary Party.* Vol. 2. London: Longmans, Green, and Co.

O'Hagan, T. (1998). The idea of cultural patrimony. *Critical Review of International Social and Political Philosophy* 1.3: 147–57

Oakeshott, M. (1928; 1993). The importance of the historical element in Christianity. In M. Oakeshott, *Religion, Politics and the Moral Life.* Ed. T. Fuller. New Haven, Yale University Press, 63–73

Oakeshott, M. (1938). The concept of a philosophical jurisprudence. *Politica* 3: 345–60

Oakeshott, M. (1948; 2004). The voice of conversation in the education of mankind. In M. Oakeshott. *What Is History? And Other Essays.* Ed. L. O'Sullivan. Exeter: Imprint Academic, 187–200

Oakeshott, M. (1962; 1991a). Political education. In M. Oakeshott. *Rationalism in Politics and Other Essays.* Indianapolis: Liberty Fund: 43–69

Oakeshott, M. (1962; 1991b). Rational conduct. In M. Oakeshott. *Rationalism in Politics and Other Essays.* Indianapolis: Liberty Fund, 99–131

Oakeshott, M. (1962; 1991c). Rationalism in politics. In M. Oakeshott. *Rationalism in Politics and Other Essays.* Indianapolis: Liberty Fund: 5–42

Oakeshott, M. (1962; 1991d). The voice of poetry in the conversation of mankind. In M. Oakeshott *Rationalism in Politics and Other Essays.* Indianapolis: Liberty Fund, 488–541

Oakeshott, M. (1975). *On Human Conduct.* Oxford: Oxford University Press

Oakeshott, M (1983). *On History and Other Essays* Oxford: Clarendon Press

Oakeshott, M. (1991). Political discourse. In M. Oakeshott. *Rationalism in Politics and Other Essays.* Indianapolis: Liberty Fund, 70–95

Oakeshott, M. (1993a). *Morality and Politics in Modern Europe: The Harvard Lectures.* Ed. S.R. Letwin. New Haven: Yale University Press

Oakeshott, M. (1993b). *Religion, Politics and the Moral Life.* Ed. T. Fuller. New Haven, CT: Yale University Press

Oakeshott, M. (2004). *What Is History? And Other Essays.* Ed. L. O'Sullivan. Exeter: Imprint Academic

Oddie, W. (2008). *Chesterton and the Romance of Orthodoxy: The Making of GKC 1874–1908.* Oxford: Oxford University Press

ODPM (2004). *The Future of Local Government: Developing a Ten Year Vision* London: Office of the Deputy Prime Minister

Office of Public Service Reform (2002). *Reforming our Public Services: Principles into Practice.* London: Office of Public Service Reform

Oliver, J.E. (2000). City size and civic involvement in metropolitan America. *American Political Science Review* 94.2: 361–73

Ormston, R. and J. Curtice (2010). Resentment or contentment: attitudes towards the union ten years on. In A. Park, M. Phillips, E. Clery and J. Curtice (eds), *British Social Attitudes: The 27th Report: Exploring Labour's Legacy.* London: Sage

Orwell, G. (1937; 1962). *The Road to Wigan Pier* Harmondsworth: Penguin

Orwell, G. (1941; 1988). *The Lion and the Unicorn: Socialism and the English Genius.* Harmondsworth: Penguin

Orwell, G. (1941; 1994). The lion and the unicorn. In *The Penguin Essays of George Orwell.* Harmondsworth: Penguin

Orwell, G. (1941; 2001*). The Lion and the Unicorn. Socialism and the English Genius: Part 1 England Your England.* In *Orwell's England.* Ed. P. Davison. Harmondsworth: Penguin, 251–77

Orwell, G. (1968a). The moon under water. In *The Collected Essays, Journalism and Letters of George Orwell,* Vol. 2: *My Country Right or Left.* Eds S. Orwell and I. Angus. London: Secker & Warburg, 44–7

Orwell, G. (1968b). Review of *A Coat of Many Colours,* by Herbert Read. In *Collected Essays, Journalism and Letters of George Orwell,* Vol. 4: *In Front of Your Nose.* Eds S. Orwell and I. Angus. London: Secker & Warburg, 48–52

Ossewaarde, M. (2007). Cosmopolitanism and the society of strangers. *Current Sociology* 55: 367–88

Ouseley, H. (2001). *Community Pride, Not Prejudice: Making Diversity Work in Bradford.* Bradford: Bradford Vision

Parekh, B. et al. (2000). *The Future of Multi-Ethnic Britain: The Parekh Report* London: Profile

Parekh, B. (2008). *A New Politics of Identity: Political Principles for an Interdependent World.* London: Palgrave

Park, A., J. Curtice, K. Thomson, M. Phillips and E. Clery (2010). *British Social Attitudes: The 26th Report.* London: Sage

Parrinder, P. (2006). *Nation and Novel: The English Novel from its Origins to the Present.* Oxford: Oxford University Press

Paxman, J. (1998). *The English: Portrait of a People.* London: Michael Joseph

Pedersen, S. and P. Mandler (eds). *After the Victorians.* London: Routledge

Perryman, M. (2006). *Ingerland: Travels with a Football Nation.* London: Simon & Schuster

Perryman, M. (ed.) (2008a). *Imagined Nation: England after Britain.* London: Lawrence and Wishart

Perryman, M. (2008b). Becoming England. In M. Perryman (ed.). *Imagined Nation: England after Britain.* London: Lawrence & Wishart, 13–34

Perryman, M. (2009). *Breaking Up Britain: Four Nations after a Union.* London: Lawrence & Wishart

Phillips, M. and T. Phillips (1998). *Windrush: The Irresistible Rise of Multi-Racial Britain.* London: HarperCollins

Phillips, T. (2005). After 7/7: Sleepwalking to segregation. Speech to Manchester Council for Community Relation, 22 September. Available online at http://www.humanities.manchester.ac.uk /socialchange/research/social-change/summer-workshops /documents/sleepwalking.pdf

Poirier, A. (2008). Know what I mean? *The Guardian*, 22 August: 35

Pollard, A.F. (1911). *The History of England: A Study in Political Evolution 55 B.C.–A.D. 1911.* London: Williams & Norgate

Pope, A. (1733; 2008). *An Essay on Man: Moral Essays and Satires.* Forgotten Books. www.forgottenbooks.org

Porter, H. (2008). *Memorandum from Mr Henry Porter* in House of Lords/House of Commons Joint Committee on Human Rights, *A Bill of Rights for the UK?* Twenty-ninth Report of Session 2007–08, Volume II: Oral and Written Evidence, HL Paper 165–II/HC 150–II. London: The Stationery Office

Postan, M.M. (1972). D.M. Joslin 1925–1970. In J.M. Winter and D.M. Joslin (eds). *R.H. Tawney's Commonplace Book.* Cambridge: Cambridge University Press, ix–xi

Powell, A. (1966; 1997). *A Dance to the Music of Time,* Vol. 3: *Autumn.* London: Mandarin

Preston, P.W. (2004). *Relocating England: Englishness in the New Europe.* Manchester: Manchester University Press

Priestley, J.B. (1973). *The English.* London: Heineman

Prins, G. and R. Salisbury (2008), Risk, threat and security: The case of the UK. *RUSI Journal* 153.1: 6–11

Radcliffe-Maud (Report) (1969). Royal Commission on Local *Government in England, 1966–69*, Comnd 4040. London: HMSO.

Rahman, S. (2009). *Muslims: Beyond the Headlines*, 'The Guardian comment is free'. Available online at: www.guardian.co.uk /commentisfree/belief/2009/dec/15/muslims-open-society-institute-europe (accessed 6 January 2010)

Ramsden, J. (1980). *The Making of Conservative Party Policy*. London: Longman

Readman, P. (2008). *Land and Nation in England: Patriotism, National Identity and the Politics of Land, 1880–1914*. Woodbridge: Boydell Press

Redlich, J. (1908). *The Procedure of the House of Commons*. Vol. 1. London: Archibald Constable

Redlich, J. and W. Hirst (1958). *The History of Local Government in England*. London: Macmillan.

Redwood, J. (1999). *The Death of Britain? The UK's Constitutional Crisis*. Basingstoke: Palgrave Macmillan

Rex, P. (2004). *The English Resistance: The Underground War against the Normans*. Stroud: Tempus

Rhodes, R.A.W., Wanna, J. and Weller, P. (2009). *Comparing Westminster*. Oxford: Oxford University Press.

Ribeiro, A. (2002). On Englishness in Dress. In C. Breward, B. Conekin and C. Cox (eds). *The Englishness of English Dress*. Oxford: Berg, 15–27

Ritchie, D. (2001). *Oldham Independent Review: On Oldham, One Future*. Manchester: Government Office for the Northwest

Robson, M. (2003). *Arthur Mee's Dream of England*. Barnsley: King's England Press

Rogers, R. and R. Walters (2006). *How Parliament Works*, 6th edn. London: Longman

Rorty, R. (1989). *Contingency, Irony, and Solidarity*. Cambridge: Cambridge University Press

Rose, L.E. (2002). Municipal size and local nonelectoral participation: findings from Denmark, The Netherlands and Norway. *Environment and Planning C: Government and Policy* 20.6: 829–51

Rose, R. (1982). *Understanding the United Kingdom*. London: Longman

Royal Commission on the Constitution (1973). *Royal Commission on the Constitution* Vol. I, *1969–1973*. London: The Stationery Office

Royal Commission on Local Government in England (1969). *Report of the Commission*, Cmnd 4040. London: The Stationery Office

Russell, A. and G. Stoker (2007), Introduction. In Political Studies

Association. *Failing Politics? A Response to The Governance of Britain Green Paper*. Newcastle: Political Studies Association, 2–3

Russell, D. (2004). *Looking North*. Manchester: Manchester University Press

Russell, M. and G. Lodge (2006). Government by Westminster. In R. Hazell (ed.). *The English Question*. Manchester: Manchester University Press, 64–95

Rye, W.B. (1865). *England as Seen by Foreigners in the Reign of Elizabeth and James the First*. London: John Russell Smith

Sacks, H. (1992). *Lectures on Conversation*, Vol. 2. Ed. Gail Jefferson. Oxford: Blackwell

Sackville-West, V. (1930). *The Edwardians*. London: Hogarth Press

Sandford, M. (ed.) (2009). *The Northern Veto*. Manchester: Manchester University Press

Santayana, G. (1922). *Soliloquies in England and Later Soliloquies*. New York: Charles Scribner's Sons

Sartori, G. (1976). *Parties and Party Systems: A Framework for Analysis*. Cambridge University Press

Schwartz, B. (2002), Philosophers of the Conservative nation: Burke, Macaulay, Disraeli. *Journal of Historical Sociology* 12.3: 183–217

Scottish Affairs Committee, House of Commons (2006). *The Sewel Convention: The Westminster Perspective*, Session 2005–06, HC 983, London: The Stationery Office

Scottish Affairs Committee, House of Commons (2010). *Commission on Scottish Devolution*. Session 2009–10, HC 255. London: The Stationery Office

Scruton, R. (2000). *England: An Elegy*. London: Chatto & Windus

Sennett, R. (1998). *The Corrosion of Character: The Personal Consequences of Work in the New Capitalism*. New York: Norton

Sentamu, J. (2008). Anglicanism. In A. Cooper and G. Lodge (eds) *Faith in the Nation: Religion, Identity and the Public Realm in Britain today*. London: Institute for Public Policy Research

Shannon, R. (1999). *Gladstone: Heroic Minister 1865–1898*. London: Allen Lane

Shaw, G.B. (1906; 1937). *Man and Superman* in *The Complete Works of Bernard Shaw*. London: Odhams Press

Skey, M. (2009). 'We wanna show 'em who we are': national events in England. In D. McCrone and G. McPherson (eds). *National Days*. Basingstoke: Palgrave Macmillan

Skey, M. (2010). 'A sense of where you belong in the world': national belonging, ontological security and the status of the ethnic majority in England. *Nations & Nationalism*, 16.4: 715–33

Skidelsky, R. (1975). The reception of the Keynesian Revolution. In M. Keynes (ed.). *Essays on John Maynard Keynes*. Cambridge: Cambridge University Press, 89–107

Skidelsky, R. (1983). *John Maynard Keynes*, Vol. 1: *Hopes Betrayed 1883–1920*. London: Macmillan

Smith, D. (1986). Englishness and the Liberal Inheritance after 1886. In R. Colls and P. Dodd (eds). *Englishness: Politics and Culture*. London: Croom Helm, 254–82

Smith, W. (2007). Cosmopolitan citizenship: virtue, irony and worldliness. *European Journal of Social Theory* 10: 37–52

Solomos, J. (2003). *Race and Racism in Britain*, 3rd edn. Basingstoke: Palgrave

Sperber, D. and D. Wilson (1981). Irony and the use-mention distinction. In P. Cole (ed). *Radical Pragmatics*. New York: Academic Press, 295–318

Stapleton, J. (2009). *Christianity, Patriotism, and Nationhood: The England of G.K. Chesterton*. Lanham: Lexington Books

Steavenson, W. (2010). Born to lead: but where? *Prospect* (May): 43–9

Stewart, J. (2003). *Modernising British Local Government: An Assessment of Labour's Reform Programme*. Basingstoke: Palgrave Macmillan

Straw, J. (2007). The MacKenzie-Stuart Lecture. University of Cambridge, Faculty of Law (25 October)

Straw, J. (2008a). Modernising the Magna Carta. Speech, George Washington University, Washington, DC (13 February), available online: www.justice.gov.uk/news/sp130208.htm (accessed 12 August 2010)

Straw, J. (2008b); Towards a bill of rights and responsibility. Speech (21 January), available online: http://webarchive.nationalarchives .gov.uk/+/http://www.justice.gov.uk/news/sp210108a.htm (accessed 12 August 2010)

Tajfel, H. (1978). *Differentiation between Social Groups*. London: Academic Press

Tawney, R.H. (1921; 2004). *The Acquisitive Society*. Mineola: Dover Books

Taylor, A.J.P. (1965). *English History 1914–1945*. Harmondsworth: Penguin Books

Taylor, A.J.P. (1977). *Essays in English History*. London: Book Club Associates / Hamish Hamilton

Tearne, R. (2008). *Bone China*. London: Harper Press

Thatcher, M. (1998). Don't wreck the heritage we all share. Reprinted In L. Paterson (ed.). *A Diverse Assembly: The Debate on the Scottish Parliment*. Edinburgh: Edinburgh University Press.

Thomas, E. (1913). *The Happy-Go-Lucky Morgans*. London: Duckworth

Thomas, E. (1981). *A Language Not to Be Betrayed: Selected Prose*. Ed. Edna Longley. Manchester: Carcanet

Thomas, E. (1993). *The South Country*. London: Everyman

Thomas, E. (2008). *The Annotated Collected Poems*. Ed. Edna Longley. Northumberland: Bloodaxe

Thomas, H. (1978). *Time and Again: Memoirs and Letters*. Ed. M. Thomas. Manchester: Carcanet

Thomas, P. (2003). Young people, community cohesion, and the role of youth work in building social capital. *Youth and Policy* 81: 21–43

Thomas, P. (2007). Moving on from 'Anti-Racism'? Understandings of community cohesion held by youth workers. *Journal of Social Policy* 36.3: 435–55

Thomas, P. (2009). Between two stools? The government's preventing violent extremism agenda. *Political Quarterly Journal* 80.2: 282–91

Thomas, P. and P. Sanderson (2009). *The Oldham and Rochdale Youth Identity Project Final Report*. Huddersfield: University of Huddersfield Press

Thompson, E.P. (1963). *The Making of the English Working Class*. Harmondsworth: Penguin

Thompson, E.P. (1978). *The Poverty of Theory and Other Essays*. London: Merlin

Titchmarsh, A. (2007). *England, Our England*. London: Hodder & Stoughton

Tocqueville, A. de (1966) [French 1835–40]. *Democracy in America*. New York: Harper and Row

Tocqueville, A. de (2008). *The Ancien Régime and the French Revolution*. London: Penguin Classics

Toulmin-Smith, J. (2005). *Local Self-Government and Centralisation*. Boston, MA: Elibron Classics

Travers, T., G. Jones and J. Burnham (1993). *Impact of Population Size on Local Authority Costs and Effectiveness*. York: Joseph Rowntree Foundation

Travis, A. (2001). Blunkett in race row over culture tests. *The Guardian* (10 December)

Turner, B.S. (2001). Cosmopolitan virtue: on religion in a global age. *European Journal of Social Theory* 4: 131–52

Turner, B.S. (2002). Cosmopolitan virtue, globalization and patriotism. *Theory, Culture and Society* 19: 45–63

Vallance, E. (2009). *A Radical History of Britain*. London: Abacus

Vorda, A. (1993). Stuck on the margins: an interview with Kazuo

Ishiguro. In A. Vorda (ed.). *Face to Face: Interviews with Contemporary Novelists.* Houston: Rice University Press, 1–35

Walden, B. (1987). In *Sunday Times* (8 November)

Wallwork, J and J.A. Dixon (2004). Foxes, green fields and Britishness: on the rhetorical construction of place and national identity. *British Journal of Social Psychology* (43): 21–39

Ward, L. and J. Carvel (2007). Growing sense of Englishness explains why less than half the country feel British. *The Guardian* (24 January)

Watson, G. (1973). *The English Ideology. Studies in the Language of Victorian Politics.* London: Allen Lane

Webster's Quotations, Facts and Phrases (2008). San Diego: ICON Group International, Inc.

Weight, R. (2008). Is it cos I is English? In M. Perryman (ed.) *Imagined Nation: England after Britain.* London: Lawrence & Wishart, 92–108

Who Was Who (1941). Vol. 3: *1929–1940.* London: Adam & Charles Black

Who Was Who (1972). Vol. 6: *1961–1970.* London: Adam & Charles Black

Wiener, M. (1981a). *English Culture and the Decline of the Industrial Spirit 1850–1980.* Harmondsworth: Penguin

Wiener, M. (1981b). Conservatism, economic growth and English culture. *Parliamentary Affairs* 34.4: 409–21

Wilde, O. (1890). The true function and value of criticism. *The Nineteenth Century* 28.163: 435–59

Wilford, R. and S. Elliott (1999). 'Small earthquake in Chile': the first Northern Ireland Affairs Committee. *Irish Political Studies* 14.1: 23–42

Willets, D. (2009). England and Britain, Europe and the Anglosphere. In A. Gamble and T. Wright (eds), *Britishness: Perspectives on the British Question.* Oxford: Wiley Blackwell in association with the *Political Quarterly.*

Williamson, P. (2008). State prayers, fasts and thanksgivings: public worship in Britain 1830–1897. *Past and Present* 200: 121–70

Wilson, D. and C. Game (2006). *Local Government in the United Kingdom.* Basingstoke: Palgrave Macmillan

Wilson, H. (1964). *The Relevance of British Socialism.* London: Weidenfeld & Nicolson

Winder, R. (2004). *Bloody Foreigners: The Story of Immigration to Britain.* London: Little, Brown

Winter, J.M. (1970). R.H. Tawney's early political thought. *Past and Present* 47.1: 71–96

Winter, J.M. and D.M. Joslin (eds) (1972). *R.H.Tawney's Commonplace Book*. Cambridge: Cambridge University Press

Wolfe, A. (1989). *Whose Keeper? Social Science and Moral Obligation*. Berkeley: University of California Press

Woolf, V. (1979). The Reader in 'Anon' and 'The Reader': Virginia Woolf's last essays. Ed. B.R. Silver, *Twentieth-Century Literature* 25.3/4: 356–441

Wright, A. (2000). England, whose England? In A. Wright and S. Chen (eds). *The English Question*. London: Fabian Society

Wright, P. (1985). *On Living in an Old Country*, London: Verso

Wright, P. (1996). England as a lost idyll. *The Independent* (16 June)

Young, K. (1989). Bright hopes and dark fears: the origins and expectations of the county councils. In K. Young (ed.). *New Directions For County Government*. London: Association of County Councils

Young, K. and N. Rao (1997). *Local Government Since 1945*. Oxford: Blackwell

Younge, G. (2000). On Race and Englishness. In S. Chen and T. Wright (eds). *The English Question*. London: Fabian Society, 111–16

Younge, G. (2009). Where will we find the perfect Muslim for monocultural Britain? *The Guardian* (30 March)

Index